D0065910

THEY
SHALL
NOT
HAVE
ME

"POWs shaking lice out of their blankets." Watercolor by Jean Hélion, 1942, after his escape. *Courtesy of Galerie de la Présidence, Paris.*

JEAN HÉLION

THEY SHALL NOT HAVE ME

(Ils ne m'auront pas)

The Capture, Forced Labor, and Escape of a French Prisoner in World War II

Introduction by Deborah Rosenthal
Afterword by Jacqueline Hélion

Arcade Publishing • New York

Arcade Publishing books may be purchased in bulk at special discounts
for sales promotion, corporate gifts, fund-raising, or educational pur-
poses. Special editions can also be created to specifications. For details,
contact the Special Sales Department, Arcade Publishing, 307 West
36th Street, 11th Floor, New York, NY 10018 or
arcade@skyhorsepublishing.com.

Arcade Publishing® is a registered trademark of Skyhorse Publishing, Inc.®,
a Delaware corporation.

Visit our website at www.arcadepub.com.

10 9 8 7 6 5 4 3 2 1

Library of Congress Cataloging-in-Publication Data is available on file.

ISBN: 978-1-61145-501-4

Printed in the United States of America

TO MY COMRADES IN CAPTIVITY
WHOM I HAVE LEFT IN GERMANY
DIGGING POTATOES ON THE FARMS
WORKING FOR LONG HOURS
AS LITTLE AS THEY CAN IN FACTORIES
THIS BOOK
THEIR STORY
IS DEDICATED

CONTENTS

Contents

Part IV — Escape

INTRODUCTION

by Deborah Rosenthal

I know of no other book quite like Jean Hélion's *They Shall Not Have Me*, his memoir of two years as a POW in Nazi prison camps. It seems to encompass a bundle of contradictions. It is an underground cult classic that was, sixty-odd years ago, a bestseller. It is a narrative written in English by a Frenchman and has never appeared in French. And it is a book about being imprisoned by the Nazis that lets us into the life of a prison camp but is not about the Holocaust, and which is as full of a sense of ridiculousness as it is of catastrophe. Most improbably—it is a book by a fiercely committed, strenuously articulate and intellectual artist that contains no thoughts on art at all.

They Shall Not Have Me is in no sense an ordinary book by an artist. Hélion's title tells us that the book is an outcry, a protest. And the absence of art from its pages serves to create a different kind of picture—a sketch of the gigantic hole ripped in the fabric of life and human culture by the Nazi assault on the world. Once back in the free world, Hélion seems to have wasted no time in setting out to write it. Although *They Shall Not Have Me* was written to benefit the Free French and the Allied war effort against fascism, the book's underground reputation in more recent years has been sustained mostly by people who are painters. Over the past several decades, painters have heard about the book from other painters, all fascinated by this French artist whose fifty-odd-year career played out in Paris and on the international scene. Hélion's *They Shall Not Have Me* reveals nothing directly about his subsequent long life in art; he died in 1987. It purports to be nothing more than his eyewitness account of almost two years at hard labor. It is, though, a book that tells us something about the artist. We see the young author as though through prison bars. His vignettes and observations serve as slivers of light illuminating the author—and perhaps even his art.

Hélion presents himself to his readers as a French soldier. His story revolves around the European conflict and all its dramatis personae are Europeans. When, after almost two years in captivity, he managed his escape from the Nazi prison ship SS Nordenham—an escape only now told in full in the afterword to the present edition—he made his way through France to his ultimate destination, the United States. He had an American wife with whom he had lived for part of the 1930s in Virginia. He must have written the book quickly, summoning up the events and conversations from two years of captivity, perhaps using notes. *They Shall Not Have Me* is a serious adventure tale, enlivened by dialogue deftly rendered in English, with smatterings of French and German. Hélion knew some German, and had particular privileges and responsibilities as a prisoner because the Nazis used him as a translator.

The book begins like a newsreel, with a scene directly from the front lines, as Hélion's platoon retreats under German fire and the Nazis sweep through France. It has the understated suspense of a really good thriller. At its abrupt end, with Hélion's solo escape, we are thrust back out into the ongoing war.

In 1943, admirers of the book would have been acutely conscious that they were reading these pages in the free world, in the United States, where its author was now also safe. Clearly, Hélion wrote *They Shall Not Have Me* in English as a cautionary tale for the English-speaking allies, particularly the Americans, who, though already deep in the war by the time the book was published, had not experienced the Nazi conquest firsthand. In his memoir, Hélion is of necessity a man of action among men of action. But the man of action is a thinker, too, who casts a shrewd and somewhat jaundiced eye on both the captors and his fellow captives, sizing them all up. He spent the year following publication traveling in the United States to do radio and live appearances and talk about his experiences. He saw himself as a messenger—an emissary—bringing dispatches from the front.

Thirty-three years old when he was conscripted into the French army in 1940, Hélion was a young painter, ambitious, talented, and energetic enough to have already cut a swath through the Parisian art world. Hélion arrived there in 1920, sixteen years old, from a year of chemistry studies in Lille and a childhood in provincial France. He was a quick study. He soon began painting. And, as he later said, he immediately found his masters in the Louvre, particularly Poussin. In the village that the Parisian avant-garde had created within the capital city, he found a tutelary spirit in the Uruguayan painter Joaquín Torres-García, who sparked his interest in the work of Mondrian. Hélion was the sort of artist, and Paris was the sort of place, where, after being turned down for an exhibition, he was able to gather together a group of artists so they could exhibit on their own. Hélion, who had had a village childhood, might have felt particularly at ease taking hold of his new milieu, acquaintance by acquaintance. Within ten years, he had had solo exhibitions, and was involved with an artists' organization devoted to abstract art: Abstraction-Création. He belonged to this international group for a few years, and edited the first of its publications. In the early years of the 1930s, he made trips to the Soviet Union, to Switzerland, and to London; he traveled and lived in the United States; and he exhibited his paintings in group and solo shows in Switzerland, Spain, England, and the United States. He made his way to most of the places where artists were forming affinity groups around the idea of abstraction.

Hélion's abstract compositions of the 1930s are unlike anyone else's. Along with Kandinsky, Arp, Calder, and Miró, all of whom he knew and with all of whom he showed, Hélion saw in the rejection of representation a key to what was modern in the art of the new century. Though he originally found his way into abstraction because of Mondrian, using reduced, flat shapes of color and free-floating lines, the relation of his pictures to Mondrian's is unique. Figure-and-ground is Hélion's game. He builds complex entities out of arrangements of simplified yet enigmatic forms. Perhaps his apprenticeship as an architectural draftsman played a part in this original synthesis, which mediates shrewdly between Mondrian's airy reduction and Léger's machine-age forms. Hélion's images suggest, in the words of his friend, the poet John Ashbery, "sphinxes erected to guard the secret of their construction." They are abstractions that loom before us in such a way as to suggest a human presence.

And after these magnificent works came the two years recounted in *They Shall Not Have Me*—two years away from drawing and painting, away from writing about art; though certainly not away from thinking of art. Is Hélion the painter there in the camps? Hélion never drew or painted scenes directly from these two years at forced labor. A single watercolor, of prisoners shaking lice out of their blankets—done in 1942 after his escape—remained his only graphic testimony to all the two years' worth of sights he witnessed.

They Shall Not Have Me can be understood as a collection of short stories—episodes and vignettes, closely observed and lapidary in their details. Hélion depicts the grim stretch of freezing barracks in a gray, Bruegelesque landscape at the first prison camp. He gives us the sights, sounds, and smells; the feel of the filth; the semi-starvation; the sense of the prisoners as cogs in the huge machine of forced labor. He is deftly constructing a world that has the texture of fiction. Here is the castle on the Pomeranian potato farm where Hélion and his comrades were slave laborers:

> The Von Z . . . castle was a large structure, with an eighteenth century character, three floors, a broad high roof, an octagonal tower, and a verandah above the main perron . . . the castle faced a park, a pool stocked with fat old carps, and a little round Adonis temple, in a Teutonic version of Versailles, set among birch trees.

And here is the description of the slaves' overseer and tormentor:

> Thirty years old, his short, powerful body oscillating so on his shiny boots that he sank progressively in the mud; his

pink, sourish, piggish face set on a thin slice of neck; his eyes glittering far apart under a low felt hat, he fully deserved his nickname of 'Tapageur' (Noisy).

Here is the peasant, Carl, the pig-keeper on the farm:

> He thought a lot of me because I asked him every morning the names of his ten children. The government gave him one hundred marks monthly, for them, and he believed it came directly from Hitler. "His name is right there on the check," he said. "He is good for the poor peasant!"

Hélion's cast of characters is large and tragicomic. There are his fellow-prisoners—Frenchmen, Belgians; the lawyer, the head-waiter, the cheese-maker, the professor. There is the Pomeranian Baroness, mistress of the Von Z . . . manor. There are the Nazi commandants of the camps, and their underlings, the guards, who range from vicious killers to the occasional man who confesses to disliking Hitler. Hélion shows us the small everyday strategies for staying warm, for getting enough to eat, for staying on one's feet, for not enraging the guards or the commandant—for remaining alive, in short. He evokes, discreetly, tenderly even, those who could cope and those who could not. He describes watching a young boy's knotting himself into a ball under the whip of a sadistic guard, thereby protecting all but his then-bloodied hands. He tells of a singing group organized among the prisoners. He recalls sitting at every meal with his pocket German dictionary; this led to his being designated as interpreter in the second year of his captivity. There are accounts—not surprising from an artist—of all kinds of ingenuity with materials at hand, to make shoes, garments, vessels, and whatever was necessary to barely survive. Here Hélion the village boy and Hélion the painter mingle. He admires artisanal skills, the know-how to work with one's hands, to improvise from virtually nothing. In the congeries of anecdotes about the men he saw every day, we find a theme common to all the best accounts that we have had from the prisons, concentration camps, the gulags, of the twentieth century. Human beings respond in a great variety of ways to the horror of systematic dehumanization.

Hélion's successful escape in February, 1942—he had tried more than once before—comes as a sudden, if expected, finale to his tale. The palpable terror in this chapter builds as, moment-to-moment, Hélion fears being recognized, recaptured, shot. But the deeper terror of these climactic pages has to do with our mounting realization that every page of the book has been, as every minute of the two years must have been, permeated with terror and the desperate wish to escape. In an afterword to the present edition of *They Shall Not Have Me*, the events of this final chapter have been amplified by the author's widow, Jacqueline Hélion. For the first time, she reveals the particulars of the story as she heard them from Hélion, mentioning both fellow prisoners who helped him organize his escape from the camp, and those in the Resistance who helped him make his way through and then out of occupied France, but who at the time of the book's publication were still in Nazi Europe, working at great peril to their own lives.

Hélion made it back to the United States in 1942, and spent 1943 in a whirlwind of activity and travel, shaping and re-telling the stories of his captivity. On at least one radio program, the broadcasters recognized the theatrical potential of his stories, and they were broadcast as dramatizations. A reviewer in *Time* magazine that year called Hélion's account "one of the half-dozen most remarkable books of World War II." Back in New York for the duration of the war, exhibiting his work again, Hélion emerged with a flood of compositions of the human figure, built upon drawings from life. The human presence in these new works is perhaps surprisingly fully articulated; they have lips, eyes, shoulders, arms, hats, even hairdos. In their unequivocal specificity, many commentators have seen a renunciation of Hélion's previous commitment to an abstract, invented world of generalized forms. But even in the early 1930s, deep in his abstractions, Hélion had written about the importance of the figure compositions of Nicolas Poussin. And the slow evolution of his abstractions had already brought him to his recognizably human-scaled "Figure tombée" of 1939. In a letter to a friend that same year, Hélion declared himself ready to take on the figure in the fullest traditional sense—to set the human figure into a social context. During his two years as a prisoner of war, Hélion, may, by sheer force of will, have dreamed up some of the never-painted compositions that finally carried him from abstraction to figuration. Perhaps *They Shall Not Have Me* is the great unpainted composition of 1943. And having composed his literary vignettes of the camps using his stored-up memories of props and action, Hélion set out to marshal the elements of narrative again in the compositions done immediately after he resumed painting. In these new paintings, presences that suggested figures in the prewar abstractions have been exchanged for men and women who act and react; whose relationships invoke the moral world of figure composition that goes back to Hélion's admiration for Poussin. For many years after his turn to representation, Hélion uses the intimate structure of the vignette to look at human society, and this may bring him closer to Chardin, to the Le Nains, even to Corot. His brush homes in on the cracked walls of urban streets populated by store mannequins, newspaper readers, bicyclists, lovers. One can even in some instances imagine hearing dialogue, of the sort that accompanies his vivid scenes in *They Shall Not Have Me*. Perhaps this is why some have mentioned, mistakenly, a comic-book quality in his work. Yet the piquancy of Hélion's vignettes never overwhelms the powerful and unremitting formal rhythm of the painting, what the artist called the "double rhythm" of Poussin or Seurat.

In the postwar decades, Hélion's reputation faded considerably, as the kind of work he had undertaken as a representational painter came to be underrated and misunderstood. He did not have consistent support from a dealer in the 1960s and 1970s, and the predominance of American abstraction meant that real prominence eluded him. A new generation of younger, mostly figurative painters, many American, discovered his work—and *They Shall Not Have Me*—and his reputation was sealed as an artist's artist. His painting continued to evolve. For a while, the Gogol-esque humor of some of his early representational work disappeared, only to return finally embedded in the extraordinary triptychs of the 1960s and 1970s. In "Things Seen In May," Hélion takes as his subject the uprisings of May 1968; his packed, exuberant flea-market triptych is called "The Last Judgement of Things." In these grand compositions—some more than ten feet across—Hélion expanded the vignette into a novelistic allegory. His urban street became the stage for a tragicomedy not unlike that played out, in extremis, in *They Shall Not Have Me*.

Through all of this, Hélion was writing about his art, and writing about the art of the past that interested him. Prolific as he was as a painter—paintings and drawings seemed to pour out of him, throughout all the phases of his long career—he was nearly as productive in print. He began to publish almost as soon as he became visible as a painter in his first shows in the 1930s. Perhaps because in France writing about art had long been part of a literary tradition—the elegant essay, the explication de texte as the models—French artists themselves did not for the most part explicate or adumbrate the new art of the twentieth century. Though there are the occasional landmark statements, such as Matisse's famous 1908 "Notes of a Painter," or Braque's gnomic observations, many Parisian artists were reluctant to give the ideas they developed in the studio a literary form. It was the painters who had come from other part of Europe and who had invented the various languages of abstraction—particularly Mondrian and Klee and Kandinsky—who consistently wrote to locate themselves and their cohorts within a tradition. Hélion, who could write in French and English, and knew artists across Europe and also in America, was, like those pioneers, fiercely cerebral. But his thought, like theirs, always seems to emerge from the experience of the studio. It is the modern young painter he seems to address, and, beyond that painter, the modern person who reads, looks at paintings, and perhaps believes with Hélion that painting belongs to what he called the "world of concepts."

Hélion outlived his career as a painter, as in the last few years of his life he suffered near-blindness. But he continued to write. He wrote to reprise his work and revisit the adventures and attachments of his life. And in an extraordinary feat, he took himself in imagination into the "yellow room" near his studio where he had kept unfinished or aborted works, and revisited those works in his mind's eye. He had always believed that art "requires all that a man has in his head and his flesh." He said this in 1938, when he was living in the United States, in an interview in *Partisan Review* entitled "The Abstract Artist in Society." When the interviewer, the artist and critic George L.K. Morris, asked him about the relationship between art and political life, Hélion made this response: "The artist cannot believe himself a solitary god creating all that he feels he must express in his work; the substance, more or less transmuted, he gets from life, from daily experience as well as from culture, from the experience of others." In *They Shall Not Have Me*, we have Hélion the artist painting a self-portrait of Hélion the man: the artist in society.

—New York City, 2012

PART I

DOWNFALL

CHAPTER 1

War Came to Us

I was not sent to war. It came to me in Mézières en Drouais, a charming village west of Paris, where, for months, I had crawled upon the hills, ducked under blank shots, dug model trenches, and absorbed soporific chapters from the infantry sergeant handbook, very peacefully.

Early one June morning, with the sixty men of my training platoon, I was sketching from a hill the valley beneath, according to the military convention of perspective, when a slow column appeared in the hollow of my model: vehicles of all descriptions — buggies, farm wagons drawn by four, six, sometimes eight horses — strangely loaded. Cattle and pedestrians followed. It dragged on towards the south, uninterrupted. Then cars, with trailers and carts in tow, shot by the horses and formed a dotted line to their left.

I recognized it. It seemed to jump out of my past. Twenty-two years ago, after a maddening night of bombing, I, too, fled from the north, hauling a cart. My mother pushed, her feet soon bled. Red and blue flares and explosions tore the sky beyond the city. Enormous and scarlet, the sun came up and washed out the lights of the battle of the Somme. Then I saw that the woman ahead of us wore a dressing gown, and carried an alarm clock, a beauty kit, and a ladle. Next to her, a girl pulled a wheelbarrow with her mother in it. Bundles were piled in the emaciated arms of the old woman, but her jaw hung open. She was dead, and the bundles fell on the road, one after the other. The girl didn't know it.

Downfall

This was the same fatal hemorrhage, running, flowing out of the deep wound that the invasion had, once more, inflicted on my country.

As if the exodus had propagated a plague, the villages around became devitalized. The population disappeared, deserting crops, stock, cellars.

Training was interrupted. We spent days ardently combing the woods for parachutists, and found none. Formed into regular companies, we expected to leave for the front, and were eager to fight; but our train never came. On the ninth of June, the next railway station, at Dreux, was neatly sprinkled with bombs by fifteen German dive bombers, hardly bothered by a weak antiaircraft fire. Where were the Allied airplanes? We never saw them any more. German observation planes took their place above us, and strafed us a bit, every day, for fun.

Paper headlines swelled enormously: Treason . . .

Our officers became nervous. Old reserve Major Galois ordered every road stopped by antitank blockades. Ridiculous obstacles of cobblestones and farm machinery were hastily built which any large tank could push away.

Men took to drinking so much that the two remaining cafés were ordered closed. Over the radio, I heard Reynaud say that a miracle was necessary to save France. He called on America for help.

On the eve of the thirteenth, a lieutenant of my platoon, of whom I was very fond, took me aside and told me that the Germans were hardly twenty miles away, advancing rapidly after breaking the main line of resistance. The order had come at last that all troops should evacuate Mézières the next morning, except a rear-guard of fifty men entrusted with the defense of the village. My lieutenant was to take command of it. Would I volunteer to stay with him?

"Yes, of course."

We were to be given two machine guns and two sub-machine guns, but no heavy weapon. If we hid well and waited until the Germans came near, we might cause them some damage, puzzle them a bit, and slow them down for three hours, until they had cleaned us up from the air, and with field mortars. The mission completed, some of us might escape over the hills, through the woods. Perhaps.

I felt hot in the head. It is so good to know that one is going to do one's best, come what may.

But in the night, the order was cancelled and, by the same valley road over which had swept the influx of refugees, we left at daybreak, in good order, full pack on the back.

CHAPTER 2

Days of Rout

June 14.

ONE has to learn to walk fully loaded. It is not so much a question of strength, as a question of suppleness. With the knapsack well installed on the shoulders, one projects the body over one leg and then over the other, smoothly. It is as if the legs were moving under oneself like a different part, gliding, rolling.

The charge must stay horizontal. Any up and down motion of the shoulders absorbs energy. The straps are devils. They cut the shoulders, the chest, the belly. There are quantities of them, from the gun, the bags, the canteen, the gas masks, crossing, overlapping. One breathes low, so as not to shake them.

With the cartridges, the blanket, the spare shoes, the reserve food, the tools, one carries fifty, sixty pounds, not to mention the "utility gifts" from the family. I had, besides, a handsome American leather brief-case full of books and drawings. My shoes were new; my feet soon cut.

A thick fog followed the night. What luck! Nothing to fear from above. We plodded mile after mile. The first twelve or fifteen are always the hardest. One has to tear through one's own crust of stiffness, weakness, laziness. When all the muscles warm up, each gliding gently over the other, carrying its own share of the total burden, it ceases to be painful. One becomes part of the column. The cadence of the steps lifts up your legs. At the first few halts one gets busy with talcum powder, adhesive tape, rubbing oil. For the toes, there is nothing better than tallow. One soon decides that one has no use for this book, or that fancy kit. "Who wants it? No one?" It lands in the ditch.

After twenty miles, we reached a railroad station. The station master was sore and sorry. The tracks had been accurately bombed from the air that very morning, as if the Germans knew that we were to embark there. He was left alone. The freight cars had rolled over the bank and smashed up the cattle awaiting shipment. Surviving animals had galloped madly away, with bloody bits hanging from their horns.

We took to the road again, now clean of all traffic, as if reserved for us; and six or seven miles farther, in the darkest night, we stopped in a village, invaded the barns and fell asleep.

June 15.

"Everybody up." What? It is still night, we have been here only a couple of hours. Hot coffee will be served in the yard. That sounds better. But where are my things, my gun, my gas mask, my bags, my bayonet, the whole mess? Fumbling in the dark — flashlights are strictly forbidden. Through any crack in the roof they would show at a great height. Hell! My mistake. This is not a barn, but a stable! Then a woman screamed. I had stepped on her face. Apparently some refugees had crawled in, too, and just lay anywhere.

Soon we were on the road again, each company now a full fifteen minutes behind the other. My feet felt much better. I had feared I could not carry on last night, but with the blisters opened, well patched, the shoes broken in, the top part discreetly split with my knife, I could manage.

We followed railroad tracks. Smoking was prohibited. No lights, you know! But at a curve, a splendid red light burst above the tracks, bloody in the dark. I was sent up to see; nothing but a regular stop signal. The lieutenant thought that it meant the tracks had been blown up beyond. Mighty strange! He would not let me shoot at it. No instructions, to do so,

Downfall

he said. A reserve officer is a timid soul, after he has made a couple of enthusiastic blunders. In the Army you are supposed to do nothing beyond your particular mission. There was another station, he said, a couple of hours away. He believed that we would be given new orders there, and were likely to be shipped south, and then sent up to where some strong line of resistance was being completed. He mentioned the River Loire.

No! What kind of a joke is this? They cannot have let the Germans pass the River Seine. It could only be a few advanced elements that had crossed it, and they should have been annihilated quickly. But why was it that as we went west towards Chartres, the few civilians left in the streets were old, and looked desperate?

Since yesterday we had passed many small towns, or villages that recalled lovely souvenirs of my old hikes: Roman churches, Renaissance city halls, blue mail boxes with 1830-type inscriptions, cafés with marinated eels and dry Touraine wine. To M . . . I had come once last month, to deliver a message for one of Darlan's officers. Naval general headquarters had been installed right here. Now, all windows were closed, shutters latched, and papers littered the street. No café open, no newspaper to be found. I could not make out what a distant radio was blaring forth about Paris: "Yesterday at . . . the Germans . . ." Had the hogs bombed it?

But the roads were gay. There were flowers, trees, spots of oil and horse dung. The birds had no bad news to twitter.

In a thicket sat two girls, blonde and red, hatless, looking pretty. The boy ahead of me turned his head, left the ranks, calling to the lieutenant that he had to take off his shoe. The girls, laughed. Somebody behind me said that he made for the thicket. I do not remember seeing him again.

Not two, but six hours later, we arrived at a station. The road crossed the tracks. There were two immensely long trains of platform cars, loaded with armored cars, guns, brand-new superb material. It always makes you proud to meet neat war machinery, well painted, with white numbers, so business-like. You feel that if you are given this, no enemy shall ever get the best of you. It looks so invincible.

There seemed to be something the matter. Though the four locomotives steamed, they did not move. And then, funny little points in the sky, too well-known, appeared, three by three, a dozen in all. They became bigger and bigger. We were ordered to scatter promptly into the fields and lie quiet. The planes dived, six of them, roared enormously and let loose. The bombs whistled. In a certain light, you could see them coming down, just after being released. Then you would duck, sure that they were aimed directly at you. The noise of bomb explosions is terrific, clattering. When it stops, your ears throb and the earth vibrates. Then stones, bricks, torn-off bits landing at last, make a gentler clatter. Next, somebody screams. Last comes the smell of powder. The planes taking height again, the humming of the engines will quiet down to a peculiar waving roar until they dive again.

Behind me, Corporal Marais, my comrade in training, his eyes out of his head, muttered: "I can't stand it; I can't stand it!"

Somebody said: "*Ta gueule.*" (Shut up!)

It is strange how one reacts to fear. Everyone feels something. One out of ten becomes paralyzed. The rich, untranslatable, Army slang says: "*Il a les miches qui font bravo,*" or "*Il a le trou du cul a zéro.*"

When the bombs whistle, I get a cold sensation in the lower backbone; later, it climbs to my neck, and I become angry: I want to fight.

Where were the officers? In that station, on those trains, no antiaircraft or, if any, nobody to man it! To protect them, it would have taken at least four quick firing guns. Where were

Downfall

our famous 90 Schneiders, which could shoot eight miles up? Where were the batteries of sharp 25's, or the new 47's, or even the old brutal 75's? All sent where the final stand was going to be, no doubt. And where were our machine guns? Somewhere beyond, with the other company! They are not much good against fast planes, unless coupled, and provided the planes fly low. They will dissuade planes from strafing, though.

Where are the lieutenants, the captain? Couldn't we do something? Men here and there started shooting at the planes uselessly, but it relieved our nerves. Then, orders were passed from haystack to hole, from hedge to tree; "Don't shoot, or they'll come after us." Too late! Two of them plunged, gracefully, and the roaring became enormous. Tatatata. The machine guns clapped the road, where some trucks had stopped, the drivers hidden underneath. Two caught fire, and the burning men ran.

The bullets whistle and render a different sound according to the objects hit. Brief, shrill, dry, vibrating, or soft when they bury themselves in flesh. Dust, little bits of pavement, torn off pieces of stone or wood fly around.

"I can't stand it, I can't stand it," shrieked Marais, again. I smacked him. He said: "Thank you. I can't help it." A good fellow, Marais, a grocer, from a small town, somewhere.

So we were not going to board a train here. When the planes left us, they had done little damage to our scattered company. A few scratches. The railroad tracks were completely smashed on both sides of the station. The trains themselves had suffered little, but would stay there. It was none of our business, apparently, for we formed again, and marched to the village, far beyond the station, where we found stragglers from the other companies, and a good warm soup.

The village was empty, except for a few groups of refugees,

silent, eating or sleeping on the side of the road. I found a house open. It was poor. There was some coffee in the pot, and I drank it. It tasted fresh. I washed and greased my feet, and endeavored to lighten my pack. On the mantelpiece I felt a beautiful *Saint Augustin* and a *Life of Eric Satie;* in a closet, a soiled shirt, a pair of pajamas, and some odd things.

The company staff looked puzzled, and grieved, around old Major Galois the creator of the funny antitank blockade, at Mézières. He wore a white beard, on a kind face. It was decided that we would not march any longer in company formation, but by isolated groups, and we were given the meeting point and general directions.

With a dozen of my friends from what was, a few days before, a brisk, shiny-looking training unit of noncommissioned officers, all but I bearing the pretty stripes of corporal, I left by a back road. We had reached that degree of fatigue where one can hardly carry more than a thought. To go on, was our only thought then.

We loaded our sacks on a small carriage found in a back yard. Half of us pulling and pushing, the others walking ahead, and whistling a song, from time to time.

*   *   *

The tallest of the group, Ernest, had fought, as top sergeant, in Morocco, sixteen years ago, and in the Sarre. He had been degraded for some minor scandal: fight with an officer, drunkenness, that kind of mistake. I thought that I could rely on him, eventually, for advice. It was so hot that, against all regulations, we laid our heavy mantles on the sacks. I was in favor of advancing as fast as possible, but the others complained they could not; and we had to stay together.

At a farm, one of those fine buildings where all the roofs turn around a central yard, with a warm dung pile in the center, we stopped. We wanted a lighter carriage. All the doors were

Downfall

open, but no farmer answered our calls. I looked around for a road map, but found only a sketchy sort of regional map on the back of a calendar. I tore it off.

Hearing a noise above, we climbed the stairs and found a young man, and a girl helping him pull off his boots. He wore a swanky uniform, and said in good French that he was a Flemish officer, from the Belgian Army; that he had escaped through the German lines, met his wife in Paris where the Germans had arrived yesterday; that, as far as he was concerned, the fight was over, Leopold having capitulated. He had found some civilian clothes in a closet, and would put them on. He invited us to do the same. "What's the use?" He said. "We are all betrayed anyway!" Indignant, none of us would imitate him.

We left them in the attic. No carts in the barn, no cattle, no chickens, no old, lame dog. A plague-stricken place. So lovely, though, so architectural; as abstract as a geometrical perspective on paper that always misses looking alive.

Back on the road, I found that Ernest had collected some bottles of brandy. I didn't like it very much, but I took a sip, and it did me good. There was a heavy cannonade north and east of us. Thank God, there was a line! That Belgian fellow did not know what he was saying. We should have taken him along, with his boots and his unattractive mate, and made him repeat his statements at headquarters. But there were so many civilians from the north, Belgium, Holland, who had said such things as we passed by.

Planes bearing German markings passed us, continually. We did not stop any more. If they began machine-gunning us, we could crouch under the pushcart. Nothing better to stop a bullet than a packed knapsack, except a sack of loose earth.

We saw a pack of bleating sheep, two or three hundreds of them. They had shaved the ground completely, and looked famished. Who had left them there? I wished we had time to kill one and roast it. We let them loose. The foolish flock stayed together, and followed us for a while. Then Corporal Durand said that they would stuff themselves with green grass and burst their bellies. He knew. He was a farmer, wrinkled, with an ample mustache, a heavy torso, short legs, no neck. From western Normandy, certainly. I felt badly. Perhaps we had done the wrong thing.

There was no traffic coming up. Everything we ever met went south.

Silly! Silly!

So the beautiful French country, its villages harmoniously gathered around a grey, golden, or pink stone church, or a *Place de la Mairie;* its carefully kept gardens behind the houses, with beds of flowers around the vegetables; its inhabitants so witty, so wise, so rich in all kinds of recipes for living well, eating well, drinking well, and, — what so few people in the world know — resting well; sitting in front of their houses, after work, or having friendly games of cards and billiards, at the Inn, while the women sip coffee and tell delightfully ugly stories about each other — so all of this, that I had loved, would vanish.

Demolished the houses, gone the parson, the mayor, the drummer, the nobleman, the teacher, the Communist leader — all gone except, sometimes, the elder of the community who had refused to be carried away, and who lay, strangely alive, in a lone bed, under a flayed roof, with a pile of decaying food on the bedside table.

Vanished, melted away!

No, no. That could not be! There had been a battle of the Marne, in 1914, in 1918, at the gates of Paris. There would be one of the Loire. We would drown all the Germans. But where were they? We knew nothing. It could not be true about Paris, or was it what I could not understand, over the radio?

Downfall

I could not bear the thought of the Germans marching down the Avenue de l' Etoile, towards the Louvre, invading La Cite, sitting in the Luxembourg Gardens, disgustingly proud.

Where was the famed French Army? Where were our generals? What had Weygand done? Where were the young officers, the grandsons of the heroes of the Revolution? Wasn't there anybody to rise from nowhere and lead us, as so often before, to victory? I almost felt that anyone who wanted to strongly enough, could have done it. Even I, perhaps. Yes, but what? One should know something. Who could know anything any more, when no plane of ours showed itself, when nothing went up to fight the German bombers from our skies? When they flew down, south or west, it was never very long before we heard a whole chain of explosions. Sometimes there would be antiaircraft, very thick. The sky would be polka-dotted with white clouds. The bombers would disappear and come back, half an hour later, when the antiaircraft guns were all gone, or silenced, and they could sprinkle their bombs, and their parachutists, in comfort.

Everywhere, the telephone and telegraph lines were cut; the electric wires were not charged. How would the colonel know anything, tonight? We never saw him any more, by the way. He had a car. Most of them had cars, of course. They went ahead. Very few walked, as did the tall, funny-faced Captain C. . . . whom I had seen once or twice, with sandals and a rifle on his back. He would not leave his new recruits, men who had barely had time to learn how to wrap the puttees around their legs. Most of them were "recuperated," as they say: weaklings previously refused by the medical commissions. They were taking punishment.

All of this went through my head, thickly. My thoughts had the shape of the road; they went one way, away, away. They faded at times, and then I would hear my own feet and the others tramping on the road, and feel tired. Also, we had had little to eat. There was nothing to be bought. The reserve food we carried was not supposed to be touched until the last extremity. In a deserted chicken house we found a whole pile of eggs, and sipped them raw.

*   *   *

Our back road ran into a highway, where we met various groups from other companies. Their appearance struck me. Did we look like that, so dusty, shabby, unbuttoned, no two packs alike? We were worse, certainly, pulling and pushing a cart, like gypsies. A crossroad suddenly poured a convoy of refugees into the highway, and it became a remarkable mess.

Automobiles tried to pass and could not. They were overloaded with mattresses laid on the top; odd things hung from the headlights and the door handles; or piled on the bumpers and the running boards: chairs, pails, stove pipes, suitcases, blankets packed like Bologna sausage, everything connected with a web of strings, as if a huge spider had taken possession of the entrails of a wandering house. The women, children, and old people crowded inside, like worms in the dark. Army trucks behind went into the fields so as to get ahead, and found themselves stuck in the high wheat, ditches, and mud puddles. The whole convoy had to stop, passed only by stragglers from all sorts of regiments. People began to swear and to fight.

Out of a stuck delivery wagon came three firemen of the Parisian Elite Corps, recognizable by their leather jackets, and their shiny helmets. "What are you doing here, handsome *Pompiers?*" They said they had escaped from Paris last night, by the Porte d'Italie, when the Germans were already there. They had found this car abandoned on the road, and had been compelled to make many detours to avoid capture.

So it was true; but the city had not been bombarded. Thank

Downfall

God! Perhaps I should return there, some day, and wander through the beloved streets.

Paris taken. Shame on us!

It was so difficult to advance in the jammed crowd that, trusting my bit of a map, we took a dirt road going to the left. One of us had disappeared. We called in vain. We were now eleven.

Ernest caught two stray chickens, cut off the heads with his knife, and plucked the feathers as he walked. We stopped to boil them, carved into small pieces. The brew tasted good, though unsalted. We decided to equip ourselves better at the next village. We were beginning to realize that this might keep on for sometime yet. Everywhere ahead of us, the stations might be blasted, or the trains gone. We fought sleepiness with alcohol.

We met a convoy of army trucks, packed with well-equipped men, and light artillery. They were dusty, but unfatigued and cheerful. They thought they were going to take positions somewhere. They threw packages of cigarettes towards us. Behind followed civilian lorries. Our comrade R. said suddenly: "I have had enough of this; my feet ache too much," and he climbed into the last lorry. "Your knapsack," I yelled. He threw his hand above his shoulder. We dumped it right there: ours were already too much to pull.

Why hadn't all the trucks been mobilized for the army so that we could be sent promptly wherever we were wanted?

According to the road signs, the objective, Bonneval, was only two hours away. There we would meet the others, eat, and rest. I had decided to speak to the lieutenant. We liked each other. He must know something and could tell us what was really going on. Meanwhile, we sang, and as is customary in any army, told each other jokes about top sergeants, and the like. It was fortunate, indeed, that Ernest had taken the cognac.

A good brand, too, with a lot of stars, — better deserved, maybe, than the silver stars on some people's caps.

When we arrived in sight of Bonneval, approximately one and a half miles farther on, it was almost dark, but suddenly became very bright and noisy. A couple of "black birds," hovering over the village, were enjoying themselves, dropping their "eggs." It was a beautiful sight if you did not mind being frightened a bit; — not so very different from Fourteenth of July fireworks, except that the pieces were expanding upwards, instead of down, and, added luxury, a few machine guns were firing from the ground, with tracer bullets. A couple of searchlights would have given the "Abscisses and Ordinates" to the brilliant show; but they were not there.

Twenty bombs or more fell before the planes went away. There was a barn in a field; we made for it. We were so tired that we had to have some sleep. We had hardly reached cover when thunder began again, but a real, a peaceful thunder, sounding like a heavy ball rolling down the stairs, with nice, friendly-looking lightning; and it rained superbly, divinely.

Damn! There were people in the hay! "Don't step on my barges, you ass." Barges, in French Army slang, mean feet. Here was old Marais as frightened as ever, with his "pants loaded" as the army says. He had snuggled under a wagon, between two bunches of straw. At least that is what he said, for I could not see. He repeated endlessly that he had met the Mézières Mill truck, and that sixteen of the twenty-eight civilians inside, were killed.

"Shut up! Thousands of others die like that every day! One cannot possibly worry over every bit of disaster. Don't you know any other tune?"

Ernest, having struck a match, was being shockingly insulted. He argued. The wind blew the match out, and settled the case.

Downfall

Some artillerymen asked where we came from, and said that they came from the Somme, where there had been some fierce fighting for days and nights, with thousands and thousands of dead on each side. The line held perfectly where they were. Suddenly the Allied planes disappeared from the skies, our men were attacked by tanks, from the rear, and that was the end. Their batteries silenced, they barely escaped captivity, and arrived here by devious ways. Now they were walking, and did we have any wine to offer them? Everybody said something in the dark. Dirty jokes, moving confidences, angry remarks. I never saw their faces.

I fell through thousands of miles of darkness, into oblivion. Ernest shook me. Tatatata. He shook me again. Tatatatata. What is that? "That is a machine gun," he said, "(better sip some cognac), that is a machine gun, and not a French Hotchkiss. It is a Maxim. I know. I have had to reckon with it, in the Sarre. Come on! Limon and Kerouan have gone already. They left, just after the shower, with the artillery fellows."

"Don't worry," said Jules. "I have served in the Army for twelve years, everywhere, and I have fought plenty. I won't let myself be caught. Better stick to me."

Old Corporal Jules, a mail carrier in civilian life, was very poor at military theory, and to give himself a better chance at the weekly exams, he shined his buttons to an exquisite polish. We used to laugh about it; but he could mount and fire an 81 mm. mortar in no time. A good old egg, his hair already white.

*   *   *

June 16.

So we left, and promptly lost ourselves, having to sit in a ditch until daybreak. Then we found a post of a dozen men. It was at them that the shots were fired last night. A German motorcycle patrol, with machine guns mounted on side cars, had come down the road. The post had killed the first ones, and the others had turned back, after letting loose a few bands. There lay three Frenchmen, pulled together gently, a mantle over their heads. For them, it was all over.

"I wish I knew what to do now," said their sergeant, "but you boys better make tracks."

We did, though that carriage, with only six of us to pull, had become a nuisance. We abandoned it, as well as the others' luggage, and strapped our knapsacks on once more. It hurt. Gosh, it was heavy! This is where I relinquished that excellent, thousand-page, grey-bound book called *Manual of the Infantry Leader*, the famous *"Théorie"* that said: ". . . keep the given direction, keep contact with the men to your left, and the men to your right. Report constantly . . ."

In the next mile and a half we had to stop again because three fat Capronis, flying so low that I could see their dirty colors, had come to finish the Germans' job. They stayed only fifteen minutes, dropped a dozen bombs, and strafed around nicely. More than the Germans, especially when there was not much antiaircraft they liked to come down at a crossroad, and play havoc with the fleeing civilians.

It is, of course, excellent business. The carriages and trucks get jammed in a mess that cannot be undone. The bodies of dead horses fill the holes. Those that are left of the terrified women, children, and old men, run in all directions, and quickly invade roads that are supposed to be reserved for military traffic. They confuse that traffic, slow it down, and when the vehicles rescued from the strafed column, arrive, finally stop it altogether. To get rid of them, you would have to shoot. Anyway, the women insult you:

"Why are you going this way, flying bastards, sons of everything low on earth, cowards . . ."

Downfall

"Lady, we'd rather fight, but where, and with what? We are told to go south. We are going. We shall find better arms there; we shall stop the invader. You will see. Get away from us. Can't you see the planes are after us? Who ever told you to take this road?"

"Somebody. A man. He said he knew this road was free, and much safer."

There was always such a man, in every column of civilians, but he could never be found. There may have been one in every village, ten in every small town, one hundred in every city, who started this lamentable exodus of civilians, that, alone, would have made us lose this war of movement, if we had not had other reasons to lose it. It would be good for one's nerves, for one's confidence in any future, to get hold of each of those men and beat him to a pulp.

* * *

Not much was left around Bonneval now. I found my comrade Barois, the bicycle racer, on a shiny bike, with one yellow wheel, and the other blue. He had arrived last night, found a bicycle store blown open, and had made himself one out of the remnants of a dozen. Kerouan and Limon had been there, too, and had helped themselves. They were there, behind the wall, when the Capronis started. They had not ridden very far.

Kerouan was good at figures, and knew better than anybody else how many cartridges of this or that sort a group should carry, and the particulars about any sort of material. His head had gone through one wheel; the spokes came out of his mashed skull, like the rays of a saint in a penny image.

A "crevard," Limon, one who never had enough to eat, and who would come back for more, with a pitiful look. They had always given him the bones, and no meat at all! He lay on his stomach, his pants torn off. His behind showed white, without a scratch; large, hairy, fascinating. A strange beast. Cruelly funny.

*   *   *

We found the staff. Fortunately, a small village, away from the railroad station of Bonneval, had been set as the meeting place. The officers had spent the night in a castle.

The company cook, on top of his rolling machine, distributed hot coffee. Nothing to complain about there. Fresh bread too; baker's bread, white, instead of the heavy brown army bread that we call "*boule.*"

I went to sleep in a barn, with my bunch of comrades. I woke up at noon to find that Léon and Ernest wanted me to roast a chicken.

I could not stand on my feet; the ground was coming up to me, first on one side, then on the other. A bucket of cool well water helped me, and I got busy. Others were investigating pens, for chickens or rabbits. There were many easy victims. All larger animals had been removed.

The officers strolled around, not shaved but looking fresh. Our lieutenant praised Barois for his good-looking bike. "Get motorized any way you can" he said to me. "We'll leave in two hours."

In a house I found a stove, a pan, and some grease. The roast soon smelled good. An old man, about seventy, came in. He wore a large cap, with ear-flaps, and muttered that he had come to get his purse. This was his house. His workshop was behind. A cooper, he had been successor to his father and his grandfather. Fine tools, well disposed on racks, handsome boards of many sorts of wood, leaning against the wall, or lying on trestles, explained the barrels, casks, and kegs, left at various stages of fabrication, on the workbenches.

Downfall

A thick layer of chips and sawdust felt comfortable under foot. Thin dust softened the light falling from the high windows; and spiders had woven deep nets on each side, ample, also loaded with dust, looking like curtains hung the wrong way.

He showed me a prize keg of oak, with shiny copper rings, his masterpiece, made at the end of his apprenticeship long, long ago.

What a pleasant old-wood smell!

Cooper, I'd like to stay here with thee, turn the wheel of the large sharpening-stone yonder, learn thy trade and keep, for my children, old cognac and fresh wines, in kegs and casks bent by thy able hands. . . .

But the cannonade rolled heavily again, and away he went, towards his death, somewhere far from the scene of his life, and away I went, irresistibly, towards a great black hole into which it was my fate to fall, three days later.

* * *

Ernest and the others were very proud. They had found a lame horse and attached him to a funny farm wagon, much too heavy. All the poor animal could do was pull the sacks, and sometimes one or two of us, over flat ground. We soon met some wounded men whom we laid over our sacks and transported until we could persuade some truck drivers to take them on. In a panic, everyone looks out for himself or his family. Ugly things happen. I had to raise my voice and threaten.

We received our worst strafing that very afternoon, and had to crawl under the wagon, several times. The old horse did not move until a car ahead of us caught fire. Everybody inside must have been killed, for no one popped out or screamed, but the horse jumped, and fell into the ditch, with the carriage and contents following. We had a hard time getting away from the heavy wheels. Léon's knee was bruised and he had to be laid on the wagon. We shot madly at the planes until the civilians became angry. They said that it made the Germans return and strafe until nothing moved any more. An anti-aircraft battery began shooting, presumably 25mm., mounted on trucks, half a mile ahead; and we had, at last, the joy of seeing a twin-engined craft drop, with a long trail of smoke, and crash in a field, with a magnificent noise. It exploded.

A parachute had appeared in the sky, and was drifting away from us. Two mad women darted out of the road and ran across the field, in its direction. Others followed. I knew what they would do, if they could: beat the flyer down, crush his face with their heels, and pull his eyes out. There were many children, many women, many old people, buried hastily on the side of the French roads — or not buried at all — and many a destroyed village where no soldier had ever been seen. It would be preposterous to fly a fast warplane, accomplish a mission calling for the destruction of everything on the road, and then come down in a parachute and say to the women whose babies you have just massacred: "Will you please treat me according to international law?" and expect them to tear the children's shirts to dress your wounds properly. . . .

Who ever spoke of humanizing war? Doesn't he who receives a shell splinter in the face suffer as much as he who is killed by an angry woman's heel? If giving death to the enemy is no crime only for properly patented soldiers, with a reference number on the collar, it should be arranged for bullets and shell splinters to be educated, like special police dogs, to hit only men whose military papers are in good order. And perhaps, above the belt only, and never in the back. Where does war stop?

During these days when I have been running away, been shot at, bombed, without the satisfaction of fighting back, giving the best in me, doing something positive for my country

Downfall

and the people I love, a wound has been inflicted on my soul that will never heal.

We left the main road and, night having fallen, slept a few hours in another barn. Up again in the dark! We found a sack of oats for the horse and, in the hay, a woman badly wounded in the foot. We laid her on the carriage and she held the reins.

What? Flashes in the dark. A light appearing at several windows, and then going away. We made for the house, knocked loudly. No answer. We broke down the door, searched every room, the basement, the attic. Nobody. We called, threatened, fired shots in the closets. Not a sound.

Hell! Everywhere something that we could not understand. Parachutists? Traitors? Only for them was the whole mess clear. They had instructions. They knew where we were going. No doubt they directed us.

The road again. It divided in two sections, right and left. We took the one to the right, but it was a dirt road and soon proved hardly practicable. I went back alone in order to investigate the other. I could not see at all. It was blacker than black, indeed. The ground was solid enough under my feet. Maybe I'd soon reach a milestone bearing the name of the next village. Suddenly I felt a stick in my ribs, and stopped short.

"What's this?"

"Quiet. A sub-machine gun. I shoot."

Now I could see something like a dark oily raincoat and a strange helmet above. A tall broad man. His French was clear, with little accent.

"Quiet. This way. Hurry."

He motioned me briskly in the dark, to a path. I turned my head. He was watching the road, instead of following me. Ahead, ten or twenty feet away, I heard approaching footsteps. A vanguard post? Violently I jumped over the hedge, undid the rifle that the fool had not taken off my back, and fired three shots in both directions. There was no answering shot. I heard something falling, or tramping in the bushes, and I ran, breathlessly, until I fell on a path running six feet below the level of the fields. Unhurt, I ran again. No one was pursuing me. I couldn't have killed them all. For some reason, they did not want to show themselves.

Half an hour later I found my friends, guns in hand behind the old carriage. They would not believe my story. I could hardly believe it myself, now. They said that I had shot ghosts. The lame woman, under the driver's seat, was muttering prayers.

*   *   *

June 17.

Before dawn, we crossed a village. On the Place de l'Eglise, a tiny streak of light showed under a door. We knocked and found some twenty men around a table loaded with food. Tankmen with leather jackets, and helmets without vizors. They let us in, after turning out the lights carefully. They were black with smoke, young, and strong. Two wore bloody bandages. A top sergeant poured me a glass of wine, gave me a thick piece of ham, asked where we came from; and laughed when I told him.

"My God, you come straight from the Jerries' lines. We fought there today. We started with fifteen tanks in the morning, and came back at dusk with eight. One had to be abandoned before reaching this village. You must have passed it. The seven others are under the trees, in the square. Hasn't the watchman seen you? Have you met any motorized troops?"

"No, we haven't, or rather we did meet many yesterday, rolling in strange directions."

"Then," said the adjutant "what is the use of fighting? We meet columns of German tanks. Ours are stronger, better

Downfall

armored. Our special 75mm. gun shoots clear through theirs; but they are more mobile, and outnumber us ten to one. We have gone back and forth through their lines, destroyed many, but no motorized troops follow us any more. Our 47mm. anti-tank batteries have vanished. Not a single plane on our side. Theirs drop bombs in our way — strange carbon dioxide bombs that stop our engines; and then it is just too bad for us. Our antiaircraft also has vanished. We are supposed to receive fuel and ammunition at daybreak. You'd better not stay around my men."

Later in the morning we met the rest of the battalion and received some hot food. The lieutenant came to me and said: "We have to pass the River Loire today. At five o'clock all the bridges will be blown up. Get bicycles, or make that horse run until it dies; but be sure to cross the Beaugency bridge before 4 P.M."

This time we had to stick to the main road. Everywhere on the left we had encountered trouble. It meant definitely that the Germans were coming from the east, above the River Loire. But as all the roads coming from the right brought columns of refugees, it meant that the Germans were coming from the west, too. Civilians said unbelievable things about Cherbourg having been taken on the thirteenth, etc. The thirteenth! We were still in Mézières. If we were going to walk all the way, why hadn't we been given orders to leave, two or three days before? Or why hadn't those many motorized units, that had passed us the fourteenth, fifteenth, sixteenth, sent back their trucks to get us? It couldn't be gasoline that they needed, for that was wasted everywhere. I had met many an army gasoline truck giving fuel to any person on a motorcycle, or in a car, who wanted it.

Things were wrong, shockingly wrong everywhere; even with the German planes. There were many of them above, following the road, or going in all directions, but they didn't bomb us any more. They flew just above rifle range, turned, and photographed our miserable column. Weren't we even good enough to kill?

Many soldiers carried half of their equipment, having dumped their knapsacks in the ditches. I picked up several packs of cartridges. Many villages had been bombed and evacuated. The main streets were disgustingly littered with empty bottles. Fleeing civilians, soldiers, too had broken in and plundered the cellars.

We were eight, now, around the carriage. Ernest, Legrand and I were the only ones from the original group. The others had disappeared in the night, boarded passing trucks, or found bicycles without bothering to inquire if their owners were around. I was wrapped in fatigue. Everything was becoming thick, and syruplike around me. Whenever I stopped, the soil balanced itself slowly under my feet, which didn't ache any more. They had healed in my shoes, or made a compact with my rotten socks. They didn't really feel like a part of me at all. I didn't try to climb on the carriage. It was enough to be relieved of my sack. It did me good, mentally, to feel so tired. Suffering was the only excuse, in my own dim eyes, for being such a wretch in what had begun as a battalion march, but had now turned into an ugly rout.

Around noon, three handsome Moroccans, tall, with wide eyes, passed with supple strides. I said to them: "Hello, boys! All right?" They nodded. No emotion showed on their yellow faces. Inside, though, they must have been scornful. So this was the country that had conquered theirs! Exhausted, beaten, sometimes drunk, the men who had been imposing what they called their civilization upon them, lay in the ditches. Or, sons of warriors, knowing that reverses come after victories, did they only go, indifferent, wherever they had been ordered?

Downfall

A lad from La Réunion was following the carriage now, a young, short, colored boy, with kind black eyes. He had taken to us, and we to him. He never asked for anything. We had to make him drink, once in a while, from the canteens hanging from the driver's seat. Léon, his knee aching, drove, and exchanged angry words with Rameau, mad about something I could not grasp, and advancing with stiff strides while pulling his belongings on a baby carriage.

I made a point of waking up the soldiers asleep on the sides of the road: "Move on, boys, the bridges will be blown up in two hours. You don't want to be captured, do you?" They would open their bewildered eyes that did not see, and drag themselves painfully out of the ditch.

*   *   *

We reached Beaugency in the early afternoon. Here was a beautiful bridge over the River Loire, and a crowd running away from it. What again? A lone German plane circled above. As the first bomb whistled, we threw ourselves against a wall. Five bombs fell, but none hit squarely, so the plane came back, lower this time, and machine-gunned copiously. Hysterical, a girl darted from her hiding place and made for the bridge. The bullets were hitting all around. Bits of pavement and stone flew in the air. She fell. I ran and dragged her back to the sidewalk, crying: "Get up, you fool!" She didn't answer. Her eyes wide open, her mouth distorted, I shall never forget the horror on her face. The bullet had entered above the shoulder. I drew a mantle over the poor young head.

"Let's go" urged Ernest "here come some heavy Heinkels that will blow up the bridge." We ran as fast as the old lame horse would allow, pulling him savagely by the bridle, on each side, beating his flanks frantically with our bayonets, as if it mattered whether our sacks were saved or not. We clung to them, as the woman in my memory had clung to her ladle and alarm clock on the Rouen road, twenty-two years ago.

We made the bridge, among the bullets, many of which hit the water and trees. Ahead of us, a machine gun fired suddenly. Here was the old drunkard Robert, our training sergeant, letting loose at the sky; alone, haggard, swearing, magnificent! When he had no more bands, he shot with his rifle, and we all followed suit, shooting at the flying beast that went so fast we could hardly follow it.

For a while, we felt proud again.

*   *   *

The chap from La Réunion fixed our next meal. Somebody had produced a sack of small chicks, smothered to death. He cut them in quarters, fried them, poured water on top and looked very professional while we supplied the wood and whatever the next open house had to offer. We had settled ourselves in a yard, a mile southeast of Beaugency, and it was exactly five o'clock. So we were safe. All the bridges would soon be blown up. Huge reassuring explosions shook the horizon.

An artilleryman showed his face. "Come in," we said, "the yard and odor are for everybody; but no fried chicken for you, dirty motorized beggar."

He scorned the pot that the cook looked very able to defend if necessary. "Get out of here, gentlemen! Our 105 guns are on the hill above, and we'll soon make this place hot. The waters are shallow; so the Jerries will try to cross."

"Go to Hell. Couldn't you fire 100 yards below; or are you incapable of any accuracy?"

Away he went, grumbling, and we started dinner. Unexpected seasoning soon fell in it: plaster, and wood, and all the

Downfall

splinters that a shell can send 80 yards away. But not a French 105mm.! A German 77! A German battery was shooting at the crossroad, presumably, between the bridge and us, and it was very near, too, probably on the north side of the river. The next shell fell so close that spontaneously we flattened ourselves on the ground. I nearly choked laughing at the brown boy who had gotten hold of the frying pan handle so that it could not upset, but was burning himself and making an awful face. All the same, we poured out the juice, grabbed the meat and left the place. It had become unhealthy.

On the hill we passed the 105mm. guns. Plenty of them, on trucks, with tanks and a lot of material hidden around, but they didn't fire a single round. The men were raging and said mean things. They could have blown those 77's to pieces. They were being deprived of their fun.

We met the whole of our battalion around seven. Two doctors were inspecting feet. I didn't want to run the risk of removing my shoes. Léon was taken away in an ambulance; his knee was worse. Already a dozen men of our sixty from the former *peloton* were missing. The new orders were to reach a woods located approximately ten miles away.

I must have looked very tired for our lieutenant said that I was to ride in his small car, and help him find the section of the woods that had been reserved for us. Reserved? So orders were coming again. That was hopeful.

We drove through night and mud, and I don't know how he could find his way, turning all the time, cutting lines of refugees, of trucks, and swearing that we were soon to fall on the Jerries.

"What are you saying? They couldn't be under the Loire too?" I asked, but he wouldn't answer.

I have never known the name of the village where we stopped. If I had, it would have fallen in the night that was slowly invading my head, together with the names of hundreds of villages that I had read on the milestones, the last four days. And what did it matter anyway, so long as it was France. Or would it soon be Spain, if we kept going south like that?

In the village, we tried in vain to locate a free barn. It had started raining and he had hoped that he could find a better shelter than our corner of the woods. Everywhere we found refugees packed in with their belongings. The inhabitants hadn't left. There were cattle and horses in the stables, and sheep bleating their heads off when I felt the ground in the dark, with my rifle.

A fat woman was sitting on a stone, outside, shrieking: "My darling daughter! They will violate her, they will kill her." I shook her. "They certainly will, if you keep on calling them like that." Somebody whom I couldn't see said: "Nonsense. They behave very well. They even feed the civilians."

I said "Sure they do," so that the woman would stop her lamentations. Then I wondered. How could he, in the dark, know? But rumors of all kinds were spreading among the civilians. They had heard radio proclamations that we knew nothing about.

In spite of the rain, we had to go to the woods. I lay by the lieutenant. He had stretched his uniform raincoat on top of me. I should have slept if the ground hadn't kept on waving under me, but I felt well enough, except when the leaves above suddenly released a puddle of rain that splashed on my face. I even joked:

"Do you remember the nice sort of pre-Christ type of war you were teaching us on the green hills of Mézières, and the fight we had about my not having respected the given dimensions of the so-called "Gamelin hole," a machine-gun nest you had made me dig in sandy ground which kept falling on the tripod? And what about the marvelous 1936 rifle with dis-

Downfall

appearing bayonets that we had to study about in books because the depot had none available? I have been taking all this training so as to become a liaison officer with the British Army, and it ends by my having come from America to run in the dust and mud, and live on stolen fowl."

He laughed rather hollowly. A young lawyer, short and strong, with clear eyes and open face, he, too, would have liked nothing better than fighting to the limit. He, too, was taking orders from somebody who was also taking orders. If a mistake, or worse, were launched at the top of the Army, it went down, amplifying itself at each degree until it fell on his shoulders, before bouncing ultimately on the *Poilu's*.

*   *   *

June 18.

Well before dawn I joined my group and we walked west, through the Sologne, famed for its hunting grounds and its castles. In vain did I take advantage of my lieutenant's raincoat to order the traffic of the civilians along the road. They didn't even want to flee any more, and obstructed the roads.

Around noon, at a crossroad, a portly major moving his arms like a traffic policeman, stopped every soldier and directed him to a dirt path ending in a thicket. We found two hundred men there, sitting or sleeping. It was Major J. . . whom I knew well. He had been my captain, fifteen years ago, when I served my term of military service, and I could tell many funny stories about him. Risen from the ranks in the last war, his huge chest multicolored with medals, he made inconceivable blunders, to the joy of his young lieutenants. He loved nothing better than acting like a top sergeant, inspecting clothes and writing in the company book. His metallic voice could shake a whole regiment to attention. Now he was grave. He rounded us up and said, with emotion:

"Men, you have always been like my own children. The war has taken a very bad turn. I fear for you, for your life, for your freedom. Go as fast as you can, taking the first road to the right, to Dhuison. See that no one stays behind."

My God! He had made us lose half an hour to say only that. Yet he seemed to have something else on his mind, something more important that he didn't dare tell. He looked all of us in the face, with a warm, faithful look, sighed, and drove away in his car. I heard him mutter: "They are leaving their knapsacks."

It was an old woman who stopped us, in the afternoon, to listen to her radio in her little, lone house that she had refused to quit. A deep, shaky voice said:

". . . I have asked our adversaries for an armistice. I shall only accept honorable conditions."

It was a transcription of a broadcast by Marshal Petain who had taken over the government.

So there was not going to be any stand behind the River Loire.

We were beaten. Shame ran in my veins, heavy as lead.

June 19.

The lieutenant woke us up at 2 A.M. and said that we must cross the River Cher before noon, at a bridge point named La Selle. We pushed along in the dark, then in the sunrise, then in the sun, stopping as little as possible. The cannonade had now begun on our left. The way seemed to be open only right ahead. As much as we could, we kept at an equal distance between the cannonade on our right, and the cannonade on our left. Planes were circling above, hardly higher than a mile. German planes, of course.

Downfall

At eight, we reached Billy. Only three more miles to go. The road turned left, through the woods, by a castle. The woods were swarming with soldiers, and the road was jammed. We were compelled to stop. A convoy of machine guns, pulled by mules was coming towards us, headed by a lieutenant.

"Lieutenant, isn't this the way to La Selle sur Cher?"

"Yes, or rather it was. The bridge is occupied by German tanks."

Back in the corner of the woods, we found high ranking officers engaged in a great discussion. Whomever I asked told me to wait. By a hedge, I picked up a general's cap, with two stars. Nobody claimed it.

At ten, a lieutenant and forty men were sent as vanguard to see if there was another way to cross the river. Half an hour later, we heard a stiff fire. At twelve, thirty men came back. The officer had been killed. The river, they reported, was occupied all around. At two, there was some activity and I was under the impression that a message had been received.

A tall major came around and said that we shouldn't shoot, no matter what happened. A soldier asked: "What shall we do with our rifles?"

"You may throw them in the river, along with the men who have carried them. What are they worth?"

So said the major. I can see his face. I can hear his words now, and I should like to make him swallow them, and his tongue, and his teeth. I'm sorry I can't remember his name. According to him, it was our fault that we had been marched away from the enemy with about fifteen hours' sleep in five days, and brought to this blind alley.

I found some water in the woods, and washed and shaved, as did most of my comrades. We ate a little, too. We discussed whether it was worth while trying to pass at any cost. No one thought so. The armistice had obviously been granted. The planes above could have destroyed us all, if they had wanted to. And we were so tired — tired to the bones, tired to the heart. Only the hope of taking part in that battle of the Loire had kept us going. Sleep was all that we wanted now.

I lay down, but the trees moved around me, as if I had been drunk, and I thought that I would vomit. I sat with my back against an oak tree. The last gulp of cognac from Ernest's bottle helped me a little. I drifted into an open-eyed dream:

Everybody was in a boat. It had a thousand masts. The skipper was Captain C. . . so tired because he had walked all the way with his men. He lifted his officer's cap. His head was so very small underneath. It looked as if he had left his forehead in the cap. The brown boy from La Réunion muttered that he would draw his old pistol if anyone came to his farm, way over yonder, to make a soldier of him. The road melted into water. It was a creek, falling in the North River, by a little cabin. . . .

CHAPTER 3

Capture

THEY arrived in armored cars, roaring so that the trees shook. It was five o'clock, the 19th of June 1940.

In the first car, a German officer stood up, his arms raised well above his head, and he shouted in French:

"La guerre est finie, vous serez chez vous dans trois jours."

Moving slowly behind their shields, the machine guns were covering the woods. Two observation planes circled above, very low.

They didn't need to be afraid. Nobody was going to shoot. The sad show was over, incomprehensible as far as I was concerned, right to the last moment. *They* lifting up *their* hands, and sending *us* home!

Out of the woods came my comrades. One by one they went towards the cars. Some of them had their arms lifted, just like the German officer. They meant, perhaps, that they agreed?

Followed by three sergeants, the German officer jumped onto the road, and shouted again:

"The war is ended. You will be home in three days." He laughed broadly, engagingly.

A few men cheered. Ernest and I came out of hiding, to see who had thus disgraced themselves. There, clad in French uniforms, five or six men had raised only one arm and were giving the Nazi salute. I heard this distinctly:

". . . wir haben nie geschossen. (We are Alsatians, we have never fired a shot.)" They smiled.

It is true that three or four others, who could not have been Alsatians, also smiled, or tried to.

From all the cars, German soldiers jumped down and lined up. They carried hand grenades ready to throw. So they had two kinds of arguments! This one was less humiliating.

Beyond the thicket, I had my last vision of the carriage, hoarding our knapsacks and our emergency rations inside. The horse grazed peacefully.

I was gathering my most important belongings when a German hit me in the back with the rifle that I had just laid in the bushes. He pushed me into the open, made me take off my helmet, my leather belt, my equipment, and hurried me towards the road. There I joined the rest of my group. A sentry put us in rows of three. There was already a long column ahead of us, and it grew rapidly while the Germans were combing the woods. Four men, who had been seen running towards the castle were shot, together with a fifth, who happened to be in the way of the submachine gun.

The rifles were gathered promptly. The old type models, held by the barrel, were broken against trees. The newer ones were piled up. They would soon be sent to Germany with our fine steel helmets and our leather harnesses.

At about six o'clock, we were marched to Billy. In front of the city hall, or was it the public school, we stopped. Above the door: "*Liberté, Fraternité, Égalité*," was painted in black. Was it irony, or could it mean hope?

A few women had dared to come out and, from the sidewalk, their backs against the wall, they were looking at us intently. What is your regiment? Do you know So-and-So? Mothers and wives whose love was stronger than shame. Their faces were washed with tears.

A group of French officers had been gathered apart. There was Captain C. . . . , no longer looking funny to me. Erect, his mouth set, his extraordinarily high three striped cap cocked over his wet eyes, I could see what I felt expressed in his face.

Downfall

He was trying to spot his men in the column. They waved at him. None of my immediate officers was there. Way ahead, beyond the Cher, rolling towards southern France, in a small black automobile, they were not happy perhaps, having failed to keep their men together, to instruct them, and to share their fate. But they were safe. If we had had a map, if we had known what they knew, small parties of us, hiding in the woods, could have forced the German line in places where it could not have been entirely tight yet, around us.

As tired as we were, after five days of rout, our captors were soon to show that we still had strength to exhaust. But all I could feel now was a faint curiosity. So these were the men who had been after us, stepping with order in our disorderly steps! Their green-grey uniforms looked neater and better conceived than ours. Their wristbands were lifted. They wore on their chests an embroidered silver eagle, with a swastika in the center; and a German flag was painted on the side of their massive helmets. Hand grenades were stuck in their boots. The motorcyclists wore long grey oilskins. Maybe one of them was the shadow I had shot at the night before last, or had I sent him down, definitely, through an even darker night, to the kingdom of shadows? Noncommissioned officers carried field glasses, hung on their breasts, and went around proudly, shouting orders. Sentries clapped their heels and said:

"*Ja, wohl, Herr Unteroffizier.*"

Soon they chased the women away. Nobody could speak to us any more. We were prisoners of war.

Two thousand at least, in rows of five, we went up the same road we had followed that morning; then we had been a poor, dusty, demoralized lot, but free. Now we had to march close to one another, so as to allow motorcycles and small cars to pass at great speed. Soon we got entangled in each other's packages. Everyone carried as much as he had been able to take from his luggage. We were going home, the German officer had said.

The guards rolled along in groups of three mounted on French bicycles. One man carried a light machine gun and two others carried the ammunition, in supple metallic bands of about fifty cartridges. They wore these around the neck, like scarves. It gave them a strange air, both handsome and ferocious. It was obvious that the German uniform had been studied on mannikins, not only for its efficiency, but also for the effect it might have on others. Our French uniforms were made of much better fabric; but they were loosely cut, and they had little style.

On a straight section of the highway, we stopped. Our column stretched for almost half a mile. We waited. Ernest pulled out a package of cigarettes, took one, handed another to me and struck a match.

"*Nicht rauchen, du, Schwein . . .*" (No smoking, you swine) His cigarette, the match box, and the package flew up in the air, and Herr Unteroffizier bellowed for five minutes, fantastically. What a noise! What a mixture of harsh and whistling sounds! The beautiful German language can be spoken in such an ugly way. He gargled with guttural consonants, and spat out the vowels. So as to make his barking more effective, he brandished his fist under Ernest's nose, and pushed a pistol in his side. I could hardly refrain from laughing. Frenchmen are little impressed by shrieks.

As soon as the Stentor's attention was distracted by somebody else, the cigarettes, deftly picked up between the ranks, came back to Ernest, from hand to hand. He put a whole one in his mouth, chewed it, and spat the paper in the direction of the next guard who, fortunately, did not see it.

"Attention!"

Before we could realize what was happening, a car passed

Downfall

by at the speed of a galloping horse, very close to the column. The Germans had found a very efficient way of straightening our lines: two men, standing in the car, were knocking protruding heads with their fists. In my row, it was Rameau who had gotten it in the neck. I helped him up and, as I was next to him, I took his place. It was my turn. We had already learned that the best place was as far away from "them" as possible, but everybody could not be in the center.

The car returned. The two sergeants seated now and wiping their brows, were smiling broadly. They had had some fun, and the whole column stood in perfect order. Later, when five officers, rigid and solemn, in shiny uniforms, with silver shoulder straps, red leather belts, high wavy caps, drove by disdainfully in a splendid low slung car, there was nothing wrong with the day's catch. The review must have been a complete success.

The column was then divided into three sections, with an armored car before and after each of them, the high coupled machine guns aimed at us. Every twenty feet, a guard on a bike kept a hand grenade ready. The chain around us had been tightened a few more links.

The guard nearest to us asked if anybody around understood German. My comrades urged me to answer. He dismounted and walked beside me. He looked fierce, but intelligent, and said:

"You are dumb. You have gone to war for the British. We have beaten you in six weeks. We shall beat them in even less time."

He repeated some of the words in French, so as to be sure that I had understood, and told me to translate what he had said, to my comrades. They made me ask him if it were true that the war was over. He laughed.

"For you, yes. Not for us."

That was clear enough.

After eight miles we paused for ten minutes. I sat in the ditch, dug a hole under my legs and buried my wife's letters. I could not bear the thought of such men fumbling through them.

We made three more miles. It was dark when we entered a village and were driven into a field enclosed with barbed wire. At each corner, a light machine gun was set on a tuffet. The gunner lay on his stomach; he had a searchlight and plenty of ammunition.

We sank to the ground and slept as best we could, lying close to each other.

Guards walked through the camp, all night long.

PART II

CAPTIVITY

CHAPTER 4

Days of Hunger

A FINE epitaph for Hitler — if the Poles, the Czechs, the Jews and all prisoners ever let him be buried — would be: "In everything he had method."

It would have taken many regiments of guards to escort the thousands and thousands of prisoners bagged every day. In the enormous confusion created by the speed of the invasion, they might have escaped easily. Here is a six day solution of this problem:

1st day: Give them nothing to eat, and march them 15 miles.

2nd day: 25 miles and nothing to eat.

3rd day: 30 miles and no food.

4th day: 35 miles and ditto.

5th day: a tiny platter of soup, and 42 especially well-selected miles.

6th day: a mere 15 miles, and a little French tobacco wrapped in a thin, brown paper.

It solves the question of transportation, also.

Of course, after the third day, you have to count on a certain amount of butt-end pounding of the ribs to keep these people from falling down. You may, on the other hand, improve their resistance considerably, by building up their morale with the reiterated affirmation that the war is over, and they will be sent home soon. Wretches will fall for the sweetest lure any time and swim into the net.

Captivity

I have checked these facts later, in captivity, and I found that all my fellow prisoners went through similar experiences. I am convinced that highly placed Germans gave the orders necessary to produce the desired results. But at the time, I needed every atom of energy too much to be able to draw any conclusions. Day by day, I plodded through increasing darkness.

*　　*　　*

June 20.

Captivity had begun at 5 P.M. on the 19th of June. We had walked fifteen miles to our first cattle park.

On the 20th, we stayed there all day. We could walk freely within the barbed wire. The men had already grouped themselves more or less by regiments, companies, sympathies. About twenty Alsatians stood together in a corner. They spoke to the guards, who brought them a little food and a few cigarettes. From that corner originated confusing news: sometimes the armistice was already signed; later, it was only going to be. In any case, we should not be kept prisoners long.

The Arabs and the Negroes had set themselves apart. The Germans pointed their fingers at them and snarled, for colonial troops are credited with taking no prisoners when they fight. They give no mercy. Perhaps it is more humane. Among them were the three Moroccans that I had met on the Beaugency road, as demure as ever.

About sixteen men of the ill-fated Mézières platoon were there. We were glad to be together again, to tell each other how we had been trapped, find out who had been killed, wounded, lucky. Had they any food? We had only a handful of hard biscuits between us. They too had lost their emergency rations with their sacks.

Beyond the field was a well. The sentries would allow one man at a time to fill a pail or a canteen.

The officers had been locked up for the night, in a stable adjoining the park. With straw in their hair, they looked more human. They had been brought in a truck.

Old, bearded Major Galois told me, over the fence, that he had inquired about food for us. A German officer had answered: "The question has not yet been considered."

A Frenchwoman was once allowed near the barbed wire. She carried a pail of small, hard biscuits, and another of marmalade. The hundred men nearest to her, fought to get a bit of food. It was ugly. We were too far away to have any chance.

A young boy and a girl cried from the road that they would try to get us some wine. We threw them our canteens. They went back and forth to their family's cellar, until a ferocious looking young guard stopped them. He held a pistol in each hand with such ostentation that it was comical. I received half a cup of wine as my share. What luck!

A guard, older than the others, threw a can half full of French corned beef to a group of prisoners. His colleague with the two pistols ran to him and spoke some very harsh words that I could not make out. He replied: "*Ja wohl*," and did not throw any more food; but he looked at us, some times, with an almost kindly air.

We neither lunched nor dined.

Almost every hour, a new group of prisoners was brought in. There was hardly any way of walking around without stepping on somebody.

I spent most of the day lying, sleeping, or observing the German troops passing almost without interruption on the highway. Tanks, bearing on the side the same cross that the planes carried under the wings; high motor cars of a special shape, with dual light machine guns, mounted so as to shoot easily in all directions; heavy trucks, the hood covered with an

Captivity

ugly flag, red with a white circle and a thick black swastika in the center; artillery, pulled by tractors, whole batteries of our own 25 mm. antitank guns, already in use against us; long busses full of men lightly equipped; English, French, American-made cars captured in Holland, Belgium, France, and repainted in uniform dark grey; and the German army wagons, with tilted sides, which looked old enough to have seen the Napoleonic wars.

The cannonade was rolling again, in two directions. Armistice or no armistice, other men were being caught. I had now understood their system: the map of central France had been divided into small sections, bound on two sides by highways. Planes went ahead and cut communications, so as to produce a concentration of troops in a few adjoining sections. Tanks and motorized artillery advanced on the highways, annihilating whatever means of resistance remained. Light armored cars and motorcycle-patrols then ran along the cross roads and cut the last way out.

Shooting occurred only when the mental poisons that the unbelievably developed fifth column had inoculated in our staffs, and news of the armistice, had not already disarmed the regiments. The method was most economical. It even looked humane. They were not out to kill us all, as they could have done. They were rounding up cattle.

In the afternoon, a German officer spoke in French: "We know that some of you still carry weapons. There will be an inspection in ten minutes. Any man found with a gun, a pistol, or a knife broader than the hand, will be shot immediately."

Whatever arms remained among us were promptly produced, or thrown away. Ernest and I went to the shallow trench that took the place of a privy. We crouched, and we buried our weapons; he, his long knife with a coupling notch,

I, my wonderful Swedish knife, as good as a poniard. Attached to a string, they could be pulled out again.

Hunger was felt that night.

A volley of shots awoke me. Somebody had sneaked under the barbed wire and crawled through a field of oats. But there were guards, beyond, that we had not seen.

*   *   *

June 21.

At 5 A.M. we started, on empty stomachs.

For once, my humorous Ernest was in a foul humor. His best bag had been stolen in the night, and one of my three handsome Moroccans wore a brand-new turban looking very much like Ernest's flannel band.

On the principal *place* of the next village, stood what had been a French army gasoline-truck. An *Unteroffizier* and two soldiers were distributing gasoline to refuges who had cars, inspecting their papers and ordering them north. They seemed very polite. An officer, peeping through a Leica camera, was selecting carefully the best aspect of the scene. It did make a fine picture for say, the *Kölnische Illustrierte Magazine*, with a lovely caption such as: "German soldiers showing the French population that Hitler will help them."

Elsewhere, they would seize the supplies of the village, install a rolling army-stove at the foot of the monument to the dead of the last war, make the refugees stand in line, feed them, and demonstrate later in the newspapers that they had come to save the starving population!

A crack shot was obtained later in the day, during a pause. Two German soldiers came around. One carried a large bone, with about a pound of raw meat hanging from it. He threw it in the midst of a group of Moroccans, who fought desperately for it. One came out with the naked bone, and licked it. He

Captivity

had blood all over his face. The others were trying to swallow their strip of meat before it could be snatched away from them. The Germans used a whole roll of film on that scene. In an illustrated section of a German newspaper, I was to see later a picture that looked very much like it, with this title: "French prisoners eating. . . ." If the bone had fallen by me, I would have fought for it, too!

Mileage is easy to compute on French highways, because a white stone marks every kilometer and bears the name of and distance to, the next village or city.

Every eight miles, we stopped for ten or fifteen minutes. I chewed some dandelions; but they were dusty and I had to spit them out.

Peasants set buckets of water for us, along the road. We were not allowed to stop, so we filled our cups or canteens swiftly, in passing.

In a village, a few six-pound loaves of bread were thrown to the column by a group of crying women. In an instant, the loaves were reduced to tiny bits. None came my way. Two thousand men is a lot, crying "Bread, bread." We threw money at children on the sidewalk, taking the chance that they could buy some bread and throw it to us. But there was no more bread to buy, or else the children could not find us again, in the long moving column. Soon this practice became forbidden, anyway. But nobody could prevent my letting fall bits of paper, on which I had hastily scribbled, while still marching: "My name is . . . My wife lives at . . . Let her know that I am a prisoner." I dropped fifteen such notes. Two were to be picked up by unknown charitable souls, mailed, and received.

At a turn of the road, my comrade Legrand showed me a house, with closed shutters, and said: "I shall try to hide behind it. If they shoot me, it will be over. If they do not see me, I have a pair of blue duck trousers in my bag. I shall mix with the refugees." He went swiftly, passed the open gate, and crouched behind the wall. Nobody had seen him. I had nothing with which to disguise myself, and I had barely the strength to keep my feet moving, but I hate myself for not having followed him then.

I have seen corpses burnt up, torn, the entrails spread out, the heads mashed to a red mud. I'd rather be one such corpse than stand in a famished column again, dragging myself towards captivity, through the country that used to be mine, while sobbing Frenchwomen on the sidewalk murmur: "Poor boys, how they are going to suffer!"

After twenty-five miles, we entered a park similar to the other, but this time the submachine guns in the corners were French, easily recognizable by their ammunition box above the barrel. Unlike a dog, a gun has no master.

The French officers were no longer near us. I asked a guard if there was any question of food for us. He did not know. We filled up on water.

Sleep came and went. Stomachs burned. Limbs ached. Anxiety grew.

* * *

June 22.

With grown beards, dusty, stumbling, everyone searching within himself for any atom of energy accumulated by years of good food, we started, around five o'clock, on the 22nd. Many abandoned bags and pouches lay in the park. Everyone was, so to speak, hanging on to himself for his very life. No crude joke about the guards ever shook the ranks any more, but words like these were passed from rank to rank:

"They want our skins. They shall not have them. *They shall not have me.*"

The column had been divided into smaller sections. There

Captivity

was only one machine-gun car ahead of us. We had a new and smaller set of guards, still on bicycles, and carrying a whole arsenal. The one near me was willing to talk.

"It will not last long," he said. "The armistice . . . a few days." He seemed to believe it firmly. That was good news for him, too. He had seen Poland, Holland, Belgium. The fight on the Somme was, he said, "Bad, very bad. Many dead!" He wanted to go home. He could not explain why we were not fed, and said many things I could not understand. My school German had not resisted the starvation diet. Words seemed to be flying towards me, and then turning away before I could grasp them.

The country was now covered with signs in German: Feldkommandantur, Feldlazaret. . . . Neat posters, bordered in red, had been stuck on the village walls. During a pause I read one. It said, in French: "Appealing to the intelligence of the population, the *Oberbefehlshaber* . . . any act of sabotage, any help given to escaped prisoners, will be punished by death."

Men had begun falling. Guards kicked them up, collected them, and forced them to join the column. It meant an extra effort. That was no solution. It was better to follow the dream that came to me, of a raw carrot — enormous, as big as a sugar beet, as big as a ham — that I would chew, like a cow, endlessly.

Twice we retraced our steps for a few miles. It looked as if they were trying to make the way longer. They were! It made us bitterly angry.

We reached the next park after thirty miles. That night it rained. Those who had fallen asleep by the barbed wires could make a sort of tent with their mantles, or anything. The others pulled the flaps of their caps over their eyes, and soaked.

*　　*　　*

June 23.

Much before daylight, we were pushed out by new sentries. Their squadrons were smaller than the previous ones. We had become easy to guard, now, but some had to be persuaded to get up. They lay in the mud, opened their bewildered eyes to the guard's flashlight, and did not even react to a well aimed blow of the gun, in the lower ribs, where it hurts so badly. Comrades had to put them on their feet. They would stumble, and finally go. A few had to be abandoned. No kick, no friendly hand, would awaken them.

Most of us chewed grass. It helped. The country passed on each side of us, like a dim moving picture. Sparing one's saliva, one muttered only for one's self now, to the rhythm of the steps:

"They — shall — not — have — me."

Many did not believe it any more.

Our speed had become very slow. In the middle of the day, they halted us for an hour. Three guards and a male nurse — or perhaps a doctor — went through the column, collected men among those who looked the worst, and put them in a truck. I saw one man, with white hair, refuse to go. No, he would walk with the others, until the end. A shudder of affection shook the men lying in the ditch, around him.

Old Marais, himself, who had been so afraid of the bombs, was taken too. He could not climb on the truck. Two sentries balanced him over the side. They swore. They were disgusted at our weakness. When men showed them on their fingers, five, while tapping on their stomachs, indicating five days without food, they shrugged their shoulders. They did not believe it, or did not understand or did not care. It was none of their business. They had filled themselves comfortably, the last few days, with the treasures of the French cellars.

It took us more than seventeen hours to make thirty-five miles.

We stopped, or rather we fell, in a field, by a castle. It was, perhaps, lovely. That day I had abandoned my last belongings.

Captivity

I had no soap, razor, spare shirt, socks. I did not care if I ever looked human again, but I still clung to my leather brief case, containing, now, a single book, and a few drawings. I put it under my head and slept.

It seemed five minutes later when they woke us up. Couldn't we even sleep? It was dark, and it rained. Now I knew that it was the end for me. I would not, I could not walk any more, no matter what happened. But a fantastic rumor ran around:

"Get your plates, cups, anything, ready! They will give us something to eat."

A new energy shook the camp. It is amazing how much people want to live, even when life has become unbearable. A smiling sentry passed around, showing a plate, and said: "*Ja, ja.*"

We stood in line, a long time. The line advanced so slowly that I knew I should arrive too late. There would not be anything for me. No face has ever looked gentler than that of the German cook who handed me a little plate of barley soup, and a thin slice of rye bread, from his kitchen truck. As if every grain were going to fill up a hole carved in my body, I chewed the bread for a long time.

We spent the rest of the night in the dependences of the castle, on naked floors that felt dry and good, though harder than earth.

A wave of hope ran through the prisoners. That little food had gone to our heads.

*   *   *

June 24.

The most naive rumors circulated when we started in the morning, originating, as usual, with the better-treated Alsatians. We were going to be transported in trucks. A very nice officer had said that he would do what he could for us. We walked almost willingly. The column was tame. It was generally accepted that the armistice was definitely signed, and that we were going to be freed. Free. Go. Forget it all. But many were very anxious about their families. Had they survived the exodus on the machine-gunned roads? For a few hours, jokes ran again, timidly, through the ranks. Then despair came back. It was to be the hardest day of all.

After some nineteen hours of march, we had made forty miles. The column was dragging itself over a forest road when the unbelievable order came:

"Run! Run!"

Guards shouting: "*Raus, raus . . .*" and shooting at our heels, made us run. I would not have believed that it was possible: the whole column ran. It was splendid, in a way, through the night, the lightning and noise of the shots, the heavy clapping of the feet, followed by the gentler clapping of whatever was still hanging from their necks, at the end of a strap, on the men's backs, and that sensation of maximum, of impossible, punishment!

When they commanded again: "March!" men began falling, one by one. I saw seven. One cannot mistake a man falling dead from exhaustion. It is as if his body had lost the backbone. It drops like clothes from a coat hanger, and arranges itself gently on the ground.

We made two more miles, and entered a camp in the darkest of all nights. We had to pass one-by-one between two Germans who ordered, in French, the surrender of all straight razors and flashlights. The man ahead of me, tall and thin, slipped a hand in his coat, as if he were going to put a razor in the hand already stretched out for it. No. He leaned away from that hand, sighed, and fell.

Death by a bullet is not so horrible, even if you have to suffer

Captivity

agonizing pains. It keeps something heroic, spectacular. It is part of a fight. But dying so, your life pulled away, torn away, step by step, breath by breath, in the dust, in the mud, in the dark . . .

I was so full of hatred that I could not sleep.

*   *   *

June 25.

We arrived at Orléans after a mere fifteen miles. I could not even lift my head to see the damage that Italian planes had inflicted on that lovely city, a few days before.

One by one, we passed a railroad bridge, over the Loire, that had been incompletely blown up, and repaired with huge wooden beams. At the end stood four guards, two on each side. One stopped me and put a package of tobacco in my hand. He smiled gently and said: "Arrived."

Each of us received a pack. The most foolish gratitude melted my heart.

CHAPTER 5

A Prison Camp in France

EVERY soldier going to war is provided with a pack of gauze, and told how to dress a wound. This simple precaution may save his life. Why isn't he also told something about regaining his freedom if he happens to lose it? Anyone at the front line is subject to being taken prisoner.

Half an hour of instructions from someone having gone through what was in store for me, would have enabled me to end my story very soon after our arrival at the huge Dunois Artillery Barracks, in Orléans. It is immediately after being taken, when you are not known or registered, when the organization is not yet tightened around you, and when the front line, or the border, is still in proximity, that the possibilities of making good an escape are the greatest.

I knew nothing. I had never thought about this problem before. Instinct, perhaps, had made me brush up my school German in the last few months; but the little I understood helped me only to fall more completely into my captors' hands. Every German standing guard in the numerous courtyards where we were allowed to circulate, was willing to talk, and repeated that we were going to be freed in a few days. It was a question of transports. The armistice was effectively signed, peace expected soon. Why not? the war was over. His officers had said so. Their predictions had never failed. France had fallen exactly when announced.

There was always a large group around anybody who could understand German. We saturated ourselves with this news,

Captivity

so in accord with our hopes. Every word was repeated, amplified. Once launched, propaganda is transmitted like a germ, by its very victims.

*   *   *

Excepting a few rooms reserved for their services, the Germans were methodically filling up the barracks, from the main floor to the fifth, with prisoners. The stable and the numerous garages were being hastily furnished with primitive double-decker bunks, with or without a little straw. The army steel cots and mattresses were removed progressively from the buildings, loaded on trucks, and replaced by loose straw. My part of the column was assigned to garage number twenty.

I had fallen in a corner and slept for two days. I woke up to be made responsible for a group of twelve, and as such, had to stand by the kitchen assigned to this part of the camp, and get the rations in an old tin can. In the waiting-line I found a dozen more of my platoon comrades, arrived by another road in five days, also. They had not been compelled to run, as we had, but had made forty-five miles on the last day.

How good to be where it smelled of food! Twice a day we received about two tablespoons of peas, of a bitter variety that I had never tasted before, or a little thin soup, one or two slices of French Army bread, and sometimes a bit of very old cheese. Not as old, however, as the bread, which, it was rumored, had come from a wrecked freight train and was perfectly green inside, or yellow like sulphur. The mold had little taste, fortunately, and we soon found that it could be eaten when toasted. We could not afford to lose a crumb, so we hunted for wood, and started fires everywhere in the courtyards. After a few days, a little meat, strangely red and smelly was added to the diet. Anyhow, good or bad, it was food coming regularly, with a cup of water. Even such small quantities meant life. The ugly fear of starvation disappeared.

Dysentery took its place. As there was no more water in the barracks, and no city cleaning-service, the lavatories had been locked. Trenches dug along the back walls had now to be filled every day, and multiplied to such an extent that they invaded every courtyard — hidden at first by low palisades; later entirely open. Of the fourteen thousand prisoners interned at Dunois at the end of June, one thousand, perhaps, were constantly crouching over these trenches, bleeding so much that maggots soon ran out, and were thick under foot all around. We took pieces of cardboard along to fight off the flies, but had not always the strength to do that.

The disease caught you suddenly; you would painfully vomit the small amount of sour peas and rotten meat that you carried in your stomach, and then you had to run to the privy. Men who arrived too late sprinkled their pants with dirt, and scraped it off with their knives, or small pieces of tin. It was so disheartening to lose the food that represented your hope of recovery, while, instead, you became green, and extraordinarily thin and weak.

At night, it meant a continuous descending and ascending of stairs, and difficulties with guards. They had orders to shoot anyone out of the buildings after curfew, and did so freely. We called them, a hand on our stomach, saying: *"Latrines, latrines!"* They came around, shouting, but we would become sick right there. They finally allowed us to go to the nearest trench, following a definite route. They would go back to patrolling, and contenting themselves with firing shots at all windows where a light showed. It was too bad if you were behind the window! As there was no electricity, you would make torches with paper to clean up the mess that you had just made around your bed.

Captivity

The infirmary had been reorganized with French prisoner-doctors, under the direction of one or two Germans. The supply of paregoric and bismuth had, fortunately, not been raided. The worst cases were sent out to some hospital, but the epidemic, dangerous for the Germans also, grew to such an extent that their head doctor inspected each kitchen, made a formidable row with his sergeants, ordered the green bread burnt up in the yard, and a horse that had just been cut up, buried by the privies. In the evening, a party of Arabs dug it out, and, in spite of the most terrific smell, roasted large pieces over bonfires, until they were almost charcoal. Then ate them, with a disdainful air. They had known worse than that, probably.

Later, better bread was provided, though in smaller quantities; all meat was boiled a long time, and men were employed to spread calcium chloride over the trenches. There was never enough of it and, in the summer heat, you contracted the disease there, if the food had not already poisoned you.

*　　*　　*

Inside the camp, wherever no guard stood to chase us away, we behaved as if in conquered territory. The Germans had removed all arms, ammunition, radio apparatus and valuable stocks before we came, but many secondary storerooms had not yet been emptied. Nobody ever knew who forced the doors, or if they were found open, but everything left was raided. We found shirts, socks, used uniforms, wooden shoes, sacks, pouches, and promptly replaced what we had abandoned along the roads. Gas mask tin boxes proved very useful to fetch the soup for a group of twelve. It gave an extra taste of varnish to it. The expensive masks were just thrown away. Everything concerning war was painfully ridiculous. We did not feel military any longer. My platoon comrades appeared one day with perfectly silly kepis, blue-black with red lines, gallantly cocked over their ears, that made them look like old-time country postmen. It was a sort of generalized flea market, where one bargained with reticent locks only: when they did not give in, we broke them.

The courtyards had a funny atmosphere of a county fair. No gaiety, but a strange animation, nervous, sneering, predominated. All possible uniforms were present, air force, cavalry, heavy and light artillery, and all branches of the infantry.

The colonial troops had been housed separately and stayed together. There were about two hundred Indo-Chinese, small yellow men, looking so young. They left at seven in the morning, in sections commanded by their own corporals — harsh, shrieking, and even slapping them, and worked all day in the city, under the care of a few German guards. They came back at night, very tired, but some of them carried fresh bread. They seemed immune to dysentery, played and laughed together in the evening. Perhaps little change had been wrought in their life.

The Arabs numbered many hundreds, and could be found anywhere that there was anything to take. Already they came around with strange things to sell, that they showed you under their coats: a knife, a wallet, a piece of leather, and sometimes a nice shirt. They lacked only a pile of rugs and a sheepskin on the back, to duplicate their compatriots who proved such a colorful nuisance on the Parisian streets, offering to people sitting on the terrace of popular cafés, a magnificent silver ring for fifty francs, and finally selling it for three francs, with a profit of two!

There was a strange party on the second floor of one of the larger buildings. They called themselves North African civilians. They had been imported from Morocco, apparently, to work on French farms, and had been collected by the Germans.

Captivity

Dressed in civilian clothes, I suspect them of having shared these with friends from various regiments, for their number increased every day. I had been sent to draw a plan of this building, and had the opportunity to see every room. In one of them, two boys with red fez and naked torso, handsome and appearing fourteen years old, greeted me by bowing to the floor, then said many things I could not grasp, and fell into a very suggestive dance with four older men, who treated them exactly as if they were their wives. Others, squatting in filthy straw, played games, or sorted odd objects, buttons, pieces of metal, empty bottles, cloth samples, scraps of paper. They had a distinguished way of scratching themselves slowly, and of fingering their chests in search of a hungry louse. It smelled of repellent soup in a large army pan, around which a group was busy. Others, lying in perfect immobility, seemed dying or dead, their brown skin having turned grey.

The Germans never interfered with them until one day when they started to jump out of the windows, with their clothes burning. They had been cooking a dog or a cat, caught in the yard, on a big stone in the middle of a room, the powdered straw around had caught fire, and it is a wonder that it could be put out. Then a squadron of guards, bayonets out, chased them away to an empty storeroom, in the garage section, where they acted as before.

The Negroes behaved otherwise. There were samples from every part of Africa. The handsomest were the Senegalese. Elegant, slender, they took great care of their long thin feet, scraping them between the toes with a knife, bathing them in a small tin can, wrapping them carefully with rags.

A group of thirty, belonging apparently to a single tribe, spent hours dancing and clapping hands in dry, fast asymmetrical rhythms. They formed a circle, three jumped in the middle, vociferating, rolling their eyes, sticking out their tongues, and suddenly throwing one foot well over their heads; then falling ritually, crawling, standing on their knees and muttering what sounded like threats; then bursting out laughing, and beginning the scene all over again. They were so pleased, they threw each other pieces of money. Fascinated, the white men gathered around. Here was another world, undefeated, untouched. They also threw money in the arena. When a five franc note had been given, one of the dancers would come near the donor, vociferate at him, and seem to include him in the sacred dance, then he would explain, in broken French, that luck had thus been brought to him forever. I learned from them that they had been captured very near, and had not been submitted to any exhausting march. The armistice did not mean anything to them. They were not concerned.

The white prisoners felt no such high spirits. When not too sick, they walked around the yard, in small groups, discussing liberation; dreaming aloud of returning home, forever; or went from room to room trying to find some old friend; or searching for something to replace a missing item in their equipment. Here and there the inevitable games of *belote*, piquet, and bridge were in progress, played without enthusiasm, but attentively, so as to keep away all other thoughts.

A few southern French officers had organized a game of hand ball, a rather hard one, where the ball is hit with the palm against a wall, and must not be allowed to touch the ground. They were lucky to be so energetic. German soldiers, sergeants, and officers, circulated about in groups, and looked at us. Curiosity was in their eyes. They looked contented, as if on furlough. To them it was a colorful slave fair. They carried cameras and took pictures of the dancing negroes, the demure Arabs, the short Indo-Chinese, and of the lines of white men squatting over the trenches. So these were the men they had just beaten! How amusing!

Captivity

Such was the aspect of the Dunois prisoners' camp during the first ten days.

* * *

Meanwhile, we had been formed into regular companies and battalions commanded by French prisoner-officers who reported regularly to a German lieutenant in charge of the camp. It was unexpected and reassuring.

I was made secretary to the Third Company, and sat in an office all day, receiving, registering, transmitting papers, very much as I had once done during active service, except that now everything seemed to be a mockery.

On heavy shelves, from floor to ceiling around the room, the administration papers of the artillery regiments that had occupied this section of the barracks for fifty years, stood where generations of fussy top sergeants had laid them with stubborn seriousness, neatly copied in the clean, thin handwriting customary in military offices, and rigorously classified. As we could not obtain any writing paper, we began tearing out the blank pages of the precious books. Soon we ruined them entirely. Then we searched for anything that could be used as identification papers for an eventual escape. Though we were persuaded that the liberation was near, that part of the mind that is never convinced stirred us into making vague preparations that might never be carried out, but were reassuring.

Every fifteen minutes, notes came from the battalion above, such as this: "According to orders given by the German *Kommandant* of the camp, Major Galois prescribes that every company furnish a nominative list of all men, with indication of date of birth, family address, number of children, profession, rank, religion . . ."

The word "Prisoner" was usually avoided.

So we had to send for the sergeant on duty, who had been sleeping somewhere, and he would search for each corporal and send him after his group of twelve men. After some delay, a fussy line formed behind the window.

"There is nothing changed; the bureaucracy continues; can't we be left alone until we go home?"

Anything recalling military discipline was unbearable. Nobody wanted to have anything to do with war again. Men felt washed-out and needed to hide. They did not admit it; took a sneering attitude, and did not seem to realize that they were prisoners. The hardships of the last weeks had been like the sufferings of a grave illness. Now that they were recovering slowly, they eliminated their memories as if they were only nightmares from a high fever.

I had to assure each of them that I believed we were asked these details in view of our liberation; and it started waves of speculation on the possible date and method. Marais, and old Jules — who had been so sure he'd never be taken prisoner — became very angry with me because I refused to admit that it was going to be next Thursday. They knew. They wanted it so much. Wherever there is a large group of men, with a strong common desire, collective illusions take on an increasing power. We could not resist them. Such wishful thinking, flashing through the camp, was called "*bouteillons.*"

All objected to being asked about their religion. Nobody had ever meddled with this private question before. Two men answered: "Israelite." "Are you sure that it is desirable to mention it?" "Yes." They wanted to.

Later, it would be a list of all farmers, or railroad workers, or state employees, that had to be furnished in a hurry. Cautious men declared themselves of every required profession. When this was found out, we had to start all over again, trust no one and verify every detail. It proved an impossible job, for many men had carried their identification papers in the knapsacks that they had been forced to abandon when captured.

Captivity

After ten days, the notes coming from above took another character: "... tomorrow, at 6 A.M., each company will furnish fifty men." Then one hundred, two hundred; and it was not long until everybody, but men officially recognized as sick, was sent to work.

Men having disappeared, had to be especially reported. It happened almost daily — in spite of the warnings posted on every wall, that anybody caught while, or after escaping, would be shot to death in the middle of the main yard—and it brought endless verification and increasing control. The counting was further complicated by the fact that no one could prevent the sick from going to the nearest privy every ten minutes.

Broad, short-necked, congested, his eyes popping out, and clad in an apple green jacket, the *Herr Kommandant* looked like a frog, and became hysterical. He shrieked, laughed, snorted, and threatened at the same time.

*   *   *

Our officers had brushed the dust of the retreat from their uniforms, but they did not shine any more. In the confusion of the last weeks, contradictory orders (originating often with the fifth column) and inability to cope with unforeseen situations, had made them look ridiculous to the extent of wiping away whatever authority is traditionally attached to stars and golden stripes.

Uniforms had grown unpopular since the World War, but some of the old glamorous feelings had been revived in 1939, for a short time. Now we held them responsible; they had led us into this hole. It had been their business to know what should be done under any circumstance of a war. They had failed. Some of them had behaved shamefully, abandoning their men.

Though they had thus saved themselves and were not around, it reflected on the others. They fared better than we. Authorized to buy some food in the city, they took their meals in what, in peace time, had been the bar of the noncommissioned officers, while the officers' bar was being occupied by the German sergeants. It was as if they had slid down one or two degrees. They were served *apéritifs* and liquors, and many came out with shockingly glowing faces. They occupied the buildings of the pre-war infirmary, at the other end of the camp, and took turns for the little service they had to do in the companies. When free, they played cards, slept, or strolled around the courtyards. Only the colonial troops, whose discipline was not yet shaken, saluted them. They answered very unwillingly. They too, did not want to play soldiers any more. They had organized lectures and German classes. I attended one of these, but it was so obvious they objected to privates there, that I left immediately.

Did they feel inwardly their guilt, and wish to isolate themselves, or were they merely anxious to maintain their privileges? It was a most awkward attitude, though. We were going through a crisis and needed very much to be talked to. The Germans would not have allowed it, but had anyone tried discreetly to build up our morale he would soon have aroused enthusiasm. No one did. They abandoned us to growing intoxication by the German propaganda.

A few officers, especially the professional, did not hide their anti-Nazi feelings. Captain C . . . made long detours to avoid meeting a German officer and having to salute him.

Old Major Galois who was much affected by the defeat, had difficulties with his colleagues, and did not understand the men. On the 14th of July the Préfet du Département de la Loire sent barrels of wine to the camp, so that each man would receive two glasses of it. Galois decided that we should have no cause

Captivity

for rejoicing on that day, but should mourn instead. The men, under his orders, received their portion the following day only, and were much irritated by the delay. They needed anything sent to them. This sudden sentimentality did not fit in with the rest of their experience. The water works had been repaired, the city service resumed, and the lavatories reopened, but their number was too small, and they were discouragingly dirty. Galois had built himself a little palisade around a square foot of trench and written on it: "Reserved for Major Galois." Soon he could not use it any more. The men had crudely demonstrated to him that they did not approve of his feelings. If he came among them, why not share their fate entirely?

All officers were called by bugle, at irregular hours, for a special nominative control; but it was relatively easy for them to escape. They were allowed two hours alone in Orléans, on written parole. They could meet friends, communicate with relatives, find a room, a suit of clothes, and prepare their way out. German patrols combed the city, and outposts stopped people on every road, asking for identity papers. You had to prove that you had not belonged to the army, or they arrested you; but, with some complicity, you could either fool, or avoid them. A few officers disappeared thus, and I learned later that they had joined the Fighting French. It ended for the other officers, as it had for us, by a serious increase in the control.

In the company office, where I spent most of my time, the officers openly blamed the men for our defeat. Not as soldiers, for they knew that these are what their chiefs make them, but as civilians. Had not the masses brought the Popular Front to power in 1936? That was the black sheep. They did not remark on the fact that defeat came to us from above, and that the great majority of high ranking officers did not originate in the masses that had supported the Popular Front; or on the fact that our downfall could be traced to a series of events beginning with the inadequate conclusion of the last war. Who is ever willing to consider such questions in their entirety?

So everybody was against everybody else. In a way, it was correct: it was everybody's fault — from the right to the left wing; from the center to those who did not fit in anywhere. But it played into the Germans' hands.

With arrogant air, high caps curved and placed exactly in the center of their heads, reddish leather harness around their paunches swelled with rare French foods and wines, the German officers looked happy and competent. They were. Everything was going their way. We had helped them to beat us, and we continued weakening ourselves. They had all reasons to believe, then, that they were going to lead the world.

*   *   *

Towards the middle of July, all officers were segregated and prisoner top sergeants took their place at the head of the reorganized companies.

All men had to be classified according to manual professions. I ended with my best friends, in a group without special qualification; but I was sent back to the office, and life started as before, except that there were no more notes, inscriptions, and transmissions. A single complete list was furnished to the *Kommandant* and everybody but the noncommissioned officers was sent out to do manual labor.

The men did not dislike it too much, because one extra plate of soup was served in the middle of the day, wherever one worked, and it often came from a German military kitchen — which is to say, it was much better than the putrid food supplied in the camp. Everyday, thousands went to work on airfields — enlarging them, and filling holes made by the last German and Italian bombings. This was hard work. Others cleaned

Captivity

military barracks, and had the opportunity to improve their equipment. Though it was forbidden, they could always hide behind one another to slide a pair of new trousers over their old ones, before the guard saw it. They soiled it right away and the trick was played. A group worked at the railroad station, loading enormous quantities of excellent French canned vegetables and meats on trains that departed very soon. They could steal, or rather recover, a few cans.

The best machinery available was moved away from the local factories on trucks or on trains. The Germans did not seem to bother the property if the owner lived on the premises, but everything else was removed immediately to unknown destinations — always north or east. Enormous stores of arms, war material, ammunition, raw materials, were thus loaded for the benefit of the conquerors, by the men who should have used them.

The patrols through the camp were now insured by a larger squadron of sentries equipped with the fine French rifle model 36, of which we had not been able to secure a sample for our Mézières training platoon.

A dangerous job was cleaning the ruins. The last, completely useless, bombing by the Italians, had destroyed priceless Renaissance houses, in the center of the city, and obstructed the narrow streets. These had to be opened again. One had to be very careful not to strike some unexploded bomb. Sometimes, also, one encountered the gruesome job of extricating, from crushed beams, corpses that had lain there for several weeks. But there were also cellars where all the bottles had not been broken. Whoever could hide something in his trousers, had an evening of forgetfulness in store, with a few friends.

French civilians, when allowed around, brought you what they could: fruits, green vegetables, and bought bread for you as long as bread could be found. Sometimes, when out in small groups, the guard could be bribed into taking you to a café, or a store. A few men better placed, or cleverer, found ways to secure appreciable quantities of bread, tobacco, chocolate, that they took back to the camp at night, and sold to the others. They took care of letters, also, and had them mailed by civilians, in spite of orders to the contrary. I suspect that a good deal of money was made that way. Men who will devote themselves to a few friends with no idea of profit, will rarely feel generous towards a multitude. It was the beginning of the black market, but it helped; and everyone in the camp was in search of such men.

Once, after a day's work at the station, a group of my comrades came back enraged. The tracks had not yet been restored between two points. A train had arrived, loaded with Germans previously interned in a southern camp. They were people who had been living in France for many years and spoke our language well. Some of them sneered openly at the prisoners who were compelled to carry their luggage along the damaged tracks, to another train beyond. It resulted in a few suitcases dropped ostensibly by accident and broken; and a distribution of blows in the ribs, by the guards.

It was generally reported that the sentries were not excessively brutal and nothing recalled our experience with them during the hunger march. A new policy had been inaugurated. It appeared, also, that most German soldiers were pleased with the soft job of keeping prisoners, and were not anxious for the work to be finished too soon. They became fierce only when anything above a corporal came in sight.

I collected this information when my friends came back at night. I had left the camp only once, when, by order of the doctor, at the height of the dysentery epidemic, we had been sent to the River Loire to bathe and wash our clothes. I had done my best to stay in the office where, at least, I did not slave

Captivity

for the Germans. But now that our freedom did not come, I was anxious to become acquainted with the city, and mail a letter to a friend in order to prepare a discreet exit.

*   *   *

One morning I swapped places with Barois and left with a group of ten. We were counted at the gate, inscribed, and a sentry led us to a hotel opposite the railroad station. It was reserved for German officers, and we were supposed to clean their rooms, and attend to whatever service they expected, then go to the kitchen and peel potatoes. A soft job.

Carlier, who showed an exaggerated familiarity with the sentry, acted as group leader, distributed the work, and had a written permission to go out alone to buy goods for the officers. It had been agreed that I should go with him, and we left with large baskets that were sufficient excuse to keep the Germans from questioning us. I had promised not to try to escape then.

It made me dizzy to be in the street again. It was painful: I felt that I would soon fall, or that the Germans would arrest me again; but if you saluted attentively anybody with something white on the shoulder: sergeants with a narrow silver border around the collar, and on the shoulder flaps; top sergeants with stars added, and officers whose flaps are entirely white, you got by all right. They looked you straight in the eye, returned your salute drily and neatly.

We went directly to a small café, in a lone street, where Carlier was well-known. Nobody being in sight, we entered by the back door, and the owner kindly agreed to mail my letter and receive the answer. Carlier would take it whenever he came to get his own mail. We left as discreetly, and went to a grocery store. Its steel curtain was down and the door opened to admit only one person at a time. The shelves were already half emptied. We got some chocolate, and two cans of sardines. One could buy only a limited quantity at prices greatly increased.

German money was now circulated. The value of the mark had been fixed at twenty francs, which is three times its value at the time of the armistice, inasmuch as French notes printed by the Germans, in apparently unlimited number, could have any value. The imposition of these special "occupation marks" at such a price was, in itself, a very effective way to ruin France, rapidly.

German privates received two marks a day, that is, the pay of a non-qualified city-worker, and twice the pay of a farm helper. They bought everything in sight. They invaded department stores, and spent all their savings on yards of fabrics, dresses, underwear, shoes of any size. They took what was there, indiscriminately, obviously intent upon investing their savings as quickly as possible. They were allowed to send home daily, a two pound package, postage free. It is easy to imagine how much the officers bought, not to mention, of course, the heavy official requisitions. With this paper money, it looked fair. The natural greed of most tradesmen is easily aroused; they charged increased prices to the Germans, but even so, everything remained astonishingly cheap for them. There had been no such luxuries to find at home, since Hitler had come to power.

The public market was open. There was plenty of fresh meat, vegetables and fruits. The Germans waited in line, mixed with the civilians. Only the officers refused to wait. The spectacle of it was deeply puzzling. It was obvious that the civilians did not think much about us, or did not realize our condition. Perhaps they considered us responsible for the defeat, or had the impression that the whole situation was a play, a fake, and was going to end happily, one of these days, with life going on

Captivity

as before. This far in the center of France, people had known comparatively little of the pathetic exodus on the strafed roads; that was a story they had heard of, rather than lived.

Everything, however, was so confused and confusing that I hardly knew myself where I stood.

We even went through a café, full of French civilians and German soldiers. We were not supposed to be served anything, but Carlier pretended to be fetching wine for the German officers' kitchen, and a waiter brought us a bottle in an empty room behind, from which we could see everything. The atmosphere was noisy and nervous. Whores, with broken voices and sick eyes, were already hunting the conquerors' money, smiling at them, laughing with them; the only ones, perhaps, still secretly at war . . .

Travellers unpacked their own sandwiches on the tables. They looked well. They came from the unoccupied territory. The men had been regularly demobilized from the defeated army, carried special armbands and passes, and were going home, anywhere north or west. Among them were, undoubtedly, some who had abandoned the ranks before it was too late, and, by jumping in passing trucks, simply deserted. It would never be found out, now. They had been right; they were free, and we were the suckers. I could see it expressed in their eyes, though they tried to look sorry when prisoners passed in the street, in rows of three, with an armed sentry at their back.

Many German civilians had already arrived, and one could not mistake them. Their luggage was being carried to apartments whose owners had fled south. They gave loud orders in German, or broken French.

On the walls, around the Squares, at every street corner, neat inscriptions painted in high letters, on hundreds of strips of wood nailed to low posts: Feldlazaret, Hauptkontrollstelle, Feldkommandantur . . . scribbled a sort of disrespectful sketch across the face of the city. It was as if the new master had begun tracing corrections on a piece of work he disapproved of entirely.

Young boys in brown shirts and Nazi armbands stood erect on the edge of the sidewalks. A terrifying sort of Boy Scouts, they looked meanly at us. We should have realized, from their faces, the stupidity of our hopes. They did not yet know how to cheat in the name of high politics. They were showing frankly that, for us, it was going to be the end.

I was glad to go back to the camp.

*　　*　　*

In spite of numerous queries from top sergeants now commanding the companies, it was still strictly forbidden to write. Twice postcards had been distributed to us, with this shocking text printed on them: "*Je me trouve prisonnier de guerre Allemand et je suis en bonne santé. Mon adresse se trouvera dans une prochaine lettre.*
Mes meilleures salutations.
Nom et prénom."[1]
We could only sign our name. I found a mass of these cards torn or half burnt, behind the infirmary, and suspected that they had never left the camp. When I asked a German corporal who came regularly to the office, he replied: "Of course, because you are going to be freed in a few days." The perfect explanation!

Since everybody worked outside, many had found different ways to have their letters posted. Wives and mothers had come in cars and, when the gasoline ran out, on bicycles; in horse carriages, or on foot. They formed a long line outside of the

[1] "I am a German war prisoner and am well. My address will be found in a later letter. Best wishes. Name."

Captivity

main gate and sent delegates to the *Kommandant*. Sometimes he agreed to let a group of prisoners be posted inside the gate, so as to fetch the wanted men, and if they could be found they would be allowed to speak to their mother or wife for five minutes, but any difficulty arising in the camp provoked the suppression of this privilege. So the women waited in the by-streets, and called the names of their loved ones when columns of prisoners passed on their way to and from work. They threw them packages that the men hid under their coats, and that the guards often willingly overlooked.

An enormous amount of mail for the camp had arrived at the post office, and the *Kommandant* was once persuaded to let it be distributed, under control of his men, but this was stopped immediately. It was, he said, too much work.

A new development proved more puzzling than any other: several hundreds of farmers were sent away harvesting: after accord with local French authorities, these prisoners were rented out to the peasants, who were responsible for them. They were fed, received ten francs a day, and ten francs went to the camp. Some prisoners went home, harvested their crops, and reported twice a week at a local *Kommandantur*. Perhaps a hundred benefited by this measure, but most of them were to be called back later and sent to Germany. The Germans, of course, were most anxious for the grain to be brought in so that they could requisition most of it.

The Alsatians and Lorrains had been segregated and sent home as free Germans. All were delighted, of course. Propaganda had worked easily on them, but they could not hide some anxiety. They were offered jobs in the camp as interpreters. Only a few accepted and received four marks a day. They behaved worse than the guards, and were cordially hated.

The Dunois Barracks were surrounded by high walls and, even from the top floor, only the roofs of Orléans could be seen. Two gates were the only openings. I never spent any time near the main gate, because too many Germans paraded there constantly. The *Kommandant's* office was on one side, and the guards' room on the other. During the first week, men clutched the locked steel bars of the secondary gate, called to the rare civilians outside, and handed their canteen to little boys who raided their parents' cellars in order to bring them some wine. This traffic was soon forbidden. An additional line of barbed wire prevented us from approaching closer than six feet. It was usually deserted. The huge piles of masonry, on each side, framed a sort of stage. As *décor*, a pleasant bit of peaceful grey street; on a wall crowned by a soft molding, a sinuous crack had the nervous quality of a child's scribble across a book.

I went there, at times, for a fugitive contact with outside life. It had revolted me in the city itself, so brutally confused and shaken, but, cut in small scenes, it had a melancholy charm. The show went on all day.

* * *

Here I had watched the pulse of the city beat again, after a week of lethargy following the arrival of the Germans. Windows furtively opened behind locked shutters. A few civilians hurried along the walls, with pails, in quest of water. Then all sorts of vehicles awakened the cobbled stones, automobiles loaded beyond imagination, horse carriages, pushcarts, followed by pedestrians carrying odd packages. They came back home, from wherever they had hidden in the country. Now the same persons went to work at regular hours, with food in a little bag. They did not look at us often. They were embarrassed. It was perhaps enormously painful for them to see us; but they had to live. So they passed in the morning and in

Captivity

the evening, like lantern slides, profiles of another world. They free, and we, caged; the public machinery was turning again.

*

Sometimes a wife, having had no luck at the principal gate would come, and from the far side of the street call the name of her husband. Thus I once heard the name of my comrade Rameau, and hurried to fetch him. When they saw each other, they lost all control. She ran across the street to the gate, while Rameau deftly jumped over the barbed wires, and they kissed ardently between the bars. Grey haired and quiet looking, the sentry, completely abashed, came and tried to push the woman away, while telling Rameau to go. A German sergeant arrived, running, and shrieked until everybody disappeared. He blew up the sentry, who was promptly replaced, and I learned, later, that allowing that kiss had cost him fifteen days in jail, with bread and water.

*

Loafing German soldiers would come too. Healthy young-sters, with rosy cheeks, well buttoned and always ready to stiffen in an impeccable salute if the silhouette of a sergeant appeared in the vicinity. They had bought strawberries in little brown paper bags, and stood looking at us through the fence, as at mannikins in a store window, a little absent-mindedly, while their jaws went up and down.

*

The evening was so peaceful in that street that a couple of very young lovers adopted it. They met at first with a handshake, and walked up and down. They would pass three times, sometimes four. After a few days, they held each other tight, and stopped to kiss. I could see them going away, much beyond the door, in the large mirror fixed against the wall that had served young recruits in peace time to verify the correction of their uniform before facing the Sergeant on duty at the gate.

*

Once, a girl, accompanied by a young man, came from the far side of the street, looked intently at a group of us. We must have been a pitiful sight, for she suddenly burst into tears and, with shaking hands, opened her purse and threw a package of cigarettes and a bag of candy in our direction. Both fell inside, between the barbed wires and the gate, and the guard threatened us with his rifle when we tried to get them. The girl grew hysterical and ran to him with her hand raised. Her friend tried to drag her away, but she managed to throw her handbag in the face of the sentry. It fell open, some letters and a lipstick rolled on the sidewalk. The Jerry yelled, some colleagues came to his help, and took the couple away. During the agitation, we snatched the candies and the cigarettes, but the handbag was too far away to rescue. It stayed there, for days, until a heavy shower washed it away, in the gutter.

*   *   *

The remnants of the Mézières platoon had gathered in the Third Company before the control had become nominative. They had furnished a raided storeroom with cots picked up anywhere, and I had painted a sign on the door: "Corporals' Room, Third Company," with a complete list of names. It had an appearance of order, and the inspecting Germans never failed

Captivity

to examine it intently, as if it meant something to them, and they did not chase us away.

In that room, three or four tight little groups had formed on an economical basis. Whatever wine, vegetables, bread, or canned food could be secured in any possible way, was shared by the group, and cooked by whoever managed not to go to work that day. This food problem absorbed all of our ingenuity, and we enjoyed deeply a sense of revenge when, by supplementing our always meager rations, strength came back slowly to us.

My group did not fare too badly.

Bertrand, a ship's purser, had received several packages from his wife. She had ridden from Paris, on a bicycle, and waved to him from the sidewalk when he went to work. Having given his word to his guard that he would come back, supplemented by a generous gift, he had sneaked away to spend an hour with her.

Barois, the bicycle racer, rather communistic, received nothing, but was diligent and clever. He had patched up an old stove, and found a cooking pan.

Lavaud, once a Florida *maitre d'hotel*, cynical, ambitious, liar, told very lively stories, had an unbreakable morale, and directed the cooking.

Portier, an engineer of good standing, had a way of securing one or two quarts of sour Anjou wine every day.

Rameau had accumulated, under his cot, an amazing collection of objects: pieces of leather cut out of army equipment, radio parts, heavy steel tools, pieces of army cloth, and objects without a name that he would soon take home and transform into valuable instruments.

Durand was a peaceful peasant. He had never read the paper except for local information, and knew that some day he would go back to his family, his fields, his cattle, and live exactly as before. Neither the war nor the defeat seemed to have meant anything worse to him than a ridiculous bother. He had obeyed the military orders, but they had not moved him. His wife had brought him butter and bacon, and the mayor of his community was trying hard to have him freed, temporarily.

All of them worked at the Officers' Hotel, emptied the chamber pots, swept the floors, carried water, and tried to hide their humiliation. The job was easy and resourceful.

The most successful group was headed by Carlier. A rather high state employee and a former well-known athlete, he had no scruples or opinions except that of sticking to the winning side, and made the best of his job at the hotel. His handsome shoulders, his bold frankness, and his persistent gaiety, prevented us from hating him, though we quarrelled endlessly. He agreed with the abominable newspapers that were sold in the camp since the last week in June. Written at first in very doubtful French, by men never heard of, they demonstrated that our government carried full responsibility for the war, but had been driven secretly by the British; that Herr Hitler was a misunderstood soul, who had been forced by the international plutocrats into a war that he did not want, and that he would make us pay for the damage we had made him do; but we could have faith in his generosity, for otherwise he had nothing against us. He would carry through the mission that we had created for him by our opposition: the unification of Europe under German command for an everlasting peace. Our country illustrated the weaknesses of democracy. He would cure us of it.

Soon these papers had sounded more French. The Nazis had found Frenchmen for sale, or who could be easily persuaded and wanted their share of the plunder of their country; others, too, who had not wanted the catastrophe, but had seen the opportunity to win a power that they had lost, or never had.

Captivity

With good, or foul intentions, they played the invader's game. All of our sorrows were traced to England. Hadn't she let us down beautifully at Dunkirk? Had we ever seen a British plane after that? History was hastily rewritten, beginning with the middle ages, to show England as our mortal enemy, enlarging her empire at our expense, and stepping in our way whenever we wanted to go ahead. But now, Hitler was going to settle all wrongs, and make her very small.

All of this was irritating, harsh, unpleasant, but had a revolutionary sound. It was no longer the flat language of our democratic papers, full of promises and compromises, high words and filthy combinations, and, in any case, contradictions. It came from one strong voice. I hated it and spoke violently against it, yet it impressed me, as it impressed the others.

The old Maréchal Pétain, we hardly knew. He had risen to power suddenly while we retreated, and signed that armistice which, we could not doubt, should stipulate our freedom. He had been last heard of as an ambassador to Spain, after the defeat of the Loyalists, and as a general in the last war, had not achieved a celebrity comparable with that of Joffre or Foch, but his pictures showed a fine face. We had no idea where he really stood.

Above all, we felt a violent disgust and distrust for the men who had led us to this shameful and miserable downfall. If Hitler had dared to be generous to the beaten Frenchmen, freed the prisoners and offered them full collaboration, he would have carried the whole country, I am afraid.

He, who seemed to have sprung from the comic strip, a corporal who wanted to be the world field marshal, a sort of grotesque and perhaps homosexual form of Joan of Arc, with an impressive voice and a Charlie Chaplin mustache, who could not be taken seriously, had come down to the Invalides and ceremoniously bowed before the ashes of Napoleon. He had attended to the business of refueling the lantern of the unknown soldier, under the Arc de Triomphe. He had ordered his soldiers to behave politely to the civilians, and organized distributions of food. Perhaps he was a genius, after all, and would unite Europe to put an end to our exhausting wars.

*   *   *

The tide changed fortunately, when the first wave of Gaulist news brought some fresh air into the camp, during the first week in August. General de Gaulle I had heard of once or twice as an armored division specialist. He was now reported organizing resistance to the Germans in spite of the armistice. Rumors of large numbers of Germans being drowned and burnt on the coast of England were brought by letters secretly received. A new kind of hope ran through the heads of my group and began fighting off the German influence. So the war was not yet over, and Hitler had not won. We would be avenged, perhaps. But how much of the rumors was true? We had no way of knowing.

One evening, the party working at the air field brought, enthusiastically, the news that it had been seriously damaged by British bombs during the previous night.

We became wary. I made plans with Bertrand to join de Gaulle in Africa, where we thought he was. Having received no news from my Paris friends, I sent pressing letters to others. I entered into several schemes of escape with David and Barois, but we had let the easiest period pass. We were now pretty well guarded. We should have gone at the end of June, like Ernest, who was smuggled out in an empty ton when the water was being fetched outside every day.

It was too late.

On the 20th of August, two thousand Arabs more famished

Captivity

than we had ever been, arrived and were cantoned in the courtyard. In spite of a chain of guards, they ran out towards us,
asking for a bit of anything to eat. The sentries pursued them
around the buildings, and beat them hard with their guns,
not only in the ribs, but on the head. I saw two broken skulls,
at least. It was strictly prohibited to approach them. We were
not supposed to learn that they came from Germany.

The next day, nobody went to work. We were ordered in
the yard with all of our belongings. In groups of one hundred
we marched to the station, naively sure that freedom had come.

CHAPTER 6

Live Cargo for Germany

FORTY men, eight horses. Such has been, since the beginning of railway transportation, from a military point of view, the capacity of the smallest freight cars.

The Germans, though, can outdo anyone else. When they locked the door on us, fifty-five pairs of feet were shuffling desperately — not all of them on the floor. There was not room enough for them and the absurd amount of luggage that had been picked up at Dunois. Narrow benches had been installed; but whereas they would have been a help for forty, they proved a hindrance to more.

Much less ambitious than my colleagues, I sat with my two small army duck bags, my canteen, and my leather brief case piled up on my knees. Rameau, fighting, complaining, disturbing everybody, had been compelled to insinuate his multiple packages, one by one, in any interstice between any two legs or two necks near him, and kept one hand running constantly from one to another, like a mother hen anxious for her chicks. At the barracks, he had abandoned enough to open a junk shop, and had very expertly thrown a bundle in the direction of his wife, who stood with a group of others at the station. Wrapped in brown paper, it did not look military, and none of our many guards had noticed anything other than a fumble in the crowd. It was, said Rameau, his only consolation; for the package contained a brand new cavalry topcoat, and she could make something for herself with it.

The women's tears had been edifying enough, but it was only when reading on the German freight car *"Stolp y Pommern,"*

Captivity

that we lost the last feather of our blinding plume of illusions. Unfit for the work expected from them, or for the German climate, or both, the Arabs had been brought back in this train, and we were sent to take their place. The fact was somewhat substantiated by itchy little things already investigating our chests and armpits.

We opened the ventilation trap on the side and, from car to car, without seeing each other, exchanged newly born *"bouteillons."*

"We are going to the north of France to clear up demolition before we go home. The sentry who speaks French has told us so," voiced the car ahead of us.

The following car protested: "No, we are going harvesting in the south." All sneered, followed though by nervous outbursts of humor.

"The '*bouteillons*' leak," one said.

"The Germans have gotten us once more, down to the core, the hateful, lying bastards."

"Some day," said Portier, "some day . . ."

"Are you cracked?" chuckled Lavaud, as cool as ever.

"Some day . . ." repeated Portier, with a bitter little smile.

Guibaut, who had been stenographer in the camp, had stuck to me. I had helped him to find a little space for the mere one hundred pounds that were left of him after prolonged dysentery. Weak to start with, brought up for auxiliary service last May, and never having carried a gun, he kept the correct, precise manners of the country estate lawyer he used to be, but looked rather like a famished clerk in some Balzac novel. He cried, now, softly, with silent sobs that shook his trench cap in the semi-obscurity. I pressed his hand.

"I'll never come back," he murmured.

Barois, always efficient, had found a place directly by the opening, and described what could be seen: civilians were boarding or leaving trains and looking in our direction, but sentries made them move away. The line of wives and mothers had invaded the hall and was now pushed outside. The obstinate Mrs. Rameau had presumably bought a ticket and paced up and down a distant platform, holding a loaf of bread in her arms, and trying to spot her husband.

It took a quarter of an hour and some hard swearing before the latter could take Barois' place and wave to her and the tantalizing bread.

As soon as a squadron of sentries had locked up its prisoners, it marched back to the barracks to get another column. Several trains identical with ours were in sight. A German station-master, neatly uniformed in blue, with red on his high cap, gave orders to interpreters who kept the French railroad employees busy. Quiet and portly, he competently managed the exportation of French machinery, crops and horses on one track, and of men on the other. When our train left, about 7 P.M. he must have gone to his office and written something like this:

"Train number So-and-So, with fifty loaded freight cars, and a passenger car for escort, left on time, the twenty-first of August 1940," and then gone to the next café for a glass of cognac.

*   *   *

During the night we stopped for an hour at a small station. The guards patrolled both sides of our track. A dozen shots burst out in the rear. There was agitation and running in that direction. When we started again, a French employee cried to the faces peeping through the ventilator:

"No use playing the fool. Four have just been caught and shot while trying to escape."

Captivity

"Where are we heading?"

"Straight towards Nancy and Germany."

Of course; but we had so much repulsion for it that the knowledge would not stay in our heads.

We slept as best we could. The most desirable place was on the floor, stretching yourself between various obstacles that would eventually fall, or step on you. The problem was to protect your face.

Guibaut, Barois, and I sat, and having passed our arms through a wide strap we had hung from the ceiling, leaned on them.

It was only at five, the following afternoon, that the train stopped in the middle of the country. Our doors opened, we were ordered to a portion of field guarded on all sides and, as Durand said from his professional point of view, this patch would not need any more fertilizer for some time. Our legs were numb. We exercised on the tracks while the men who had not been able to wait so long for halt, cleaned up the mess they had made during the night. No water being available, they sprinkled handfuls of dirt on the floor.

A sewer, half full of stinking slime, crossed the embankment. Barois and I eyed it for a moment. Why didn't we crawl through it? It would have been possible if a few friends had stood opposite to shield us from the nearest sentries.

An interpreter, wearing a French colonial uniform and an armband with the word *Dolmetscher* on it, collected a man from each car. Lavaud went along and brought back a blanketful of war biscuits that we divided immediately. Each of us received nine. They arrived in time, for most of us had no food in reserve, and after twenty-four hours, we wondered if we were going to be starved again.

The doors were locked, and the guards looked carefully around for anybody hiding. One of them glanced through the sewer, but without a flashlight he could not see much. He did not fire a shot through it, as I had expected. That was the last view of France that I was to have for nineteen months.

Life became organized in the freight car as if the trip were going to last forever. Everyone had created his own vital space between himself and his belongings, and found two or three possible positions for his body, none of them straight so as to relieve legs or arms when they became numb. There were small zones in common, for the use of which we took turns. Only a dozen men cared to stand by the window. They had their hours, and had elaborated a complicated but precise way of reaching it, between, above, under heads, arms, feet, bundles belonging to their comrades. They paid their way by telling what they had seen.

A corner had been adopted by the sick. They got along as well as they could, and helped each other. They would beg pardon politely, once in a while. One of them, laboring obstinately with his knife, carved a little hole in the hardwood floor, between two pieces of iron, through which most of the filth could with some patience be eliminated. We urinated against both doors, at the joints.

It was rather dark and stuffy, but it had a sort of coziness. The groups had tightened, though their members often stood far apart. They shared tobacco, food, confidences. At times it became very noisy and one would cry *"Vos gueules, la dedans!"* A boy you had never met before would suddenly grow tender and tell you the most intimate story of his love. Another would boast about his former situation, which appeared high and far away like the Himalayas. Someone would unroll a moving film of bad luck and misery. Silly jokes would suddenly shake the whole crew with irresistible laughter, especially at the hour when it became darker through the unique hole than inside.

Captivity

"Some day . . ." yelled Portier, once in a while.
"Some day . . ." echoed the others.

* * *

On the third day, the train stopped at a short distance from a farm. Two German girls, arm in arm, came down across the fields. A sergeant and a corporal, whose job seemed to be to survey the sentries, had called to them. It was not long before they joked merrily, tickled, embraced, and kissed, no more concerned with us, crouching in the grass and clutching our trousers, than if we had been grazing cattle. We did not count for those girls. We were booty — cattle, indeed, brought back to Germany by their playmates. These had obviously lost all anxiety about us. Now that we were in Germany, there was little chance of our getting away. We could not go far, clad in French uniforms, and without food.

The rations were given daily, at the halt, and improved a little. We received a small can of potted meat, and twelve or fifteen small hard biscuits. That was enough for men accustomed to drastic restrictions.

I went back to the freight car without repulsion.

The rumor ran that two men had succeeded in unbolting the protective grill around the ventilation window, and jumped during the first night, when the train was not going very fast. The guards had seen nothing. Perhaps they had not broken their necks. The impulse to do anything like that had not arisen in me.

This was a jail, but I felt better in it than in the market at Orléans, the day that I had spent out with Carlier. The bars of the ventilation were like long teeth. The little light they admitted had the dullness of a chewed material, and fell equally upon us. We were at the bottom of the world. It felt hard, but solid, underneath. I was mentally cleansed, having cleaned myself of all parasitic hopes. I had the healthy sensation of travelling light, outside as well as inside. From the motion of the train emanated a slim atmosphere of venture, but I did not want to arrive anywhere. Unwashed, ridden with lice, growing whiskers already scratching my neck, I would have been content to spend all my captivity in this wandering prison, cut off from a silly, inconsistent world.

*　　*　　*

My daily hour at the window had proved unsatisfactory. The landscape, I already knew fairly well and unfortunately it had not changed. Except for a bridge blown up a little beyond Zweibrücken, and seven bomb holes at a short distance from the tracks, beyond Worms, no reassuring demolition could be seen. Only batteries of antiaircraft guns on the roofs of the stations and a very serious black-out at night, suggested that a deadly aerial warfare was going on, as we had heard lately. Not even when we passed near Berlin, on the third evening, did the suburbs show any sign of destruction.

It would have been so comforting to see enormous fires destroying factories, and habitations, with corpses hanging from steel wreckage, carbonized, exactly like the passengers burnt in their locked cars on the French road to Beaugency.

We should have laughed merrily, all of us, even Carlier of whom we had made fun ever since we left Orléans:

"So you did believe the foul papers published in Paris by handsome Adolf? You must be pleased that he is calling you a bit nearer to him, you dirty bootlicker. . . ."

But Carlier never failed to recall that whatever newspapers of recent print had existed on the train, had been left at the first sanitary halt for the scarabaeus.

Captivity

Sour jokes now predominated. We had toughened considerably. Even Guibaut was catching on with "Some day . . ." That had become the general motto. One shook a fist and it meant:

"Some day it will be their turn. I shall volunteer to pack them in, not fifty-five, but one hundred Nazis in a freight car, one on top of the other. Breathe who may!"

When they opened all doors, one morning at ten o'clock, after four whole days of voyage, an indomitable column formed on the platform, sneering so obviously at the guards that they became riled. A corporal went around shaking his fist and saying in good French that we were not going to laugh long. The Germans would teach the lazy Frenchmen how to work hard.

We stood impeccably in rows of five, at attention.

We had learned how to get by with the minimum of damage to the ribs. They could not do anything to a thin little smile that meant:

"They shall not have me."

CHAPTER 7

A Concentration Camp for War Prisoners in Pomerania

No WONDER that the Germans had kept us seven weeks in Orléans, with the help of bayonets on one hand, and of fairy-tales on the other. The concentration camps in Germany, were not yet ready to absorb and distribute the huge army taken captive between the day that the armistice was signed and the day that it was granted. Masons and carpenters were busy adding new barracks to the *Stalag* II B when we arrived in Hammerstein.

Carved in a woods of meager pines, it stretched on a wide patch of sand, so arid that the solenoids of barbed wires spread between a double line of fences standing six feet apart, seemed an adequate vegetation for it. At intervals, thirty feet above the fence, observation towers showed, on each side, the glassy eye of a searchlight and the stingy nozzle of a machine gun. Beyond the large and low administration buildings set up near the gate, a main alley, twenty feet broad, rigorously straight and paved with concrete, divided the camp in two. One-story barracks, grey, neat, and sad looking, faced one another symmetrically. Each element was reduced to a glabrous minimum. The barracks number nineteen and twenty were not yet completed.

Everything in the camp moved at a quick pace. We were driven through a system of parking lots along the outside fence. Enclosed by a single line of barbed wires, these lots communicated by a small gate, where a sentry stood. One was assigned to my column, and shouting prisoner interpreters, standing at

Captivity

attention, beside fierce sergeants, directed us to a line of vast old tents. We jammed into these, like sheep, everyone dropping automatically wherever a little straw hid the ground, and then crawling around in order to avoid the biggest holes in the canvas above.

My little team had hardly organized its narrow plot when we were called out and hurried through a system of operations that was to last three days.

Arrived as an indefinite mass, a loose cargo of bewildered captives, we were to be transformed into permanent prisoners of war by successive manipulations of our body, our identity, and our luggage.

*   *   *

Of the body, the Germans took a complete care, in a dry, hard way. The soup was distributed individually at a large, clean, well equipped kitchen. Led there in groups of one hundred, we waited in line. Inside and out, sergeants saw that the prisoners working in the kitchen did not pour more than the three quarters, or full quart of brew allowed that day, in whatever container we still had. Fortunate were those who carried the old army iron mess kit, with plate inside, for the guards liked the newer handsome aluminum sets to the point of confiscating them. They substituted enamel plates, in exchange, if they did not forget. Many of us ate in old tin cans.

Back in the tent, we were now counted by groups of fifty men. An accredited prisoner-interpreter, wearing a white armband, received a distribution ticket for each group, from a controlling guard, and fetched the cold ration. We received: 250 grams of very heavy bread (a little more than half a pound) in which rye predominated. This made about three standard slices. Then, a tablespoon of artificial marmalade, and a teaspoonful of shortening. Twice a week, a tablespoonful of lard, or very dry cottage cheese. This was all for the whole day. We divided it as we chose. It required considerable self-control to keep a piece of bread to accompany the pint, or half pint, of unsweetened barley tea that we received at 6 A.M. for breakfast. The best way to absorb the sickening, tasteless fat was to mix it with the chemically red marmalade.

This small ration was cleaner and probably better than that distributed in Orléans, but we could not supplement it with a little food smuggled in from outside. Still, one could live on it. It would maintain the body at a sort of minimum weight. Posters in every building said that our diet had been scientifically determined and that we should, in no case, weaken it by exchanging part of it with a comrade, for such delicacies as tobacco.

How humorous!

*　　　*　　　*

In the middle of our first night under the tent, my group was awakened for delousing. I was delighted with the idea. Filthy up to the whites of my eyes, I felt ridden from toes to whiskers by strange little visitors that I could not catch.

Impenitently joking, we stood outside until 2 A.M. before being admitted to the disinfection barrack. In the vestibule a sentry and a prisoner-interpreter made us surrender all of our clothes and belongings. Everything in our possession had to be processed. The interpreter warned us that we would not recover all of it, for every operation in the camp was a pretext for confiscation. No one could tell exactly what we were allowed to keep, he said.

Rather anxious about this, and as naked as worms, we entered another waiting line. "As a worm," is saying too much in the

Captivity

case of Guibaut, for he was not that fat. He was naked to the bones, desperately yellow and embarrassed. We felt gaily ridiculous; he was pitiful.

Here, we were to get a very smooth haircut. A prisoner-barber officiated with an electric clipping machine so large that it must have been conceived for horses: in five main strokes the job was accomplished. Around the edges, some little traces of the old appearance might remain, as he had no time for a finishing touch.

Bertrand, ahead of me, cursed his entrails out. He had tenderly nursed a thin patch of dwarf hair and, at great expense for lotions, maintained a greyish effect on his skull. The timid little fuzz would never survive such treatment!

It is funny how, in the midst of distress, minor worries will over-shadow the things that burn your heart. We put on as good a face as we could.

Our next stop was under a shower so cold that we wriggled while trying to restore our feet, hands, and face to a decent color. Our skulls felt uncomfortable, bare and blue. We made fun of each other. Portier, with his high shoulders and a deep frown on his forehead, looked guilty of maniacal assassinations. He did not spare me any joke either: "Isn't it the first time that your hair has ever been groomed?"

The establishment furnished no towels. We had to wait and shiver in the next room until our packs came out of the disinfecting machine. We stood another hour by the delivery window, where a second interpreter, a Fleming, was being very discouraging: "There will be numerous searches; they take away belts, boots, extra shirts, trousers, coats, and tobacco when you have more than one package."

When Rameau's lot came out, his high boots were still on the top of it, to his great exultation, and the interpreter tried in vain to swap a pair of plain shoes for them.

"You will not have them long," he said. "They are bound to go. As a camp employee, I could manage to keep them." The piece of leather-wear was so dear to Rameau that he would not part with them. He could always cut off the tops, if necessary.

It is true that the Germans took a heavy toll of the prisoners' belongings, but we had no way of knowing then, that there was no official search during the disinfection. Beastly prisoner-interpreters had gotten together with greedy guards and discreetly selected what they liked, while sorting the clothes. Out of my luggage, they stole one shirt, one package of cigarettes and, what was worse, a precious can of sardines that I had carried since Orléans and which was to constitute the group's breakfast the next morning. Undoubtedly they sold most of their booty at the black market of the camp. We had expected such harsh treatment from the Germans, that we were rather relieved to find they had taken so little.

Clad in our damp uniforms, our caps sunk down to the ears, we were led to another tent exactly as filthy as the one we had left a few hours before. We felt so sleepy that we sank in the powdered straw, with only a faint hope that the smell of chemicals would preserve us another day from the vermin.

*　　*　　*

Three hours of sleep were found sufficient to prepare us for the investigation of our identity. We joined a line behind a building named *Kartei* and, as usual, waited for many hours.

A prisoner of war is either working or waiting. The Germans make him stand endlessly, on the slightest pretext. Instead of dividing us in small units and allotting definite hours to each of them, they call everybody out, form a long line, and enjoy

109

Captivity

the job of keeping it according to their conception of order, while it moves like a slow belt, one notch at a time.

Every one of several hundred men had to pick up his belongings and advance one step each time that one man was admitted inside the building. When my turn came, I was told to deposit my bags in a corner and join one of the short lines hanging, so to speak, from a dozen tables. There, fellow prisoners, supervised by German secretaries, were installed on chairs, as if they belonged to them. They had pens, pencils, a square foot of table to themselves, and an inch of hair on the head. Old-timers, men taken in Belgium last May, they were necessarily shrewd or clever, to have been able to grasp or retain these soft jobs, in proximity of the *Kommandantur*, where all information — this intoxicating sort of mental sweets for captives — originated. They looked competent, a little distant, and did not strike me as particularly devoted to us. They formed a breed apart, and talked together while filling out our papers. It sounded like little intrigues and combinations that could lead, eventually, to getting a pair of shoes from a storeroom or to obtaining his soup from the bottom of the huge kitchen kettle, where it is thick, instead of from the top, where it is thin.

The different inscriptions comprised all possible indications of name, date of birth, rank, regiment, date and place of capture, address of family, number of children, and religion. In exchange for a set of finger prints, I received a little rectangle of grey metal, with a greasy string attached that had already hung from someone else's neck. It bore the following words: "*Stalag II B, Deutschland. Kriegsgefangenennummer:* 87.461." From now on I should be prisoner number 87.461.

Stalag is a contraction of the German word *Stammlager*, which can be translated as "nucleus camp." It is the heart, the base, from which radiates a system of smaller working camps called *Kommando*, where the prisoners are quickly sent. No one is supposed to remain in a *Stalag* longer than necessary for disinfection, matriculation, or consignment to a *Kommando*. The administration employees, a few sick men recognized as permanently unfit for work; and, until February, 1940, noncommissioned officers unwilling to work (according to the Geneva International Convention), were the only prisoners staying permanently in the *Stalag*.

There is a score of such *Stammlager*, scattered throughout Germany, and their location has been publicly announced; but no one is supposed to know anything about the numerous *Kommandos* where at least ninety-five per cent of all prisoners of war stay the whole year around.

At another table of the *Kartei* of this *Stalag* II B, all money in our possession was supposed to be surrendered. A poster on the wall proclaimed that any amount exceeding one thousand francs (twenty-two dollars at the 1939 rate of exchange) would be considered as war booty, and confiscated. Smaller sums would be returned at the time of our liberation. It felt good to read that word "liberation." So, one day, we would give back the medal and the number, and go home, with nobody pointing a bayonet at our back! The last paragraph, however, mentioned that undeposited money would be confiscated. Why couldn't they let the poster end with the sweet word above?

I handed out one hundred and ten francs to a German cashier and received a long pink slip from a prisoner-secretary. I had a little more, though, hidden crudely in my cap until I could do better. Some of my comrades carried several thousands of francs but none of them declared more than one thousand.

Back in the vestibule, I picked up my bags and went out through another door. At no time of the procedure were we allowed to go back and inform the others of what they had to face. This time, I was incorporated in a line leading to the culminating ceremony. A civilian photographer, riding the

Captivity

tripod of an old camera, showed nothing of himself but a broad behind sticking out of a black sheet, as ample as a shroud. A sentry assisted him and prepared the prisoners, five at a time, bareheaded, each holding a slate upon which his matriculation number was written with chalk. I distorted my face as much as possible, without arousing the suspicion of the noncommissioned officer on duty. There is always one of these around, keeping the sentries on the alert, and making the air vibrate with shrieks, as thought fashionable in the German Army.

*　　*　　*

The dreaded inspection of our belongings remained.

We had not been in the camp two days without picking up information about everything. Our tents were completely separated from the lodgings of the veteran prisoners, but we had come in contact with some of these in various offices. We knew, now, that the Germans confiscated cigarette lighters, fountain pens, checkbooks, passports, and anything, according to their views, that was not needed by a prisoner.

While waiting to have my picture taken, I had buried my passport, my American re-entry permit, a checkbook and a few hundred francs in the sand. Two comrades had shielded me while I pretended to tie my shoe. I had figured that I could always return to the administration section on the pretext of giving extra information about my wife's address, and collect them, if they were still there. I did, and had luck. Many ways to juggle small objects, at the time of a search, become classic, and are constantly used in the camps.

Upon our topcoats spread on the ground, we displayed the contents of our sacks and bags with great art and no symmetry, so as to minimize the appeal of our most treasured objects. I was most anxious to save my leather briefcase. It had been taken from me once, already, during the last night of the hunger march, by one of the guards collecting the razors and flashlights. He was going away proudly with it, when I sneaked behind him and briskly snatched it. I disappeared in the crowd while the thief went through a complete dictionary of curses. Ever since, I had carried it wrapped in a dirty piece of burlap, having understood that such a handsome satchel, in the hands of a dusty, shabby, captive-foe, was a provocation. I was as attached to it as to my passport. It embodied all the comfort I had known. To increase my chances to pull it through an attentive search, I had soiled it with mud, and had written my name and address in large letters everywhere possible, inside. It would give remorse to anyone at all honest. Besides, I had discarded my two duck pouches, and it constituted my only baggage. A rusty mess-kit, a cup, and a spoon hanging from the handle, ruined its appearance even further.

I trusted that my little exhibition looked miserable, but having consulted a leaflet of special instructions, the guard who inspected it removed a German grammar, a midget water-color box, a shirt, a good pair of socks, and a score of recent drawings that I shall regret all my life. They landed on a pile of confiscated stuff.

The German searched my wallet, my coat and trousers pockets, and felt my legs with a minimum of decency. He was doing his job seriously, but did not enjoy it. Having pressed the top of my shoes, and, convinced that only my toes dwelt there, he told me to pack up. The briefcase remained mine.

Now we could understand why the Germans had not reacted much to the raiding of the storerooms in the Orléans barracks. The prisoners had collected and sorted this extra booty for ultimate transportation to Germany. Now, they offered it themselves, in this new kind of a flea market, where bargaining was out of the question, the picking being free.

Captivity

Not only were we miserable, but also ridiculous. The feeling of being thoroughly fooled was settling upon us, bitterly. Our captors gave a respectable name to this confiscation: *"fouille d'allègement,"* which means search to lighten our burden! As a finishing touch, we were to be sifted once more when sent out to work.

*   *   *

Cleaned, registered, streamlined, we were now directed to the barracks. My little group was assigned to number eighteen, into which more than five hundred men were jammed. The bunks were made of boards crudely nailed together so as to offer three decks, in groups of six units, with a narrow alley around. It was unpleasant to climb to the top, but nobody stood above you, and you could enjoy a little more space. No bunk being free at any level, we arranged ourselves on loose straw, under the small windows. It had one advantage. When my stomach ached with hunger, in the early morning especially, I searched under me and sometimes collected in an hour as much as a palmful of rye seeds. About two thirds were stale, but the rest, once properly crushed between two stones and soaked in barley tea, could be digested.

Around 7 P.M. a staff of brisk, impatient noncommissioned officers entered. The first man to see them called "Attention." One prisoner-sergeant, elected as chief of barracks, was responsible for the roll call, and for the order of the beds. Then, until curfew at eight, we could exercise in an empty lot, between the main latrines and the fence. Little groups turned around, at a quick pace, for the weather was already growing cold. Icicles hung from the roofs every morning.

*

Around one prisoner, a hundred men prayed aloud, ardently. He said a verse alone, accentuating certain words, and they repeated it with the same rhythm, five, ten times in succession: *"Je vous salue Marie. . . ."*

The prayer was like a garland hanging from their mouths and waving in the wind. Hoarse, hypnotizing, it went on endlessly. Outside the fence, a sentry stood immobile and listened intently. He was, perhaps, muttering the same words, in German: *"Ich gruesse dich, Maria. . . ."*

Yet, if any prisoner derived the necessary faith from them for a wild attempt to jump over the fence, he would shoot all the cartridges of his gun at him.

*

In the latrines, and at given spots where one stayed only a few seconds, the black market went on, feverishly. I have seen an ounce and a half of French Army tobacco, worth one franc, offered for one hundred, and overbid three times up to eight hundred francs, namely eighteen dollars. A single ounce has been sold for as much as twenty-five dollars. Shirts, socks, were bought by men attached to a unit working for the moment in Hammerstein. They slept in a special barrack, and were not constantly searched. They would smuggle the goods out of the camp and sell them to certain German workers for good civilian money, or for loaves of rye bread. But spies were rumored to exist in the camp, and special patrols were on the look-out. The transactions were nervous, merciless, and ugly.

*   *   *

Our next call was the registration for work. Everyone had to go, unless holding a doctor's exemption. It was useless to

115

Captivity

present oneself at the medical inspection without an obvious symptom, such as high fever. Here we waited again, but not in line. We gathered around a door, several hundreds at a time. A prisoner-employee came out, once in a while, and called: "Thirty men together," or "Twenty-five men for farm work," or "Fifty men, one of them speaking German." Professions were rarely stipulated. Volunteers lifted their arms and went first. The necessary complement was simply dragged in. Each man received a ticket of assignment indicating that he would leave in a day or two.

My group was now reduced to ten men. Many of our old comrades were still engaged in the incorporation process, and others had been segregated as "Bretons." This was quite a laughable invention. In view of keeping for himself very important Atlantic bases, Hitler pretended to separate the old province of Brittany from France. Prompt liberation was promised to the Bretons. They were delighted.

Born in Brest, Carlier went along with them. He told us later, across a discriminating fence, that he had just been informed that Brittany had always been shamefully mistreated and that the downfall of France would mean the rise of his province as an independent country. "Think of that," he snarled, "but I shall have to learn how to speak Breton!"

Something must have gone wrong, for the Bretons were never freed. In the various *Kommandos* they are still registered as belonging to a special nationality, but to no advantage.

When one called out for ten men for farm work, we lifted our hands. Durand had convinced us that we would be better fed on a farm. He would show us how to work. My ticket bore my name and number, and the following indications: "*Kommando* 86. Place, Bornzin, via Stolp. Employer, Von Z. Date, August 30."

We felt relieved. In thirty-six hours we would leave this

Stalag where too many guards had nothing else to do than bother us; where the rations were dangerously scant, and where we had witnessed a demonstration of Nazi discipline never to be forgotten.

* * *

Smoking was forbidden when standing in line, when lying on a bunk, and anywhere in the main alley, or under a tent. A few of us had a little tobacco left and, to enjoy it longer, we often kept an unlit cigarette in the mouth. Under the tent of our first parking lot, a young French sergeant lay on his back and sucked a cigarette that he was in no way preparing to light, when one of the guards, with a police dog, peeped through the door and saw him. Pulling on the leash, and shaking his whip, he ran towards the sergeant who understood promptly enough to get up and race through the other door. He made for the latrines, as the only possible hiding place, but the other had followed him. He drove him out, tracked him until he fell, and whipped him with all his might. Fortunately, my comrade had set his head between his legs, and covered his neck with both arms. Clenched like a fist, he was taking the punishment with the minimum of damage. The dog barked, but did not bite. Animals do not attack motionless beings. His mouth twisted in the brutal effort, the two little tails of his Wilhelm II mustache wriggling above, the guard beat the human bundle as long as his arm could endure it.

I made myself look until the end. Then I helped the boy back to the tent. Thanks to his position, only his hands were cut. The cigarette reduced to a pill, and soaked with blood, stuck to one palm.

*

117

Captivity

Attentive sentries surveyed the soup line. It was strictly forbidden to come for a second helping, but a boy, having no other container than an empty sardine tin, and thus being deprived of four-fifths of his ration, sneaked into a second line, and was recognized by a guard. The furious German hit him so hard with his gun — in the ribs, as customary, but a little too low, and with the nozzle instead of the butt end — that it went through the thin coat and tore open his stomach. The poor little tinful of soup came out, a red mixture. The boy had passed out, when they took him away, perhaps to the hospital, and we knew that he would not stand in the soup line any more. He had had his last helping.

*

Most of the Poles were demobilized, assigned to a place of work, and given a semi-freedom; but a certain number were kept in uniform and treated with constant brutality. A huge P was painted in red on their coat, and we were not supposed to approach them at any time. They dug trenches for the camp sewers, or extracted sand that they carried away on narrow rail tracks. Often punished, they were subjected to the kind of exercise called, in French *"la pelote."* It is a succession of regular military movements, but at such speed that it becomes a torture: "March, stop, run, stop, lie down, kneel, jump, run, turn around. . . ." They became dizzy and fell. This breach of discipline was repressed with a few blows and kicks. It was better to obey, if they could, and not openly refuse to work, the next time.

I wonder what he had done, the wretch I saw at a distance, entangled in the solenoids of barbed wire, between the two lines of fences. On both sides, guards kept him moving, hitting him constantly with their guns. They shrieked, he crawled.

His clothes were reduced to strips, and left on the thorns a trail of torn off patches. His face and hands bled. It took him a long time to advance ten yards. I was ordered away, but came back later to learn what had happened. Condemned to crawl all around the camp, he had not been able to make it. He, too, had been carried away on a stretcher.

*   *   *

There is a little cemetery, near the camp. Whether a prisoner dies of sickness, or of "accident," the Germans are ceremonious when it comes to his burial. They send a delegation of soldiers to render full honors. A prisoner-priest officiates. His comrades are allowed to buy a wreath of flowers for the grave.

FORCED LABOR

A) A Prison Farm on the Polish Border

CHAPTER 8

Fall

ENTER TEN FARM HANDS

THERE was a frown on the Baroness' face when, from her perron, she saw us wearily entering the farmyard, followed by a
sweet little sentry, who had not so much as yelled at us once
since we left Hammerstein, in the early morning.

"What a puny lot!"

What she expressed with a highly distinguished wrinkle,
her general overseer expressed with a wide gamut of howls.
Thirty years old, his short, powerful body oscillating so on his
shiny boots that he sank progressively in the mud; his pink,
sourish, piggish face set on a thin slice of neck; his eyes glittering far apart under a low felt hat, he fully deserved his nickname of *"Tapageur"* (Noisy). He started in a slow, smiling,
monotonous tone and suddenly made your ears drum with a
wild outburst. He became as congested as a stormy sunset. His
voice climbed at full speed through a series of hoarse, chromatic
tones and battered its pitch obstinately, for a while, as if trying
to bore a hole through it, and so go half a tone higher. Then it
slid back to a low murmur, far more disquieting than his shrieks.

Our presentation to him gave us the first opportunity to view
the show. We stood at attention. The guard said:

"Gefreiter Rohr, mit zehn Kriegsgefangenen vom Stalag II B."

"Does anyone understand German?" asked the overseer.
I came out one step.

123

Forced Labor

"What is your profession?"

"Artist painter."

I could see "Oh" written on his face.

"Are all the others farmers?"

"No, Herr overseer." His eyes became smaller.

"What are they?" I began with:

"Portier, engineer."

"Next?"

"Barois, bicycle racer; Rameau, cashier; Bertrand, ship's purser." The overseer's mouth was so tight that his face became broader than it was high.

"Georges, insurance agent." Georges was very thin, but he looked an athlete compared with Guibaut, who came next:

". . . real estate lawyer." Gentle, and in no way disconcerted, Guibaut produced a transparent little smile that was a sort of translation of the courteous "Won't you sit down?" that he would have said to *Tapageur* if the latter had ever come to his office.

The explosion came right there: "*Rechtsanwalt, was? . . .*" and many things that I could not exactly grasp but that referred furiously to the one hundred pounds left of my comrade who, meanwhile, looked at me reproachfully as if to say: "Are you sure you have translated correctly?"

Automatically, the sentry had clapped his heels and stood in respectful position. He had recognized something military in the overseer's technique. The sunset effect was produced when I said, imprudently:

"Lavaud, head waiter." Lavaud was strong and I counted on his making a good impression, but he was trying so hard not to laugh that he wriggled like an epileptic, with the expression of a complete ass.

The subsequent roaring seemed to be about calling up those people at the *Stalag* and giving them a piece of his mind for sending such a crew of starving lawyers and idiotic head waiters, when the Baroness had applied for ten husky farm hands.

In order to save the situation, I came out promptly with:

"Normand, gardener." Standing almost six feet tall, with broad hands, his short thumbs sticking out, he could not be objected to, but it was only with:

"Durand, farmer," that the storm decreased and melted away. Durand's ample mustache, stocky chest, and earnest face constituted our best chance not to be sent back to the *Stalag* right away.

Tapageur looked at him for some time, appraisingly, gave a last quick glance at the rest of us, muttered unintelligibly, turned around briskly, and hurried back to his office, in the castle's basement.

"March," sighed the sentry.

* * *

Beyond the chicken pen, at the end of the lower yard, a new set of heavy, hand-forged iron bars designated a rather cunning little house as our next jail.

A fellow prisoner came out, arrayed in a blue apron and said without enthusiasm: "Hello, boys!" He was the cook, he explained, and the fourteen others were in the fields. They had already been here two months, and did not like it. Had we, by any chance, anything to smoke? No, we had not, but what was he going to give us to eat? We had received no ration for the trip, and felt weak.

The main room of the little house constituted the farm bakery. The oven was a primitive construction at the end of it. On each side was an ordinary room and a tiny one. The

Forced Labor

veterans' bunks occupied the entire left side. The kitchen and refectory occupied the right room, and we were expected to crowd into the remaining eight by ten feet.

To the cook's disgust, we found everything lovely. He gave us a plateful of potato soup that was the finest thing we had tasted for a long time. He refused to give us more, though he had plenty.

"You would get sick. Your stomach has shrunk, you'd better go slow."

Sick? What did we care? We felt the hunger in our heads even more than in our stomachs. We would have forced him to help us again if another guard had not come in.

"Watch out," warned the cook, "he is no good."

Gefreiter Schwoll was mean and tough, and looked it. He made as much noise as the overseer and many more gestures when I told him what our professions were.

"You will not stay here long. Meanwhile, if any one of you escapes, I'll shoot three others." He patted his gun and showed with his fingers exactly what he meant.

A civilian — an old cap over his ear, a twisted smile showing very decayed teeth, and one useless arm in a sling — entered. He looked suspiciously at everyone, and took us to a storeroom. Each received a straw sack, made of woven paper string; an enamel plate, a cup, a spoon, a fork, and as much straw as we wanted. Clean, new, bugless straw. How marvelous!

Even with the best intentions, each contenting himself with twenty-four inches of bunk, we could accommodate only eight in the small room. Normand and Guibaut had to go with the veterans, who were just coming back from work. Farmers, or manual workers, most of them tall and strongly built, they looked tired and thin. They inquired about comrades left in the *Stalag*, and complained about the *Kommando*:

"The work is hard, the food is not substantial enough, the

overseer is hateful, the civilians detest us, and the *Wachmann* is terrible."

"Fellows," we retorted, "haven't you forgotten what a *Stalag* is like?"

We had made up our minds to be pleased. To have a room for eight, with a few square inches of shelf for each was a forgotten delicacy. It is true that between the bunk and the shelf there remained only room enough for four, but the others could lie down. Besides, there was a window with a view of a large field and a forest beyond. As a playground, we had a ten yards' stretch between the tool shelter and the privy. The latter looked like a sentry box, and from each of the three holes inside, one could view the farm and the castle through the cracks.

The farm buildings were large and fairly well kept. Some had four floors and massive gables. The main body of the stables and granaries was in the form of an H, open under the bar. A large sawmill, a blacksmith shop, a wheelwright shop, a sheep stable and an imposing *schnaps* factory, with a high brick chimney, were set apart.

The Von Z . . . castle was a large structure, with an eighteenth century character, three floors, a broad high roof, an octagonal tower, and a verandah above the main perron. A narrow lawn, adorned with bushes and high trees, seemed to announce another perspective than the horse stables opposite, and the pig sties at the left. One could survey the whole farm from every window on this side. On the other, the castle faced a park, a pool stocked with fat old carps, and a little round Adonis temple, in a Teutonic version of Versailles, set among birch trees.

Bornzin was made up of about thirty-five houses, each having its own little yard, a stable, a shed, and a chicken pen. The old ones, with high gables, the masonry whitewashed and the wood-

Forced Labor

work painted black, were attractive. The new ones were low, grey, and neat, and reminded one a little of the Hammerstein barracks. They were more comfortable than the average peasant's house in France. They succeeded each other without giving the village any form. There was no church, no city hall, no inn around which they could have gathered their roofs. A long muddy pond divided Bornzin in two, and that was all. Along a very poor dirt road, the houses stood at attention, so to speak, but did not dare face the lady dressed in black, dry, slender, many feet tall, like a medieval tower herself, watching the horizon all around that belonged to her, who could be seen often around her manor.

Bornzin was only one of four villages, each including five thousand acres of fields, meadows, and woods, for the exclusive benefit of the Von Z . . . family. Hay wagons, machinery, tools, buildings, bore the inscription: Erbe von Z.

With the exception of an old widow handling the small village store, and a little farmer, whose independence we could not explain, every man, woman, and child worked for the Baroness, had worked exclusively for her, or was going to. She practically owned every family, exactly as she owned every house.

Yet she too had a lord. High on her chest, so high that it may have meant her heart had little to do with it, a small enameled swastika testified that she had sworn allegiance to a wild Austrian house painter haunted by a Prussian dream. He had taken away, for his armies, the best of her serfs, and had very politely lent her a score of French slaves.

*   *   *

ILLUSIONS

Contrary to all advice, my team went to bed stuffed with potato soup as entree, boiled potatoes as vegetable, and cold potatoes as dessert. Guibaut and Georges were soon compelled to part with their dinner, but Portier, Lavaud and I built castles in Spain, on the foundation of a Pomeranian manor.

"Please move away so that I can breathe," said Portier, on the exiguous bunk, "and listen. I have been directing a milk and cheese factory for five years. When they see my profession on the *Stalag* list they won't think about sending me harvesting. I can show them a few French tricks for producing unique cheeses. Boys, I'll make you some, too. Just wait!"

Lavaud was a thoroughly trained hotel man. He knew French, Italian, and American cookery. Provided he had the opportunity to dip his ten fingers in the sauce, behind somebody's back, he was ready to turn out marvels, any style, even for a Junker's widow.

"If she has any sense, you know she won't send a French chef to feed the horses."

If I had twenty-four prisoners working for me, and one of them were a pianist, I would keep him busy at the keyboard, rather than at the threshing machine. I felt ready to paint the whole family, with the barking overseer in the background, with every hair in evidence, and even a little swastika in the glitter of their eyes; to restore any old coat of arms; and to decorate the walls of the castle, for an extra slice of bread a day, with a little fat on it. All things for which I would not have taken a lot of money, before.

Who couldn't see what an exceptional lot we were, and what a chance it was to get much for little? Who, but a Pomeranian?

The only job Portier was ever given in relation to cows was to remove dung from the stables. Lavaud made no soufflé of potatoes, but for two months, dug them on his knees. I, by special attention, was given a job in my line: I whitewashed everyone of the cows', horses', and pigs' stables, from 7 A.M.

Forced Labor

to 7:30 P.M. There were two hundred and twenty-five of the latter, lodged in a vast room divided in little square sties. I had to move them from one sty to another in order to renovate their quarters, and I never felt secure with the old sows. With a sack around my shoulders, as a smock, I was paddling through a foot of the most stinking dung when the Baroness entered on her daily inspection. She spoke excellent French and, after patting the horses and cows, would say a few words to the prisoners. Well measured, distinguished, interesting statements, falling from her great height, such as:

"Our Pomeranian soil is not as rich as the French soil. We have to give it twice as much work and fertilizer; but we produce the best potato crop in the world, and our milk is the richest!"

She asked Carl, the pig keeper, if I was the artist-painter who spoke German. He nodded, and I turned my back on her, feeling as free as the pigs around me to do so. I thought that I would grunt if she came near me, but she left. That was better. At the last second, I might have felt bound to show her that a Frenchman in a hog pen could outdo her manners. Angry with her for her feudal manners; mad with myself for my stupid readiness to expect anything else, I whitewashed a whole litter of pigs in their own pen! The bewildered little animals squeaked and grunted, upset my pail and ran desperately around me, trying to shake the lime from their hides. Carl hastened to me. Frantic, he could not understand what had happened.

"*Schnell, schnell, Wasser* (quick! quick! water) . . . if the Baroness saw that . . ."

A good old serf, Carl looked like his charges, and received a small share of their sales. In the good months, his salary reached forty-five marks. He thought a lot of me because I asked him every morning the names of his ten children. The government gave him one hundred marks monthly, for them, and he believed it came direct from Hitler.

"His name is right there on the check," he said. "He is good for the poor peasant!"

*   *   *

TWENTY-FOUR HOURS OF A PRISONER'S LIFE

After two weeks, the whitewashing completed and my hands eaten raw by the lime, I joined my comrades at the threshing machine. What a hard job! In three days, the raw spots on my hands were surrounded by thick calluses, and I felt my bones on the fork handle. With no other antiseptic than the straw dust on the tool, they healed.

The threshing machine was set under a barn and stuck out through both doors. The bundles of rye were taken down to it, on one side, and the bundles of straw piled up on the other side. The men were placed in the morning by "Half a Gallon," a civilian so nicknamed as a diminutive of "half a gallon of schnaps." Shaped like a Vichy water bottle, with deeply sloping shoulders and a cork-like little head, he went on terrific sprees, recovering just enough in the morning to come to work. He had lost a son in Poland, the previous winter, and told me several times a day that the boots he wore belonged to his boy. He had been a prisoner of war himself, for four years in Siberia, and promised us to get his revenge at our expense. He excited the guards against the prisoners, on the pretext that they did not understand his orders on purpose. Things went a little better after I came.

A man of habit, he put each of us in the same place, every day, without discrimination. Three of the biggest men of the older batch of prisoners went on the platform with the comparatively light work of untying the bundles, collecting the

131

Forced Labor

strings, and feeding the machine. My team was formed in line on the huge stack. One or two of us pulled out the bundles while the others kept them going with their fork, towards the machine. Untrained and underfed, it proved exhausting. Half a Gallon came around and bawled: *"Schnell, schnell"* every fifteen minutes. We had to keep the darned machine full, and when Guibaut or Georges slackened the line, the others had to compensate for it. The work was considerably complicated by the fact that the bundles of rye had been stacked irregularly by prisoners who knew as little as I did about it and tangled in all directions.

At nine-thirty, the steam engine whistled for *"Früh-stück."* We had half an hour to eat a snack. The civilians' smaller children brought them handsome sandwiches of ham, butter, and cheese, while we could hardly do better than chew a thin slice of slightly smeared bread. I could not always eat. I lay on the ground, trying to recuperate. The next whistle seemed to come in five minutes.

At twelve-thirty, we went back to our barrack and sat down to a bowl of warm potato soup, one and a half ounces of venison, and a plate of boiled potatoes. Everything came from the same big pan: the soup from the top, and the potatoes from the bottom. Everyone hurried to his bunk and slept until one forty-five, when Schwoll cursed us up. At exactly two, the threshing went full blast again. The first three hours of the afternoon were the hardest of the day. How often have I felt that I could not carry on, and tried desperately not to fall, not to give in, not to be defeated.

Wading through the stack, my feet sank as if they were in the mud and dust of the Beauce and Sologne roads. It was like retreating again, with no hope or goal. Were we condemned to retreat forever? Up and down, up and down on the stack — squirrels in a cage — we marched without progressing a step.

Like a golden belt, the bundles of rye moved along our forks, with our arms for legs. To lull myself to hypnotic sleep, I counted them. Pick up the bundle, five hundred and one, pass it on! Pick up the bundle, five hundred and two, pass it on! We handled as many as eighteen hundred an hour. "*Schnell, schnell,*" roared Half a Gallon. The sickening potatoes danced in our bellies. Pick up the bundle. . . . With each one, we broke wind, or belched.

When he saw me ready to give up, Durand would come, rectify the position of my fork, and show me how to swing it low, so as to economize energy. The gestures were so familiar to him that, though he had taken as much punishment as I had since we left Mézières together, he could endure hard work better. His muscles were intelligent; mine were dumb and numb. He liked handling a fork again. The smell of the straw, the dust of the grain, the cough of the steam, recalled the good old days to him, when, on his farm, he gaily emptied his barn and filled his granary, with the help of all his neighbors. Jugs of cider were passed around, the girls laughed and the men plotted practical jokes for the traditional threshing festivities that last all night. He dreamed off his fatigue!

There was no feeling of such stimulating joy for the civilians around here. The old mechanic, almost blind, running the engine; the horse drivers rolling away the sacks of grain; Half a Gallon bullying everybody — all worked only to fill the coffers of the Baroness, and earn a bare living for themselves. Accustomed to it, they did not complain, but passed as much of the hard work to us as they could. When a discreet whistle warned that "*Tapageur*" was in the vicinity, they rushed breathlessly, as if competing for a raise, or for praise. The prisoners, on the contrary, slowed down as much as possible to demonstrate their weakness.

At five, we stopped for "Vesper," a thirty minute rest. The

Forced Labor

last two hours were the easiest. Every five minutes, one of us managed to glance at our watch. Half a Gallon softened. He had thought only for his date with a bottle of *schnaps*. At seven-thirty we dismounted the belts, closed the gates, and went back to jail, for the best moment of the day: sitting at supper.

There was no surprise about that meal. On Monday, we had potato soup, and potatoes browned in a very little lard. On Tuesday, potato soup and a plaster-like cottage cheese, incredibly dry, with the green top of an onion mixed in it. On Wednesday, potato soup and our best dish of the week, a sort of boiled barley flakes with a little sugar and skimmed milk. On Thursday the sequence started again. The cook received almost as many potatoes as we needed, but no ingredient to help his cooking. He boiled everything. That gave him time, after the dishes were done, to help around in the farmyard, and to walk the big bulls on the dungpile in order to ram it down. Greens or fruits never appeared in our diet.

Immediately after supper we began peeling potatoes. It required about half an hour and we fussed about So-and-So who did not do his share, or left too much peeling, or all the eyes. Gefreiter Schwoll rushed us so as to spoil any little tranquillity that we might have derived from this domestic occupation, and, as soon as the peelings were swept away, made us take off our shoes and trousers, and lay them one by one on the benches in the bakery. He counted them, counted us, and bolted the doors. They were so ridiculously barred with heavy iron that there was no chance of our sneaking out and picking up our clothes. As an extra precaution, the bakery door was locked and padlocked, and the guards slept in the attic above.

An old steel barrel was used in each room as a night toilet. The potatoes had a strange action on our bodies; each of us had to get up two, three, and as many as four times in the night. Our bowels were swollen with gas and the atmosphere consequently infected. I tried hard to behave correctly the first few days, but it proved impossible. My arms and legs ached. Stretched as straight as possible on my narrow share of bunk, I could not move a leg without kicking someone. He grunted, broke wind, and sank delightfully back into oblivion.

Not a born *Wachmann*, Gefreiter Rohr was such a gentle soul that he would have hated to wake up anybody; but his colleague Schwoll came at a quarter to six, unbolted the doors and bellowed:

"*Aufstehen, aufstehen!* It's a blooming shame," he said, "to awaken prisoners so late. This is a soft *Kommando!*"

Before or after a little washing, very moderate, to be sure, for we had only one small basin for four, and the water had to be carried fifty yards — we waited in line by the privy. Stags and hinds grazed in the low fields, extremely near us.

A pint of toasted barley concoction, unsweetened but discolored with a white liquid — part skimmed milk and part water, probably — constituted our breakfast, with one or two slices of bread, at the expense of the *Frühstück*, or Vesper sandwich. Our bread supply amounted to one pound a day. The rye flour was mixed with potato flour and other ingredients, so the bread was very compact and heavy. We received with it enough marmalade and butter to make a teaspoonful of each a day, sometimes more, and a round of sausage half an inch thick. We worked cautiously with the slicing machine! Our two loaves of bread lasted through the week only if we marked the days on them, with a piece of chalk. Six thin slices a day, at the most. Both ends of the oval-shaped loaf meant considerable loss. Two slices could be covered with the marmalade, if one did not mind a few bare spots, and two with the butter. The cows had little responsibility in the latter, according to Portier. It contained a large quantity of potato flour, and perhaps some skimmed milk. The daily ration would fully veil the dark faces of two

Forced Labor

slices of bread only if the operation were undertaken near enough to the kitchen fire. The last two slices could be clapped together so as to make a prisoner of the round of sausage, like a small oyster in a big shell. A breadless lunch or dinner is so unusual for a Frenchman, even captive, that some of us preferred to save a cold boiled potato for Vesper, and keep two slices of bread for the meals. We wrapped the sandwiches in paper borrowed from the fertilizer sacks, for there was none other to be found.

At a quarter to seven, both guards would come down, order everybody out, and distribute the tools from our special shed. Five men with a "*Shippe*," ten with "*Forke*," five with "*Harke*" and the rest with "*Hacke*." Everyone knew that *Shippe* meant shovel, but there was always confusion between a mattock and a rake. This gave Gefreiter Schwoll a second opportunity of the day to clear his throat. What a fuss he made about a single "r."

In rows of three, we climbed the sloping kitchen yard towards the stables. From his house, to the right, the castle valet, a thoroughly abject, born spy, eyed the correctness of our manoeuvres. He would report, later, that Gefreiter Rohr told me "*Guten Morgen*"; and any other little incident. At five minutes to seven, sharp, we stood in line for the overseer and his staff. Cleanly shaven, his thin high boots irreproachably polished, *Tapageur* wore the same soapy smile every morning, and fingered his riding whip. At his right, the *Hofmeister*, very tall, his eyes sticking out of a narrow forehead under a felt cap, had an air of authority, without distinction. We called him "The Ox." He represented the Pomeranian routine, and enforced it, though it fell upon him to see that any new idea of *Tapageur*, an engineer of the modern school, be carried out. Instead of a whip, he held a stick, and his boots were neat without shining. Grade B, so to speak. He could pour a lot of noise through his long, flat teeth, as his position required, and roll his beefy eyes accordingly. Not mean, he was afraid to look soft, either with the prisoners or with the peasants, from whose ranks he had risen. His house in Bornzin was the best, and nearest to the castle.

Half a Gallon came next. When he was drunk, his cap was way down over his eyes. His dead son's boots were the only part of his equipment he took care of. His clothes were made of an incredible number of patches of all colors, neatly sewed together. He carried a tool.

The eight drivers stood next, a whip around their necks, with a few older men, four boys between fourteen and sixteen, and from five to ten girls less than twenty years of age.

"One Arm," as we called the cripple in charge of the storerooms, watched from a distance. He never left the buildings and was a sort of watch dog.

On the dot of seven, *Tapageur* distributed the work: Ten men threshing, two on the dung pile, ten in the hay, etc.; and we departed. The castle coachman held a handsome black horse. *Tapageur* sprang acrobatically on it, and rode away galloping. The Ox slid a bike between his endless legs, and went away pedalling. . . . Another day.

*   *   *

POTATOES

"*Kartoffel*" means everything to a Pomeranian. While turning a miserable hay rotting in swampy meadows; while hurrying the bundles of rye through the threshing machine; while alternating a bite of bacon with a gulp of ersatz coffee, the peasant talked about the potatoes.

Forced Labor

"They are coming on. They will soon be ripe. They are ready . . ."

One Arm took all the prisoners to the blacksmith shop, one evening, and each of us received a short three fingered hoe, newly reshaped, a wire basket, and an old sack. At seven, the next morning, we lined up apprehensively on the edge of a hundred-acre potato field. *Tapageur*, on top of his black horse; The Ox, on top of his huge self; and Half a Gallon, sober for once, presided at the distribution of the work. Each prisoner, considered as inexperienced, was assigned two rows; the men at our right, three each; the women and children knelt beyond them.

A whistle, and the mad dance started: crawling on your knees, along the rows, you dug with one hand, pulled up the vine with the other and, dropping the hoe, picked up the potatoes, put them in your basket, and advanced to the next plant. When the basket was full, you got up and emptied it into a metal basket called a *"Kippe,"* its capacity about a bushel and a half. These *"Kippen"* were to be kept in line, behind us, and as near as possible. Wagons drove by constantly with two prisoners who had the hard job of emptying the *"Kippen"* at full speed, while the castle valet, promoted to the dignity of controller, pulled a ticket out of a roll and dropped it in each of them. These were to be kept individually and produced on pay day.

Dragging the sack under our knees, sweating and swearing against the sentry tormenting us from the rear, and against The Ox bellowing from the front, we advanced as best we could. It was not long before we found that it saved time to bury some potatoes under our knees, but it must have been an old trick. The Ox caught on to it, and with a long hoe, controlled our rows from time to time, and made us, under showers of insults, do the job over again.

At the extreme right, the women seemed to have caught fire. Holding three rows each, they advanced with an extreme rapidity, faster than most men, and filled eighty *"Kippen"* a day. Guibaut finished twenty, I, thirty, and Durand forty-five. *Frühstück's* time had been reduced to fifteen minutes, but they hardly ate, and had already filled a *"Kippen"* when the hateful whistle startled us. The whole year they awaited the time when, instead of making seventy-five *pfennigs*, or at best, one mark a day, they could be paid according to their efforts. In the two months of potato digging, the fastest of them made as much as one hundred and fifty marks, which is about thirty-five dollars of buying power. The average man produced fifty or sixty *"Kippen"* and the children over ten years of age, from thirty to sixty.

I soon had the opportunity to watch the best of them for, as soon as they reached the end of a field — after one day, or two, according to its dimension — they started towards us without waiting for a new distribution of the rows, until we finally met, they, expert and valiant; we, weary and disgusted. It is a matter of suppleness rather than strength: digging the whole plant with one single neat stroke of the hoe, pulling it out with a certain jerk so as to scatter the dirt and detach the tubers, gather them with both hands, and deftly fill the basket. The potato queen, a huge gal of twenty, with no neck and a broad, thin mouth, became pretty when she did it: her hands played a sort of smooth piano around her, at a constant speed. In a turn, her basket was full. She ran up to the *"Kippen,"* and was very clever at filling the latter without ramming down the potatoes, so that fewer did the job.

Once in a while, one of the women walked ten yards away in the field and, in full view of all, crouched for a second, or a few minutes, then got up, arranged her skirts, went back to her place and hurried to make up for the lost time.

Forced Labor

Lunch was whistled about one o'clock and lasted only forty-five minutes. The cook brought us the soup and plates in an obsolete buggy, driven by the oldest man who ever sat on a seat. Indeed, his horses drove him, and the cook had to wake him up at both ends of their trip.

We hated to start again. Whether it rained or not, we rode the rows until we could no longer see the potatoes. The peasants did not mind the showers. They were making their best money of the year; and they had a good fire and other clothes at home, if one can call "clothes" the thousand patches that they wore. We had no way of drying our unique uniform quickly. When we were wet, it was for days. We had found out how to turn our sacks into overalls by cutting them and sewing with a string, in the middle; and we used old pieces of burlap as raincoats; but once soaked, they proved more of a hindrance than a help.

Exhausted, muddy up to the chest, we marched a few miles on slippery dirt roads, and arrived at the farm after eight o'clock. The worst, as expressed by Portier, was that, after having pawed potatoes all day, we still had to pet them for half an hour at night, peeling them.

*　　*　　*

During October, fifty new prisoners arrived. Thirty were parked in a stable, near the hogs, and the rest occupied the rooms above us. The two guards, quite delighted, went to live in the attic of the castle, and had a rather good time with the pretty maids and kitchen helpers. Now they locked us up as soon as we came back from work, with the compensation that we saw them one hour less a day.

So that all possible hands would clutch a hoe, the mechanical rakes and the heavy harrows that followed us on the fields were driven by little boys, aged from six to ten. They sat proudly on the seat, whipped the horses, and pulled on the reins with all their little weight, to stop them. They could not always manage it, and resorted to swearing exactly like their elders. They worked all day, while everybody over ten was kneeling. The line in the field often comprised more than one hundred and thirty diggers. Mothers of large families dug in the afternoon only. Many girls from distant villages came to the rescue, too. The Bornzin youngsters knelt by them, and joked in a true Pomeranian fashion, namely with very little subtlety.

When the weather was clear. the Baroness and her younger daughter came after lunch, in a coach driven by an old crow: he was assistant *Wachmann*, carried a pistol; and showed it to us, once in a while. He jumped to the ground, lowered the collapsible steps, and the Baroness descended. Wearing high riding boots, she went around, said a few words to *Tapageur*, who bowed to her from the top of his horse; to The Ox, who blushed and stammered; and, here and there, to the peasants. The daughter, seventeen or eighteen, her long hair flying handsomely in the wind, borrowed somebody's hoe, and dug a few potatoes, neatly, as if she knew how. She just stooped, of course, and lifted the potatoes one by one, with the hoe, built a little heap, handed back the tool and said with a smile: "Here you are."

The peasant answered respectfully, "*Danke schön, Gnädiges Fraulein*," as if she did not mind hurrying to make up for the ten minutes lost.

"I wonder how long you would keep lovely, *Fraulein* von Z . . . crawling on your knees, and your arms embracing the mud?" Who said that, behind me? She rarely looked in our direction, but she always set herself where we could see her pretty, disturbing silhouette against the sky. The prisoners grunted, threatened, and joked about her in a sharp obscene tone. She knew it, I'm sure.

Forced Labor

Three of her older brothers were in the army. The eldest was a lieutenant, the second a sergeant, the third, a private. The lieutenant came on furlough, from France. He visited the potato fields, and cried *"Heil* Hitler!*"* in a voice that echoed to the woods. Then he inspected every yard of the digging line. He objected to our dragging somewhat behind, as usual, and Half a Gallon blew us up accordingly, to no avail. The Junker then galloped away, an unusually tall figure on the horizon, towards his ancestral wealth, towards glory in the Nazi ranks, and, probably, towards a little wooden cross, somewhere south or east.

In November, it became very cold, and we froze at the potatoes. So did they. The damaged ones were immediately carried to the *schnaps* factory. The others were piled in long silos, covered with straw, then dirt, then potato vines, and finally dirt again. With a good blanket of snow on top, they would stand 30° below zero, Fahrenheit.

The digging machines were set in action, late, when the vines had been pulverized by the frost. Driven by tractors, they plowed very fast, but the dirt, falling back in thin dust, partially buried the potatoes again. Each prisoner was allotted about thirty paces along a straight line, and had to gather everything on the ground. It meant faster work than with the hoe, and was very hard on the back, but any potato on which we stepped sank half a foot immediately. So, picking with two hands, and burying with two feet, we could cheat The Ox. It proved only temporary. Each field was deeply harrowed and raked, later on, and we, formed in long lines, had to march over all the ground on which we had previously crawled, or stooped, to collect what had come up. Frozen to the ground, the potatoes had to be unearthed with the foot. They would produce only half of the normal quantity of *schnaps.* Our subtle manoeuvres had not been useless.

142

During potato time, the meat ration was increased a little. The head forester went to the woods, every week, and killed a deer or a boar, from which enough meat was given to our cook to make three ounces a day for each prisoner. The meat was heavy, but nourishing.

This forester was six feet tall, very husky and jovial. Dressed in apple green, crowned with a funny twisted hat of the same color adorned with a brush of boar's hair, he filled a field of a hundred acres with crude jokes that shook the girls on their knees. He was added to the valet for the control of the "*Kippen*" and they were rather jealous of each other. While the valet eyed suspiciously the contents of each "*Kippe*," and refused it if the top was not evenly flat, the forester could sometimes be fooled into allowing a ticket for a "*Kippe*" packed only on one side. A former professional soldier, he was correct with us, answered greetings willingly, and proudly showed us the herd of roebucks grazing in the fields, every morning. They retired only with the mist.

Once when I became sick in the field and had been allowed to rest a while in a thicket, he made me drink *schnaps* from his own flask. I was almost drunk when we marched back to the farm, under the moon, and my comrades were full of envy. It was everybody's dream to drown himself in alcohol and wash away, for a few hours, the shadow of the *Wachmann* and the bars of the windows.

*   *   *

SUNDAY

Sunday was the only day of the week that had any sense for us. We got up as late as seven thirty, which felt luxurious. It took us a good hour to do our laundry in the castle wash-house. Each was allowed one small package of washing powder and a cake of facial ersatz soap, a month. We took turns heating the

Forced Labor

water and cleaning up the place, afterwards. Lack of strings, or wires, made drying a problem. If we spread the clothes on the bushes, the wind blew them away into the duck pond.

Then we oiled our shoes, when we could persuade One Eye to let us have some oil. Grease was not to be found. Shoes constitute the main clothing problem for a prisoner of war. We had no nails, no string, no leather for repairing them. Mine had burst open near the tip, and took water better than a pail, for they sucked it out of the mud, as well. Barois got busy. From the horse stables he stole a leather strap. I obtained, so to speak, a nice bit of wood from the wheelwright shop. We cut it in two and, with our knives, carved two things that could be used as soles. Barois made a very fancy top with overlapping pieces of strap. The nails came from a carriage seat. It was an expressive piece of work, and suited my condition, if not exactly my feet, but I could tuck them in there and, when sufficiently wrapped in rags and old newspapers, they felt almost comfortable, except at the heel, where the back was missing.

It is difficult to realize to what extent every bit of metal or leather has been collected in Germany. On this huge farm, not a rag, not a nail, not even an old sole, could be found. To hang our clothes from the walls, we had to pull out nails from the barns, when nobody was looking. We fumbled everywhere, even through the garbage cans when we saw any, in search of any bit of anything that could be used in our quarters.

It is fortunate that we had a little yarn for our socks, and we proudly showed each other the funny spider webs that we wove at the heels and toes. Later, the only remedy would be a patch with a bit of handkerchief, or thin burlap, if one could be cut out of a sack, in spite of One Eye. It seemed to have rained confetti on my jacket, for about once a week I sewed a new patch, at the expense of my shredded puttees. I rather liked the looks of them, with their fancy stitches.

Shaved and washed, we stood in line at eleven o'clock for the regular inspection. The *Wachmann* made us take off our caps so as to decide who should have a haircut. We had a clipping machine, and anyone of us did the job. It consisted of running the instrument around the ears and on the neck. The little hair above did not amount to much as yet. The *Wachmann* looked at our shoes and clothes and made a list of what he thought was needed. Whether he sent it to the *Stalag*, or not, it rarely brought anything other than a few very poor shirts, and only occasionally a pair of trousers for the worst-off of the lot.

Then, ritually, I read the following rule, worded in French and German:

"The prisoners of war are warned that it is absolutely forbidden to approach a German woman. Anyone convicted of relations with a German woman, whether married or single, will be condemned to ten years hard labor. In case of pregnancy, the penalty will be death." I signed on the back, and the guard wrote the date. Everyone of us had signed such a sheet, on the first Sunday. We did not even laugh about it any more.

Once dismissed, we cleaned the house, and our section of yard, and dug a new trench for the privy. The hut had two handles and was easily carried farther. The new excavation-dirt served as covering for the old one.

At twelve-thirty we sat down to a peaceful meal. When some fat had been found on the meat allowed for that day, Lavaud tried something like a sauté of boar, or deer, and it had a taste that we greatly appreciated. The conversation ran regularly on the elaboration of the farewell meal that we would take together, when landing at the Gare de l'Est, in Paris. All were in favor of going to the nearest place so as to lose no time in ordering: a few dozens of oysters for each; a huge Chateau-

Forced Labor

briand steak with water cress and a pile of French fried potatoes; an enormous bowl of lettuce perfumed with garlic; a collection of cheeses and a few French pastries. Anjou, Burgundy, and Bordeaux wines, coffee and cognac would be the drinks. Lavaud knew a place where we could get this banquet for forty francs each. Now, that would avenge us of this watery dish of potatoes!

But when? We had no information whatsoever. The guards said sometimes that they had heard our captivity would not last long. We made bets. The general opinion was that we had been brought to Germany to handle the potato crop and would be sent home afterwards. There was no doubt that they would want France to pay a much heavier price for her defeat than had ever been asked — but not collected — from Germany. How could they hope that we would pay if they did not send us home to work for the taxes? That much was clear.

I greatly compromised my popularity by saying, out of mere prudence, "Boys, it may not be for this year, and who knows if there will be any wine left for us when we go back?"

Do you remember, Lavaud and Bertrand, how ridiculous it seemed to you? Yet, three years later you are still captive, and the above banquet would cost one thousand francs a piece, if you could get it through the black market in Paris, with only one sort of wine, and that not of the best.

After lunch, we hurried back to darning, sewing, or washing, so as to be free for the most important operation of the day: writing home. We received special paper four times a month: two letters comprising twenty-five lines, and two cards with five lines. No extra line could be added and the writing had to be done exclusively with pencil. The letters cost three *pfennigs* the cards, two. After November, this letter included a similar page for the answer. No ordinary letter would be accepted. We received two special stickers a month, that should be sent to our families, and pasted on the packages that they would send us.

Writing home meant a great sucking of pencil and meditation about how to say the most in the minimum space, and how to overcome the censorship. There are many ways, if one thought about it, but a letter refused by the censor is destroyed and not replaced. Everyone soon found that besides "Much love, how are you and the children and the relatives, I am fine, I hope to be with you soon," we had little to say. Who would be cruel enough to write that he felt like a wretch, that working all day for your enemy, eating poor food, and sleeping like a cow did not constitute a worth-while existence?

No news from home had yet arrived. Anxiety grew. Everyone had his moments of despair, during which he would refuse to speak to the others and would just lie on his bunk as soon as he came back from work. Everyone let him alone. After two, three, four days, sometimes a week, he would come out, of his own accord, and say: "Hello, give me a little clover for my pipe."

All the herbs around had been tried as a substitute for tobacco. The Pomeranians used potato vines, but the smoke stank, though it did not taste bad. Clover blossom was found quite sweet. I contented myself with the two German cigarettes that we could obtain every week. As our *Kommando* was too small to support a canteen, we were allowed to buy beer and tobacco at the village store. I went there every Saturday evening with the *Wachmann* and two prisoners. Our maximum ration was two small bottles of non-alcoholic malt beer, one of three per cent beer, and two cigarettes a piece. The storekeeper was a harmless old bird who had lost part of her mind. She could not count and robbed herself. I soon showed her that a prisoner would never think of taking advantage of her, and whenever she could she sold us three cigarettes instead of two.

Forced Labor

The whole supply amounted to about one mark per man, and meant our Sunday comfort.

It felt good to open a bottle, while playing bridge or *belote*, and besides, it was slightly nourishing. The two or three cigarettes, mixed with ten times their weight of clover, produced a lot of smoke. If the *Wachmann* was considerate enough not to show his face for a few hours, then this was the nearest to a sensation of freedom we ever got.

Dinner was potato soup and a round of sausage. While peeling the potatoes, a few boys hummed or sang, something sweet and ugly, a little out of tune, and we went to bed.

The feast was over. He who felt like crying hid his face in the bundle of underclothes that was his pillow, so that no one could hear him.

*　　　*　　　*

MAIL

Taken prisoner in Belgium, or in the north of France, most of the boys of the *Kommando* had had no opportunity to communicate with their families. They had been reported missing. Missing implies lying in a ditch with hardly enough dirt to cover his skull, and no stick to mark the place where an unknown man has fallen uselessly. The first batch of letters from home arrived one evening in October and shook them with fresh life. It was as if they, too, were now sure they were not missing. So much of their life had been borne in someone's heart, that to be thought dead meant a sort of death.

The letters said: "I am well. So are the children, and your parents. The house is only partially demolished, and we have lost only five cows and all the sheep, but are getting along fine. The newspapers say that you will soon come back. We all need you." Or "Our boy is well and goes to school. Our little girl was killed by a bomb. She did not suffer. I have sent you a package of woolen underwear, tobacco, and cheese. We live in the back of the house because the front part is occupied by the Germans. They are polite."

Every man, on his straw, took an inventory of his life and made a first draft of his next letter: "I have received your letter and it makes me so happy. Do not worry. Wait for me. I shall arrange everything when I return. I shall work hard. Send me a little sugar if you can . . ."

Our comrade Roland received the first package. It contained some food and one single package of "gris," the dark tobacco that every Frenchman loves. Every man in the *Kommando* got a thin cigarette of it. Then Roland hung the empty brown wrapping above his bunk, and it made us homesick.

When a whole load of packages arrived together, the *Wachmann* had a painful job. According to the booklet of instructions remitted to each *Kommandoführer* (military chief of a *Kommando*), every package must be opened and investigated for forbidden contents such as razor blades, fruit juices, ink, paper, arms, toothpaste, and hidden letters. One cigarette in each pack must be cut in two. Cans must be opened at once, etc.

Some guards found it amusing to keep the prisoner waiting while they endlessly pawed the box in which a dear hand had packed attentively some delicacies from home, but most of them understood our emotion and acted decently. Every one of them, though, suffered from the smell of chocolate, coffee, cakes, and from the touch of the pure woolen socks and sweaters — all products that could rarely be obtained in Germany. If they did the job as thoroughly as required by the regulations, they had to spend hours. As it could be undertaken only in the evening, after we were back from work, it cut the good time promised by the maids of the castle to the handsome *Wachmann*, and the control slackened, to our advantage.

Forced Labor

The lucky prisoners waited in line by the table in the bakery. Clad in rags, dragging wrecked shoes, often of different sizes, a threadbare cap flapped down on the ears, their faces barred by the scornful expression common to all prisoners worthy of that bitter name, meaning "No" to whatever a guard may say to them, and tenderness mellowing their eyes, they went away, one by one, holding the wrappings and strings in one hand and the precious package in the other — an incredible luxury in our *bagne*.

There would be banquets, next Sunday, each man inviting his own little circle, and the sandwiches would be substantial during the week. It was strictly forbidden for the guards to take, solicit, or accept any part of a prisoner's package. Confiscated items should be sent to the control office of the *Stalag*. Even so, some Germans had a way of smelling the chocolate and rolling their eyes that meant clearly: "It might be to your advantage to give me a bit of this for my girl ..." The prisoners understood the bargain. If this guard ever caught them smoking at work, in spite of *Tapageur's* orders, his trap might easily be shut. A puff of smoke slowly and deeply swallowed is like a soothing veil hung around you when it becomes unbearable to shuttle the hay with a rake, in a thin sun, in an endless landscape, for a litter of seven-feet-tall Heil-Hitlering Junkers, in exchange for a bellyful of potatoes and a bundle of straw for three, on a jail bunk.

*   *   *

GUARDS

I have never been able to read any German regulations concerning our rights, but I had deducted from conversations with the guards that one full day a week should be given us for washing, repairing clothes, having haircuts, getting ready for the *Kommandoführer's* inspection, and relaxing. Exceptions should be made in case of urgent work, only, and then another day should be given to us, as compensation, if possible. That was the catch. *Tapageur* could not resist making us work at least one Sunday out of three. There was always urgent work, such as unloading freight cars of coal at the station, or this or that, and it was never possible to give us another day in exchange. My protest amounted always to a fresh edition of this motto: *"Ihr seid Kriegsgefangenen . . ."* Prisoners of war, to them, meant men without rights.

The *Wachmann* was our only protection. To avoid any difficulty with him, the castle had a policy. The old cook took good care of his food. He ate supper with the maids, and his sandwiches were coated with ham, sausage, and butter of the real sort. The valet invited him to his house, where he had good *schnaps* and a gay fat wife. *Tapageur* received any new *Wachmann* in his office and told him how to make us work more. We were so lazy and slow, he said.

Gefreiter Schwoll had been a *Wachmann* to his liking, loud-voiced and quick on the trigger, but he had been called back to his regiment, in September. Gefreiter Rohr was not born to be a *"VACHE-mann"* as we said (*"Vache"* is French for cow, and our current expression for meanness). In the morning, when he loaded his gun in front of the prisoners and slid an extra cartridge in the barrel, he looked at us as if to say: "This is the regulation. I'm sorry." He had lasted only a week.

New guards came from Stolp every five or six weeks, two together until November, and then only one. Some were severe in the matter of discipline, but none as mean as Schwoll, or as dishonest. When he went to Stolp, about once a week, he brought us little items on which he made enough profit to pay for his train ticket. He sold Roland a cigar that cost nine *pfennige*, for one mark.

Forced Labor

Franz was really lovable. He had to be reminded constantly about his duties. He fumbled through the packages without looking at them at all. He came down one morning without his rifle and marched us out. I had to tell him. He never said anything while we worked, except to repeat *Tapageur's* words when the latter ordered us to work faster, and even argued with him, in front of me:

"You can't expect city people to know how to dig potatoes." In the evening, rather than stay in the kitchen of the castle, he sat among us. The boys did not mind him at all. He spoke a few simple words, such as: *"Gefangenschaft, nicht gut,"* and smiled. They brought him candy. He shared his tobacco. He had a wife and four children, somewhere in a large city, and often said to me: "It is all rotten anyway. When shall we all go home?" or: "I earned a hundred and forty marks a month in a factory, before. Damn, that wasn't enough. How much shall I get after this?"

Disgusted with such a poor specimen of a Nazi, *Tapageur* had written to his company, in Stolp, to have him removed. Two German lieutenants came down at lunch time, and inspected the *Kommando*. Franz made me tell them what we received for food, and how *Tapageur* behaved. They listened politely and objected openly to the exiguity of our quarters.

"If the prisoners work for Germany," said one of them, "Germany will treat them correctly."

"They do the best they can, *Herr Leutnant*," lied Franz.

Our food remained the same, as did our quarters; but we received another *Wachmann*, not quite so mellow.

*   *   *

LAST OF MY GROUP

Another week. Another month.

Another week. Another month. Comfortable calluses lined

my palms and there was a place for each tool on my shoulders. Never having sat at a meal without a pocket German dictionary, and having taken every occasion to improve my German, I was promoted to the rank of interpreter. At first it meant only such responsibility as ordering my comrades to attention, in the morning, and translating the *Wachmann's* and *Tapageur's* orders and opinions on our efficiency.

Pay day meant the extra job of standing with the cashier, calling each man by his number and counting his money with him. We received seventy *pfennige* for a full day's work. Any day of sickness was deducted. This, by the way, meant a real scandal. When a boy did not feel well, he said so to me in the morning, and I had to report him to the *Wachmann*. The latter came down to investigate and tried to get the man up with a few sound threats. When that didn't work he registered him as sick. During his morning review, *"Tapageur"* would ask:

"How many are sick?" He would accept one. For two or more, he would go to the barrack, yell loudly, and drag the men out of bed by their feet. One had to be really very sick to withstand this demonstration of Pomeranian authority. If sick more than three days, the prisoner was sent to the German military doctor in Stolp. He would walk six miles to the next railway station, and pay for round trip tickets for both himself and his guard. He might be granted three days' exemption, or be sent back to the *Stalag*, if recognized as incapable of working. While the guard was away, the coachman officiated in his place.

Every few days, the *Wachmann* received orders from the *Stalag*, to make a new list of our professions, or our religions, or former regiments, etc. and it fell upon me to get it ready, and fight the illusions that it aroused among my comrades.

Once every two weeks, I deposited in the castle kitchen, a list of items that we wished to be bought for us in Stolp, such as combs, razor blades, pipes, playing cards. We had little inter-

Forced Labor

est in the coupons that we received instead of money. They were not good at any civilian store except with the authorization of the *Stalag* and under control of a *Wachmann*. The oldest daughter of the Baroness exchanged them with the castle cashier and ordered the things for us when she went to Stolp, but we could not buy any food, or clothing, and rarely more than one or two cigarettes a piece. We collected enough money to buy an accordion, and one of us made a racket with it during the peeling hour.

At work the Germans called me Johann and wanted me to translate their remarks. It made them feel important. The Ox was almost friendly to me, but he certainly started to explode when he found me at the foot of the granary steps, sitting on a one hundred and sixty pound sack of barley, instead of carrying it.

"Johann, *was?* . . ."

"*Herr Hofmeister*, I don't understand you any more."

"What is that? What did you say?"

"Carrying those heavy sacks is what does it. When I have to climb these steps with a load on my back, I forget my German completely."

For a moment he hesitated between bursting with anger or laughter, and finally compromised by saying softly:

"Go get a shovel, and ventilate the grain."

I made the grade. Now there would be only soft jobs for me, in as much as soft jobs exist on a Pomeranian farm. I was discovering the prisoners' technique.

*   *   *

Guibaut, too, had managed pretty well. The first time that a big load of hay had been put on his back, he had valiantly climbed ten steps and then given out. The hay had fallen on the head of *Herr* Half a Gallon, and Guibaut had saved himself by clutching the banister. Another trial had been so disastrous that Guibaut had been sent to help the gardener. It proved a blessing for us. He was so thin that he could hide a lot of things under his topcoat without attracting attention. He never came back to lunch without a little head of cabbage, a couple of carrots, or anything else that he had been able to snatch while cultivating the Baroness' garden.

"You should make a successful lawyer, Guibaud," sneered Bertrand, "I see your talents."

"If you are mean," retorted the thin man, "I shan't show you a nice little turnip that I have in my hip pocket. I must admit, though, that I ate a fairly good apple in the cellar this morning."

All of Guibaut's booty ended in the huge kitchen kettle, and gave a little taste to the potato brew.

"See, boys," said the cook, "what you would all do, if you had any sense; bring me something from the farm, every night. But you are hopeless."

We repaid the mocking Breton in full. The next evening, Lavaud, Barois, and I each brought him a little bag. Mine contained some hay, Barois' contained some straw, but Lavaud had filled his in the hog stable. The cook became so provoked that we had to fight in order to restrain him from putting the whole thing in the soup. The guard hurried down with his gun, and found everything looking normal: I, patting the cook gently, Barois poking the fire, and Lavaud smiling.

"What is that racket?" he asked me, "and what stinks so in the stove?"

"Just wood, *Herr Gefreiter;* just Pomeranian wood."

*

Rameau had not lasted long. On the eve of the "Potato Crusade" as we called it, he had developed a very bad rupture and

Forced Labor

been sent back to the *Stalag*. His face, during the last meal, was even more pitiful than it had been during the fatal search of his supplies in Hammerstein. We all regretted the leather, the nails, the material, the thread that he had lost then. Now it was his daily portion of soup that was taken away from him. He certainly filled up on it before returning to the meager ration at the *Stalag*.

Guibaut always smiling, Georges always fussing, Bertrand always pointing at every ugly Pomeranian with his thumb and saying: "Look at our conqueror," had been warned many times that they would go too, after the potato season; but Portier and Lavaud were also discarded.

Tapageur kept me as necessary interpreter, with Durand, good all around, and Barois clever with any tool. Only remnants of the old platoon, we formed a queer, but intimate trio. Durand told me about his slow struggle to acquire a farm of his own. Barois confided the tricks, the pains, and the glories of a little bicycle racer. I had nothing to tell them about painting, but they liked hearing about luscious watermelons eaten in Ukraine, and rattlesnakes tasting better than eels, in Virginia.

They read their letters to me. From home, I had none to show them.

Durand's wife wrote: "I have plowed the fields, sown the winter wheat, and sold the apples. What do you want me to do in the little patch above the woods?"

Barois' wife wrote: "I receive a small allocation from the new government, prices are going up, and many things can't be bought any more, but I'll manage all right. What do you want me to send you?"

"What in the world can she do" Barois said to me, "with two children and no savings?"

His reply to her letter was: "I am very well on this farm. The food is plentiful and substantial. I don't need anything. As I have lost the habit of smoking, don't send me any more packages."

He had spells when he would work savagely, as if trying to break his tool. Sometimes he dug potatoes as fast as the women. They turned their heads, abashed, and wondered what was the matter with him.

CHAPTER 9

Winter

WINTER WORK

Snow suddenly changed the pine trees edging the landscape, from a mournful black hem to a luxurious lace, and life on the farm took on a quieter pace. Only sixteen prisoners were left in the little house by the duck pond, in the care of a cross-eyed phthisic sentry. When he came to wake us up, in the dark morning, his voice vacillated like the flame of an exhausted candle:

"*Au-u-u-f-stehen-n-n, aufstehen . . .*"

He had taken a liking to us, and was, next to Franz, the best sentry we ever had. He didn't stay around any more than was necessary, nor did he dally in the castle kitchen. Ascetically, he confined himself to a row of Nazi prayer books. While Hitler represented for *Tapageur* a thundering Alexander the Great; for Half a Gallon, an avenging Attila; he was a visionary virgin, armed with a lily switch, for our tender *Wachmann.* Any little conversation gave him the chance to comment on the kindness, the understanding of the world's sufferings by his Adolf, and to quote meek words flowering here and there in some of the latter's orations.

When it became very cold, he warned us to be careful and keep our toes moving all the time, in our wrecked shoes. He obtained from the *Stalag* six pairs of good trousers and some light sabots for us. They looked indecently clean among the others, for almost a week. We had tailored, for ourselves, some comfortable underclothes from old paper fertilizer sacks, by cutting three holes, and poking our arms and head through them, but they stank persistently.

We spent much time fitting our footwear, obturating openings with crumpled newspaper and patches of burlap, and tying strings all around. When the shoes were large enough, a layer of straw inside gave fine protection.

After interviewing the castle staff several times, I had obtained a handful of rags that we shared judiciously. I made a hood to complete my cap, with a small hole for my nose and eyes. Later, I had to enlarge the hole for my breath formed a sharp knife on the cloth, under my nostrils. On windy days, I added a whole newspaper attached at both ends under the collar of my topcoat. When the wind has rolled across Poland and slaps your right cheek, it seems to go through the left one as well, leaving your teeth cold.

On January nights the thermometer went down to 37 Centigrade, or 34° Fahrenheit below zero. We went to work in temperatures oscillating around 10° below zero Fahrenheit. The hour of walk through the fields, to a distant barn, was torture. When both doors were open, and the threshing machine set in motion, there was no use for Half a Gallon to *schnell* us up. We forked as fast as we could, to keep from freezing. Mittens of army cloth, carefully darned, didn't prevent our fingers from becoming numb, and feeding the machine was dangerous. It swallows the bundle irresistibly. If a hand is caught under a string that your knife has missed, the arm follows and the man too, until his skull stops the flapping wheels and causes the belt to jump off the pulleys. Many a prisoner has lost his fingers, his hand, or his arm at the sawing wheel, as well.

Going to the next thicket for a few minutes wasn't the pleasant distraction it had been in warmer weather. One couldn't smoke on the stack, either. Only dreaming was possible.

Forced Labor

Around nine o'clock, local war time, when the sun emerged from behind the plains, I knew a minute of enthusiasm: a vermillion flare brushed the earth, the foot of the trees, the legs of the prisoner raking under the machine, the lower pulleys, and ran on the belt towards the steam engine on the other side. Everything turned to red hot iron. Then the sun climbed up the tender blue sky where it became shockingly pale, while the grey mists retreated under the pine woods, like a woolen blanket put away for the day.

Lined with immaculate snow, torn by a unique track for the sleighs on which all carts were now mounted, the fields showed magnificently their form of a cross, or a star, carved in the woods, so as to give protection on all sides from the wind. Sometimes, a single high tree stood in the way, marking a spot where a famous Lord von Z . . . had made a big kill. Long ago, it was, when hunting was a ceremony. Now, the hunter's face blemished on a decaying painting, and the tradition lived only under the funny green hat of the forester, so respectful of the heavy deer, so careful to have straw set in the woods to keep them from starving.

We didn't pause any more for *Frühstück* or Vesper. We hurriedly ate our lunch sandwiches around a barn fire deftly built by Half a Gallon with a bundle of straw and a few limbs downed by the storms.

Since one of them had frozen his toe, no *Wachmann* idled with us all day. He brought us, and then came back after us. Wouldn't the snow promptly take care of anyone foolish enough to escape, even if the civilians didn't notice him immediately?

Another winter occupation was spreading manure in the fields. Eight prisoners remained on the farm, to dig out the dung pile. After all the output from the stables of the cows and horses, and from the pig sties, had been dumped there for six months, and rammed down daily by the two heaviest bulls, it was a hard job. The lower layers had to be sawed vertically, with a special blade. The sleighs and big wagons brought the dung into the fields and dumped it in heaps, on a straight line. It was divided up equally among us, and we got busy energetically shaking our forks all around. The Ox and Half a Gallon paced along to see that each lump had been carefully broken into tiny bits, and spread incredibly far. If a load of sheep manure tenaciously caked had been dumped on your lot, you were in for a rough time. I was pretty good at sprinkling snow on the large spots of manure, so as to retouch the face of my job. The Ox fell for the trick every time.

Three or four girls were often lined up with us, and that was no fun. Not only did they do the job very quickly, with a supple agitation of the fork all around them, but they shortened their share of the line, at our expense, by removing the sticks limiting the lots. I appealed to The Ox and after some argument he undertook to rectify the divisions. Each was to have about fifty yards, but due to the surprising inability of these peasants to count, he never succeeded in dividing the huge fields exactly. Meanwhile the loads kept coming, and we shook our elbows as if trying to throw them out of joint.

When the dung pile was exhausted, and the snow too thick in the fields even for a Pomeranian, we collected kindling in the woods, for the year's supply of the castle baker. It wasn't hard work, but we froze to such an extent that no civilian would stay with us all day. We dragged the branches through the snow to the nearest forest road, and loaded them up to the sky on the carts. When the weather was absolutely impossible for work outdoors we chopped wood in a cellar.

To prevent the carp from suffocating in the castle pond, we bored holes in the two-feet thick ice and stuffed them with straw. During a whole week, we sawed the ice in blocks, one

Forced Labor

foot by three, so as to fill up the ice-house, dug deep in the soil, which served as a giant year-around Frigidaire for the meat supply, exactly as was practised on the plantations in the South a century ago.

Once a week, at least, we had to reopen the way leading to the main fields, by shoveling away the snow brought by the wind, and carving a six-foot-deep tract; typical convict labor, while our watch dog paced above, cursed the weather, and talked to the drivers of the sleighs, loaded with potatoes from the silos, passing at regular intervals. These were delivered to the *schnaps* factory, where a couple of prisoners shoveled them into the reserve cellar. All work around there offered the advantage of warming oneself, once in a while, at the chafery. The stoker, a graduated peasant, was very fond of French tobacco.

The director of the factory was an agreeable little man, broad and portly, and rather odd looking in his short boots. He was Mayor of Bornzin, whatever that could mean in a community so entirely dependent on the castle. Every three weeks, the *schnaps* was shipped away, and it sometimes fell upon two prisoners to fill up the two-hundred-gallons steel barrels with ninety-four per cent alcohol. One manipulated the hand pump, the other rolled the empty barrels in, and the full ones out. They were duly weighed, verified, sealed, and registered by a custom's officer, in impeccable black uniform: a curved cap, a green hem around a coat adorned with military insignia and riding breeches. According to the talkative mayor, he carried the fermentation of the potatoes to such a point that two hundred and twenty pounds of them produced twelve quarts of ninety-four per cent alcohol. I verified it several times by counting the average quantity of potatoes unloaded in three weeks. Twenty-four barrels at a time were usually driven to Radamnitz and sent by rail to an ammunition factory.

The barrels came back empty, ten days later. The truck

driver shook every one of them to find out if any alcohol had been left inside. I have seen him pour about a glassful of it into the truck shovel, soiled with dung and dust, and gulp it until his eyes became bloody.

The distilling circuit of the factory was sealed and carefully checked by the custom's officer. Posters threatened death to anybody stealing alcohol — the property of the *Reichsmonopole* — but the peasants managed it whenever employed in our place. One filled a tin can behind the officer's back; the other suddenly taken with colic, ran to the privy. At closing time, both would hide from *Tapageur*, the valet, or One Arm, and intoxicate themselves at great speed, either with pure or diluted spirits. The first man to drink seemed to be struck by lightning: he swayed on his feet, and fell. His comrade helped him up, and then he, too, fell. When the stunning effect had settled a little, they would leave through the back gate, plodding in the snow, close to each other, their backs covered with a hundred patches, only playing the comedy of being very tired, their faces lit under the old felt caps, their entrails tormented by silent shrieks and savage joy.

THE PEASANTS

Brutality, shrieks, and gallops are the natural expressions of the Pomeranians. They don't signify meanness. Life is hard for them; they are hard with it. They have less than six months of good, or tolerable weather, in which to do all their work. That may be the reason for their speed mania. As prisoners, we received an extra dose of *"Schnell! Schnell!"* but the peasants were not spared by either *Tapageur* or The Ox. They dug, shoveled, loaded, unloaded, cut wood, cut straw at a fast pace, but — excepting potato digging, at which they were excellent — their ways were awkward. I learned to manipulate a shovel

Forced Labor

from my comrade Charlot, a Parisian excavator, with a broad back and heavy neck, a true professional who wore, in civilian life, ample black corduroy trousers tied around his shoes, and a wide red or blue flannel band, with a garland of tassels, around his stomach. "It is the tassel that counts," he used to say.

He leaned lightly on his shovel, pushed it through the dirt, or coal, or fertilizer, lifted it, balanced it, emptied it, without a jerk. The shovel moved slowly along a harmonious cycle. Wherever he worked, the ground was neat and the pile had an architecture. He spat in the direction of the Pomeranians with a double contempt for their messy work and their fear of *Tapageur*.

During the harvest, my comrade Roland, animated by a fool- ish zeal, had begun stacking the bundles of rye the French way: several bundles standing upright, the grain above, and one bundle spread on top so as to cover entirely those underneath. When the rain came, only this bundle would get wet, and then dry quickly. The Bornzin fashion consisted of piling the bundles any way. The Ox came around, looked intently, and finally blew up Roland for spending so much time at the job. "*Schnell! Schnell!*" and what does it matter if the rows are not straight?

They loaded the hay wagons with so little care that they upset often at the curves on the dirt roads. Everybody was called to the rescue, and the whole thing was put back on its wheels and hurried along.

Except for the most elaborate machinery, such as the two tractors and the mechanical potato diggers, the farm equipment was built by the smith and the wheelwright, on very simple patterns. The wagons were composed of a chassis with four small wheels on which boxes with tilted sides could easily be set. The heaviest wagons had comfortable tires of artificial rubber that must have been excellent to withstand the most careless treatment.

Whenever *Tapageur* could be seen surveying the scene, from the top of his mount, the drivers beat their horses to a mad gallop, over the most impossible dirt roads. No vehicle of any size ever entered the farmyard otherwise than at full speed. The horses knew it so well that they took to galloping when in sight of the gate, no matter how heavy the load — a tradition, dating, I'm sure, from the time when a ferocious von Z . . . , perched on a medieval tower, hurried his serfs around. I hated those galloping hoofs on the cobblestones. They reminded me of the invading war material thundering on the French roads.

*　　*　　*

Elsa was my friend. She had never been afraid of me, and it was on her that I tried my stumbling German, months ago, when she brought her daddy's sandwiches to the farm or the fields:

"How old are you?"

"*Ich bin acht.*" *Acht.* How sweet the guttural sound "ch" can become in an eight-year-old's throat. I made her say it every day.

All children had been warned to beware of us, and, the first two months, they didn't dare fool around us, so it was a secret between Elsa and me. She was ugly; her neck too short; her face too pink; her hair too red. I loved her. She got the first piece of candy I ever received from home.

Squatting on a truckload of coal, I came back from the railway station one biting cold day, and saw her, by her parents' house, carrying a pail of water heavier than she. I threw a block of coal at her, to make her laugh, but she did not. Instead, she dropped the bucket, and dragged the coal into the house. I was valiantly leveling the dung pile, the next morning, when her father, a little man with heavy features and timid eyes, came

165

Forced Labor

to me, looked around, and swiftly handed me a small package. It contained one sandwich with a luscious little tongue of meat inside. A virtual pact had been sealed. I never passed through the village with a load of straw, or coal, without dropping a bundle or a block at every door behind which lived a sympathetic peasant. As if they had stood guard behind the window, small children darted out immediately to pick it up. After discussing the fact with my comrades, we made it a point to help the peasants out whenever we could, and their attitude towards us changed accordingly. Not only had they taken the habit to work with us, get wet with us under the showers, freeze with us in the snow, compare patches with us — theirs better sewed only because they had wives — but they realized, though perhaps vaguely, that we stood together on the same side of the castle: the slave quarters. I told them so, openly. We became friends.

Sawing wood, and splitting it in a special cellar where the sentry left us alone with five or six of the oldest peasants, gave me a good opportunity for this:

"Men, are you much better off than we are? A little more and better food, a wife and a score of children, who all have to slave for the castle. Isn't Germany the land of a new socialism? When are you going to share these thousands of acres that you have tilled for generations, for the exclusive benefit of one family?"

The most timid retorted: "It's not too bad. The Baroness gives us a good house, a cow, a sheep, two pigs, a little rye and barley, some straw, and some potatoes, as part of our salary. We know that we'll never starve."

"Yeah," said another, "Johann is right. Each one of us should have his own farm, and be a member of a village co-operative."

"That will come, Johann, after this war, when Hitler organizes all of Europe."

Hitler must have spoken the language of the peasants, for they believed in him. I had to carry my points cautiously:

"How many of you will have to pay for it, with your lives?"

They dreamed and, because a prisoner can never be on the side of his captors, I tormented them, viciously perhaps:

"Look at my comrade Durand. He owns sixty acres, three horses, ten cows, a house and all his farm machinery. He will hand it down to his children and they will increase it. Men, you will get only what you take yourselves."

Yet I liked them, and they knew it.

Slowly I discovered that everyone, from the lowest horse-driver to the foreman, stole what he could from the farm. Sacks of potato flakes, still hot, disappeared from the factory. The men had their sandwiches for *Frühstück*, and Vesper brought by their children who could then fill up their pockets. They played under the threshing machine and collected a few handfuls of rye seed "for my chicken" they said to me. During the winter, a few sacks of barley migrated towards the inn, located entirely outside the village, where some of the peasants dashed, once in a while: they stood at a counter made of a board laid across a door, and ordered ⅛ — sometimes ¼ — of a quart of *schnaps*, which they drank, one glass after another, without stopping, without tasting — like shoveling fuel.

We downed trees for them, to increase their wood supply; and they said: "Frenchmen good. Comrades."

The argument between Alphonse and Charlot about which horse-driver was responsible for the pregnancy of a girl working at the mill, was settled when, one evening, I found her stuffing her wide skirt with a comfortable little bag of flour. In fact all the women were decidedly thinner in the morning. Not that the above accusation was at all irrelevant. Everywhere the peasants mixed freely. Since the days were shorter and the work easier, I felt like knocking at every door, before entering

Forced Labor

a stable or barn. It was unpleasant to hear the giggle of a girl assaulted in the hay. Old man Karl, my friend from the pig sty, was one of the worst. The young girls never went alone to his quarters; he chased them around his hogs. Pink, round and heavy, though often with pretty features, they looked rather like his charges. They wore red, blue, or grey kerchiefs on the head, men's jackets and boots. Charlot had nicknamed the fattest of them "Potato-blossom."

Charlot had an eye for everything. He warned us of a strange romance occurring, he said, in the sheep stable. The shepherd was a romantic sort of thin young man, coughing his lungs out, and wearing a large hat and long black cape when he walked his animals through the fields, to eat up the remaining potatoes. Charlot had found him kissing the hand of the Baroness' oldest daughter, in the dark, with a shocking enthusiasm. Perhaps because his strength was slowly coming back to him, this affair was worrying my husky comrade.

The guards pursued the chamber maid. She looked dainty, well groomed, in black dress and white apron but, according to *Wachmann* Franz, they couldn't compete with the youngest lord of the castle, hardly fifteen and still wearing short trousers, occasionally. Our cook told us that the guards found consolation with the valet's wife. Her eyes were small, her mouth large, and her waist ample. When a guard sneaked in, during the day, she sent her children out, and drew the curtains tight.

The stable boys wore short pink rayon blouses over their shabby clothes, and it gave them an elegance contradicted by their old twisted caps and their way of sitting in the stable litter. Their work was often controlled, and we never had the opportunity to persuade them to give us milk. Neither could we milk a cow behind their backs.

The wheelwright and the smith lived above their shops, and

mixed little with the others. Through working only for the castle, they had almost graduated to the rank of artisans; yet they were the most subjugated. The peasants warned me to watch my tongue when they were around.

Due to the lack of teachers, the children went to school four hours a day, two days a week only, until the age of fourteen. Between fourteen and eighteen, the working boys received two hours' schooling, twice a week, in the evening, when they didn't come back too late from work. I have often found, when asking them for a word, that they couldn't agree on the spelling. I told them to get away from this farm where they had no future at all. They were anxious to go, but didn't see how they could make it. The army seemed to be the only hope for all of them. Wasn't a former stable boy already a sergeant? But a horse-driver, who had come back, a little lame, from the Polish campaign, said to them, in front of me:

"A year of hard work on a farm is softer than a day at war."

In spite of the pretension that Nazi social laws guarantee adequate pensions to old people, men in their late sixties worked on the farm. One of these stood over six feet, and was so incredibly strong that he lifted up Roland who happened to be stepping on his shovel; but two or three others could only be employed at minor jobs, such as ventilating the grain. Like their very old clothes, they looked mildewed. In the high granaries, they stood on shovels, used up, tired of life, doing very little, and waiting for Death to come.

One morning, the white-bearded miller failed to come. Two days later, at 4 P.M. the peasants gathered in the yard, and it took me some time to recognize them: each wore a long black cloak, a curved cap with a shiny vizor, and a vermilion armband with a swastika on it, ferociously black on a white circle. They were so proud, so happy. They collected a green wreath from the basement of the castle and in rows of two, The Ox

Forced Labor

and Half a Gallon ahead, away they went: "One, two, one, two, one, two . . ." to bury their old comrade.

WEIHNACHTEN

Our Christmas tree should have been an ersatz tree of barbed wires wrapped around rusty rifles. The green should have been borrowed from the sentry's uniform. The red should have been blood sprinkled over all; blood from the French roads. I could have filled my canteen with the blood that leaked from the strafed cars upset on the Beaugency road. The silver should have been clipped from our heads. Many a scalp had whitened in these few months of captivity. But there is a deforming process in the world, persistently hiding the face of reality. Events show their faces only for a fugitive instant, then a mask is laid over them. Everybody is afraid of life as it is. Like a tracked bandit, every man wipes off his finger prints and obscures his traces: he wants to forget, to be forgotten, to be thought somebody else, somewhere else.

It was a green pine, five feet high, that the Baroness' oldest daughter ordered brought to us, with a dozen shiny glass balls made in Hamburg, one ounce of aluminum icicles, and twelve birthday candles with nice little holders. The boys were shy at the idea of any form of festivity. They simply wanted to enjoy three days with only two hours' work around the stables. "Let's play at it," I told them. Barois and Roland set the tree in a corner of the room where we ate our potatoes, now mixed fifty-fifty with coarse rutabagas. I wonder if it was a trick of the youth in the castle, or just a coincidence, but there was no infant Jesus in the little box of figures for the holy stable. I arranged them.

On Christmas morning, tall, blonde, discreetly painted, and ornamented with a swastika, the Baroness' daughter appeared

170

in our quarters, on the arm of her brother in uniform of a sergeant of the Reich. I greeted them with a military salute.

"*Glückliche Weihnachten*," they said.

"Merry Christmas," I answered.

They wanted to see the tree. I showed it to them. The girl, with a sweet expression in her admirable blue eyes, remarked that Jesus was missing. She knew it, but thought that I might make one. Carved out of a potato, perhaps?

"It is better like this, *Fraulein*. The Saviour has not come for us, this year."

She wanted to be kind. She talked to me as nicely as she could, about the Christmas customs in Germany, and how she wished everybody to be happy on that day. Two cakes and a few cigarettes had been added to our diet. The brother, to say something, commented on the war biscuits that the French Red Cross had sent us, and said that he enjoyed them in France, every morning, with his coffee, as well as our corned beef, (that we call monkey meat) though he found it a bit dry. After a while they went away. I showed them to the door, like a gentleman.

"Good-bye."

Damn it! I almost said, "Come again."

Gnädiges Fraulein, I am sure that you felt happy to have been so generous on this day of generosity; but if you had wanted us to be happy, you would have let us alone. All alone.

*　　　*　　　*

We had three days to meditate on our past hopes; and that was worse than working all day. No one had believed that we would be behind bars on Christmas day.

The mail had brought us a special number of the *Trait d'Union*, a four to eight page paper published twice weekly,

Forced Labor

in French, for the prisoners. Most articles were signed with initials, followed by the mention: *Stalag*. II C, or *Stalag*. XIII, or *Oflag*. VI, etc. Either clever or naïve, they were masterpieces of bootlicking, pathetically colored by illusion, the infernal disease of the captive. Without naming him, they extolled the glory of the *Reichsführer*, the saviour of the world from a democracy apparently so rotten that it would let everybody be happy or unhappy in his own way, and so stupid that it would let anyone fight against it without liquidating him right away. They usually missed the stronger possible attack on our former governments, by omitting the fact that they had led us to war without adequate preparation. All wrongs were traced to the British, of course, and many disagreeable things were bitterly recalled. They omitted to say that whatever the share of other countries in the responsibility for our defeat, our own was sufficient and should always come first in our eyes. Whether the discreet initials in the *Trait d'Union* hid traitors bought by Goebbels, or sincerely convinced Fascists, their lack of dignity in associating with our captors, invalidated them. A leading mind could be felt behind. The name of Marshal Pétain appeared on each page, adorned with words of patriotism, faithfulness, and hope in this shepherd who, like Hindenburg, would not abandon his defeated people. It had sounded reassuring, at first, but the news of a strange revolution taking place in France in our absence was equally disquieting. Measures opposed to our traditions and habits were taken. Anti-semitism showed its ugly torch. It was a strange mixture.

The German and Italian communiqués were given on the first page. We were told that London and Coventry were burnt to ashes. It seemed an entirely one-sided affair, and it was only curious that the British hadn't yet surrendered. It was only when back in America, two years later, that I heard about the "Battle of Britain."

We read the *Trait d'Union* because we had nothing else to read, and also because it felt good to receive something printed especially for us; but it lacked the only convincing argument: our liberation. Even so, it may have revived, in many heads, ideas that centuries had not completely erased. I made a point of hanging my copy in the privy, with a little string, and I never distributed the new issues without telling my comrades:

"Remember that this is given free, as a prospectus, and that all of it is said on the last page, in the last line: 'Printed in Berlin.'"

It had taken me three months to formulate this simple statement that should have been spontaneous. The bitterness of the defeat, the hunger march, the atmosphere of terror during the first days in the *Stalag*, had left their marks on me. I had been reduced, mentally more than physically, to a pulp, a frightened animal. Later, when the Germans fed us, and only kicked us once in a while, if we didn't obey quickly enough, the considerable betterment of our condition had been unexpected to the point of appearing generous. We would live! They only wanted us to work for them! The Nazis were kind! It wasn't their fault if we had imposed war on them. . . .

From a bewildered animal, I had become an ox; a working ox. I had adjusted my steps to the furrows. I forked, I shoveled, I dug, as if I had done it all my life; as if I were going to do it forever. I enjoyed the smell of the earth. And then, what had survived as a feeble light in the back of my head, had shown brighter. I had been defeated, not vanquished.

A SHELL ROAD MAP IN A GARBAGE CAN

Durand was resigned to his fate, Barois was not. Here was my man. His great strength was in his hard muscles, but his

Forced Labor

judgment was sound. I was stronger in the head, but my body was enduring. We'd make a fine pair.

"Let's escape together. . . ."

We dreamed about it, a little vaguely, and soon pooled all of our resources. My torn shoes were a great problem. He worked on them at night. To build up our resistance, we needed either milk or eggs. I failed in my attempts around the stables, but Barois discovered a hen of secretive habits. She didn't like her nest and went to a little bush of her own, on the edge of the slimy duck pond, at ten o'clock sharp every other day. The difficulty was in getting there after her, without attracting attention, either from the farm personnel and the sentry, or from the other prisoners. The first haul brought three eggs, that we sipped raw, with joy, being careful to hide the shells. Then we took turns for the precious food. It was usually easier for me to go after it, because I could argue with anyone who might question my presence in the vicinity. Three days in succession I failed to find anything. We decided that I should model a couple of eggs with newspaper soaked in water, to lay in the nest, in case the disappearance of her works was discouraging the hen. Or was it the doings of a rat? I found him, on the fourth day. It had rained, and his boots had sunk so deep in the mud that he could hardly get out. There was a bulge in his pocket, the villain, the thief, our own new guard! He looked at me, very mean, and blew me up:

"What are you doing by the duck pond, with a load of hay on your back?"

"I was looking for you, *Herr Gefreiter.*"

He would have eaten me, if he had dared but, alas, he did eat the egg!

From then on, whether we were engaged in rolling barrels of *schnaps*, carrying blocks of ice, or chopping wood, we never saw a lone hen without irresistibly drifting in her direction.

Half a Gallon and One Arm didn't look low enough to find the magnetic reason for our loss of direction, but our comrades did. Alphonse beat us to the goal several times with unsportsmanlike ways. I caught him once in the tool-shed, surgically investigating our hen to see if she had already laid, or was going to. He stifled her desperate cackling with his cap. The farm flock lost all privacy. Sixteen men and one *Wachmann* knew each fowl by her gait and habits.

We found our greatest treasure in the garbage can: a map of all Germany and the northern part of Switzerland, a Shell road map. We worked over it, feverishly. Our itinerary followed the woods and small rivers, in the direction of former Czechoslovakia, turned, and reached Switzerland. We would try to cross the border beyond the source of the Rhine. It meant about 900 miles. We might do it in two months, or three, walking all night and hiding in the woods most of the day. We would live on raw grain mashed and soaked in water, and on fish. I had curved a few pins, and made fine hooks, with a sharp dent, out of them. The lining of my coat would furnish enough linen thread for the lines. To dig worms for bait, we would need a tool. We might take along a fork and shovel, and, some days, risk walking along the road, openly, in our uniform, as if coming from a field en route to the next farm. Passersby might take for granted that our guard was not far away. So the scheme was taking shape. The main problem was to leave the farm early at night, unseen. We had figured out a tricky way to fool the *Wachmann* and the heavy bars of the windows. He would search for us the next morning. We would be far away, out of his reach.

One of the peasants had two bicycles in his shelter, in the center of the village. The padlock was not very secure. With them we could make eighty miles before daybreak, then dump them in the river, to leave no trace. As the peasant was a good

Forced Labor

man, I couldn't bear the thought of his believing that I'd rob him, so I'd leave a check in American money, covering the price of the two bikes. How fortunate that I had been able to get my American checkbook through every search of my belongings. The idea of the check made Barois and me feel comfortably right. It would bring us luck.

Our tentative plan was to take place as soon as the grain ripened in the fields, late in June. We had a few months in which to get ready. We secured a pair of hair clippers. It was important for us to look fresh if we met anyone. We lived our scheme. We recited every move to each other: you watch, I crawl out. . . . The farm was slowly disappearing around us.

But on the first of March, the *Wachmann* brought me the sudden news that I was individually recalled to the *Stalag*, and should pack up immediately.

Barois kept the map, and never used it.

FORCED LABOR

B) Prison Camp in a Big Harbour

CHAPTER 10

Bound for Nowhere on a Banana Freighter

WHAT a fate for a ship built in Great Britain to haul bananas from tropical islands, to end as a prison, anchored in the harbour of Stettin-on-Oder!

What a fate for a man used to crossing the seas often on fine, gay steamers to be condemned to float and never move! Yet, as soon as I found English marks on the steel structures, I knew that I would stand life here better than on the Bornzin farm.

The *Nordenham* had come from Hamburg, a few weeks before. A British bomb had barely missed her, leaving a few scars on her bow. She carried a complete staff of officers, a crew of ten men, a cook and a steward, all housed in the central castle.

The huge hold, both foredeck and afterdeck, had been divided by four light floors, furnished with double decker bunks and could swallow 750 prisoners. A rectangular patch of pier, 100 yards by 200, neatly fenced with a combination of chicken and barbed wires, looked like a sterile garden for this silly house, where the windows had been forgotten, safe in the lone attic above, to which we had no access.

I arrived at midnight with 300 men from the *Stalag* II B. We climbed the chicken ladder leading to the deck, and poured down the hold in a great confusion that was rather exciting. The vibration of the engine commanding the dynamos persuaded everybody that we were going to sail. But where? Meanwhile the sentries filled the ship, beginning at the bottom. The floors, the bunks, the stools, the straw sacks, the blankets were new and neat. A certain number of cabinets, irregularly distributed

Forced Labor

promised the luxury of an individual shelf. Each man received an enamel soup bowl, a fork, a spoon, a knife, a cup, and a towel. The ship was warm and an insufficient number of electric light bulbs made it seem immense, especially to men just released after spending twelve hours in a freezing freight car, packed to the last cubic foot.

Already selected as interpreter, I was given a choice place on the first deck, but every one of the fifteen sentries called me at the same time:

"Dolmetscher. Dolmetscher!"

I ran down the stairs to tell a group of men who had just laid their baggage in a quarter where there was a little light, that they would have to move to the darkest corner. Half an hour later, another sentry would make them move to the deck below. Soon I was the most unpopular personage. Wherever I arrived, it meant bringing new orders from guards intoxicated with fresh authority and most anxious to have the last word over their comrades. The agitation ceased only around 3 A. M. when these all agreed that they wanted to sleep. I retired last, and had hardly become unconscious when I was shaken to my feet again by the *Kommandoführer*: he wanted me to yell in every corner, on each floor, that smoking was absolutely forbidden on the ship.

Such is the life of an interpreter. For one year, day and night, I was to know less tranquillity than any other prisoner.

*   *   *

For a few days, prisoners arrived in more or less important groups from various *Stalag*. As soon as the boat was full, the slave market was held in the yard. It was a dim day. Everyone had been driven out of the ship: Afterdeck by me, foredeck by a Frenchman with a northern accent who was also interpreter, and more effectively by a dozen guards yelling *"Raus, raus"* and terrifying the slow ones out.

We lined up our comrades in ten rows parallel to the ship, and the sentries tried in vain to make them stand at attention all at the same time.

The *Kommandoführer* was a stocky man in his late forties, with a round face crowned by a cap a little too large. His ears stopped it, but his skull made an awkward bulge on the bottom of the cap. The silver border of sergeant had recently been sewed on his collar and shoulder flaps, and his hands were not yet familiar with the mutation lists. He let them drop, then wiped off the mud with his sleeves, stuck them in his various pockets, searched for them in vain, and made me call off the name and captivity number of hundreds of people, several times, until my voice gave out.

A scrappy demon, five feet tall and four feet broad, with a fantastic baritone voice, a Charlie Chaplin-Adolf Hitler mustache, acted as his assistant, contradicted his orders, galloped around on his tiny stumps, and considerably increased the confusion.

From the central door of a long barrack set perpendicular to the boat and housing the camp services, a paunchy, bearded petty officer of the German Navy, wearing much gold and a broad swastika armband, looked at the scene with gravity. This was the *Lagerführer*, civil commander of the camp.

On the opposite side of the yard, the door of a long barrack reserved for the latrines, opened an unique eye and looked tempting.

The Jerry on duty at the gate admitted several small automobiles; they roared through the yard and came to a dead stop almost on the same line, in the center. Two dozen men, with brief cases and a competent air, got out; and the auction began.

Forced Labor

"All professional concrete workers step out of the ranks."

One by one, a little dazzled at being in the open, a few men advanced. One civilian said: "I'll take this one." Another said: "Then let me have this big fellow."

According to face and width of shoulders the prisoners were sorted and formed in separate lines behind sentries. "Ten helpers" or "twenty-five helpers." The prisoners volunteered in groups so as to stay together, regardless of the meaning of the bidding which they didn't understand. Nothing is ever explained to a prisoner. He is ordered to come, or to go, and is separated from the comrade who has become dear to him. With everyone incorporated in a group and assigned to a sentry, our new routine began.

CHAPTER 11

Life around the Kommandofuhrer

EVERY two months we received a new *Kommandoführer*, usually a sergeant, but sometimes a staff sergeant, in his late forties, having fought in the last war. He seemed to be chosen according to his military record rather than his ability or experience in any form of organization. A mason's helper, a chauffeur, a cigar store clerk, suddenly put in charge of a battalion could make our life miserable by applying the *Stalag* regulations to the letter. They could make it hell, and still look right. If kind, or just indifferent and lazy, they could lighten our plight by overlooking a few of the most trying points. The life of the camp went up and down with their temper.

*   *   *

UNTEROFFIZIER SCHUMANN

Unteroffizier Schumann was tall and sportive looking, from the top of his very large cap down to his chest, and there his personality seemed to change. He expanded towards a very ample waist, parked low on legs that were just a little too short. While his arms balanced impressively at each side, his legs shuffled tiny steps that did not match or keep time. The contradiction expressed itself by a coquettish bouncing of the rear, not altogether masculine.

The articulation of his neck might have been built on ball bearings, so swiftly did he move his vast face, a little empty, with no angle, and two small eyes, nestled happily in fat eyelids.

Forced Labor

He felt no hatred for the French prisoners, and would have showed them much of his happy disposition if he had obtained from them the satisfaction he yearned for: salutes — plenty of them — from morning to evening, any time he was met; respectful salutes, complete from the dry tap of the heels to the final upward motion of the chin. He himself saluted beautifully, but for the sharp Prussian technique he substituted something mellower, a little round on the edges, so to speak. It began with condescension that melted into familiar kindness. A fifty-year-old hosiery dealer in a medium-sized city of central Germany, manners appropriate to fitting pretty legs, showed through the pride of a man put in charge of a battalion. He studied his mirror a lot. The French prisoners felt only disgust for that sort of stuff. In vain did I explain to my comrades that this old bird, a little fairy-like, was not a bad egg. They affected not to salute him, or to do it as badly as they could, and that irritated him. They cut the remaining buttons off their top coats because he wanted everyone buttoned up to the neck. He ordered those buttons replaced at once, but they reported, an hour later, that none could be found in the camp. What should they do?

His conception of a soldier's cap was that of a fragile vase set carefully on top of the head, in a horizontal position, so that it wouldn't fall. A prisoner's cap is a rag that he puts anywhere above himself, between the ears. To baffle *Herr* Schumann, the fashion was started to wear the trench cap across the head, in a Napoleonic style, but cocked a little, with hair sticking out, like feathers from a burst pillow.

The reaction was an order to every one of the thirty-five guards to see that the caps of their charges be set correctly. There was little they could do about it. They knew from experience that bothering the prisoners in the morning, brought bad will at work, as revenge, and in the end, trouble for the guard with the overseer. So Schumann, provoked to the point of furor, went through the ranks and viciously twisted the nose of every Napoleon until it became purple. Every eye became so obviously a bullet that wanted to kill him, that he kicked three men in the seat of the pants. The whole assembly hissed, and I ran to him to say that if we had to be punished, to punish us as soldiers, not as dogs.

Compressing his paunch like a powerful bellows, he flooded the yard with imprecations, and made every sentry drive his herd out to work immediately. The ship's captain, leaning on his bridge, sneered. The *Lagerführer* stuck his beard out of the kitchen, and expressed the Nazi point of view on this scandal: jail, with bread and water to everyone for a month, but Schumann was not fond of that swastika bearer, and the storm subsided into a silly quarrel between the two.

Much hurt and red in the face, he climbed up the collapsible stairs leading to the ship's castle, retired to his cabin, and asked for the prisoner barber, whom he always used as his valet. He wanted him to inquire in the kitchen if a little porridge couldn't be boiled for him. No perturbation affected his stomach.

He forgot the scene, but the prisoners hated him forever. A year later they still talked about the brute who twisted their noses. It had been more insulting than painful. In spite of my conviction that he would have been a better *Kommandoführer* than the average, my comrades did not want to pay the price that he required; and it is only as a joke that he got one single satisfaction.

Kiesgruben was the name given to a group of thirty-three prisoners used by the city to extract gravel somewhere along the Oder. They had been collected at the end of the slave market, after the masons, carpenters, and mechanics had been selected. Men of little manual value, they were intellectuals or

Forced Labor

craftsmen of delicate professions, and formed an exceptional bunch of undaunted rascals. The handles of their shovels always had a defect and broke like glass. The wagons they pushed, on narrow tracks, fell into the river, most unfortunately! They never refused to work, but were expert at producing very little while looking active. In the truck that brought them to work, they sang loudly and pretended to be very gay whenever the civilians looked at them. In the evenings, they showed their rutabagas to the *Lagerführer*, when the latter crossed the yard, and made starved faces.

Three personalities dominated this fine group. Morelle had the build of a weight thrower, a slow voice, and no fear in the world. He was a Socialist and spoke German well, but hated his captors so much that he had refused to replace my colleague when the latter, unable to cope with the endless responsibilities, had asked to be sent to work.

Ramon was long and thin, with something of a bird in his long nose and high pitched voice. He was a Royalist and could exasperate any *Wachmann* by his way of standing at attention. His heels didn't quite meet, his hands were crooked, and his little fingers stood alone on the seam of his trousers.

Rosatier was serious and poised, with large eyes facing you like a supreme court. As a Communist, he had had much political experience and knew how to carry out a mission. Staff sergeant in the army, he took care of the *Kiesgruben* group and reported its needs and problems to me, together with his views on a possible solution. He despised Schumann whom Ramon wanted to whip, and Morelle to drown. Having once agreed with me that we shouldn't allow him to believe that Frenchmen were incapable of discipline, they entered the gate, one evening, in a sensational fashion.

I was pacing the yard in the company of *Herr* Schumann, who, between the formalities of control of the returning firms, was describing his views of world affairs. When the *Kiesgruben* truck pulled up outside, the thirty-three men jumped down and, to the astonishment of everyone, Rosatier put the men in order, slowly turning the column around, making one of them advance and the other back up, and while the sentry wondered what to do about it he set himself on the side and shouted the commands:

"*Repos! Garde a vous! En avant, marche!*" Like a platoon of candidate corporals eager to ornament their sleeves with a couple of red stripes, Morelle first and Ramon last, these men in their late thirties entered the yard. "Left, right! Left, right!" with a marvelous enthusiasm. Snap! snap! the sabots — those long boxes of soft wood, heelless and looking truly like barges — made sparks. The hands balanced together and sawed the ice of the air on each side of the column.

"*Gauche, droite!* left, right! section, halte!" One, two, and at three, all the heels clapped, all the hands went down, all the noses went up. Silence swept the yard, and emotion shook *Unteroffizier* Schumann. Rosatier advanced three steps, saluted and announced:

"*Kiesgruben*, thirty-three men back from work."

Schumann set himself at attention so nobly that half a foot of his paunch transferred itself to his height. His salute was an illustration out of a manual. Having sent back his hand slowly so as to show that he was not exactly bound by the rules, he told me softly:

"*Lassen sie weg treten.*" I translated and turning briskly on his wooden heels, staff sergeant Rosatier dismissed his men. Each paused to salute, and ran off at full speed, to release an explosion of laughter. Meanwhile the *Kommandoführer*, his chest swollen with delightful pride, his head turned a little upwards, his eyes mellowed like candied fruits, was muttering:

"*Schön. Wunderbar.* Wonderful! These men are soldiers!"

Forced Labor

Not yet awakened from his stupor, the forgotten sentry approached and got ready to accomplish his little act: to report. But it was a statue of disdain that faced him, with an arm stretched towards the *Wachmänner* barrack, and meaning: "Ape, this way."

*   *   *

He took me as witness to his most intimate life, and didn't seem to remember that I was a prisoner. I think his only objection to me was the little care I took of my appearance. I could go to the *Kommando's* storeroom and choose the best clothes available. Instead, I had replaced my torn coat of the confetti patches, with a decent but modest one, being careful not to distinguish myself from the mass of my comrades, otherwise than by my white armband. He had allowed me to replace the former interpreter by Paul, a cultured Belgian professor — a fine man and a warm patriot — always so neatly clad. His confidence in me was unlimited; and as long as he remained our *Kommandoführer*, I handled the accounts of the camp, with my colleague. I wrote the current mail to the *Kontrollstelle* and the *Stalag*, placed it under his nose and offered him a pen. He loved to scratch a few words, correct my mistakes or my gallicisms, and sign with a handsome flourish. To replace the thundering Jurk whom we had lost, he selected among the guards a *Gefreiter* (corporal) who became a strange shadow to him. His name was Asiatic, but my men nicknamed him "The Gnome." Incapable of writing three lines that anybody else could make out, he could hand the telephone to his master and follow him, three steps behind, anywhere, like a tail. Schumann wanted everyone of his secretaries to have a secretary, and be like the top of a mountain expanding indefinitely downwards. He never referred to me otherwise than as his "*Oberdol-*

metscher." As super-interpreter, I had a first interpreter in the Belgian professor. Later, as was necessary for such a big camp, we had another Belgian teacher, an excellent man from the coal country, who took the title of second interpreter, and had to assist the sentries and take charge of the cleanliness of the ship.

Rather than call the camp-barber directly, Schumann sent someone for him, and the latter, busy making his boss' bed, called one of the prisoners charged with sweeping the floors and washing the decks, to fetch the coffee from the kitchen. I wondered why one of those whose nose Schumann had twisted several times was volunteering for this, and I asked him.

"Haven't you guessed yet?" he said. "I go to the kitchen, get the coffee, and take it to his room, but on the way I stop in the washroom and pour out one fourth of it."

"But why do you think that makes any difference?"

"It does, all right, but not in the quantity, because I fill it up myself."

"What?"

"With the coffee that I drank yesterday."

The man was deadly serious. For one month he had been avenging himself and the camp for the insult of the kicks and of the twists, in his own way, without telling anyone. I have never looked at Schumann since without thinking that he buckled his belt around a chamber pot.

*   *   *

Schumann felt towards the telephone as one intoxicated by tobacco feels towards his pipe. He couldn't resist picking it up and filling it with all the tones of his throat, and all the fog of his soul. He had three mistresses — chiefly I think to call them up.

Forced Labor

"Irma? It is I. You know, I. Yes. I am in my office, with my *Dolmetscher* and my assistant. I have so much to do. . . . Are you in bed? What have you got on?" For an hour or more he waded through swamps of sticky sentimentality, seasoned with inquiries about the menu. When she would at last hang up he turned to me, sitting on his left in the narrow office and said: "That was Irma, you know; a charming person. I ought to call up the others, too, but I'm so tired. However I have to say a word to my Luischen."

While fingering the dial, he lifted up his monstrous thigh and broke wind loudly, making this unavoidable comment: *"Nicht schön aber gesund."*

Whether it was as he said, not pretty but healthy, my colleague, sitting with his back to him, got up with an angry face, clapped his heels in the direction of *Herr* Schumann and disappeared for ten minutes.

*   *   *

My re-entry permit to the United States of America had expired while I dug rutabagas out of the frozen fields around Bornzin, and I had in vain applied for renewal. The censor of the *Stalag* had refused to pass my letter. I had persuaded our first *Kommandoführer* to present my case to the *Kontrollstelle* and to show that, through lack of a simple formality, I would lose the right to live in the country where my wife and son resided. The reply of the major had been most clearly worded:

"A prisoner of war needs no visa."

In each of my weekly cards or letters to my wife, I had asked her, either openly or in a dissimulated fashion, to do what was necessary in Washington to obtain a prolongation; but until I received her answer in about five months, I would wonder if she had received these cards or understood what I meant.

The morning mail brought a letter from the *Kontrollstelle*, underlined by a phone call from the same office, recommending Schumann's special attention: it was a transcription of a message from Von Ribbentrop, the Nazi foreign minister, informing me that I should report at a certain American embassy in a neutral country as soon as I was freed from captivity. I would find there all the means necessary for my return home. It was a few months before Hitler declared war on America, and his newspapers were soaked with information attesting that Roosevelt, not the American people, was against Nazism.

Though it meant only that a kind American diplomat, interested in my case, had taken high steps to help me whenever my captivity should end, Schumann read the letter several times, and looked at me in awe. I had hardly signed the transcription and sent it back as required, when the proud hosiery-dealer confided to his third girl, over the wire, that "he" had received an important message from Hitler's friend. Then he paid a visit to the *Lagerführer* and impressed him with the extent of his relations and mine. The thirty-five sentries heard the story, illuminated by much beer that Schumann had absorbed with Opferer, and I'm afraid that they insulted me with the idea that I had something to do with their government. The keenest among them, who might have been suspicious of some of my activities in the camp, were thus reassured.

Schumann felt bound enough to me to touch me for a couple of cans of "Monkey meat" from the little supply that we had received from the French Red Cross. He knew that I controlled the distribution, and it didn't occur to him that I would mind. I gave him my own share, and that of the other two interpreters. They understood that it was better than risking his annoyance, for he had many ways to make the whole camp pay for it.

Forced Labor

Some day I might use this as bribery to save a comrade from trouble: one little ace up the sleeve. It would be ugly, but I would do it, in spite of the sympathy and pity I couldn't help feeling for this grotesque character when he called up Irma to say:

". . . I shall bring you something tonight that you haven't tasted for many years."

∗   ∗   ∗

One June evening, the sentry in charge of the eighteen men working for the firm Grün und Bilfinger, found only seventeen when he counted them in the ranks, before marching them back to camp. Whichever way he undertook the operation, it brought the same results. The men knew nothing. He swore, threatened, prayed in vain, and telephoned to the office. Schumann rushed to the scene and didn't find any trace of the missing man. He came back, abashed but not too anxious, because, at work, the responsibility for the prisoners is shared by the firm. I knew where the boy was, and that his chances of reaching his home village in Belgium were fairly good. The police and military inquests brought no results, and six weeks later, another Belgian received a letter from his "wife" which she had not written. The visiting fugitive was giving direct news of his own health. A wave of joy and pride animated the camp. One of us had fooled "them."

Another evening, after a communication from the *Kontrollstelle*, Schumann called general assembly in the yard. The men formed a circle around the camp staff, and he produced the following statement, in German:

"We have received the information that the escaped prisoner So-and-So was shot to death when attempting to cross the border four weeks ago. Let this be a lesson to anybody tempted to imitate him."

My translation improved a bit on the original:

"I have received orders to tell you that our comrade was shot to death four weeks ago. Please don't laugh when I specify that that was one week before he wrote to us."

No German around spoke French well enough to follow me, and my men behaved very well. They did not explode, but they hardly looked impressed. Schumann remarked on it afterwards, and admired their pluck.

*   *   *

In July, following more or less fantastic predictions in the letters received from France, what I had considered another *"bouteillon"* proved a reality: by order of Hitler, the Frenchmen having fought in the World War 1914-1918 were recalled to the *Stalag*, in view of their repatriation. Out of 650 men present in the *Kommando* at this time, eleven men in their forties were affected by the stunning news. Highly excited, they were assembled in the yard, and Schumann saw the opportunity to deliver one of his grandiloquent speeches:

"Frenchmen, I am sincerely hoping that you will tell your families that the Germans are not brutes; that you have not been badly treated, and that we want to be friends with you. Once more our *Führer* shows you his generosity. Your comrades will follow. . . ."

I translated the "once more" carefully, but my comrades weren't critical any more. They had suddenly forgotten the miseries of their capture and early captivity. They didn't cheer, only because they were not quite sure that there wasn't a catch to this. They had already believed several times that the blessed hour had come. They would have said *"Ja, Ja"* to anything,

Forced Labor

without listening, in order to get nearer to the gate. The oldest, in the name of the others, asked me to thank the *Kommandoführer* for his kind address, and to say "Good Luck" to the remaining comrades; but he was so nervous, so impatient, that he stammered. Even Schumann realized it, and though he had been counting on playing the scene a little longer, he ordered the sentry to march the men out to the station.

"*Ja.*" Someone had said "*Ja*" in their name, I fear, to a condition put on their liberation by the German *Führer*, for among the 60,000 Belgian "Walloons" remaining in captivity, the veterans of the last war were not to be sent home. Fallen entirely into Nazi hands, their country had nothing more with which to bargain.

*   *   *

Kermadec was a Breton of medium height, looking taller because he was underweight, with a small wrinkled face and eyes so pale that one couldn't read anything in them. He had a cunning little smile, and something in his voice reminded me of a hen. His hobby was making rings. He was astonishingly clever at finding material for them. I shouldn't be surprised if he had shortened some copper pipes from the boat machinery in order to feed his passion for making hearts, diamonds, and clover leaves with only a small file that he had filched from some workshop. He polished them with sand sieved through a piece of burlap, and sold them for 5 mark-coupons, or gave them away.

He had been explaining to me his difficulties with a *Wachmann*, and I told him to report to the office at curfew, when I knew the boss would be in. At nine o'clock sharp, Kermadec knocked on the door, and from the telephone through which he was cooing to his number two sweetie, Schumann said:

"Come in."

Kermadec was no fool. He had polished his shoes, brushed the lime and mud off his uniform, and a high Norwegian cap was set correctly on his small skull. He saluted, took off his cap, and stood at attention for a good twenty minutes until the telephone was finally hung up with a metallic cling and a slippery sigh.

"What do you want, Kermadec?"

"I want to complain about my sentry."

"What's the matter with him?"

"He's too nice."

Schumann seemed to swallow his tongue when I gave him the translation.

"What? It's the first time a prisoner has complained about any sentry being too nice. Is this man crazy?"

"He is much too nice," said Kermadec, "he puts his arm around me."

"Someone," retorted the *Kommandoführer*, "is looking for trouble. Tell the fool," he suddenly howled, "that I can give him four days in jail, and ask the captain to add his bit to it."

"He puts his arms around me," continued my comrade, quietly, "and he tries to kiss me, just like a girl. I am no girl."

Schumann leaned on his chair with a sumptuous gesture and, much interested, invited him to keep on.

"I am no girl and I ask to be sent to another firm where no one will make passes at me all day."

"Send for *Schutzer Grosz*." My colleague Paul who had been silently working on the daily report at the next table behind us, got up and ran to the guards' barrack, on the other side of the yard.

Grosz arrived in his undershirt over which he had hastily slipped his trousers. Narrow black suspenders barred his chest. He had no chin; his face was twisted, and his sleepy eyes so far apart that they didn't seem to belong together. His shaved

Forced Labor

skull grew purple when he saw Kermadec. He clapped his heels at attention but he wore slippers and they rendered only a soft sound.

"Tell the prisoner to repeat his charges and translate everything the guard says."

"He follows me on the ladder," said Kermadec, "and he puts his hands between my legs. I don't like it."

"*Herr Unteroffizier,*" stammered Grosz, "it's a lie. I was only pushing him because he worked too slowly."

"This is how he did," and my comrade opened and closed his hand in an obscene gesture.

"What have you to answer, Schutzer Grosz?" Schumann looked like a doctor investigating remarkable symptoms.

"A lie; this prisoner lies. I am a German soldier. *Herr Unteroffizier,* you will believe me, not him."

"*Ich...Sonntag...*" and in laughable German slang Kermadec hemmed and hawed a crude proposition. "He tells me this every day."

"*Ich ... Sonntag ...*" repeated Schumann word for word. "This man couldn't have invented it."

"No, no," cried the guard in despair, and waving his arms, though the rest of his body remained in a respectful position. "No, he has misunderstood me."

"The declaration is perfectly clear, guard, but where on the boat did you expect to carry on this affair, on Sunday, when 650 prisoners are around? Did you think about the possibilities of an enormous scandal if you had been caught?"

Schumann didn't raise his voice. He didn't seem to doubt the charges, but he wanted to know every detail.

"You could be sent to martial court for this, and I'm afraid the judges would believe this man and his interpreter, not you. Are you married, or have you a girl in town whom you could present to me?"

196

"No; but this man won't make a charge against me, *Herr Unteroffizier*. I've been good to him. I gave him half a pound of bacon. He's ungrateful. Ask him if I'm a mean *Wachmann*."

"Half a pound of bacon!" Schumann looked at me in wonder.

"He's a good *Wachmann*," said Kermadec, "and hasn't brutalized anyone but me; or at least he's been pawing me, like this."

He renewed the gestures in Grosz's face, and looked him in the eyes until the other grew pale, as if much remained to be said.

"Tell the sentry on duty in the yard to lead this prisoner back to the boat," ordered Schumann.

When I came back, an instant later, I found Grosz on his knees, imploring: ". . . it would ruin my whole life. Be kind, *Herr Unteroffizier*."

So deep was habit that his naked heels, from which the slippers had fallen, were still clamped together.

"Remember the *Führer's* own best friends have been shot for this," pronounced Schumann softly. "You will be placed at another firm. Get up. This *Dolmetscher* is the prisoner's representative. I couldn't prevent him from reporting to the controlling officer when he comes here. Though there is no legal proof against you, I hope he won't. Now go."

Paul had resumed his work, and his pen creaked on the rough paper. His eyes almost closed, Kermadec's identification card in hand, our *Kommandoführer* was meditating. I was rather impressed by the comprehensive way in which he had handled the painful scene, when he concluded:

"Risking his neck for a forty-year-old mason prisoner, yellow and homely. If only he had been a handsome youngster. . . ."

*　　　*　　　*

Forced Labor

Our *Kommandoführer* was setting himself higher every day. He now commanded assembly from the bridge of the ship, as if he had been the admiral of a fleet of prisoners. The sentries had to yell the name of their firm and the number of their men while he probably verified by counting the caps and made a red mark on his list. Interpreter Number Two ran up and down the ladder carrying papers that Schumann thought undignified to keep in his own hands.

Whenever he entered the camp, coming back from the city, he gave his brief case to the sentry at the gate, and later sent a prisoner from the cleaning squadron to get it. In the office he wouldn't even pick up his pen on the table. He asked me for it, and it had to be dipped in the ink to only half of its height. In exchange for my complaisance he signed his name on any complaint that I would address to the *Kontrollstelle* in behalf of my comrades: questions of back salaries never paid by their former *Kommando;* of packages failing to arrive; requests, authorization to buy a basket-ball, etc. He backed me up in difficulties with the *Lagerführer*, and was even beginning to listen to me when I explained to him that Frenchmen would rather be shot than kicked, and that, to them, nose twisting constituted an irreparable insult. He seemed surprised at what he called our childish susceptibility, and didn't kick my comrades any more; but he couldn't resist their noses. He derived a sadistic pleasure from grasping the tender appendix in the center of the face, but felt the impulse only in connection with a misplaced cap. As my comrades wouldn't give in, I could never help them otherwise than by being very cold with him until I had something else to ask.

He bought a new uniform cap, so large that he looked like a caryatid under a capital. Pride and contentment illuminated his voluminous face. On the contrary, tormented and oppressed by obscure ambitions, his assistant The Gnome was like a receding shadow to the big man. One saw him less every day, and his voice was not strong enough to compensate for this diminution. He was gentle in the office, but he never appeared in the yard without causing some damage, and provoking the suppression of one of the little privileges that I had obtained for my comrades. He frightened Schumann with the articles in the *Kommandoführer's* handbook.

A few days after the escape of our Belgian comrade, he brought to the camp a strong police dog, so fierce that he bit two prisoners and a guard — the latter to everyone's joy — the first evening. I made as much of a fuss over this as the *Unteroffizier* would let me and, unable to obtain the removal of the dog, my best friend and I were considering ways to kill him discreetly, when one man asked that the matter be left to him. A professional dog trainer, he promised to tame the handsome brute. He began with the meat in his soup and little bits of cake from his packages. Two weeks later, the dog licked his face. Another week and he leaped amicably at anyone who would throw him a piece of war biscuit that we received from the French Red Cross. He was already showing a decided inclination to bark at every German uniform, when the embittered Gnome took him away from camp.

Renouncing his dream to be anything more than an office boy in the camp, the little man found consolation in painting portraits of Adolf Hitler on small panels. He had some talent, but his eyes were defective, and what he thought an accurate copy of a photograph, turned out most comical. He exhibited his works in the office, and every German visitor admired them. Who would have dared to laugh at anything looking the least little bit like the *Führer?*

*　　　*　　　*

Forced Labor

The sun set in Schumann's sky a little before the normal time for his mutation to another *Kommando*.

Discontented with the daily one mark thirty pfennigs of his sergeant's pay, he called personally on each firm and impressed the director with the following facts: the prisoners constituted a very important help; he, as their chief, was in a position to see that the best craftsmen among them be selected for this firm; for lack of any allowance from the army, for the expenses of his office — wasn't it a pity? — he couldn't render all possible services. In short, what would the firm think about spending a few marks on the *Kommandoführer?*

While most didn't mind adding a little to what they already gave to the sentry, so as to devote him to their interests, one of the contractors refused categorically, and called up the *Kontrollstelle.* The Secretaries in the military offices couldn't help knowing of this practice from which they eventually got a cut, but the protest coming from an influential firm and worded by a reserve officer, couldn't be ignored.

The majestic hosiery-dealer was summoned by his captain, and came back very dejected from the interview. Discharged from his post, he left us, the next morning, for a private holiday behind bars.

As a supreme humiliation, he carried his own suit case.

*   *   *

UNTEROFFIZIER EHLERT

Not a stranger, but our former chauffeur-sergeant Ehlert, succeeded the misunderstood Schumann. He was unpretentious; and that was a relief. He knew already that I did my best in the office — as did Paul — in exchange for a little indulgence and comprehension for my comrades.

He drank quite a lot, but outside of the camp. He had recently acquired a mistress, but fortunately didn't call her up all day: she did the telephoning; he had little to answer. She came often; a pleasant face on a huge torso, with legs strong enough to hold a tournament billiard table, set on small feet. She was interested in having him bring something along when he came to dinner. The German Army receives more food than the population, and with the ladies the popularity of the uniforms has consequently increased. Ehlert was honest, and I don't think he shared more than his earned portion.

His most dangerous defect was timidity. Greatly afraid of his superiors, he became frantic when anything arose for which he could be blamed, and resorted to wild measures. He spent hours and days on the *Kommando* books, before admitting that he couldn't make head or tail out of the accounts. As I had been in office since the foundation of the working camp number XIII/226, and seen many guards and several sergeants come and go, I was the only one completely informed. It gave me some influence with the succeeding *Kommandoführers*.

* * *

The prisoners of war constitute a splendid business for the German Reich. Not only do they solve its labor problems and permit the mobilization of more men for the fighting armies, but they produce a net income.

The employers have to pay a nominal salary, equal to two-thirds of the minimum salary of a German worker of the same category, for a prisoner's work. Prisoners without a specialty, earned thirty-three *pfennigs* per hour. Masons, carpenters, electricians, mechanics, earned as much as fifty-five *pfennigs* per hour. The average day being ten hours in the cities, daily earnings ranged from three marks thirty *pfennigs* to five marks

Forced Labor

fifty *pfennigs*. Each prisoner received only part of them: seventy *pfennigs*, or as much as 1 mark when the firm chose to pay a premium for production above the hourly tariff. In certain factories in the vicinity, the premiums could raise the daily allowance to one mark fifty *pfennigs*. With it, one could have bought five small bottles of weak beer if such had been available.

The excess over the sum paid to us in *Stalag* coupons was distributed daily in the following manner:

One mark for food and twenty *pfennigs* for lodgings. The city received this one mark twenty *pfennigs*. Nine *pfennigs* was for our clothing. The *Stalag* received it. The rest constituted the net profit, and went to the *Stalag*, for the *Stalag*. In the case of a helper at thirty-three *pfennigs* an hour, the net benefit amounted to one mark thirty-one *pfennigs* per day of ten hours. In the case of a specialist, at fifty-five *pfennigs* an hour, the benefit amounted to three marks fifty-one *pfennigs*. Considering that half of the prisoners were reckoned as helpers, the average income that everyone produced for the Reich was two marks forty-one *pfennigs*.

We had believed that this sum would be kept for us as a slave peculium — a savings account to be given at our liberation — but it is not so. It sometimes happens that an employer gives only half of the seventy *pfennigs* normally allowed as salary to the prisoner, and sends the other half to the *Stalag*, where it is kept for him. This was frequent when working on a farm. I have failed to find a sound reason for this complication, except to prevent prisoners from buying anything.

Anyhow, out of the 1,300,000 Frenchmen thought to be in the *Oflag* and *Stalag*, at that time, let us figure that only 1,000,000 went to work every day. That meant a daily income of 2,410,000 marks. I believe the figure is conservative. The boarding of the guards in the *Kommando* is covered by the employers. Only the expenses of the *Stalag* should be deducted from the prisoners' production. The expenses are not large. The camps are considered as permanent, and to be used, after a victorious war, to keep the dissident minorities, and to train the German youth for the hardships of the next conquests. Most of the repairing of buildings is done by prisoners.

The officers and guards are members of the regular army, and are paid as such. The *Kommandos* and *Stalags* are rest-posts for men having been wounded on the various fronts. After a few months, most of them go back to fighting.

The food for the non-working prisoners may cost half a mark daily, at the most. The expense in fuel is negligible. During a short stay in the *Stalag* II B in December 1940, I found that one small stove only was lit in a barrack housing 500 men. They froze.

According to the Geneva Convention, the officers and the noncommissioned officers are exempt from work; but most of the latter are sent to *Kommandos* anyway. I received the explanation, in the *Stalag*, that their food was charged to France.

The clothing comes from the enormous stocks that the Germans have seized everywhere in Europe, and the French Red Cross has been adding new clothes made especially since the armistice.

An average of two per cent of the prisoners are sick every day. The expense of their temporary upkeep, together with the loss of benefit on their salary, may reduce the total income by three or four per cent.

I am convinced that at least 2,000,000 marks, net, are contributed to the Reich's resources, daily, by the French prisoners, in addition to the value of their work. This figure should be sufficient to make one realize that Germany will release the prisoners as late as possible, or only with the assurance that they will produce more for her somewhere else — as civilian

Forced Labor

workers in her war factories, for instance. And not only will France be deprived of the labour of this mass of young men, but her population will always lack the children that will not be born to them during three, four or perhaps five years of absence.

*   *   *

The magnificent tastes of *Herr* Schumann had been expressed by many irregularities, such as keeping two or three prisoners in the camp for a week, working for him, or lending them to a friend of his in town. They had been listed as sick, but lacking a doctor's order, their food couldn't be claimed, beyond the maximum of three days blindly covered by the firms, according to regulations. Now who was going to pay for those extra days?

The controlling city office found a nest of such problems, a few months later, and it fell upon *Unteroffizier* Ehlert to answer them. In vain did he spend a night getting prepared, when summoned by the city *Amtmann*, a high official, for he made a very poor showing. He finally proposed bringing me as the only man who could see through the maze.

I should have liked to go in the worst outfit possible, in rags and sabots, but I was ordered to polish my shoes and replace the missing button on my coat. Carrying a brief case, I followed Ehlert and his pistol to the city hall of Stettin — he on the sidewalk, I in the gutter. A prisoner of war is not allowed to sully the sidewalk.

We were admitted to a series of offices where people looked at me with some astonishment, and, after a reasonable pause, to an audience with the *Herr Amtmann der Stadt Stettin*. I had forgotten how neat and sumptuous the private office of a distinguished official could be: heavy desk with several telephones, deep cushioned armchairs, enclosed files. He invited me to sit down, and I wondered, for a second, if he would offer me a cigar; but he did not. I had brought a written statement, and was in a position to answer his questions; but I needed documents and figures. A pretty woman secretary and an old employee, brought them. For half an hour, I, miserable *Kriegsgefangene*, had a staff of civilians around me. I even proposed a solution that the *Amtmann* thought acceptable and, having dismissed his employees, he gave me instructions on the new ways to present the accounts. The missing cigar excepted, he treated me exactly like a civilian, while paying no attention to *Herr* Ehlert, sunk in an armchair and not altogether comfortable. He concluded the interview in praising France for sending some volunteers against Russia. A good answer came to my lips, but I couldn't afford the joy of saying it. It would have cost me my post, and I had not yet accomplished all I had planned. I answered nothing.

I followed Ehlert back to the boat, he beaming, on the sidewalk, over his solved puzzle; I, exasperated, and mentally telling the gutter what I thought of Frenchmen parading in German uniforms, while we . . .

*　　　*　　　*

Most of my packages came from America, after wandering across the seas and continents for a period lasting from three to seven months; and my *Unteroffizier* didn't like to see them. It was my privilege to have them opened right away, instead of waiting for the evening distribution. The prisoner-nurse-postmaster brought them to me in the office, and I pushed them on the table, under my chief's nose. He made me wait, sometimes, for an hour or two, but couldn't avoid opening them at last; and then his troubles began.

Forced Labor

He set the wrappings and strings aside, as items of great value in Germany. If the strings were made of hemp, he asked to be presented with them. He trusted me enough to believe that my packages couldn't contain anything forbidden; but not daring to admit this, he fumbled in the box, and couldn't help seeing a pound of coffee, a pound of tobacco in a red or blue tin can, a few candy bars, some canned fruits and meats with shockingly suggestive labels that extracted a succession of guttural sounds from his bosom.

Sometimes it happened that three or four packages for me would arrive together, and, covered with their contents, the table looked like a pre-Hitlerian grocery. If by chance a book-keeper from the city, or anyone of the large firms, came in to exchange cash for *Lagerscheine* (*Stalag* coupons) Ehlert showed him the table and said: "It's not mine. My interpreters live like princes." My reply had become classic: "Like princes in captivity." In spite of all rules, I offered them a piece of candy, and they couldn't resist it:

"Don't let anybody know . . ." and they would look around with the air of fugitive convicts.

A little bit of sweets and a good cigarette were excellent weapons against their Nazi morale. These men had enough to eat, but the monotony of their diet was discouraging.

I received enough coffee to supply four of my best friends with a daily cup, the concoction of which had long been a problem. With two empty meat cans, I had made an acceptable dripolator; but boiling water was not available in the camp kitchen. The ship's crew had, for cook, a sympathetic little German, much underweight, who had fought against France in the previous war, and had been taken prisoner. He understood life, and the smell of the precious beans persuaded him to enter into a pact with us: he would grind the coffee, provide boiling water, and accept a cup for himself. The transaction was conducted daily by one of our cleaners, a tall, handsome boy who liked nothing better than appearing like an ass, though he was very brilliant. When sabots were distributed, the biggest size was too small for him, so he had to enlarge them with his knife. Their soles were soon so flat that he seemed mounted on skis. His name was Finot, and he had studied law.

At four o'clock every day, he would knock at the office door until Ehlert ordered him in, noisily clap his footwear, and produce a face that was a combination of mockery and respect. No *Kommandoführer*, no *Wachmann*, had ever been able to get angry with him, though he made them feel uncomfortable. He held a pretentious tray, made out of an old board, with two cups of the steaming nectar and one or two slices of toasted bread. He set one by me, the other by Paul, and then waved his tray, professionally, with a wink at me, and another demonstration of discipline at the door.

The office, the shelves piled up with daily reports, instructions from the *Stalag*, files and all expressions of our loss of freedom, as well as the green uniform of Ehlert, faded behind the fumes.

Very particular, Paul would tell me, in German:

"Will you please ask your wife to send us the other brand? The proportion of mocha in it was more satisfactory, don't you think?"

I have no doubt that this daily provocation would have brought me trouble if, every third or fourth day — "he" never knew which — a third cup hadn't appeared on the tray. The dear Finot would set it in front of Herr Ehlert, tap his sabots lightly together once more — to excuse himself for the liberty he had just taken in approaching the supreme chief of the camp — and vanish without a word. Only when the door had been closed behind our comrade would the delighted Jerry come out with a few grunts and the silly question:

Forced Labor

"What's this?"

"Only a little bitter water, *Herr Unteroffizier*."

Then he would add some of his own sugar to it, stir well with a pencil or a knife and, over the telephone, murmur to his voluminous girl friend:

". . . *etwas wunderbar* . . . I wish you could smell it."

Holding his arms apart in the position of a driver at the wheel, and holding a *Lohnliste* as he would have a roadmap, the poor man dreamt of better times; and I felt sorry to have to play this mean little game.

But every third day, he would wonder:

"Will the hog give me any today; or only tomorrow?"

Whenever he got tough with my men in the yard, he knew that there would be no cup for him on the tray.

*　　*　　*

When, after fall 1941, Servian and Russian prisoners replaced a large number of Frenchmen on the farms, the latter took over the jobs of newly mobilized Germans in the cities. Fifteen prisoners from the *Nordenham* belonged now to the city street-cleaning service. They emptied the house garbage cans into trucks, and though the rubbish is thin in a country submitted to intense rationing for many years, they would find a good book in them, once in a while, and bring it to me.

In this way I obtained a magnificent English-German dictionary, and an old edition of the three Fausts, by Goethe, that I laid on my shelf in the office, with a few other German books that I had been able to secure. Together with Paul, I owned a good collection of works by Goethe that I studied when I had a moment to spare. Ehlert didn't object to this display. If any visitor asked him in awe:

"Are you reading this?" he would reply somewhat proudly:

"Not I, but my *Dolmetscher*."

He contented himself with penny novels about love-martyrdom and wandering orphans.

I worked more, but fared better, than my comrades. I could get as many potatoes in the kitchen as I needed to fill me up. No sentry would openly bother me. I took orders only from the *Kommandoführer* and he showed me some consideration, but he made me pay for it by many small vexations. Perhaps he realized, as I did, that regardless of the sympathy we might feel spontaneously for each other, we did not belong to the same side; and I could no more dissociate myself from the sufferings of my unhappiest comrades, whether Belgian, Polish, Servian, Russian, British or French, than he could avoid being proud of the successes of the German armies.

When I pushed under his eyes a pile of urgent requests in behalf of my comrades, addressed to the *Kontrollstelle*, the *Stalag*, or the pitiful French Ministry for War Prisoners, he would set them aside and delay signing his name on the transmission note, for a week or two, until I had begged him a sufficient number of times to do so.

Used to the small salary of a factory chauffeur, *Unteroffizier* Ehlert was considerably afraid of keeping any large sum of money. Since the beginning of 1941, a *Stalag* regulation enabled the prisoners of war to send their salaries home: a minimum of thirty marks, and a maximum of eighty, at a time. Once a month, I posted the information that the office would be open until curfew for the necessary formalities. The men who had bought, from the camp canteen, no other trifle than the razor blades, tooth powder and laundry chemicals replacing soap, could save enough to send thirty marks home every two or three months. The *Lagerscheine* (money coupons) that they brought, were locked up in the office cabinet, by Ehlert. We collected as much as 4000 marks in a few days, for the application had to be made in three copies, signed by the sender. Once

Forced Labor

the papers were ready, Ehlert would ask the largest firms to exchange the *Lagerscheine* for *Reichsmarks* (real money). The firms would use the coupons again to pay the salary to their prisoners, and we would send the *Reichsmarks* to the *Stalag*. With a delay of three, four, five months, these would be transferred to a German clearing bank in Paris, and distributed to the prisoners' families with remarkable regularity.

The conversion into *Reichsmarks* often took as long as a week, during which time the poor *Kommandoführer* hardly slept for fear of fire, or theft. He fingered his keys all day long, and never opened the cabinet to give me an envelope, or a pencil — these precious items were always under bars — without opening the money box and ascertaining that the bundle of notes had not been disturbed.

One evening, the "Gem of His Eyes"— the one mounted on stout pillars — told him over the telephone something so exciting that he left in a hurry, and forgot his keys. Late at night, when I abandoned the office to the care of a night sentry, I pocketed the precious bunch of keys. I had forgotten all the unpleasantness of captivity when someone shook me on my straw sack, shook and shook until I opened my eyes. In the pestilence of the ill-ventilated boat, it took one a long time to wake up. It was, so to speak, twice dark in this hole. When at last I came to my senses, there stood Ehlert with a flashlight, looking as tragic as an apparition, and hammering:

"My keys, my keys! Have you seen my keys?"

"They are in the pocket of my trousers, over my feet."

"Good Lord," he said, "I've been so worried about the 3000 marks!" and he sat down on my stool to recover.

He knew that I wouldn't steal them; but there were a few men among his own bunch of guards that he would never have trusted with his keys for a single minute.

* * *

LIFE AROUND THE KOMMANDOFUHRER

SENTRIES

The best men of Germany being more and more absorbed by the Russian fronts, the level of the sentries fell progressively. Older men; men who could see only through half an inch of glass; and weaklings, replaced the better soldiers in the little brown barrack on the left side of the yard; and it was not, so far as I was concerned, a progress.

Young, strong men were stiffer about discipline, and kicked more readily, but were less fussy. When an old farm hand, a mason's helper whose lack of strength has deprived him of a better job, a little bank scribbler whose back will never stand straight any more, are suddenly put in charge of twenty or thirty men, with such authority over them as they wish to exercise, the glory of being rulers at last, goes to their head. They avenge themselves of the humiliations of their own life, at the expense of the prisoners.

This would happen in any country. There are many ways, outside of direct brutality, to drive a prisoner mad: at work, by seeing that he always gets the worst place, and keeping on his back all day; in the camp, by provoking repeated searches of his belongings, and spoiling any leisure he has. Life in any prisoners' camp in the world is, and always was, a nightmare. Like jails, prisoners' camps are schools of hatred. When the sentries dismissed their columns, after the evening control in the yard, the men would mutter after them:

"When it'll be my turn to guard you . . ."

They believed that they would make them pay for all that they were now suffering. They imagined them captive in their own place, not looking as they were now, well fed, provokingly well clothed, with leather belts and shiny boots. But a prisoner of any denomination is so much like another, that I wonder if, having to guard their former conquerors fallen in captivity, they

Forced Labor

would not recognize their own past miseries under the discolored German rags, in the sabots, in the wrinkles of the emaciated faces, and pity them instead.

Now that I have regained my freedom and tasted the joys of which I had been completely deprived; now that life has again become worth-while to me, I can look with interest, and perhaps enthusiasm, at a newsreel showing torn houses, burnt German corpses, and demolitions of any sort. But whenever a column of newly taken prisoners — without belts, without helmets, dragging their weary feet towards captivity — appears across the screen, I cannot stand it. I close my eyes.

*   *   *

When the sentries remained long enough with the same firm, they became possessive. They would say, "my column," "my prisoners," and brag about them. They had the strongest man, one who would rather carry 200 pounds at a time than go twice for 100; or the funniest, who had cut and sewed his high Norwegian cap so that it would look like a frying pan with a vizor in place of a handle; or the cleverest.

It was considered fashionable to have a school teacher. The teachers of any country have the same manners, the same qualities, the same manias. A country boy, a small factory worker, now promoted to a sentry, would enjoy bullying a teacher in whom he saw a brother to the one who used to tap his fingers so effectively with a ruler.

College professors, or such intellectual people, had no color. They were not usually demonstrative. Lacking manual ability, they served as helpers to masons; dug trenches, pushed carts, piled bricks.

Cabinetmakers were quite an asset. When an intelligent overseer was warned by the sentry that one of these was around, he would take him aside a few hours a week, and make him build a desk in his office. Delighted to have in hand again the tools of his trade, the prisoner would amuse himself by constructing something very fine. It might cause him to be smuggled out of the work-yard for a few days, to replace a decayed chest of drawers in the overseer's home. A precious reward, paid in sandwiches and cigarettes, could be expected by the craftsman, while the guard would cash in on a few marks for his discretion.

*

Reipsch was a mean little guard who believed himself handsome, and had the looks of a phthisic crow. He understood a little French, was very suspicious, and hated me especially, because I occupied a place that he would have liked. Wasn't it a shame that a prisoner could sit all day in a comfortable office, with a pen in his hand, while a good Nazi had to freeze, to soak, or to sweat, running around a work-yard, like a cattle dog?

I was shaving in the deck washroom on his day of rest, and he asked me, rather reluctantly, to help him with a translation. His prisoners, he said, sang a strange song all day, and they had taught it to him; but he couldn't quite make out the meaning. I told him to sing it to me. He began, in a tremulous voice, a sentimental drawl, and an accent that turns every p into a b, s into z, and q into g, the following verse:

> J'ai le trou du cul qui me démange,
> Je ne sais ce qu'il y poussera,
> Mais s'il y pousse des oranges,
> C'est Adolf qui les mangera.

With a few concessions to decency, it might be translated as

> Something is itching in my back,
> I wonder what is going to grow,
> If it turns out to be oranges,
> It is Adolf who will eat them.

Forced Labor

My work as interpreter had long given me a poker face. I didn't even smile. I made him repeat it once more, and then I translated as accurately as I could. His horror was supreme.

"My God," he said, "Adolf Hitler?"

"Oh no; have no such fear, *Schutzer* Reipsch; it couldn't be and it isn't. Adolf is for us a classical figure from the funnies. In fact it's a gold fish in a glass bowl."

"Are you sure? You aren't kidding me?"

"Not in the least and this little song is hollered, in France, by all students and drunks. It's a good one, don't you think?"

He thought so; and greatly reassured by my ridiculous story, immensely proud to know a French song, he went down the chicken ladder, singing:

> "... *mais s'il y poussait des oranges* ..."

while my excellent comrade Finot, now engaged in washing the decks with a hose, marked time with his sabots, and joined in the last line:

> "*C'est Adolf qui les mangera.*"

*

Schlegel was a brute and a swastika fanatic. He drank until his eyes were bloody, and his face waxy. He had spells of such violence that his prisoners, protecting themselves with their shovels, called the overseer for help, and showed him that he kept them from working. But a prisoner cannot be right, and nothing prevented Schlegel from hitting a few of them viciously again, and reporting them for having threatened him with their tools. I sent several of his victims to the sanitary inspection, hoping to raise a protest from the doctor; but he gave them only a little box of vaseline with which to rub their bruises.

A prisoner has become such a valuable animal, for Germany, that a sentry might be severely punished for killing one uselessly; but anything short of a wound is considered a trifle. Ehlert, to whom I presented the case as pathetically as possible, did not react. He admitted that Schlegel was brutal but believed that the prisoners provoked him. Though he wished the prisoners to be fairly treated in his *Kommando*, he approved of the most violent measures if taken in the name of discipline.

One night Paul and I were working alone in the office, where there was no end to the scribbling, especially around the middle and the end of each month. Schlegel pushed open the door and stumbled in, drunk as a lord. He raised his arm in the Nazi salute, advanced one more step, and bawled:

"It is magnificent! Alone you keep the office going. You work all night. Prisoners, you are worthy of Adolf Hitler! I salute you," and the mad hog clapped his heels and lifted up his chin. We had to render him the military salute while he poured his drunken look on us, like a repugnant slabber.

This hurt me more than a blow.

*

Unlike most others, little man Kellner was not proud to be a soldier. He didn't like polishing his gun any more than his boots; and saluting his superior was no fun to him. He had a good time only when invited to sign his name, on the company pay roll, to receive ten marks for his ten days of irksomeness.

As soon as possible, he called for his *Urlaubskarte* (authorization to leave the camp) and came back only after having poured so much beer in his stomach that two quick *schnaps* would make him thoroughly drunk. Thanks to this economical process, he could make his spree last two evenings. He would

Forced Labor

then go to bed and bother no one. Again broke, he would content himself with picking up the prisoners' butts, in the yard, to keep his little pipe going, and spend his days inoffensively dreaming. He was entrusted only with a very small firm, and his men woke him up in the evening when it was time to return. They kept him more than he kept them, and they would not have caused him any trouble.

It was his turn to be on watch by the small night gate behind the office when, around 1 A.M. another *Wachmann* found him dead drunk on the ground. It would have been a swell chance for a prisoner, hidden under the foredeck chicken-ladder, to break out; but no one had known it, or been ready to take advantage of it.

I could understand that a patriotic sentry would become indignant at such failure to accomplish one's duty. From this point of view, the good old Kellner deserved to be driven to bed with a few sound kicks-in-the-pants by the comrade who would find himself compelled to take his place. But it was a complete surprise to me when, the following morning, a guard appeared in the office and said:

"*Herr Unteroffizier,* I have to report that *Schutzer* Kellner was sleeping while on night watch, at one o'clock."

Kellner got three weeks in jail, on bread and water, from his captain. When the major would receive the report, he would add to the punishment; and it might have become a long stretch when the colonel would finally put his name on it.

I slipped him two cigarettes when, after presenting himself at the office, he left the camp to go on his new diet.

I asked Ehlert if the informer were in danger of getting his neck broken by the other sentries. He looked at me in astonishment. Where in the world had I gotten such a silly idea?

*　　*　　*

When a new sentry reported to the *Kommandoführer*, I wondered:

"What is he like? Is he going to be tough on my boys, or lenient? Is he Hitlerian or not?"

I could find the last answer easily enough, with a standard question, the first time that I should see him alone:

"How long do you think it will take Germany to beat Russia?"

If he were a very hot Nazi, he would say:

"It's already done."

If tepid:

"It may last some time yet."

If against:

"Well, I don't know," and look at me intently.

Then I could risk:

"Quite an expensive proposition, don't you think? There were many black crosses on the obituary page of the *Pommersche Zeitung*, today."

We would soon understand each other. Out of thirty-five guards, there was never more than one at a time who would admit that Hitler was not his man and, of course, only after looking around to see that no one could hear. It was difficult to realize how many of the others were not enthusiastic Nazis. According to their answers to a series of questions offered during their stay in the *Kommando*, I believe that twenty per cent were hot partisans of Hitler, sixty per cent followed him with confidence, ten per cent did not praise him, and ten per cent could be considered as decidedly against him.

The Oberschutzer who replaced Kellner, confessed to me that he was a Communist, and ready to give his life to kill Hitler. He informed me on the exact results of the British bombings in the vicinity, and called my attention to the fact that many of the antiaircraft buildings seemed to have been conceived as

Forced Labor

inner-fortifications. Was Hitler expecting to have to fight inside Germany, in spite of his successes of the moment? The Allies might find, some day, that the tender borders of the Baltic sea have been secretly fortified, and that the cities have been converted into strong points, as has been practiced by the Russians.

CIVILIANS

The way in which visiting civilians lifted their arm when saying:

"*Heil* Hitler!" was a barometer of their convictions. The austere, one hundred per cent Nazis, stretched their right arm stiffly, slightly to the right and above the shoulder. Showy characters, such as *Lagerführer* Opferer, threw their hand in the air, very high, while they joined the heels. Moderate people made only the gesture of showing something in the far corner. It was automatic, but I could tell when it was easy, when slightly unpleasant.

From his seat, Ehlert answered "*Heil* Hitler!" without any gesture. Soldiers in uniform, wearing a cap, make the military salute; but when they had no cap they set themselves at attention, and lifted up the arm.

"*Heil* Hitler!" is a general password that no one can ignore. Business letters always end, and sometimes begin, with it. It cannot be overdone, while its omission would mean lack of submission, and prove dangerous. The Nazi faith has engendered numerous bigots who, with the sly keenness of village sextons, spot the unbelievers and report them.

Instead of pronouncing "*heil*" as "hi-el," some provincial Germans pronounced it almost "hell," and that had been the origin of a joke in my little circle of friends who spoke English. We would greet each other with a good, hearty: "To Hell,

Hitler." A poor joke it was; but prisoners are accustomed to poor samples of everything.

*

Once, a controller came from the city while I was alone in the *Kommandoführer's* office. A tall man in his late fifties, he was neatly dressed, but his clothes showed wear and patient darning. He held the leather brief case that Germans relish and carry everywhere.

"*Heil* Hitler," he said.

There was a polite intonation in his words, and it felt sweet to my ears. I got up, tapped my heels, bowed a little, and answered:

"*Guten Tag, Herr Inspektor!*"

He looked at me, and to show that he had understood, corrected:

"*Guten Tag, Herr Dolmetscher!*"

Then, smiling, a little sadly, perhaps, he added:

"In Germany, one never bids Good Day any more."

*

The bookkeepers of many firms came twice a month and, their business completed, liked to sit down for a welcome chat with Ehlert. They had seen me so often, on my stool beside him, that they lost all arrogance or embarrassment, and showed me their sympathetic German middle-class features. Good men they were, so much like my own men; slower perhaps, but more methodical; also concerned with the fate of their families; with the problems of the future, and their own individual hobbies. Meeting no hostility in my eyes, they would tell me something pleasant about my comrades.

Forced Labor

"When they want to, these Frenchmen can certainly work. They are marvelous craftsmen."

"But why don't they always want to work?" Ehlert would ask.

"Imagine yourself in their place, *Herr Unteroffizier*, and you will find all the answers."

But they couldn't quite see it. They belonged to the winning side, and no victor can think like the vanquished. Ambition is a contagious disease. Hitler had promised them the products of our farms and factories; the grain of the Ukraine; the oils of Baku; and provided them with reasons and principles, with true documents and convenient lines, that made the kindest among them accept his worst brutalities as expressions of necessary discipline. It was the victims' own fault! Why wouldn't they give in?

*

A map of Europe hung in the office and it was I who planted the little swastikas mounted on pins, along the front line as defined by the daily communiqué. It had been a joy, in the fall of 1941, to set back a few of them. I was rectifying the line after the Germans admitted withdrawing from Rostov, when the overseer of a small firm nodded and said:

"Russia is an infernal place."

"This is going to be the end of it" protested Ehlert.

"Yes, but listen" said the man, and he held one hand upright, the fingers stretched apart. "I am from Stettin. I grew up and went to school with five boys of my age, living in the vicinity. Life took them to all parts of Germany, but we kept writing to each other, regularly. As a building specialist, I haven't been taken in the army yet, but they have fought all over Europe. In June, they were all sent to Russia. During each month of the war with the Bolsheviks, one of them has been killed. Only one remained. I heard this morning that he too, has fallen! Once I had five friends. Now, I am all alone."

He closed his fingers, one after the other, until it was a clenched fist at the end of his arm, suddenly looking like a threat.

*   *   *

THE SLOBBERER AND THE SICK

His jaw was twisted, his teeth protruded, his mouth couldn't close, he slobbered. Save for the nose out of center, his face would have looked normal if his neck had been able to support it upright. Due to some deformity of the spine, his head fell on the side, like a heavy fruit on a weak twig, without being able to rest on his shoulder. He shook it upwards every few seconds.

His voice had a sweet sound, but the words entangled themselves in his teeth, perhaps because his tongue hadn't enough space to move freely. It was worse than stammering. Only after a few trials could he produce some clear words.

The other guards made fun of him. However careful he might be in getting dressed, his uniform looked ridiculous: the back of his coat remained hooked on his belt, or the bayonet fell out of the scabbard.

Each time that he had been sent out with a working group, the firm had called up the office to have him replaced. He couldn't cope with the least little difficulty. His ideas were perhaps fluid inside his skull, but their expression followed a deforming process similar to that obscuring the sound of his words. While other sentries changed *Kommandos* every two or three months, he remained with us endlessly. His one job was to march the sick to the sanitary inspection, every day.

At 5:45 A.M. I gathered all the men inscribed on the sick list, and called their names. This didn't mean that every sick man

Forced Labor

was included. From 7-7:15 P.M. only the prisoners that The Gnome, or whoever was assistant to the *Kommandoführer* at the time, would recognize as sick, were inscribed. It was a question of appearances, except in case of high fever, verified several times on the spot. When more than twelve men were presented to him, the German doctor complained bitterly. I had to fight hard to persuade The Gnome to accept men who were very sick, while he chose others who had nothing serious, but made the proper face. Anyone refused, could call on the prisoner-nurse who handled a little store of the most necessary medicines, and, besides other functions in the camp, dressed slight wounds. No one was allowed to stay idle without orders from the doctor. Unrecognized patients went to work, and it was often pathetic.

The Slobberer counted his troop in vain, for he never found the number that I announced. He counted again — starting this time at the other end — and obtained a third figure. He finally had to trust me; but if I failed to come near him and refresh his memory when he was ready to present his column to the *Kommandoführer*, he called out no matter what number, and the day began very badly, for him. He was told, for instance, that he was going to be eaten raw, or at best, sent to jail for eight days. The prisoners laughed and soon got a share of the imprecations.

Once outside the gate, the Slobberer was so afraid of losing a man on the way, that he kept turning around and hitting the men on the outside, so that the column would stay very compact. He had no control over his blows with the butt end of his gun, and the only way to avoid them was to walk faster than he. Then he needed all of his strength to follow, his mouth wide open, and calling in his indecipherable dialect to slow down. This was possible only when no one was injured in the foot.

When absolutely incapable of walking, a prisoner would be spared the five-mile walk, and sent by streetcar, with a guard carrying a special written authorization of the doctor.

*

The sanitary visit was held in a wooden shack behind the huge Kreckow Barracks, on the other side of Stettin. The patients waited outside for two, three, four hours, regardless of the weather and with not a single bench to sit on. Only those with wounded feet were allowed the privilege of waiting inside with the guards who had brought prisoners from all *Kommandos* of the district. Men with fever as high as 103°, have stood in the snow until an indignant comrade succeeded in getting admitted, and called on the infirmary interpreter for help.

The compensation of waiting was the possibility to communicate with comrades from other camps. This was forbidden, but no sentry cared to stay outside long enough to effectively prevent it.

Their turn having come at last, the men were inspected by French and Belgian prisoner-doctors, who could only propose work-exemption for a few days. Every decision had to be submitted to the German doctor captain, who came very late, and signed the diagnostics and prescriptions in each *Kommando* book. He blew up fiercely the men that he didn't consider sufficiently sick; but those recognized as suffering from a definite disease, were well treated. They were eventually admitted to a clean infirmary, where the food was scarce, but the medical care serious. The price of it was another hair-shave and a two-hour wait, naked, in the unheated delousing department, while the clothes were being disinfected. When his disease was contagious, or when his injury necessitated an operation,

Forced Labor

the prisoner was sent, by ambulance, to a hospital in Stargard, a few hours away.

Until the war with Russia, a German or a French doctor, accompanied by a sentry, would drive to the ship in case of indisputable emergency, and take the man away; but later, due to lack of cars, this practice was drastically reduced.

During one year, one of the prisoners died of disease, one was killed by accident, two lost a hand, three were sent home in desperate condition from tuberculosis, and five others were liberated when found incapable of working any more. Any such decision could be made only by the *Stalag* doctors, and then not altogether seriously. I am under the impression that there were definite quotas, not to be exceeded, and that it was a matter of luck if you arrived at the proper time.

Men whose legs had been broken in several places, while in a *Kommando*, and, treated too late, left with a permanent limp, would be sent back to work. One little man on ship was becoming blind, and the pains in his head drove him crazy. It took me six months of incessant requests, protests, explanations, to have him sent to a special hospital, from which he ultimately returned to France.

I am willing to believe that the written sanitary regulations for the prisoners' camps are acceptable, but one should realize how they are carried out. Their execution occurs by successive steps, taken by different persons. Any one of them can stop the process, and place the responsibility on the others. No one is in a position to help the individual prisoner, except his fellow *Vertrauensmann* (representative) who is not informed of his rights, and has no means of enforcing them. For example, some of my comrades whose stomachs had been cut several times for major operations, were incapable of lifting weights, or digging with a pick-axe, without reopening their wounds. Presented at the medical visit, they would come back with a bandage, and the note: "to be given light work." The doctor had done what he thought was correct.

But there was no "light work" in our *Kommando!* The cleaning of the ship was done by four men in similar condition. Other posts couldn't be created, and the *Kommandoführer* would return them immediately to their respective firms! The only defense for the disabled men was to lift up their shirt, in front of the overseer and the guard, and try to persuade them that it was not just a matter of unwillingness on their part. As long as the bowels didn't leap out, the men in charge claimed that laziness had something to do with the case! The men were soon shifted to another firm, where they didn't get along any better. They caused the *Kommandoführer* so many difficulties, that he would get rid of them as soon as possible, *i.e.* the next time an order came to send some prisoners to another camp. He would round up the sick, and ship them away in the lot. It was the easiest solution; but the other *Kommandoführer* knew it also, and did the same. When it was our turn to receive a column of new prisoners, I asked them prudently:

"Who is incapable of working?"

There were always two or three having a similar story to tell. They drifted from one *Kommando* to another. Once in a while, a local doctor would order them back to the *Stalag*, and the *Stalag* doctor would send them back to work. Some day, they might fall on a job that they could accomplish without too much pain.

On the whole, the death and sickness rates were not abnormally high, due to the fact that the major part of the army was made up of men selected for their health and strength, and the weaklings had been eliminated during the hardships of the first three months. The prisoners are now accustomed to meagre rations and hard work, but after a few years of privations, they will bring home tired bodies, weak hearts, rheuma-

Forced Labor

tism, and neurasthenic troubles that may considerably affect the length of their lives.

*   *   *

The prisoner-doctors disliked very much their position. Their pharmacy was reduced to a small collection of pills; very little antiseptic; paper bands; a little gauze, and no cotton. Deprived of medical equipment and, worst of all, of professional independence, they lost interest in their patients. The German doctor-captain treated them outrageously.

My comrades often complained to me that they didn't find the sympathy and comprehension with the French doctors that they normally expected of them. I well understand that they had many troubles, and that the imaginary diseases some of us claimed in order to meet someone in the infirmary yard to receive or transmit secret information, proved very embarrassing to them. Even so, I regretted that they didn't devote themselves to their more unfortunate compatriots. They have failed to realize what spiritual, as well as physical, help they could have rendered; and this betrays again the lack of preparation of our officers. One should not train an army for victory only; instructions should be given for the reverse also. No one had any doctrine about what could be done, in captivity, by the captives for themselves, and for their country.

To render the medical visit even less pleasant, a corporal would come from the *Kontrollstelle*, located in the vicinity, and collect one or two dozen sick prisoners for any sort of work, such as unloading a freight car of *Stalag* clothes, or gifts from the French Red Cross. Although it was obviously in our interest, it proved no cure, and was exasperating.

CHAPTER 12

Life around the Lagerfuhrer

(THE CAVE OF ALI BABA)

Lagerführer Opferer showed so much of himself outside, that nothing but a hollow mannequin remained inside. Even his viscera tried to leave his carcass, and projected his front line so far, that only a stout leather belt prevented him from bursting altogether.

I believe he spent all of his Hitlerian faith in his Nazi salute. It was colossal, *"überkolossal."* He threw his right hand with such violence, that instead of stopping as it should, slightly above the level of his shoulder, it flew beyond his head, while his back curved in, and his knees gave way a few inches. Bent to the extreme, his arm would then have a spring action, and his hand would be sent forward to stabilize itself, for a fugitive instant, at the level of his cap. Then his arm would slacken like a fishing line when the artificial fly, deftly whipped, stays immobile for a second, before falling down gently on the water.

A reserve petty officer of the German Navy, he wore the insignia of the different branches of the service, in which, for fifteen years, he had tried in vain to become an officer. He had the splendid commanding voice of a man accustomed to shouting orders through the heavy fogs of the northern seas; but all his authority was exhausted in the tumult. He had none beyond his words. How splendidly, though, he shook his short, dyed beard, while he made his mouth square, and clapped his jaws after each word, as if he had spat out little cubes of noise. It

Forced Labor

was most impressive while it lasted, but it all vanished as soon as one looked in his fishy little eyes.

I was in a position to get frequent doses of his poisonous invectives, because my men did many wrong things around his quarters. For instance, they pocketed as many potatoes as they peeled, in the evening. They took them to the workyard, and managed to cook them over bonfires. Civilian workers would bring the salt, lend a lenient hand to the cooking, and get their share. One of the results was that the kitchen kettles would be only half full, and I had to argue with the *Lagerführer* that the difference came from the excessive number of completely frozen potatoes that had been discarded with the peelings.

Sometimes a pot of fat, that had been imprudently set on a table near the kitchen window through which the buckets of peeled potatoes were handed, would vanish. It was, as voiced by the boys, a very small return for what had been stolen from them, and was being stolen every day by the Nazis in France. I could blame them only when they let anybody see them!

The disappearance, however, led to frightful scandals. Opferer called for me, in the kitchen, showed me, with an avenging finger, the empty spot on the table, and hollered at me what he thought of my comrades, in terms so vile that I wouldn't listen. I snapped myself to a rigid position of attention, looked him quietly in the eyes while repeating silently to myself:

"You barking swine, growling dog, most obscene thief of the best part of our rations, don't you realize how ridiculous you are?"

What could he do to anybody so respectfully silent as I remained? While he fulminated, my own monologue helped me pass the time, and gave me a humorous feeling. He would tire of it before I would, and finally go back to his private office, while letting out supplementary curses, sounding, in the corridor, like a rear-guard fire. Alone in the field, I would smile while the German employees laughed, and join my comrades who had contemplated the scene through the distribution window, with more amusement than anxiety, though no one could guess what punishment might result from the intense telephoning now going on between the *Lagerführung* and the *Kontrollstelle*.

Adjoining the guards' own barracks, was a storeroom, beautifully locked, but so poorly constructed that the potatoes froze in it in winter, and fermented in summer. Occasionally, vegetables destined for the sentries' menu, would be kept there. I shall not reveal how my men extracted two cratefuls of red cabbages from this stronghold; but the brilliant deed was discovered that very evening, and though it seemed impossible that prisoners could have been guilty of it, *Herr* Opferer tumultuously convoked me. I soon quieted him by proposing that he be on the lookout for any fire that my comrades might attempt to build in the camp, in order to cook the cabbages, if they had any. It sounded like good advice, to him. If the swashbuckler had thought about investigating on the ship, he would have found the prisoners on their bunks, in the night, bravely chewing the raw cabbage, stalk included, so that no trace remained! Though much less palatable than after marinating in oil and vinegar, it would still supply some greatly needed vitamins.

The disappearance of the precious vegetables remained a mystery that was still commented upon around the *Lagerführung*, when I myself disappeared.

*　　　*　　　*

If *Herr* Opferer had not been able to decorate his Nazi brown shirt with the insignia of an admiral, he had partly real-

Forced Labor

ized his other pet dream: being a Bagdad sultan. He had a harem.

The bags of sugar, the boxes of margarine, the pails of artificial marmalade, stored around, attracted many flies — or should I say butterflies? Some were pretty, some ugly, some fresh, some rather worn; but all of them had handsome legs. It seemed to be on this basis that the *Lagerführer* engaged them to work, as their weekly pay check said, for the city of Stettin.

The prettiest one was his private secretary, and I had thought her distinguished — until I went to the office to tell him that I couldn't supply the ten men he wanted for unloading sacks. He joked about the word with a vulgarity, a crudeness, and a complacency in the details, beating even the stories of the Bornzin potato diggers; and not only did the lovely stenographer giggle, but she also added to them. Sometimes I found the office empty, but Opferer's private room, next to it, was locked and, the panelling being thin, not entirely silent.

I have known eight women employed in the kitchen at the same time. As a German head cook and the prisoner-helpers did all the work for us, the women sat in the best corner nearest the windows, smoked, laughed, shook their bobbed hair while looking at the sentry passing in the yard, and occasionally peeled some vegetables for the guards. They would also cut the rounds of sausage for us and weigh the portions of marmalade when, once in a while, we were allotted some, wrapped in paper. With eyes rounded in black as far as the middle of the cheeks; heavy, soft limbs that seemed to melt on their stools, and lips deteriorated by long use of cheap paint, two of them would have looked more natural in a pink dressing gown, awaiting sailors, behind closed shutters. These two were sometimes entrusted with dragging a mop over the tiles of the *Lagerführung* corridor, which they did with a voluptuous slowness, stopping at every door to beg for a cigarette. The others — excepting one who had distinction, but also mannerisms — were more of the slum-girl type, unprofessionally gay.

They were supervised and hated by a horsy old woman, dry and incorruptible-looking, who exercised some control over the supply room. She saw no objection to their bringing their children, once in a while, to meals. Two little girls who had been claimed by no particular father, came oftener than the others; but their mothers wore a little enamel swastika. In Nazi Germany that is a more effective moral guarantee than a marriage license.

They didn't dissimulate the sort of work that the *Lagerführer* gave them as a preliminary test of their abilities, or whenever the fancy took him. I had many opportunities to hear them, and talk to them when I came around to complain about the exiguity or the regularity of the portions that they handed through the window to my men.

One blond head was completely lost to a prisoner who had no feeling for her. She first asked me about him — who he was, if he spoke German, if he was grateful for the double portions she had slipped to him. She would have taken dangerous steps to have him. She sighed and looked through the window at him, like a sheep, when he stood in line among the others for the distribution of soup.

There is something in the prisoner's rags that attracts women. It may be the mystery: they are from far away; none could guess their situation; they may be rich, but now, all are miserable. Or is it their continence?

The four boys working in the kitchen fared well, to the disgust of the German guards who, not allowed inside, guessed, rather than saw, that the women diminished their better rations in favor of our cooks. The penalties for relations with a war prisoner are very heavy, but each of these women knew so much about the others, that the danger of denunciation was

Forced Labor

small; and, besides, there was little possibility to carry on anything but a very platonic intrigue.

To most of the camp, the female figures behind the panes were far more irritating than pleasant. There was one in the canteen located on the other side of the distribution room adjoining the kitchen. She, also, handed the items through a window. Razor blades, pencils, cigarette cases, breast pins and odd objects that couldn't be sold in the city, were bought at high prices by the prisoners each anxious to bring anything as a souvenir to his wife and children.

On two evenings, salted cucumbers, Italian lemons, and little pots of potato syrup were sold. The whole camp lined up as far as the barbed wire, for them; but this exception was not repeated. The only thing with a nutritional value was a small bottle of saccharined sparkling water, for twenty *pfennigs*, or an occasional bottle of weak beer. Even so, the business of the canteen was so good that it justified the presence of a manager, besides the sales girl. He was a man in his late forties, not unpleasant, but sticky with Nazi pride. His assistant may have been a tired girl of twenty, or a young looking woman of forty. Her hair was strangely groomed to form a Louis XIV wig. She was much underweight, febrile, unhealthy, but graceful. I have no doubt that she would willingly have extended to many of the prisoners the favors that she granted to several of the guards and to the ship's steward, besides her other obligations around the *Lagerführung,* if it had been feasible. She, too, locked herself up with the canteen manager, in the back room where the reserve blankets for the prisoners were kept. Almost each time that I brought back the sleeping-and-eating-equipment of a prisoner moved to another camp — this happened daily — I disturbed some passionate traffic. They must, by the way, have caught some of our lice and fleas.

*　　　*　　　*

The *Lagerführer* held his parties rather privately, either in his cabin on the sunny side of the ship's castle, or in his various rooms, in the *Lagerführung*. One of these opened directly on the yard, near the gate, and the incoming prisoners stepped on the little items of pink rubber that he simply discarded through the window.

He had an understudy called *Unterlagerführer*, an agreeable little man with only two passions: stuffing his large stomach, and preaching the Hitlerian creed. He, likewise, had an assistant, also fond of abundant food, and of Nazi quotations, but whose chief interest was centered on the kitchen flock. A fat girl, with enormous eyes, who might have been beautiful if everything about her had been reduced — here by an inch, and there by ten — was his, principally. Her German was poor, because she came from Ukraine and was considered a German protégé.

After 7 P.M., when work for the women was supposed to end, the *Under-under-Lagerführer* transformed himself into a ballet master for them. The whole gang raced through the kitchen, entered the distribution room packed with prisoners calling for their bowl of soup, elbowed their way across to the canteen, where all business would immediately stop. The window went down together with a thick shade. Then beer would flow; *schnaps* would come on top, and a scandalous noise would soon shake the wooden walls.

Meanwhile, burning their hands with their platter of rutabagas or barley, the prisoners went away, one after the other, both envious and disgusted at the libations going on so near, and making such a violent contrast to their own privations.

Once or twice a week, the feast in the canteen was prolonged by a banquet in the *Lagerführung*, most obviously supplied by the best part of our rations. The women got busy around the stove with an enthusiasm they had not shown during the day,

Forced Labor

and their spirits were already high when three of the kitchen prisoners went away at 9 P.M. The fourth prisoner remained until eleven, to prepare the barley drink for the morning. I arrived around ten, through for the day with my endless work in the military office, to eat the potatoes that he kept warm for me. It felt good to sit in the large kitchen, now deserted, without a guard, and without a crowd of anxious comrades bringing problems and worries that I could help so little. The tumult of the camp would cease in me, as it had outside. It was the nearest I came to privacy.

Suddenly, completely drunk, a couple in search of accommodations would break into the kitchen, and fall on the butcher's table, as if on the tender moss of a thicket. A lone, staggering figure, having lost her partner might come in and crack them on the head with a plate, or a cup, and to the two of us sitting at the other end of the huge room, give a sordid show. They would fight, and fuss, and kiss, and cry, and laugh, and, arm-in-arm, return to the banquet, to renew the fire of their entrails with a fresh dose of rash alcohol.

A tall woman, so powerful that we called her "The Bull Woman," brought her ten-year-old daughter to these sprees. She put her to bed in another room, but the laughs and disputes would keep the poor child awake, so she would come in the kitchen looking for her mother, now lying under a table somewhere, and inquire about her so pitifully that we made her sit down, and gave her a little candy, if we had received any in our last package. She was grateful, and so intelligent, as are children who see too many things, but she wouldn't stay long. She would explore every room, every dark corner, until she found her mother, and beg her, ardently, to go home.

*   *   *

To the queries of the International Red Cross Committees,

the Nazi administrators may well demonstrate that, though small, the rations allowed the prisoners are sufficient. Because they don't visit the working *Kommandos*, and don't see it happen, they cannot realize what we really receive. During all my captivity, I have never seen any international investigator, or heard of any in the vicinity, and none of my prisoners had ever seen any in the various *Kommandos* where they had sojourned.

A substantial amount of meat arrived, twice a week, at the camp, and was unloaded by my comrades of the kitchen. The German cook weighed it in the presence of the *Unterlagerführer*. Then the butcher called on the *Lagerführer* with a handsome leg of lamb, or roast of beef, and received a stamp on his bill of delivery. The weight was surely correct, for it would have been too dangerous, otherwise; but what about the bones? There was a surprising quantity of these, on which a substantial benefit could be realized. Indeed they increased progressively, as if a new kind of animal had been raised with only a skeleton under the skin.

Not only were the private banquets of the *Lagerführung* to be reckoned out of the little amount of lean meat, but also, no woman ever went home without a plump little package. That is why they were willing to work here; and it was also a judicious indemnity for their special services to the *Lagerführer*. As they didn't like the horse-meat sausage, they couldn't get anything but margarine out of our cold rations. Even the tall, dry old woman supervisor didn't go home without a black bag stuffed so full that the others commented bitterly:

"She takes too much at a time."

Of course the head cook had a family to think about . . .

We received the remnants from this flock of greedy buzzards.

Comrades from the cleaning-squad reported to me, several times that in exchange for the beer that he brought almost en-

Forced Labor

tirely for the use of the *Lagerführung*, and for the *schnaps* that the prisoners never tasted, boxes of margarine were remitted to the truck-driver. Alcohol and fat, being equally hard to obtain, were very valuable items.

However well informed I was of this traffic, I couldn't prevent it. In vain did I tell everything I knew to the successive *Kommandoführer*. They knew it too, but thought it best not to have anything to do with it.

The rations finally became so small and so poor, in the fall of 1941, that my comrades became very nervous. I plotted with them to show their daily sausage and margarine to the overseers of their firms, before eating their lunch. Several of these reported to their employer who, estimating that any diminution of the food they paid for, out of our earnings, was equivalent to robbing them of a certain amount of our energy, to the use of which they were entitled, protested to the *Kontrollstelle*. The controlling officer came down to investigate but, by a miracle only too easy to explain, our rations for that day were considerably increased.

There was nothing to do. Either this officer was initiated to the black business going on in the city camps, or else he was one of those pure types, blind to any fact, and who would see only virginal smiles on the drunken lips of the whores in the kitchen. Perhaps, though honest, and conscious of the wide-scale robbing in the *Lagerführung*, he knew that he couldn't change it.

Even if he were invulnerable in what concerned our administration, the *Lagerführer* had too many intrigues with his female employees, and though he managed to replace them often, they finally united against him, and caused a scandal. After many scenes, he was sent to take charge of another camp. I saw the repugnant creature behind his desk, his small eyes full of tears, telling someone that it was a gross injustice. He had worked enormously to organize the *Gemeinschaftslager Nordenham* and now that it ran smoothly, he was to be deprived of enjoying the fruits of his labor. And he turned to me, as witness!

CHAPTER 13

The Vertrauensmann

Soon after our installation on the *Nordenham,* my comrades chose me as their representative. A certain International Convention of Geneva, of 1929, relative to the treatment of prisoners of war, stipulates their right to elect what the Germans call a *"Vertrauensmann"* — literally, Confidence Man. About the other stipulations of this convention that the prisoners hear about, but never see, I could learn only what the *Kommandoführer* himself knew or admitted, which is to say, very little.

One *Vertrauensmann* is elected freely in every camp or *Kommando,* by the prisoners themselves, but if the *Kommandoführer* does not approve of him, he can make life unbearable for him, or simply send him to another *Kommando.* Often he is interpreter, too; but this is not mandatory. The interpreters are chosen by the Germans, and as such, are in a better position to deal with them; but they are more susceptible to bribery or influence.

The *Vertrauensmann* of each *Kommando* is registered in the *Stalag.* He represents all his prisoners at both the *Stalag* and the French Embassy for War Prisoners — an institution entrusted with all our problems, but controlled, like the others, by the Germans. It is headed by a man completely blind from wounds received in the last war. That is symbolic as well. The prisoners expect that if he is ever replaced, his successor will be deaf and dumb, too. He is supposed to send envoys to all the *Kommandos;* but I have never seen any.

The *Vertrauensmann* acts as a notary public, or a justice of the peace. He may perform marriages, by proxy, file petitions for divorces, and legalize any documents. Two prisoners chosen among the noncommissioned of the camp, or among the oldest, serve as witnesses. The transmission is assured under the control of the *Kommandoführer*, first to the *Kontrollstelle*, then to the *Stalag* censor, and finally to France, where the papers end their complicated journey after several months. The prisoners were very fond of this procedure. It gave them the illusion of being citizens again. They told me their often intricate story, asked me for advice, for which I would send them to one among us who might be a lawyer, or have had some legal experience. The ultimate solution of their problems was, most of the time, to grant full power of attorney to a member of their family, to settle the dead father's estate, or sell a piece of property so that the wife could live on the proceeds. This may prove to have been disastrous when they return home.

The *Vertrauensmann* also has the privilege of standing up for his comrades' rights, under any circumstances; which means that he can protest a little about difficulties occurring at work or in the camp, but, submitted to the same discipline and obligations as the others, he can be easily curbed. He may write to the controlling officer, but his letters, transmitted by the *Kommandoführer* himself, could hardly disclose anything that the latter would not approve of. Eventually, when this controlling officer comes to the camp, he can demand to speak to him.

His official power is indeed very small, but, if his comrades are united behind him, he can apply some discreet pressure on the *Kommandoführer* by making him realize that fewer incidents happen at work, or in the camp, when he shows a little more tolerance. A prisoner cannot refuse to work, but he can fall and break the handle of his tool, or drop a sack of cement, or let a stone fall in the wheels of the mixing machine, and make himself decidedly unpleasant, while looking very contrite about the accident.

Frankness, honesty, are possible only for free men who have

Forced Labor

rights, know them, and can claim them. How often have I heard, in reply to a moderate request, the fatal answer:

"Ihr seid Kriegsgefangenen." You are prisoners of war; in other words, you have nothing to ask.

The fundamental virtues of man take on a different expression in captivity from that in free life. Where a free man would shout his indignation, a prisoner shows a blank face. He cannot say what he thinks: he has to lie. But where an ordinary prisoner could save himself by refusing to answer, his *Vertrauensmann*, in order to defend him, has to speak.

Would I ever admit, except when the evidence against him was complete, that one of my comrades had stolen a loaf of bread, or some civilian trousers, when I knew that he needed them for his escape? I would violently deny it, confuse the facts, build up wild stories. Hadn't his own existence been stolen? Hadn't he the right to try to get it back? The fact that the Germans punished the whole camp when one man escaped, should in no way prevent any one of them trying to escape.

Sometimes, also, one of the few abject individuals always present in a crowd, would steal a loaf of bread from a comrade. I couldn't let the Germans know that. I would inform the whole camp that if the disgusting thief were found, his neck would be broken, and then I'd go to the *Unterlagerführer* and beg him for another loaf, on the pretext that the missing one had fallen in the river. The victim couldn't stay three and one-half days without bread.

Though from the day of my capture, to the day of my escape, I have hardly heard anything but lies from the Germans — all truth being carefully altered to serve the interests of their *Führer* — the perpetual comedy that I had to play with them, has sometimes been very painful.

Such is captivity, the most unsung of all the calamities of war.

CHAPTER 14

Nazi Propaganda in the Camp

OF ALL the duties of a *Vertrauensmann*, the least official of them was the principal: to keep up the morale of the camp; fight the Nazi propaganda among us; and, lacking other doctrine, unite my comrades against our captors.

The Nazis must have attached a great importance to our opinions, for they took many steps to switch us to their side. These seemed to contradict the very character of our captivity; as if we were to believe that, in spite of the bayonets and barbed wires around us, we were not considered as enemies. Besides the prisoners' paper *Trait d'Union*, distributed freely, twice a week, we could read certain German magazines, such as *Das Reich* — Goebbel's own organ — *der Adler*, etc., offered at very moderate subscription rates.

Hitler never delivered a speech without our receiving a translation of it, beautifully printed for French prisoners. It came either from the *Stalag*, or from the city of Stettin, and sometimes from both, as if there had been a competition between the military and the civil branches of the main Nazi office for propaganda.

The *Führer's* harangues, and the other leaflets sold to us by the canteen, kept enough foreign character to be shocking; but the newspapers from Occupied France and Belgium, to which we could also subscribe, were more insidious. Dealing with local problems in which every one of us was interested, they showed the Nazis at their best, our former politicians at their worst, and the Allies in their most embarrassing positions. My comrades admitted their disgust with these foul newspapers, but they couldn't resist reading them for the same reason that

Forced Labor

a prisoner in a cell looks through the bars of the ventilation hole: there ran the life denied them. They said they didn't believe a word of it, but it intoxicated them slowly, as the fumes of alcohol when you breathe them, even though you don't drink any. There are such things as written poisons.

No cleverer measure was ever taken by the Nazis than the authorization to send our savings home. When it had been announced, in the early spring of 1941, I hadn't taken it seriously. I wondered where the catch would be, and how we could be robbed of the little indemnity granted us daily for the loss of our freedom. Rumors ran in the *Kommando* that the exchange was going to be as poor as six francs for one mark; but letters from home testified that the money had arrived and been computed at the official rate of twenty francs for one mark. Instead of a few, almost every prisoner applied to send the minimum thirty marks every two months. With 600 francs, his wife or his mother could buy very little food, under the existing conditions; but she could pay the rent of an average apartment in the big cities, or of a house in the small ones.

This measure was beautifully played up by the enslaved press. The reaction in the camps was one of gratitude, but even more so in France. Nothing has a more reassuring effect than a little money coming in regularly. The husband, the father, the son, were captives, and yet sent their salary home. It was a little as if they had only gone away to work.

The Nazis have made considerable efforts to make themselves accepted in France. As often as they could, they have dissimulated their brutal egoism. The plunder of our national wealth has been covered with French bank notes, (printed by the Germans, of course) in unlimited number. Now they paid for the prisoners. It was unexpected and appeared generous.

At the end of June 1941, at the conclusion of a resounding tirade, Hitler ordered all men having fought in the previous

World War, freed. Later he extended the measure to the father of five children, and the elder of seven brothers. Only several tens of thousands were thus restored to their families; and I have no doubt that measures were taken for the direct, or indirect, integration of these men in the German war effort in France.

It is because I believe that the Nazis are very dangerous, that I am trying to identify them completely. Too much simplification in their description plays into their hands: it prevents them from being recognized when they come around with hearty smiles.

Nazism has showed us two faces: one of utmost brutality, carried out particularly well by the SS, the advanced sections of the armies and the Gestapo; and one of comprehension, and humanity carried by certain administrators and propagandists. The method is perfectly clear: first, the invaded country is frightened into complete submission; second, it is reassured and induced to collaborate. Nazism works at its best in a mixture of fear, confusion, and hope. Special agents see that these conditions are produced.

It is perhaps the greatest originality of Hitler to have used well-measured generosity, in conjunction with terrifying horrors, in his endeavor to deepen our defeat.

One can never understand the apparent apathy of the French people after the rout, and until the American invasion of North Africa, without realizing their condition, and the double character of the Nazi methods of conquest. After a thorough demonstration of overwhelming power by the *Wehrmacht* who had, in one month, invaded even more of France than they later occupied, and America having failed to answer favorably the last-hour call to help, it seemed obvious, in France, that the British would soon share our fate. Then the Nazis, from whom everyone expected only horrors and destruction, showed

Forced Labor

themselves apparently understanding and even helpful. They stretched a hand towards their victims, instead of crushing them completely as they had done with the Poles. They reserved their well known cruelties for the Jews and the active Communists. These two groups were small in France, and the misinforming press has disfigured their martyrdom. Shot every day as hostages, they were identified as terrorists, inspired fools, dangerous to everyone; or British agents, causing only "justified" reprisals.

The Germans have failed to bring the great majority of Frenchmen to their side, but, for a time, they have convinced them that the best policy is to lie quiet, and not render entirely impossible a collaboration with the new European masters who held their sons as hostages. The increasing privations imposed by the occupation, have been blamed principally on the pre-war politicians responsibile for our defeat.

The opinions in the camps followed similar trends, because the prisoners reasoned in terms of their families, and of their homes that they hoped to regain soon.

Remaining alone at war with our captors, England had everyone's sympathy, but when the German-controlled newspaper reproduced British news saying that an Allied flyer had succeeded in bombing both ends of a tunnel, so as to trap a whole train, somewhere in the north of France, my comrades said:

"My mother, my wife, my children, may have been on that train!" And they anxiously awaited the next letters.

Most men in the world are willing to face death for their ideals; but how many would sacrifice their mother? Many of the British measures taken, very logically, in the interest of victory, worked against the French. The British couldn't help it if, when bombing a German war factory in France, they killed many French workers; but the latter couldn't be expected to approve of it. I was already in occupied France when the first mass bombing of the huge Renault factories, near Paris, killed 600 civilians, including many women and children, living in the vicinity. While the bombing was going on, the enthusiastic Frenchmen waved their arms through the windows; but not so in the quarters that were being demolished. The Germans, of course, saw there the proper occasion to play one of their favorite comedies: they sent military delegations and flowers to the funerals of the victims. They shook hands with the crying families, and looked indignant — as if they had not killed many, many more French mothers and wives! They contributed to the relief fund. Their attitude amounted to this: we have killed you and robbed you as much as we wanted to and now we are going to be your friends. Look at the bandits now attacking you, preventing supplies from coming to you from your colonies! Of those supplies, the Germans, of course, requisitioned eighty per cent, but twenty per cent went to the population which, in great need of this little supplement, could not possibly be happy to lose it.

The beaten Frenchmen felt that even their friends were against them. Three thousand miles away from where the bombs fall, it is much easier to realize what necessary sacrifices must be made in order to beat the common enemy, but one could not hope for a complete independence of views from a semi-starved people exposed to constant propaganda, and to whom three very hectic years have brought many extra reasons to be confused.

A majority of prisoners, to which I have never belonged, was ready to make concessions to the victor, to try to live with him as long as there was no other sound possibility, and as long as he, too, showed himself willing. Until America was at last swung into the war, it seemed to be a normal attitude, dictated by the average man's will to survive, and by his con-

Forced Labor

fidence that the fantastic ascension of Hitler would be followed by an equally fantastic fall. It lacked heroism, but it was objective. It revolted me, yet I believe that any other large democratic country, in the same situation, would have behaved the same way. France, as a whole, should hardly receive more blame for her attitude than should America until Pearl Harbor, for having waited so long in order to be strong enough to face the powerful Axis.

Since Pearl Harbor, the possibility for a democracy to win over fascism, has reappeared; and the resisting minority in France has suddenly increased. In my camp, December 7, 1941 was a day of tremendous joy. I made fun of the fairly accurate details given by the German Press on the American naval losses. So great was the confidence of every prisoner, in the United States of America, that not one of us could believe that they would repeat our mistake. Fortunately, Pearl Harbor was in the middle of the ocean.

*   *   *

The incarnation of the special intentions of Hitler, concerning the prisoners, is the *Sonderführer*. Every *Stalag* has been provided with an officer in charge of the mentality of the prisoners in the main camp, and in the numerous *Kommando*. Representing the *Stalag* II C, *Sonderführer* Lingsch, a lieutenant, had no other function than that of travelling from *Kommando* to *Kommando*, bringing books, helping the formation of theatre groups, sport teams and libraries, and convincing us, by his charming and considerate manners, that the "honest face of Nazism" was not a mere shadow of the brutal one with which we were better acquainted.

In his early thirties, Lieutenant Lingsch was a professor of languages, and had spent enough time in a French University, before the war, to speak our language with a rare perfection. He first brought us a two-hour-long moving picture show that proved rather disappointing, because it consisted of documents of the life of youth in Germany: healthy youngsters marching like soldiers, with a shovel on the shoulder, digging trenches, living in camps. It is rather characteristic that the first expression of national socialism is to give everyone a spade, as the Egyptians did to their slaves, and the lords to their serfs. Debunking the show was only too easy for me, and I told the *Sonderführer* that my boys would rather see Charlie Chaplin.

"They work with a shovel all day, so it represents something decidedly unpleasant to them."

He didn't bring us any more shows, but instead, a box of fifty books, to serve as a lending library. It contained thirty French novels of the last century, carefully combed by the censorship of the *Stalag*, and bearing its stamp: "*Geprüft.*" A few recent books, written by French traitors, reviewed our downfall with some accuracy, but, disgustingly, drew all conclusions in favor of the Nazis. One of them initiated us into the stupidities and horrors of anti-Semitism, now renewed and shaped into a religion, a philosophy, and a mode of government. The collection was completed by a few books written in German: one Schiller or Goethe, a few speeches by the big Swastikas, and a couple of picture books on old German buildings.

Twice a week, my comrades could call at a little storeroom latticed off in a corner of the ship, for one of these books, or for any from another library that we had assembled with all the books individually owned by the prisoners. But, Herr Lingsch, as long as I supervised the library, I saw to it that only the thirty French novels were offered to my comrades. I read the German classics with pleasure, but I examined the other books, with a little committee of fine men who were

Forced Labor

anxious only to find arguments against you, or at least study your methods so as to oppose them better.

It would be unfair to omit that the *Sonderführer* obtained a basketball for us, and provided our theatrical group and orchestra with badly needed material. After the fall of 1941, he visited my camp once a month, and spent hours talking with me. He greatly praised, and seemed to appreciate, the efforts that I, and a group of devoted comrades, made to organize distractions for the others. He was gentle, discreet, earnest. I would have liked to like him, and perhaps he would have liked to like me.

No better evidence could be given that the *Sonderführer's* efforts were aimed at increasing our subjugation, than his attitude in the case of the non-commissioned officers of the camp. The 1929 Geneva Convention granted them the right to refuse to go to work. At first, this was accepted in the *Stalag*, though a certain number of sergeants and top sergeants had preferred the active life of a *Kommando* to the starving stagnation in the barracks, and volunteered for work, thus losing definitively their right to idleness. But when, in the early part of 1941, the increased mobilization in view of the campaign against Russia increased Germany's need for workmen, the Geneva Convention was forgotten, and the noncommissioned sent to work. The *Stalag* II B, for instance, had sent fifty-five sergeants, along with the few hundreds passed over to the *Stalag* II C, to form this *Kommando Nordenham*. Given as workers to the *Kommandoführer*, the latter would not listen to their complaints. He sent them to the various firms; and there was no controlling officer around to whom one might complain. As soon as I had gained a sufficient experience as *Vertrauensmann*, and realized the possibilities left to me, I raised the issue at the *Kontrollstelle:*

"Fifty-five sergeants are compelled to work in my camp,

though they have never volunteered. They ask to be returned to the main camp."

The *Kontrollstelle* replied that on one hand, no collective reclamation could be made, and on the other, that the prisoners having come a few months ago from another *Stalag,* it was not known whether or not they had volunteered before. So I started a few individual reclamations. They went as far as the colonel commanding the *Stalag,* and he sent me the following answer:

"There is no place in the barracks of the *Stalag.* These non-commissioned officers must wait."

Wait, of course, while working for Germany. . . . But the conclusion was that, very soon, an individual mutation arrived for them. They were sent to work in another *Kommando* — a smaller one, where the *Vertrauensmann* has fewer chances to see a controlling officer, and less experience in bothering the authorities. In this way the prisoners who bring any difficulty are disposed of.

Another method to obtain the same violation of the Geneva Convention, and yet keep the possibility of fooling any International Committee of Control, has been the creation of special camps for noncommissioned officers, where great care is taken to keep them from growing fat, or losing their suppleness. In the name of health, they are forced to exercise at all hours of the day or night. They do only military exercises: run, stop, run, jump, lie down — but they lie down in a mud puddle, jump over obstacles a little too high, and run too fast. . . . Any refusal would be a breach of discipline, and harshly punished.

When they have enough of this camp, they volunteer for work!

I interviewed the *Sonderführer* on this question, and gave him all the necessary details. He showed himself abashed and indignant:

Forced Labor

"Why didn't I see all the efforts he made to improve our distractions in the camp? Was all of that in vain? Weren't we willing to co-operate a little? Germany needed help to 'realize the greater Europe' in which we could take for granted that a good place would be reserved for us — but of course, only in the proportion that we, ourselves, would have made it possible."

The conclusion was given by our own blind ambassador for war prisoners. The *Trait d'Union* published an article by him, urging the noncommissioned officers to volunteer to work, so as to render possible the liberation of all fathers of more than four children, generously agreed upon by Hitler. A little later, the same blind man announced that he had obtained a great improvement in our condition in the small country *Kommando:* the sentries would be suppressed wherever possible. The prisoners would be locked up at night by their employers, and their *Vertrauensmann* would be responsible for them. In exchange for this, they should not try to escape. We *should not* try to escape!

A fine idea to economize a few German sentries. Such a measure was never taken in Stettin; but it has been realized in several *Kommando* in Berlin, and great publicity given to it.

*　　*　　*

The *Sonderführer* always spoke of Marshal Pétain with the highest respect, and once brought, as a special gift, a beautiful portrait of the old man, printed in full color, five by three feet, with the recommendation to give it a good place in the camp. I did so, but added a little strip of paper with the inscription: "Offered by the *Stalag*." Some of my comrades suggested that we frame it with barbed wires.

Though most of them were convinced of his sincerity and love for our country, the publicity that the Germans gave him, the very reactionary tendencies of his decrees, and his association with the most hated and despised Prime Minister Laval, weakened and confused his influence. Yet so great was the need to believe in one man representing the country, that it was not infrequent to see, pinned at the foot of the bunk, on the boat, one of the post cards that the French Red Cross included in the packages, representing the Marshal with seven stars on his sleeve, and a worried look on his face.

The collective gifts that were sent to us from France were called "Pétain Gifts." The *Trait d'Union* spoke of him as the Saviour. In many camps, but not in mine, Pétain Clubs were formed. Every month, a little inquiry came from the *Stalag*, about the *Vertrauensmann*, worded thus:

"Name, first name, age, profession. Is he a follower of Pétain?" to which my *Kommandoführer* answered "*Ja*" without asking me — thus sparing me one more lie.

In the fall, the *Trait d'Union* made considerable propaganda about some prison camps that had given large sums to the French Winter Relief. I could not help asking my comrades what they wanted to do about it:

"Do you want me to organize a collection for the benefit of this new organization that we know very little about? Do you feel confident that this money will be employed exactly as you'd like it to be? Don't you believe it might be better to send whatever money you have, to your own family, with the recommendation that they contribute if they think it's a good thing to do?"

At the same time, one of our comrades was killed accidentally while working on the pier, and I took advantage of it to unite my comrades in their sympathy for the widow. In no time, a sum of 1100 marks was collected for her, to the astonishment

Forced Labor

of the Germans, so accustomed, already, to count on government agencies for all relief. For another comrade, who lost his hand, we subscribed a fund of 800 marks to help him start a little business in France as soon as he'd be sent back home. No contribution was sent to the Pétain Winter Relief, but a permanent fund was created in the camp, for the benefit of our most unfortunate comrades.

I realized that this attitude towards Pétain resulted from hesitation, rather than conviction, lacking material on which to found any.

We spoke often about De Gaulle, "the Number One traitor" as the *Trait d'Union* called him; but, most unfortunately, we knew little about him and the Free French Movement. He was represented, in the German papers, as having delivered part of the French Colonies to the British, and attacked several of the others remaining faithful to the other France, to which Hitler gave orders. Never did we get hold of a Gaullist tract dropped by British planes, though they would have had great influence among us. The only British tract I could ever see was one dated in the spring of 1941, and indicating the contribution of the United States of America, not yet at war, to the war effort of England. We made as many copies of it as we could, and they circulated as important secrets. No prisoner ever met another, belonging to a different *Kommando*, either at work on the pier, or in the hospital, without transmitting the comforting information. It may have stretched very far.

De Gaulle was naturally sympathetic, in as much as the Germans hated and feared him, but how much I could have done if I had had a little material. He would have become the symbol of all resistance against them.

I had to limit my efforts to annulling the Nazi propaganda exercised upon us. Every two months, the *Kontrollstelle* sent a magazine called *France Allemagne*, written partly in French, and partly in German, and accompanied by a form on which the *Vertrauensmann* of the camp should testify that he had kept the copy in circulation for three weeks. There are now quite a few copies of this subversive publication, bearing an ominous lie followed by my own signature and captivity number, for they did not go beyond my drawer in the office. Before transmitting them to another *Kommando*, as required, I soiled them with dust and ruffled the pages. I hoped that the next *Vertrauensmann* would do the same.

With a better literary content, this magazine was more venomous than the translations of Hitler's speeches. It played a European Dream Song, so to speak: Men (victims of Hitler), let's take the great German victories as an opportunity to unite Europe once for all, and rid our future of any other intestinal war. There is a strong argument in the fallacious words. Also, all that could be written about Hitler's positive achievements was heightened by clever juxtaposition with what could be written against the past policies of his enemies. Everything was done to render inconspicuous the inhuman principles and barbaric methods of Nazism, that render urgent and unavoidable its complete abolition.

I'm afraid that my elimination of such magazines was a rather dictatorial act, although I had warned my comrades that I would spare them as much enemy-propaganda as I could. In fact I feared that the subtlety of our literary traitors, or Fascists, would impress the prisoners who were insufficiently prepared against them — and that means the majority of them.

Yet, ignoring our own mistakes as well as the good points of our enemy, to concentrate only on his more obvious vices, may prove a poor policy, and leave the door open to an attack in the rear. It is possible that some day a few good aspects of the Nazi administration and its better achievements, now ignored by the public, or denied, or simply decried, together

Forced Labor

with its failures and abominable crimes, will be most conveniently discovered, and that a consequent reversal of opinion may be used to wreck the new victory of the Allies, as was the case after the other World War.

In camp, I have observed that moderate little speeches, delivered in a corner of the yard, in the latrines, in the washroom at night, to little groups of comrades who would later repeat and circulate them around, were more effective than furious invectives.

"We suffer many privations, but we don't exactly starve. Though no one in the world would be willing to swap his freedom for our captivity, we fare a little better than our legitimate irritation at the guards and the barbed wires allows us to realize. The Nazis do not steal our individual packages, as we had feared. They authorize, and even encourage, Sunday distractions. They let us send our savings home, and it is rumored that our salaries may be increased. What does that show? It shows that we are essential to Nazi Germany, as horses are necessary to the farmer. An improvement in our condition means that we shall be kept captive a long time, and that any promise to the contrary is as much of a lie today, as it has been in the past."

Thus the little advantages granted us by the *Stalag* lost the character of favors that the *Sonderführer* tried to give them, and appeared what they were: *newer, cleverer means of oppression.*

*   *   *

While the *Sonderführer* represented the Propaganda Service of the army, the *Unterlagerführer* represented the civil administration. He was equally anxious to influence our opinions.

Much shorter than his superior, *Herr Lagerführer* Opferer,

he was as big, but didn't look it because his fat was regularly disposed around his spine. He was very much like a pot. He claimed to have been one of the first followers of Hitler, as early as 1923; with a sweet voice betraying no ferocity. He seemed fond of Frenchmen, and as long as he remained in the camp, I always went to him in order to patch up any difficulty. He soothed Opferer's constant furor against us. It was indeed, after he had been sent to head another *Lager*, that our portions thinned out so dramatically. He probably had enough sense to keep the plunder of our rations within reason.

He never met me without assuring me that the fate of France would be excellent under Nazi rule, as soon as we should have understood Hitler's message and eliminated the elements soiling our race. When I asked him what had become of Hitler's earlier intentions to wipe France off the map, he protested that these were only consequences of the bitterness created by the Versailles Treaty, but that the *Führer* also had evolved, and now realized the possibilities of my country. His story varied a little, though, from day to day. One evening when his heart was bursting with enthusiasm, he took me to his room and showed me, on a world map, the highest schemes of his Idol: a line joining the lower border of French Brittany to Rostov, on the Azov sea; and another, joining Rostov to the North Cape, in Norway.

"This will be the Great Aryan country," he said. "It will be wonderful, and so powerful that the whole world will receive its directions from it."

The *Unterlagerführer* believed what he said. As a person in love registers the object of his passion through one dominating aspect that gives a new color to all other aspects, he saw in Hitler as pure a figure as the French lass, Joan of Arc. He was full of love for the world. He excepted, though, the Jews and the Poles. The Jews, for him, were men that Lucifer had for-

255

Forced Labor

ever poisoned. They could not be considered as men, any more. When I asked him if getting rid of the Jews had cured Germany of all her troubles, he admitted that it hadn't; but explained it by the crimes of another category, that he called, comically enough, the "white Jews," as if the others had been green, or violet, or black. They were Aryans poisoned by the Jewish culture, but they might be redeemed; otherwise they should be erased.

The Poles were impossible people, treacherous and decadent. I could recognize that he placed on them all that Hitler had once said about the French — perhaps because they had resisted him so well. The Russians belonged to Asia, and should be more or less repulsed towards Siberia — except the Ukrainians, so deeply influenced by the Germans, etc.

Unfortunately, the Germans I have talked to were unanimous against the Jews and the Poles, so persistent had been the propaganda against them, and perhaps, also, because it is agreeable to anyone to have a black sheep on which to pin the responsibility for all troubles. Even in Bornzin, where the farm hands had never seen a Jewish person in their lives, they despised the Jews. When the prisoners sat at their meals with their caps on, the Germans said, quite often:

"Look at the Jew."

One cannot hope that it will be enough to beat Hitler's armies in order to suppress all the wrongs he has created. His influence may remain, even among his very victims. Old trends of injustice and brutality have been dangerously revived.

The *Unterlagerführer* accused the British of all the horrors that are attributed to Hitler by the rest of the world: they were inhuman, brutal, and stole the wealth of the countries that they occupied. He quoted the daily communiqué saying that every British bomb fell on a church, on a school house, on a hospital, or on a lone house with old people in it. I suggested that if the

British flyers could be so accurate and never miss these deplorable objectives, it seemed rather strange that they wouldn't, once in a while, aim their bombs at a big war factory. But that didn't disturb him. He knew his Nazi catechism; he recited his holy texts: "Hitler has said, on such a day" or "Goebbels has written . . ."

"You may not approve of our methods," said the *Unterlagerführer* "because democracy has rendered you weak; but you cannot doubt the gravity and purity of our intentions."

A most dangerous fellow, the little fat man with his clear eyes and candid smile. Not only did he attribute the systematic starvation to which I had been subjected, in June 1940, to technical impossibilities, but he declared that since the Armistice, the Nazis had done nothing at all against the French population. I once had the opportunity to checkmate him.

We kept a shoemaker in the camp to repair the shoes and sabots of the others, with whatever little material we could obtain from the *Stalag*, or that the men would pick up here and there: old tires, pieces of tin, etc. He was from Lille, and showed me a bunch of pathetic letters from his wife. She informed him that two of their three children had been taken away from her and sent to Germany. She was in the movies with them, on Sunday, when a newsreel of a British bombing of Berlin had been shown. Part of the spectators applauded. She had not; but the show was interrupted, everyone pushed out, and at the door, her two boys, eleven and fourteen years old, had been taken by German soldiers, as were all other boys in the crowd. She had had no news of them for several weeks. Finally the elder had written from Germany that he was following an apprentice course, and would soon work in a factory. The little one was restored to her later, but forced to work in a near-by factory. All of this information was not given at once, but divided in several letters, each one giving a brief

Forced Labor

but clear reference to the other, so that the facts stood out clearly when one read all the letters in succession. Without that precaution, no letter would have passed through the *Stalag* censorship. The mother didn't comment. She had only written:

"I am so lonesome, now, without them."

I copied the letters, made as accurate a translation of them as I could, and took the papers to the *Unterlagerführer*. He was shocked, but concluded that the boys must have made manifestations against the Germans, although the letters denied it. When I assured him that this measure was generalized in the so-called "Forbidden zone of France," and too obviously a complementary solution of Germany's lack of manual workers, he promised to make an inquiry through the Nazi party.

By a fortunate coincidence, the elder of the two boys was sent to a Stettin factory, and while walking through the city with other boys in his situation, during their few hours of freedom in the evening, he called to every column of prisoners passing in the street:

"Do you know my father, So-and-So, from *Kommando* XIII/226?"

This was reported to me and I was able to manage a secret exchange of notes between the two. The boy gave many details about his capture, making it even more shocking; but of course I could not produce them as supplementary evidence.

Each time that I asked him about the results of his pretended inquest, the *Unterlagerführer* said that he had had no answer; but he looked sincerely sad. He couldn't have helped finding out that the facts were true, even if he had never heard of them before. If he hadn't the face to admit this comparatively mild example of Nazi repression in France, how violently would he have denied the many crimes that everyone knows, and, what is worse, how fanatically would he have hidden them under mysterious stories, guaranteed by his own kindness.

So even the German people are deceived by kind propagandists — for he was kind. Several times he gave me an extra loaf of bread and a piece of sausage, for some of my boys who never received packages from home.

CHAPTER 15

The Prisoners

For the *Kommandoführer*, a prisoner was essentially any one of perhaps 1200 green cards, four inches by five, in a file. These cards were divided into ten compartments. In the upper left stood the captivity number; next came the surname, first name, age, nationality. The last compartment to the right bore the name of the employer: Kronibus, Brandt, Mast. . . . At the bottom, a long space was left for such remarks as:

"Eight days in jail from . . . to . . ."

More than 500 of the cards were barred by a heavy red line meaning that they were no longer in our *Kommando*. The remark would be:

"Transferred to *Kommando* X on . . . ," or "admitted to the Stargard Hospital on . . ." or — and what pleasure it gave me to inscribe it! —"*Geflohen*," meaning: gone home without asking the *Kommandoführer's* permission.

When a prisoner came to the office, for one reason or another, I would extract his individual card from the file, and hand it over to the *Kommandoführer*, who would say:

"Is this he?" as if all the reality of this being had lain in the paper, and the living man was only an identification of the card — a better photograph, too big to be attached in the corner. From the man himself, he required only a voice to answer "Here" when his name was called, and a pair of arms to wield a mattock or a hammer for the firm mentioned on the green card.

Kind to the man sitting next to him in the office, *Unteroffizier* Ehlert was particularly indifferent to what might happen to any other, provided that the little rectangle of paper, of the same name, stood in good order. When the prisoner left the office, his number would be delicately set in its place in the file, in a nice box of clear ash, and the top drawn over it. As far as Ehlert was concerned, this prisoner would now fall into the hold of the ship, like an enormous sardine in a big can, sealed at night and unsealed in the morning, by sentries whose bayonet was a better kind of fork.

It is only when the man disappeared — when a dozen Germans combing every corner of the *Nordenham* and of the yard attached to it, could not find any trace of him — that *Unteroffizier* Ehlert became conscious of the place he had occupied in space. The card laid on his desk made a shocking spot. Why hadn't it, too, disappeared? From it he had now to realize what kind of man this was who had suddenly found legs to walk in a direction that the bayonets didn't point out for him. He discovered that he had never seen him, and yet would have to talk about him all day, as long as the inquest should last; telephone, write down information for which he would have to count on the sentry and on me — that is to say most confused and contradictory. When the disappearance should have been accepted by the *Kontrollstelle* — whether the fugitive had been caught, killed, imprisoned, or whether he had not yet been found — the *Kommandoführer* would derive an immense comfort from watching Paul or me driving a thick red line across the card, that would squeeze all the trouble out of it. Now it would go back peacefully to the file, and the ship would again be filled with only a long, monotonous chain of numbers.

To me, it was the opposite. When I had arrived — lost in the column at first, then picked out and confronted with it — the *Kommando* had seemed to be a mass also; but a mass of beings identical with myself. Each time a prisoner had come to me for any reason, I had registered how he differed from me: stronger; more timid; shorter; what he did that I wouldn't do;

Forced Labor

etc., and, progressively, I became very conscious of his personality, without completely eliminating my own image that I had first recognized under his brown coat; it remained like a core. That is perhaps why I resented so violently anything done against my comrades, and why they have so magnificently helped me to impress the Germans with the incoercible vitality of a race previously described to them as utterly decadent.

During one year, my *Kommando* had absorbed all my energies, to the extent of a passion and a mania. I felt it constantly around me. I bore it in mind under many different aspects, each of them offering two versions: the open one, that anybody could see; and the other, carefully hidden from the *Kommandoführer*, and which only a few sentries may have vaguely suspected.

The 600 or 700 men of the Kommando were divided into two main bodies: the boys lodged in the foredeck hold; and the boys lodged in the afterdeck hold. For the Sunday review, they were lined separately. This was one aspect. Both offered different characters according to the influence of the best men they contained, and to the *hasard* of the various personalities. The foredeck crew was more intellectual, a little cleaner, and considerably tougher. The afterdeck crew was always inferior in number, more ingenious, more fussy, and more romantic. Among the latter there were more attempts to escape as well as a greater percentage of sick. There had been some exchanges between the two. To join friends — and in spite of regulations to the contrary — men had taken their straw sack and belongings to the other side. Each side had settled down, and achieved a certain individuality that the men knew and appreciated.

The division of the whole camp in thirty odd "firms" produced a very different aspect. Prisoners from both sides were mingled inside one firm. I saw them, every morning, in the yard, around their sentry, and waiting for the man, in every group, who is always the last to come. They were counted, presented to the *Kommandoführer*, who gave the order to go, and made a horizontal bar on the daily control sheet. When they came back at night, he would complete the cross with a vertical bar.

The word "firm" meant to me exclusively this particular group of men, alike and yet different, who suffered together all day. Two stood out. One was the man that they had openly chosen as representative, a devoted comrade who handled the difficulties at work and reported them to me in the evening. He went for the cold rations for the "firm," helped in the repartition of the gifts from the Red Cross, helped me to establish the numerous lists always needed, and communicated to his men the changes, occurring quite often, in the camp rules. It meant extra work; but he was exempt from the obligation of peeling the turnips or potatoes in the evening.

It had taken me five months of requests, explanations and pleas, to have this idea of a man responsible in each firm, accepted by the *Kommandoführer*, and, at the same time, to persuade the *Lagerführer* to have the cold portions distributed in boxes, by "firm," instead of to one man at a time.

The second man was equally devoted to his comrades, but more important to me. He should remain inconspicuous to the Germans. He was the soul and the nerves of the growing resistance of his group against them. I had chosen him myself. His was the real face of the firm: blank and patient on the surface, violent underneath.

I considered the sentry, the overseer, and finally the employer, as secondary accessories to each of the thirty-odd working groups; but they influenced its character. Whatever the individual quality of the prisoners assembled in one firm, if the sentry was mean, the overseer grumpy, and the work hard, they would enter the gate at night, provoked, bitter, emaciated,

Forced Labor

hard to handle. They would be revolutionary only if my trustee was strong, convincing, popular. If the sentry was comprehensive, and let them walk slowly, and talk in the street, they wouldn't look like mad dogs, as did the men that Guard Schlegel — to name only one — handled so brutally. According to their work, they would be very muddy, discolored with cement, or comparatively clean. They might be in a position to see much of the harbor, and bring me substantial information, or, on the contrary, working underground, they would only meet rats and old skeletons.

Each unit became a family, with its colorful types: the clown who provided the jokes; the *"elegant"* who provided the fashions, such as the way to set the cap the most shockingly possible, or the replacement of the collar button of the topcoat by a string, so as to be able to wear it as a cape, in spite of regulations. Another was the practical man, who found a solution to the problems of how to cook stolen potatoes, and how to protect one's old shoes from burning lime, by dipping them in mud every morning.

*   *   *

Of the thirty "firms," employing each from four to sixty men, five of the largest were the hardest. None was worse than "Kronibus." For eleven hours a day, its fifty-five prisoners dug a huge tunnel under the main railway station of Stettin, to be used as underground communication, as well as air-raid shelter. One week out of two, they worked at night. Forty men from another Kommando, and some Belgian civilians, dug with them.

Especially where a large number of men is employed, in Nazi Germany, a heavy staff of superintendents, inspectors, overseers, and controllers is kept on their back. For ten men, one at least has no other function than to bother them, report them, and provide them with the shouts that are thought indispensable in order to obtain more work.

Digging is always hard, but in tunnels, more so than anywhere else. It is dangerous, and the ventilation is either nil or terrific. It was so cold in the Kronibus tunnel, in winter, that little coke-stoves were kept burning, but the fumes were so poisonous that the men working on scaffolds, near the ceiling, fainted: freezing would have been better. When, by chance, and only too rarely, an air-raid alarm was given, the lights went out in the tunnel as well as outside, and the prisoners enjoyed a voluptuous hour of rest, nestled against each other, soon asleep, and dreaming that the whole city was being obliterated.

While some employers had found it to their advantage to distribute an extra bowl of vegetable soup to the prisoners, in the middle of the day, or at night, to complete the sandwiches they brought, the Kronibus group was granted only a cup of unsweetened ersatz coffee. They came back to the *Nordenham*, around 6 A.M. exhausted and furious. The whole camp had agreed that a little of our daily portion of soup should be kept as an extra for the night firms, but it was not substantial enough to help them much.

While the day-firms gathered noisily in the yard, the night shift would wash a little, then get inside the boat and try to sleep; but they were to be disturbed all day. The cleaning squad came first, to sweep the floors and set every stool at the foot of the bed. The assistant *Kommandoführer* came later, for a loud inspection. The sick, allowed to stay in camp for a day or two, went up and down the stairs. When the postal wagons brought a few hundred packages — on an average of once a week, but sometimes three days in succession — it meant a cavalcade of all available men carrying the sacks to the storeroom, and going back for more. The sabots made a thundering noise on the steps. Nothing, however, was worse than the

Forced Labor

mania of the ship's captain to keep a little part of his crew tapping off the paint from the sides of the rusting freighter, with little steel hammers. All day long, the sailors worked outside, on hanging platforms, and the hammering resounded in the holds like static in a gigantic loud-speaker. Even with ears filled with cotton, and the flaps of the cap turned down on top, one could not rest.

Captivity is hard on everyone, on account of the privation of many little joys of life that compensate for its pains, but when one is driven to utmost fatigue, it is an infernal condition that no free person can realize. An obstacle, light for anyone else, may prove insurmountable to him. The level of a prisoner's life is already so low, that any new diminution of his very little share of tranquillity is excruciating. A hardened prisoner whose ribs have often been pounded in the past, and who is now comparatively better treated, may well not sleep for a whole night, simply because a sentry has just told him a current insult. He had heard it 1000 times before with indifference, but always at his work. It had been part of the unpleasantnesses of the day. He was not accustomed to it when he had retired on his straw sack. Proffered without particular meaning, perhaps, by a sentry provoked at having been ordered to a curfew inspection of the boat, the well-known insult had caught him unprotected, off guard, when he relaxed from the sneering attitude that renders a prisoner invulnerable to vexations. I have known an excellent man become fiercely mad because there had been no meat in his bowl of soup for the fourth successive day; and he spent more energy in his rage than the missing ounce of protein would have given him. Others became vexed to the point of speaking to no one for days, because I had been unable to find trousers big enough for them, in the storeroom, to replace theirs completely torn, and which they had refused to mend any more.

THE PRISONERS

One might say that a man can take a lot of punishment provided he is left a little margin of privacy, a small source of
pleasure in which, and with which, he may retire to recuperate when he feels downtrodden. The smallest attack on this vital
minimum, will prove more cruel than direct brutality. What
constitutes this indispensable privacy and pleasure, no one else
knows, exactly. The prisoner keeps it a secret, or perhaps is
not even conscious of it. That explains how someone you have
known as strong, patient, well balanced, will suddenly break
down before a difficulty that you can hardly realize, but which
happened to hit his only comfort. I have heard my best man
among the "Kronibus" cry like a small child because of the
endless tapping on the steel plates. He hadn't even the energy
to go to the fourth floor, and lie on any bunk in the corner
where the noise resounded less.

I went daily to the ship's captain, and begged him to stop it.
He would, once in a while, for a couple of days. Then it started
again.

"That work has to be done all year around," he said. "Why
bother me with it? It's your own fault. Why did you let yourselves be taken prisoner?"

*   *   *

In vain did I try to have the men belonging to such hard
firms replaced periodically, but the employer would not allow
it: the prisoners had now acquired a valuable experience in
building their scaffolds, and protecting themselves against the
falling earth. Neither *Kommandoführer* Schumann nor Ehlert
was really mean, but they wouldn't exert themselves in behalf
of the prisoners. They had signed my letter to the employer,
on this subject, because it was already written; but they
wouldn't telephone and oppose such an important personality.

So, while most of my men had regained some weight — thanks

Forced Labor

to the packages received as often as twice a month from their families, and thanks to the contributions of the Red Cross — 180 of my comrades, sharing the harassing jobs, stayed emaciated and desperate.

During the summer of 1941, one of the easiest jobs was to transform the house-cellars into air-raid shelters. Distributed in a row of small houses, a few in each cellar, with perhaps one civilian, the prisoners could slow up their pace considerably. The overseer and the sentry couldn't be dogging them all day, and the German worker himself would not be over anxious to get through quickly with a pleasant job. Also, any German is far more understanding when alone, than when there are witnesses — so afraid is he of being reported as insufficiently Nazi.

Prisoners having had the luck to fall on these better jobs, returned from work in a good mood, ready to go through the evils of peeling vegetables, in the kitchen, and submitting to various camp obligations. In the evening, they might even play cards, or follow one of our classes.

In the fall, most mechanics and industrial workers were shifted to factories where their day lasted rarely more than nine hours. Sleeping on the premises, their accommodations were better. There would be an increased danger of bombing by the Allies. The old banana freighter was no more signaled to enemy aircraft as a prison camp than are all other *Kommandos*, and, like most of them, it was placed in a dangerous spot, namely, a railroad bridge over the Oder on one side, and an enormous depot of coal on the other, but it was a difficult target for a bomber, while most factories extend over a large area and can be recognized and destroyed more easily. A number of prisoners have been killed by the planes they were so happy to hear in the German skies.

The mental condition of the prisoners certainly varied with the conditions that they had met, and these were very irregular.

Some had always known harassing jobs and foul lodgings. Others had been moved every month, and known at least variety. Most prisoners will be more anxious to forget their captivity than talk extensively about it; but some of them may report on it with moderation, because they have had the double luck to get, and to stay in, bearable places.

I believe that such will be the case of a saddler who worked alone in a little shop, 100 yards from the *Nordenham,* and whose boss was so pleased with his work that he did his best to supply him with a little extra food. Sitting in a comfortable shop, manipulating the tool of his vocation, our comrade felt "prisoner" only at the end of the day, when he found a lousy bunk as a reward for his efforts.

Hard or light, the work imposed on us may not be worse than that of a civilian laborer, anywhere in the world. But the latter accomplishes his with good will, to raise money for his family, and build up his future. When tired at night, a wife, a few children, or a few friends, offer him affection and distraction. He enjoys good food and, for a few hours, he is able to do what he wants: walk around in the city, go to the movies, or sit down in a comfortable chair. Not only do prisoners get no other compensation for their forced labor than a few cents a day; but they have the discouraging feeling of working against themselves, by increasing the power of the men who keep them captive, and to be paying for the crimes, the faults, or the mistakes of others who now sit quietly at home, in France.

"Why should we, and we only, pay so much for a defeat of which we are no more responsible than the others?" asked my boys. "When we go back home, everything will have been changed. The best jobs will have been taken, the best girls married, and our own children will say, while pointing at us: 'Mother, who is that strange man?'"

*　　*　　*

Forced Labor

Every few days, an order came from the *Kontrollstelle* to send ten, twenty, fifty prisoners to one, or several other *Kommandos*. Though it is contrary to the interest of the employers, there is a constant shift of men from one place to another. After one year, only a third of the column with which I had arrived, remained on the boat. It may be that the Germans hope thus to render difficult relations with civilian workers, connections with the black market, and preparations for an escape.

Coming back from their day's work, my comrades would find, pasted on the panel by the distribution window, this sign: "Attention! Mutation!" and look anxiously for their name. The delay was always small. It would be the next morning, at the latest — perhaps in half an hour — that they would have to leave the little group whose intimacy had been precious to them. The *Arbeitsamt* decided how many men should be withdrawn from certain firms only. The large ones were rarely touched. Also, though many prisoners were not really employed in their profession, we had orders to keep around anyone of them who had manual qualifications: masons, and carpenters especially. The bulk of the mutations was always carried by the others: employees, teachers, business men, and peasants — the latter being liked everywhere for their all-around abilities.

With great effort, and all kinds of small pressure put on the *Kommandoführer,* I had been able to keep the major part of the men who played in our orchestra, aided in this by the fact that most of them were manual workers. I lost regularly the professors of the night classes, and it was difficult to find other men devoted enough and capable of teaching no matter what, after their ten or more hours of digging. The disappearance of some of the most colorful figures made holes, here and there, among the firms. Having lost its clown, one group became sad. Having lost a boy who always got in trouble, another became quiet. Having lost its directing head, another didn't respond any more to my efforts to give everyone a clear view of his fate, and of his possibilities. I would have to look for a strong man among them, pour faith in him, until his own would rise, and he would become capable of replacing the other.

So, sorry to leave a place to which they were now accustomed, and shaken by a little spirit of adventure, the boys ordered to go, would pack up. Fastidious, some of them put their clothes in good-looking paperboard suitcases, bought for six or eight marks from the canteen. If it rained, the handle would come off and the sides tear open gently. How much more practical was a burlap sack, attached at both ends with a strong cord, but everyone hadn't the chance to meet with one of these in a workshop or on a farm.

Extra bundles, of all descriptions would contain the rubbish accumulated in eighteen months of captivity: empty boxes, pieces of tin, wood, leather, rubber, strings, an old shoe, a sabot — all material most valuable in our precarious life. Its amount and quality was directly proportionate to the pioneering ability of the prisoner. Where one will constantly find something to pick up, another sees nothing. The best of the lot had gotten hold of marmalade pails — so priceless for soaking clothes, before washing — and hung them from their necks, with a string. Thus loaded, and lined up in the yard for the final review, the departing prisoners looked like a squadron of freshly recruited tramps. The *Kommandoführer* counted them, while I called their names and gave their individual clothes-lists to the sentry.

Every uniform item belongs to the Reich, and is recorded on this *"Bekleidungsliste"*: coat, overcoat, trousers, puttees, cap, shirts, sabots, shoes, and those square pieces of cloth that the French call *"Chaussettes Russes,"* and the German, *"Fuss-Lappen"* (literally foot rags. One wraps up his foot in them,

Forced Labor

like a pound of bacon, and pushes the whole thing in the shoe. It is most comfortable). A detailed list of all pieces of uniform existing in the camp, either on the back of the men, or in the storeroom; in good shape or reduced to a few buttons hanging from a patch, must be given to the *Kontrollstelle* every month. Each time a prisoner goes away, or arrives, his equipment must be added to, or subtracted from it. There is positively no end to the bureaucracy in the *Kommandoführung*.

When a prisoner receives a piece of clothing or a pair of shoes, in a package, he must show them to the *Kommandoführer* and obtain a certificate of private ownership. Otherwise they could be taken away from him.

The *Lagerführer* came around, too, with a couple of assistants, to make sure that every blanket, fork, knife, had been restored. For a missing spoon, the guilty prisoner would be compelled to pay half a mark. A cup cost one mark fifty *pfennigs*. If he claimed to have no money, this amount would be withdrawn from his back salary.

Collecting these back salaries was often complicated. There were contestations, and the little bundle of *Stalag* coupons would be forwarded, with a receipt that might not come back. In many small *Kommandos*, the sentry would not go to such trouble. The prisoner would lose his money, or wait until he met a *Vertrauensmann* obstinate enough to file back-claims, and protest to any possible office, until he obtained a result. With a heavy correspondence and much swearing – done exclusively at me – I have obtained the refund of salaries due for one full year. More than the few marks at last received, the impression of being defended and scoring one point over their captors, was gratifying to my comrades.

So strong is the bureaucratic system, with its files and printed rules, that a *Kommandoführer* who thought nothing of driving a prisoner wild with multiple punishments, could not refuse to spend hours for him, going through back pay rolls in search of the little sum that had not been handed out. Sometimes it was found that a sentry had received it, and simply pocketed it.

Hardly had I shaken hands with the departing comrades, whom I was likely never to meet again — than others, more ragged, equally loaded with strange belongings, as well as personal problems that I'd try to solve when I found time, would arrive to take their place. It is easier to obtain clothes-replacements in a large city *Kommando,* than in a small country one. The *Kontrollstelle* distributes them, but it is up to the *Kommandoführer* to claim our monthly allowance in time, in the proper forms, and exercise some subtle influence on the storekeeper, in order to avoid getting the worst lots.

Having welcomed the newcomers and searched in vain for some old comrade of the *Mézières* platoon, or the Bornzin farm, I took them, one by one, in the office to fill up their green identification card. Then, after advising them to get promptly acquainted with the multitude of rules posted in the distribution room, the Interpreter II, Maurice, directed them to their bunks, either foredeck or afterdeck. They climbed the chicken ladder, remarked on the fine view from the deck, opened the admission doors, and went down. Then, even the hardiest shriveled with disgust.

*   *   *

When I had arrived, months ago — or rather centuries ago — one freezing night, the boat smelled of old varnish and new wood. Now it stank of unclean bodies, of cheese rotting in cardboard boxes, and of all the emanations that the clothes had absorbed in the tunnels, in the workshops, on the piers: coal, oil, tar, mud, fertilizer.

The weak carbon bulbs shone less and fewer than ever, and

Forced Labor

one guessed more than saw, the strange constructions made of strings, canvas, paper, flattened crates, old board, invading the boat exactly like spider webs, but with more variety. The little alleys between the bunks had become impractical.

Every few weeks, a controlling officer would make a row, and order everything taken down; but the fancy shelves, hooks and screens, would grow again, irresistibly. They were needed for the clothes and the food, but even more, spiritually. More than ever, uniformity meant subjugation. With a little odd installation between their straw sack and the ceiling, the prisoners convinced themselves that their precious individualism survived. In fact, captivity had increased it to the point of exasperation.

The access to each hold, fore- and afterdeck, consisted of two double doors and simple steps divided by a banister. One was supposed to go down one side, and up on the other. When, in the middle of the night, a few hundred men, tormented by the potatoes and turnips, or occasional sauerkraut, opened the door, one after the other, a violent staccato of drafts swept the first floors and incommoded the men located, unluckily, in its course, without driving away the stench. It was deadly — in winter, especially — and amply justified the queer awnings, screens, and panels hung around the bunks like mosquito nets. Real mosquito nets would have been needed, also; for plenty of those insects flourished in the summer months, in our damp hole, and added their mad buzz and infected itch, to our torments.

*   *   *

When Finot and the other three prisoners consigned to cleaning the boat with the help of a few sick prisoners, dragged around their pitiful old brooms, their job was greatly complicated by the undergrowth, eating like a cancer into every corner, every narrow interstice where it could take support. It was to the advantage of the fleas.

Contrary to my predictions, the lice had not completely over-run the old boat. They stayed in the blankets and the straw sacks, undisturbed for six or eight months, for, in spite of many protests, I could not obtain new straw oftener. It was not straw that they brought us as replacement, but a very hard kind of kindling that reminded one's ribs of a regiment of Lilliputian sentries hitting with the butt end of the gun. One hesitated between the two unpleasantnesses, and sometimes preferred the old lousy nest. Besides, everyone fed colonies around the belt and armpits.

By washing my clothes very often, with the hot water run-ning from the exhaust pipe of the ship's engine, I could stay as long as a week without seeing any louse on me; but suddenly, the itching came back, and there would be half a dozen little ones rallying around the neck of my shirt. I spent part of the night investigating every crease of my clothes, until I found the big one responsible for the thriving litter.

Some of our comrades, especially the country men, were not that careful. They came back tired, at night, washed little, and were covered with enormous insects. Their chest was attacked by a repugnant eczema, provoked by the exasperating parasites. They would smash only the biggest of them between two fingernails — it made a pleasant little click — before going to bed! Others had a strange modesty, and would hide in the latrines, for this hunt; or renounce it altogether, rather than admit that they shared everyone's condition.

Every month, I would inscribe twenty or thirty of the worst to compulsory delousing. Loaded with their blankets and clothes, they would follow the sick column—led to the infirmary by the Slobberer, bewildered at this increase in responsibilities, and more brutal than ever. Whether the delousing system was

Forced Labor

insufficient, or the Germans in charge lazy, my comrades came back only a little less lousy than they had gone. It was of little use and, on account of the ten miles round trip, quite painful.

Much worse than the lice, though less disgusting, were the fleas. You had no chance to keep your own herd for yourself. They dwelt in the floors and jumped on you when you walked, and especially when you undressed. It was almost funny to see ten or twenty of them shooting, like fireworks, at your bare feet, and racing swiftly to the shelter of your underwear. Body cleanliness was no defense against them. By carefully washing the floor around your place, hanging your blankets in the icy air, in winter, or shaking them hard, in summer, you could get rid of some of them; but they would be as numerous two days later. I had obtained a few gallons of disinfecting product from the infirmary, but it was far from enough for the whole ship.

My comrades were partly responsible for this condition, because they could never be persuaded to fight the parasites all at the same time. I understood only too well that after ten or eleven hours of work, one or two hours spent waiting in the yard in the morning and evening for all the stupidities that the camp rule comprised, another hour waiting for their packages or letters, or at the office door to see me about their private troubles; they had little time, and even less energy, left for an hygiene otherwise hard to practice. It is doubly unfortunate that the more calamities inflicted on one man, the less able he is to defend himself. We lacked pails to carry the water; mops or rags to wipe it up. In most corners, there was no light.

The ventilating machinery could have been efficient enough if set in action regularly and all day long, instead of once in a while. It took one week, at least, to dry a pair of cotton socks hanging from your bunk; but a woolen one never dried.

Suddenly dumped in this atmosphere, the newcomers felt

frightened and much depressed. Yet they would become accustomed to it. Soon they would perceive the anarchic poetry of this cursed freighter that the sentries could not completely control, and learn to like it. It had a spirit, as well as a figure, of its own. We were known among the *Kommando* as *"Le Bateau"* (The Ship). The boys of the *"Bateau"* were tougher, more patriotic, determined, and experienced, than the others. A *Stalag* officer has paid me the honor to tell one of our fugitives unluckily caught on the Belgian border:

"You were from the *Nordenham,* in Stettin? I know; that's a school for escape."

There were, indeed, possibilities, that better lodgings could not offer, for hiding things that the Germans shouldn't see. They didn't like staying very long in the fetid hold, but one could disgust them even more by giving them a little taste of the evils imposed on us. When you sat on your stool, bare to the belt, and fingering your shirt — what had been a good French Army shirt and now bore, in thick, black, shameful type the hated notice: *"Stalag* IIC" and you held a healthy specimen of the German louse between your thumb and index finger, wasn't the temptation to put it back where it belonged, on a German uniform, absolutely irresistible? The fleas didn't need any help. They jumped of their own accord on the visiting sentries and *Kommandoführer.*

When I went around the floors, at night, in search of one or another of my comrades, they stopped me and made me tell them beloved bed-time true stories of the life in the *Kommandoführung,* such as this:

Unteroffizier Ehlert was more susceptible than anyone else to fleas. When he returned to the office, after the shortest visit on the boat, he would soon grunt, scratch, wriggle on his chair, and finally take down his trousers. He would search in there as one does for a lost item in a drawer full to the top: pushing,

Forced Labor

lifting, twisting, and squeezing his hands in the most awkward positions. The show became supreme when the telephone rang and then, holding it with one hand, and searching with the other, he answered:

"Who is this? *Ja wohl*, Herr Hauptmann" and setting himself mentally at attention, he became confused, and mixed his words. He soon heard a few remarks on his stupidity, so strongly worded by the said captain that he blushed, which made his bare paunch look even more sickly white. He could hardly wait for the end of the call, to release from his bosom all the oaths contained in the German language.

Then he would go back to his intimate explorations and, once a guilty party was deftly extracted from a crease of flesh, or of underwear, he would put it on the desk, hold it tight with a sharp pencil and say to my always disgusted colleague, Paul, and to me:

"Look at the brute. Isn't he big?" before avenging himself fiercely for the little itching red spots lining his loins.

CHAPTER 16

Distractions and Intellectual Life

I LINED the walls of the distribution room, adjoining the kitchen, with posters hastily scribbled with a stick of wood dipped in ink. One panel was covered with the camp rules: medical visit, care of the bed, where it was forbidden to smoke; warnings that the sentries had orders to shoot anyone seen between the latrines and the fence, or attempting to get across it; on getting off the boat after curfew, and as many equally unpleasant things that the *Stalag* had suggested, or the successive *Kommandoführers* invented. My boys would come in and say:

"Let's see what new thing has become forbidden today."

Another panel was devoted to the mail. Our tall comrade Lamy, a man of multiple functions — male nurse, storekeeper, postmaster, etc. — hung there the lists of lucky names for whom letters or packages had arrived.

A complete wall was pretentiously reserved for what I called the *"Ecole du Bateau"* (School of the Boat). It made a great impression on the newcomers to see there, under thick black headings much better written than the rest, all indications concerning our evening classes: German, English, elementary and superior French, building construction, mechanics, fencing, boxing, wrestling, and gymnastics. They would select one or two, note the day and hour and, in the evening, decide to go and find out what it really was.

The space between the canteen and the heavily barred bread storeroom concerned the shows particularly: comedy, singing, music, each had a long column of little posters.

In one corner, a curtain hung before a crude stage built of old boards that stuck out, two feet above the paved floor. It

Forced Labor

was made of green paper, with yellow ornaments both awkward and pretentious. It was ugly, but the camp was proud of it. Its story was that of a long fight with *Herr* Opferer, the foulest of all the *Lagerführer*.

* * *

THE THEATRE

No space had been reserved in this camp as recreation room. We were supposed to eat on board ship, either at the few tables placed here and there, or simply sitting on our stools. When it was not too cold, most of us preferred to eat outside, quickly, standing near the hot water exhaust pipe of the engines. It jutted out above the water, and by doing some acrobatism on a precarious board, we could wash our plates without getting too much of the shower on ourselves. The boat slid on its anchors on very windy days, and then it was impossible, but on calm days it almost touched the pier.

As we couldn't smoke on the boat, and as the latrines couldn't accommodate more than eighty men at one time, we had gradually invaded the distribution room. The *Lagerführer* had in vain chased the men away, many times. As soon as the distribution of food was over, and until curfew — when the sentries pushed them back to the boat — they stayed there, in an atmosphere of the main hall of a busy railway station, smoking like locomotives, with this difference: no pleasant trip was in sight.

On the very first Sunday, one comrade had climbed on a stool in the corner, and had sung. Others had followed. A little group had been formed. With a few benches, a little platform had been created. The others had brought their stools from the boat, and sat around. Unfortunately, not more than 350 men could be packed in, but the others could enjoy more space in the boat, and play cards or read there.

Those first improvised shows had been the best. One boy emerged from the crowd, got on a stool, looked around, a bit impressed, made a few "squawks" and let out a little song, always silly but touching. It seemed like a poor calendar picture copied by a naive amateur who, in the boldness of his ignorance, would make it beautiful, with vivid colors and frank lines. Thus they sang, putting their heart into some words, and their timidity into others, while sometimes lifting their hand in a puny gesture, awkward and sincere.

Then they had become ambitious. A few clever comrades had smuggled in enough board to make a floor, in the whole corner, and with a few pictures on the walls, it looked like a stage. The *Lagerführer* made us dismount it entirely in the evening; but once I obtained the authorization to line up the materials against the wall. They increased considerably, and took up so much space that it made little difference whether the stage was up or not, for the corner could not be used any more. Twice, the *Lagerführer* had all our material transported to the yard. It came back under everyone's coat. He thought it a good trick to transform this corner into a depot for potatoes: they disappeared so promptly, in our pockets, that he had to give it up. We had won. After three months of hazardous juggling, the stage remained permanently.

I interested the *Sonderführer* of the *Stalag* in our efforts. He sent us little plays and sketches. I took advantage of the official recognition he seemed to have granted our theatrical group, to induce the *Kommandoführer* to let us acquire some rolls of paper. A little artistic team was formed, and with the help of carpenters and some driftwood — drifted from the work-yard — the stage received settings and accommodations. Both were far from my own taste, but it was important only to keep my comrades active, and as many of them as possible. I admired if not the results, at least their candid efforts.

Forced Labor

There was a tall boy who once had a bay window. He was a cabinetmaker, specializing in luxurious coffins. It had borne little influence on his mentality. He was good humored and full of indomitable vitality. Gifted for clowning, he imitated the best music hall singers, and made everyone of us laugh heartily. In addition, he inspired the others, and organized them. With all the unavoidable quarrelling, jealousies, and troubles, that such affairs involve, we composed a theatrical unit of ten actors; a singing one, of fifteen. From one harmonica in March, the orchestra grew to twenty-four instruments by December. With the complicity of a sentry particularly anxious to make ten or twenty per cent profit, we found and bought all sorts of old instruments, in the city: horns, violins, banjos, accordions, bugles, drums, with money collected from the spectators.

At first, a rather disturbing noise resulted from all of that, but a miner proved a good maestro. In France, or Belgium, no coal mine exists without choral and instrumental societies. He had had experience along these lines and, with a little stick, of which he was proud, and patience, and a determination that I admired, he gave order and rhythm to the racket. Aided by three or four acceptable soloists, he ended the year with a band able to play a dozen tunes correctly.

I had obtained a special favor from Ehlert, who liked music: to rehearse in the distribution room for one whole hour after curfew, and I answered for every one of them. There, proud of the distinction, and with a most admirable devotion, they rattled, blew, scratched, and polished their tunes, while the maestro waved his little stick above their heads. At times, it would go well, as if they were all sliding down an easy slope; it became music; it took on color; the violinists bent their heads and stretched their souls along their bows. Serious, and appearing to blow their heads into a big red bubble, the horn players sat stiff. The mandolinists scratched a strange itch in the middle of their instruments, and a former boxer — with cauliflower ears, and a nose floating, like an empty pouch, in the center of his face — battered the drum with exquisite gentleness, as if he had exhausted all his brutality, during his fighting days, on his opponents' faces.

The singers rehearsed too, with a good Belgian accordionist — a professor who composed some of the songs. The performers looked at the ceiling, in their effort to reach high notes, and seemed to sink when working in the other direction. Powerful, big boys had wee sweet voices. Small, dry sticks of masons or bank employees, tried so hard to make a formidable noise, that perspiration dripped from their brows. They retired to the corner with a bit of paper, and shaped their expressions and gestures like museum mannequins.

Nobody has ever explained where the boxers had gotten hold of a marvelous rope, but they had a ring, with four posts, and stretching wires and screws. In five minutes, it could be set up in the center of the room, and a few insufficiently nourished men, weakened, and tired from a day's work, demonstrated that strength is more moral than physical. No matter what the weather, the room was never heated. They stripped down to a pair of shorts, and found again the emotions of their youth when, as amateurs or professionals, they had danced in what they call sentimentally, "the enchanted ring." The rounds were reduced to two minutes — and there were only two of them — after which they sat or stretched out, completely exhausted. It was often beautiful. Formerly, they had only put their youth and vitality in it. Now it was to be their expression, their feelings, their escape from ugliness. Instead of spending thus their hatred of the guards, they seemed rather to exhaust their kindness. A little blood ran sometimes, but it was friendly. They loved each other. There would be pairs of intimate comrades who fought unwillingly against anyone else. The excep-

Forced Labor

tions were found only among the men who didn't know how to box, and had no feeling for it.

A little beyond, there would be fencing. I had bought a mediocre pair of swords and masks for the camp. We had two specialists — one of them excellent — who gave lessons. The boxers would join them, after a while, in a gymnastic lesson, and they would patiently bow, lift up their legs, and, together, go through the figures of an intense training.

I spent ten minutes there every evening, and sometimes joined in the gymnastic lesson. It was the aspect of the *Kommando* I treasured the most. This mixture of efforts, this naive earnestness, had for me much more reality in the rehearsal than in the Sunday shows of which they were all so proud.

*   *   *

Whether it was to be an exhibition of sports, a play, or a music-hall fantasy, I presided and delivered a little speech. The boys were lined and packed in awkward positions. They looked intently at the curtain. They were ready to forget everything else; and did. It was the time to tell them some good news: it wasn't going so well for the Germans in Russia; Berlin had just been bombed; a new class had been formed. Time also to praise the efforts of one group, and explain the difficulties of another. The band played a couple of tunes, and the show began. The comedies — mostly Labiche, Courteline, or light satirical pieces — were played in uniforms, a little transformed with paper garments. No male civilian clothes were allowed in the possession of a prisoner, but with special permission, female ones could be.

Two of our boys put these on, looked frankly ridiculous, knew it, but had no other pretense than making the others laugh. A third man was quite different. His name was Dutheil, and he was a butcher by trade, a little man with a broad mouth, and brown hair curling on a low forehead. One of his combat-comrades, met here again by chance, said that he had fought with bravery, even fiercely. But he loved to dress up like a girl. He had obtained a complete outfit from home, and wore it with a strange gravity. He was stiff and so impressed that he could hardly produce his ample bass voice. It quavered. I thought it was stage fright, until he appeared on the stage in uniform, with excellent poise.

Only the feminine garments produced this effect on him. He became another person. Homely, with strong arms and powerful red hands, when white had been smeared over his face, his lips barred with vermillion, a yellow wig drawn over his curls, a bit of lace tied around his neck, and a rayon dress pulled over his underwear, he made a surprising doll. His appearance was a mixture of physical brutality and of indefinable gentleness. These hands could have killed — they had — this mouth could have bitten cruelly, and yet this painted face and this clumsy body were tender. When he stood, wordless, blushing under the make-up, and looking far away beyond the small room, he expressed something of us, of our conditions, of our feelings, battered down to a bitter pill and rolling inside of us as if in an empty box. Perhaps this ridiculous figure was the real image of our efforts to resist captivity, to feel, to love, to live the dream behind which we hid from the ugliness of the day.

It was moving, and far deeper than an inverted sexual appeal. Of the latter, we had experienced a touch, one Sunday, when, after many requests, I had been permitted to invite the theatrical group of a *Kommando* located on the other side of the street.

One of the actors of this group had appeared so well clad as a girl that he could have fooled anyone. He waved his hips and hands, he placed his high heeled shoes on the floor, and

Forced Labor

smiled, like a woman. With a falsetto voice, he sang sophisticated songs very well. He had impressed the room exactly as would have been expected. He was shockingly charming. He appeared a cheap edition of femininity, a translation into a medium accessible to the prisoners, while the real women were not. He was a substitute, but not, like our boy, an expression.

A diet of turnips and potatoes, long days of work, and incessant bickering of the sentries, helped us to be free from sexual worries. This had proved easier than I feared with such a vast group of men. Each of them carried along with him a vision, a continuous apparition of his loved ones, that he superimposed on his surroundings. He leaned on them, he talked to them. The most ardent urges of his flesh were, so to speak, delayed. They were postponed to the time when life would again become sweet. He found a provisory transmutation in his unique will for freedom: an escape if he were bold; the illusion of being soon released by the Germans, if he were not. Yet, if any boy such as this too-successful travesty from the next *Kommando*, had existed on board ship, I have no doubt that he would have caused trouble. Other comrades might have discovered in themselves what had been, until then, a weak, or unsuspected inclination, and they would have attracted the others, like a strong drink — a poison perhaps, but better than none, and less bitter than the solitude devastating their hearts.

*   *   *

CLASSES AND LECTURES

French reserve officers are selected according to University degrees, the least being a B.A. or a Normal Teachers School diploma, but not every University-graduate is an officer. The generation of Frenchmen having come of age between the first

World War, and the remilitarization of the Rhineland by Hitler, has been strongly pacifist. No liberal youngster serving his military term, would consider accepting a commission in the Army, so convinced were we that only reactionaries could think about another war. Thanks to this, many learned men, engineers, professors, teachers, ministers of all creeds, were to be found among the privates and the noncommissioned officers in the *Stalag*. Of course the average scholastic level of an *Offlag* (special camp for officers) remained considerably higher than that of a *Stalag*.

Not compelled to work, the French officers were free most of the day within the walls of their barracks, and could consider themselves involuntary monks. They could seek consolation in studies. Books could be obtained through the International Red Cross, from home, or with the help of the *Sonderführer*. They could found an unlimited number of classes, and begin them above tedious and elementary generalities.

I don't doubt that the advantages rendering their captivity lighter than ours — exactly as their physical share of the war had been lighter — were far from sufficient to prevent them from hating their condition. Yet, instead of slaving for their enemies, as we had to do, they could improve their mind and acquire a definite knowledge that they could count as a small compensation for their loss in happiness. Leaders could rise freely among them, and fight the evils created by endless leisure — the loss of physical and mental alertness, for instance — and organize activities with which we could not compete. I read about their fine theatrical and musical groups, and their camp universities, in the *Trait d'Union*, and obtained complementary information from some of my men who had worked in an *Offlag* as kitchen helpers.

Our own intellectual efforts began at 7:30 P.M. and involved men with hands gnawed by cement and lime, or stiffened by

Forced Labor

excessive intimacy with a pickaxe-handle. We could have done better than we did, perhaps, but we had strong odds against us. It took me five months to open the first class. Until July, the illusion of an early return to our families had been strong, and very few men had been willing to undertake any extra effort, especially one requiring time. Beginning to study a language, would have amounted to admitting the probability of a long captivity. The demobilization of the World War veterans, followed only by that of a small number of fathers of large families, had settled the matter; and I had been able to gather a dozen pupils for a course in German. The *Kommandoführer* understood the advantage of having a few more prisoners knowing some German, so granted the necessary authorization. English is the foreign language currently spoken in France; and most of our best men would have preferred learning Chinese to German. They despised anything sounding like the *"Raus, and Los,"* and *"Schnell, and Schweinhund"* that they experienced daily. If they couldn't save their ears from them, they would at least save their throats. So it was among our masons and carpenters, anxious to make the best of their acquaintance with German workers in the work-yard, that I found co-operation.

Maurice, Interpreter II, agreed to give the course. A country school teacher in the coal region of Belgium, earnest and devoted to our comrades, he understood the necessity to occupy their minds. His duties in the camp left him some leisure during the day, in which he could prepare his lessons. He did so well, with such patience and pedagogy, that the class rose to thirty-five pupils; and he divided it in two sections, giving each of them two lessons a week, from 7:30 to 8:30 P.M.

This was my occasion to make the first poster relative to the Night School of the Boat, "German, elementary and superior," that I hung in the distribution room. The *Unterlagerführer* was intrigued by it. I took him to the lesson one evening, and the sight touched him.

By pushing the bunks away, the boys had created a free space of fifteen by ten feet, behind a stairway. They sat on stools and learned "*die, der, das*" as they had "A, B, C." Happy to be doing something conforming to his vocation, Maurice did his best to interest them, but two had been unable to resist sleep. Their heads had fallen on their knees, between one hand clutching a pencil, and the other rumpling a bit of paper. I woke them up. They blushed and said that they were sorry, as they wanted very much to learn, but they had unloaded one freight car too many. Considering this course as an excellent omen for his propaganda, the *Unterlagerführer* let me borrow a blackboard that was of little use in the *Lagerführung*. We bought a box of chalk; and this corner was consecrated as "The School."

Of the sixteen grammar school teachers who had been gathered in my Kommando in the spring, only four remained, and with them I created an extensive course of French. A few prisoners had hardly been to school in their time; others had forgotten that they had been. To the others, I said that we all had been so brutified by this first year in captivity, that we needed to start life all over again. Why not return to grammar school, to begin with, and to high school afterwards? If the Germans kept us long enough, we might all become Ph. D.'s. They laughed. It was a good beginning. I campaigned through the boat in order to get pupils. To prevent them feeling ashamed of having to improve their spelling, I circulated such sayings as:

"Let's demonstrate to the Germans that, in spite of their efforts, they haven't reduced us to the state of oxen," or

"Let every one of us join a class. Whether it's bridge, gymnasium, wrestling, arithmetic, mechanics; let's go back home —

Forced Labor

whenever this happens — having learned something that we didn't know before."

I induced the interpreters, and professors of the other classes, to join me as pupils in a class of linguistics, opened by one of my friends who, reticent until then, took such interest in teaching again, that he spent considerable time revising his Latin and Greek roots, and preparing notes on phonetics. This impressed our comrades, and created a certain mysticism of intellectual effort.

I needed it myself, as much as they did. The only difference between us was that they had pushed me to a place where I had a bird's eye view of the camp; of its lacunae and its aspirations. I was not generating these aspirations, but rather expressing them as soon as I discovered them. This mass of battered flesh and soul, packed in a banana freighter, contained a wealth of buried knowledge, academic or technical, and of human experience. It needed only to be stirred to revive. It responded like a violin to the bow of the player, in proportion to his efforts.

After six months, so many professors volunteered courses, that the problem was to find space for them. There were as many as three successive classes in one corner. The men of the last class took a two hours' nap while waiting for their turn, so as to lose as little sleep as possible. We taught mechanics, a complete course in automobile engines and repairs, followed by one on electricity in the house and small machinery; English; French history; fencing, boxing, wrestling, gymnastics, elementary music, bridge, chess, and whatever could interest a few persons.

I charged a priest, having come to the *Kommando*, with uniting the men interested in religion. It took many requests to the *Kontrollstelle* to obtain permission for him to hold mass, on certain Sundays. It scandalized the *Lagerführer* very much because it was held in the distribution room, and he swore that it would not happen again, but I complained, in behalf of my Catholic comrades, to the *Stalag*, and to any German officer I saw, until the authorization was granted. The priest worked all day like the others. Only priests, or ministers having served as army chaplains are exempted from work. This one, like many others, had served as a private.

The traditional faith lived in about 200 men of the camp. They sang the hymns together. Sermons were prohibited, but the priest had opportunities to talk to a little group at a time. I had given him this chance to form a *Bible* class; but it didn't work well. No one could persuade my comrades, religious or not, that their fate was not unjust:

"What have we done, that the others haven't, to be punished alone?"

If the war had kept on, they might have thought:

"We suffer in captivity, but we don't risk being killed as our comrades, still at the front, do."

Now, it was bitter to all that one third of the army should be kept prisoner, while the rest was back in civilian life.

Once a month, the *Kontrollstelle* sent a few copies of an evangelical sermon to the Protestants of the camp. I read them, hoping to find indications for my own efforts. I did not. They spoke of resignation. This was not a language for men whose duty had been yesterday to kill, and today, should be to do everything possible to be once more in a position to shoot at their captors, until our own country was free again. One could talk of patience to my men only when adding:

"Our turn will come."

Between the various classes — the sport teams, the theatre group and the orchestra, the chess and card courses and competitions — from 200 to 250 men were constantly kept busy. It was especially for the inactive rest, that I opened a series of lectures on all subjects.

Forced Labor

Every Saturday night, the school corner was reserved, and one comrade rose to talk about something that he knew. From the peasants, I asked for talks about the life of the bees, the raising of horses, and such questions with mass appeal; from the industrial workers; the fabrication of silk material, of automobile engines, of shoes, etc.; from employees, the management of a bank, or large hotel; from government employees, the administration of a community; from the engineers, the building of a bridge, the planning of a city; and from the others, whatever they could offer.

I made a point of presenting the speaker formally, addressing my comrades as "Gentlemen," and defining the special interest of the coming lecture. He spoke. If he was inexperienced, or embarrassed, I would ask him questions, and thus extract the precious knowledge that every man contains, but cannot always express. About 150 comrades followed these talks with obvious interest. They had to stand, or sit on the steps, and they lined up in the alleys between the bunks all around, as far as the voice could carry.

After half a dozen lectures, the best speakers created emulation, and soon, men who had never spoken in public before, did a tolerably good job of it. When, towards the fall of 1941, the *Stalag* gave official encouragement to the intellectual efforts in the camps — as a means to appease the growing resentment of prisoners at their everlasting captivity, and to diminish the attempts at escape — I obtained permission to hold a monthly lecture in the distribution hall. Three hundred and fifty men could be accommodated there. The *Kommandoführer* insisted on receiving a translation of the outline of the lecture, before allowing it. He showed up often while it went on. If, at the time, I was giving an interlude on politics and what I called the right spirit of a prisoner, I promptly shifted to such subjects as the death fight of the black bass, in the rivers in the Alleghanies.

Five days before escaping, I talked about the belfries and towers of the old Russian monasteries, shaped like pears and onions, sparkling with gold, and casting enchanting reflections in the Dnieper river.

The prisoners liked nothing better than to be transported, for an hour, far away from their own life, including the past one and the present, and wander through bed-time stories of happiness and illimited space.

*   *   *

Nevertheless, all of this didn't go without bumps or accidents. There were periods of sudden atony, during which the classes thinned out. Fatigue, spleen, or, as the French say, *"cafard."* The next Sunday I'd have to open the show with some invigorating words, and try to revive in my comrades an enthusiasm fading in me, also. At times, it all seemed so stupid, so primary, so far from anything that I personally liked, that disgust fought my best intentions. Instead of seeing, in the comedy being attempted on the stage, the expression of the will of my men to buck up, I now saw an example of their mediocrity. All their patience and ability had transformed the crude but expressive platform, improvised on four stools, into a masterpiece of bad taste and pretensions, with valueless ornaments invading the once healthy panels like an eczema. There was a chimney, now, with a little kindling, and a red bulb behind it. The vase on the mantelpiece came from the German Woolworth's. The singers liked to lean on a little table with twisted legs, so as to resemble some imbecile picture they had once seen in a photographer's shop.

The classes followed a similar decadence. I had explained a short poem by Goethe to the pupils in the German class, and

Forced Labor

done my best to make them realize the beauties of the language of which they had heard only the guttural accents. I tried to make them learn this poem. Only two did. The others were more eager to learn a foul joke. In spite of the efforts of the professors, the elements of healthy architecture, given to the masons, did not fight off the reminiscences of the fancy cottages sickening the skyline of the Parisian suburbs.

I felt the impulse to get up, shake down this edifice of classes and groups that had cost me so much patience, insistence, and energy, and let them return to the savage beauties of despair. But they turned towards me with such naive hopes, they expected from me so much help, encouragement, and a solution to every one of their difficulties, that they raised me out of my own individuality to the rank of their doctor. I had to help them to be the men they were, and not the man I was.

Once in a while, quarrels occurred. Boys who had so far gotten along very well in the same group, would fight brutally for no other reason than that they had seen each other too long. It ended quickly, with an exchange of blows and reticent apologies; but a few unpleasant words let out of sheer exasperation, can wreck the best intentions. This kind of trouble was frequent around the theatre group, where a marked tendency towards conceit grew parallel to progress. The boxers were as susceptible as old maids. Everywhere, I had to apply patches, sweet words, or angry ones. I became especially angry when my boys let the Germans see their quarrels. I had told them many times that if they had to come to blows, they should go down to the bottom of the ship, ask for the fighting gloves and get rid of their exasperation with a few rounds, in the presence of Lamy, the *Kommando's* nurse.

Other difficulties came from the *Kommandoführung*. If anyone escaped, or if a prisoner's fist landed in some overseer's face, all the privileges I had patiently extracted from successive and reluctant German sergeants, were suppressed. Curfew was advanced to 7 P.M. instead of 9, in summer; and in winter, set immediately after the distribution of the soup: no more rehearsals, or late classes.

The sentries would comb the yard, peep in each latrine cell, and push everyone on board with more stiffness that usual. The night watch would be doubled. It was repeated that anyone leaving the boat at night, or seen in the vicinity of the fence, would be shot without warning. Guards like Kellner and Grün would have done their best to miss you, but others, like Schlegel and Reipsch, would have aimed carefully. Then the *Kommandoführer* and his whole staff went through the boat at 8:30 and made sure that no one was out of his bunk. From bottom to top, the boat resounded to oaths and threats. The boys would simply draw their blankets over their heads to shut out the stupid commotion.

My duty was to follow the hollering team, and translate from time to time. I looked as disgusted as I could, within the limits of discipline. This would be a week when, at four o'clock, Finot would bring only two cups on his tray — one for Paul and one for me; none for *Herr* Ehlert or his successor — until the atmosphere moderated in the office, and I could endeavor to regain our lost advantages, one by one, paying for them with renewed patience and diplomacy, and with an extra cup of my delicious American coffee.

One rule of the camps is: that prisoners not working outside must exercise, militarily, for half an hour at least, every day. The cleaning squad, the shoemaker, and the few others employed in the camp, weren't fond of it at all. It wasn't amusing to the sentries either. I convinced the *Kommandoführer* that a game of volley ball, played daily during lunch recess, would be much better than a melancholy succession of steps around the yard.

In sight of both the military office and the sentries' barracks

Forced Labor

— that is to say, quite near the water — I had two slim posts planted, and a rope stretched between them. Thanks to the *Sonderführer*, a ball was available, and from noon to 1 P.M. we enjoyed a little action.

Our game was noisy and attracted attention. The first officer of the ship — scrappy, red in the face, and bearing a name that sounded as though spoken through a mouthful of scrap metal — looked at us every day. He was one of the men I would have found it sweet to kill. He thought it funny to call every Frenchman he met "Little Napoléon." For him, everything that wasn't German was wretched.

"What are the Americans," he said when war was declared on the United States, "but a mixture of Negro gangsters, Jewish robbers and trash expelled from the other countries? We're going to blow them off the earth."

He hadn't exactly invented his insults. I had read most of them in the daily *Pommersche Zeitung*, hardly more carefully worded. His work on the ship amounted to showing his three stripes to a crew of rude, but sympathetic sailors. From his castle bridge he had a complete view of the camp and of its fence, and paid attention to everything the prisoners did. How joyfully he would have shot at anyone seen trying to break through the fence, or swimming down the Oder! He commented on our game, and mocked us when the ball fell.

The women of the kitchen and the *Lagerführer* liked to watch, also.

"Aren't the prisoners having a fine time in Germany?" groaned Opferer, fat on our meat.

We roared and shrieked like Walpurgis witches, while running after the ball, and jumping to stop it; it was so good to be absorbed entirely in the exercise.

There was indeed something a little bewitched about this volley ball affair, for every time a big truck brought potatoes or rutabagas to the camp, one of the posts was afterwards found down. I reported the accident to the *Kommandoführer* and, swearing about such miserable driving, asked permission to set my posts again, a little farther, out of the way!

CHAPTER 17

87,461: Justice of the Peace and Public Scribe

When Morelle, whom I admired for his energy and clarity under all circumstances, was reported to me as having become sulky and fussy, I was disappointed. Could it be that he, too, was sinking? Breaking down was a current disease, but how I would regret losing one of the men who had helped me to fight it by his example and influence. He had never been loquacious about his private affairs, so I couldn't ask him more than:

"Everything all right, Morelle?"

"Why not?" he answered.

That "why" turned out to be a paper, bearing many legal stamps, that the Embassy for War Prisoners forwarded to me, to be signed by Morelle, legalized, and sent back through the usual channel. Its title left no doubt: renunciation of paternity. I didn't need to read further. Such sad stories had happened before.

In August 1939, a girl, blond, dark, or red, tall or small, pretty or ugly, but for Morelle beautiful, had kissed him a warm good-bye, in a Paris railway station packed with soldiers. He had filled up his heart with her looks, her tears, her passionate words. He had lived with these ever since: during the long wait on the Rhine, the thrust through Belgium, his capture on the Meuse. She had been his only thought while he dug out new German roads — the hardest work, next to the salt mines. She had come with him on the *Nordenham* and, on the bunk that was his, she had lain immaculate, as fresh as she was two years ago. Then a letter had come — probably from his mother — saying:

> My dear boy, I can no longer delay informing you that your wife gave birth to a child, last week. I have learned it from the doctor himself. The father is. . . . If you agree, my lawyer will take the necessary steps to avoid his registration under your name.

"She, she! How could it be? I had kept her so well in me."
There is a French saying: "He who stays away, is always wrong." A young girl, secretary in a large office, maybe she loved him; maybe she hated herself now; but why had her young life been so dull since he had gone? What could she have done with one lonely evening after another, and no child to fondle? The other men had come back from the lost battle. If only they had left her in peace; if they had not always come around her, trying to be pleasant; being pleasant; suggesting that there would be no harm in going to the movies once. It is perhaps with genuine passion that one of them had pressed her, confused her, and suddenly pushed her out of the prisoner's life; while he, trapped in a tepid hold, deloused his shirt and swore. But her love had been the foundation of his patience and his strength.

Morelle distributed, among his comrades, the pullovers, the socks, that she had knit for him — everything she had sent — as well as 135 *Reichsmarks*, a substantial heap of civilian notes so difficult to obtain, and to hide. Home had lost its meaning. This man, afraid of no one, would not try any more to escape.

He asked me to send him to another *Kommando* as soon as I could. When he left, he had hardly anything in his sack. He waved indifferently to us. I never heard of him again.

* * *

299

Forced Labor

I filed eleven petitions for divorce, on similar grounds. The boys had the same look when they came around with the same words:

"When you have time, I'd like to show you a letter."

Often, it came from the forgetful wife's own mother or sister. She wrote:

> I am grieved and indignant at what my daughter has done to you. She has gone off with a neighbor, and with him has spent her prisoner's-wife pension. She has begun selling your furniture. I have taken your children with me. If you mail me the two monthly package-labels that you are allowed, I'll send you what I can. . . .

Sometimes the wife herself wrote crudely:

> . . . Do you remember Dorothy? You never fooled me. I knew all along you were deceiving me with her. Now it's my turn; so you can't say anything. If you want to, you can ask for a divorce. It's easier for prisoners than for anyone else.

Others wrote more carefully — out of pity, perhaps, or out of shrewdness:

> We have never been really happy together. I have found the man I should have married. It will turn out better for you too. I didn't want you to learn this from indiscreet friends. I'll keep sending you packages until your return, and you'll find your belongings in good order.

There was nothing to say except such trivialities:

"Boy, she wasn't the proper wife for you. You'll find a better one when you're released. Until then we can protect your interests."

I established legalized copies of the different letters, and sent them as evidence, with an application for divorce, to the court nearest my comrade's home. From his city hall, I requested that the government's pension be withdrawn from his wife, and paid instead to the children's guardian. I wrote the Embassy for War Prisoners, explaining the case, and asking them to find out in what condition the children were, and make sure that their father received news from them regularly. When I knew that he was attending the occasional masses given in the camp, I told the facts to our comrade priest, hoping that he could comfort him. If this kind of help was not suited to him, I tried to make him take an active part in our organisations, specially the secret ones.

*　　*　　*

The marriages were far more pleasant. Men decided to legalize unions kept strictly private until then; or young boys decided to marry the sweetheart who, after two years' absence, wrote to them tenderly. It had material advantages: only as a wife could they receive the small pension allowed by the government to prisoners' families. Also, it would greatly facilitate their inheriting the prisoner's estate if he died in captivity.

The formalities were simple. The betrothed would apply to the city hall for a certain form, and forward it to the prisoner. I would fill it out for him and he would declare, in front of witnesses, his decision to marry her. As soon as she received the paper, she needed only to present it to the city hall, in place of her absent groom, and the ceremony could be accomplished.

Francois, our champion at the game of balls, had left in Marseilles a treasure about which he had sometimes spoken to me: she was tall, slender, dark, marvelous; perfect! Hoping to im-

Forced Labor

prove his chance to keep her faithful, he decided to marry her. As he was a popular figure, I arranged with the theatre-group a surprise for him.

On the evening that he was to sign the papers, when he stood in line for his bowl of soup, a complete wedding appeared in the distribution room. The father wore a fine long beard of shredded burlap, and a top hat of cardboard. The bride was Ducrocq, perhaps the worst looking boy in camp: small, sneering, and with a complexion so intensely purple that theatrical lipstick didn't show on his mouth: they had to paint it black. Two shirts made him a distinguished white dress. Socks stuffed his chest where charms had been lacking before. Torn rags hid his wild hair with their luxurious lace. His train, of newspapers sewed together, was carried nobly by two pages, with high Norwegian caps.

Two violins, two accordions, two horns, and two mandolins followed, squeaking, blowing, and scratching a wedding twaddle. The stage curtain lifted on a very dignified mayor, dressed as a judge because it was the only dignified outfit, cleverly made of black paper, that we had on hand. François was seized by the legs and feet, and carried on the stage in spite of his protests and shrieks. I made him sign the papers. The mayor gave him the bride, and she smeared his face with noisy black kisses. She promised to give him thirty-three children, and let him know in time.

I explained that however funny the ceremony, this had been a real wedding. François was legally married. The crowd cheered and began a well-known saw referring to possible unpleasantnesses of married life, and particularly thirty-three other children that his wife would give him without his approval.

The witnesses were being compelled to kiss the bride, when *Unteroffizier* Ehlert and *Lagerführer* Opferer, notified by a

302

sentry, arrived in a hurry to find out what the scandal was about.

"Let them kiss the bride, too!" shouted someone.

What Ducrocq answered was neither virginal nor dignified.

*　　*　　*

If Ducrocq was not quite married this time, he was one of the very few in the camp who had ever carried on a love affair in Germany. A good mason, he had been left alone, with a helper, to transform the cellar of a private house, when a woman tenant came down to deposit a few bottles of wine in her compartment. Ducrocq didn't speak more than three words of German, but must have been eloquent with them, for she came again the next day and, while the comrade helper stood in the stairway, on the lookout for the sentry, the two locked themselves up in a coal cellar.

The work dragged behind schedule, and soon a German worker was sent along. Ducrocq brought me the little notes that his lady love had now to content herself with. I translated them for him. They were rather passionate, but the answers he proposed were decidedly too much so. I reduced them to less confidential contents, and had them copied by somebody from another firm, so that there would be less danger of locating the author if the notes were ever found. They would have been sufficient to send the woman either to hard labor for life, or to the firing squad, and the prisoner to a ten years' stretch in a fortress.

Ducrocq came so often with such work, that I had to ration him to one translation a week. He soon lost interest in the woman, but not in the wine. She had given him some, and it had revived other glorious memories. He wouldn't touch her own supply — out of gratitude, I suppose — but couldn't resist someone else's. While the German worker was away for a moment, Ducrocq and the helper lifted up a board of another

Forced Labor

compartment, dropped a noose and fished out a few bottles. There must have been a very unusual traffic around the latrines that day, for the eight men of Ducrocq's group came back to the *Nordenham* completely drunk. It was a wonder that the sentry didn't notice it, in spite of their brave efforts to walk straight, and not let out a single word, for fear that a whole song would follow. He may have believed they were very tired.

Warned in time, I ordered them to stay in the ship and send comrades for their rations. The next morning, I obtained the story from sobered Ducrocq, now quite worried: they had emptied some fifteen bottles, and feared that only five or six remained intact. Were this discovered, a frightful scandal would follow. There was only one solution: bribe the guard and the civilian. The last bottles were extracted, and given to those two, one at a time, of course, and without saying where it came from. After the third, neither cared at all. It was the sentry who had a difficult time entering the camp without attracting attention, that evening.

A few days later, the robbed woman, who turned out to be an old drunkard, shook the vaults with her shrieks when she discovered the plunder: not even an empty bottle remained. She wanted to kill someone, and accused the prisoners. Very indignant, the guard swore that he knew his duty, and that none of his men could have done it. The civilian worker testified that he had been with Ducrocq and his helper all day long, and suggested that either someone else had taken the bottles, or the woman was building up a story in order to obtain twenty-one bottles free from the firm.

We weathered the storm and, the work finished in this house, the prisoners were taken somewhere else, leaving behind two German women with broken hearts.

*   *   *

Bruneau was handsome, excessively so, but there was nothing equivocal in his manners. He spent his evenings darning his uniform, or washing his shirts. At work, he protected his hands with rags. He did less than anyone else, because his charm acted even on the overseers. They found something soft for him, such as cleaning the yard or pouring cement and sand in a small concrete mixer. He spoke so slowly that he seemed to be late everywhere, even if he were there. What he said was shallow, but the words so well chosen that their emptiness was refreshing.

When he waited for his soup, the kitchen women came to the windows and eyed him appraisingly. Two or three of them gave me sandwiches for him. He didn't care at all. He took the sandwiches and shared them with others. It happened, too, that his very sweetness irritated his comrades, and they became very rude to him; but he didn't mind. He smiled it off. Soon they were glad to have someone around who was neither dirty nor uncouth, as the best of us had become. His game of bridge wasn't brilliant, but his distinction was worth an extra trick. I liked to have him along, on Sunday night — the only time I could count on two or three hours to play cards with my friends. While he shuffled the decks in the best manner, he told his love stories, simply, and without appearing to realize how exceptionally he fared.

His firm, also, had been busy in private cellars, and during the whole month of July, three women had fallen madly in love with him. The first one was a twenty-year-old girl, who wrote him exquisite letters, which I helped him to decipher. She did her best to keep a friendly tone, but asked so many questions about him — his past, his ideas, his ambitions, his condition — that they revealed a violent passion. She had the courage, and the folly, to sign her full name. She had pinned snapshots of herself to every note, trusting that he wouldn't show them to anyone, though he did to me, at least.

Forced Labor

One day, the guard came into the cellar where Bruneau was mixing mortar, and led him up the stairway to an apartment, and rang the bell. The girl appeared, with her mother, and, all curtains drawn, they served tea. As his German was very short, and their English very bad, they spoke very little. The guard stood at the door, ready to explain, in case of trouble, that the prisoner was a mason doing some repair work. He received a considerable amount of money for that. One can only wonder how the girl had induced her mother to enter such a plot.

All day, from her window, she watched him pushing a wheelbarrow or dragging sacks. He found her even in the cellar where, perhaps, she had never been before. He smiled and she blushed. That was all. He could have obtained anything he would have cared to suggest from her — even help for an escape. He didn't think about it. His letters to her, that I had to translate, were like him: elegant, careful, shallow and charming. She cried, I'm sure, when she received them. It was a desperate letter she wrote to announce that her mother was taking her away to the beach, for a month.

Bruneau's second admirer was in her thirties, and gave him to understand she wasn't free. A German major came to see her every day. She wrote notes to tell him at what time she'd be able to come in the courtyard. She bribed the civilian foreman and sentry lavishly, so that they'd pass packages to the prisoner. They contained the most expensive cigarettes, and this rarest item: chocolate. Only her officer could have obtained it for her. In a single week, she wrote ten notes and confessed her passion frankly: she wanted him, and would do anything to have him. She too had to leave, for only a few days, and promised to bring him something he didn't expect.

Bruneau wondered what it could be: perhaps a fine suit of civilian clothes, with a bunch of false papers?

The third was neither distinguished nor highly placed, but

for love of one, she brought sandwiches every day to the ten prisoners eating lunch with him. The others told me about her careless ways, and how they feared that she'd cause our comrade trouble. Her spelling was doubtful, but her enthusiasm unlimited. She wrote she was going to manage to have him spend a whole day with her.

The house cellar being duly transformed into an air-raid shelter, Bruneau's firm was sent to another quarter, and contact brutally broken. All one week, a desolate woman paced the sidewalk, up and down, as near the *Nordenham* as she could, trying dangerously to spot our handsome comrade in every one of the incoming columns. We could see her from the foredeck. It was useless. Bruneau had been assigned to another *Kommando*, and had left Stettin without the possibility of sending each of them a cool and distinguished word of adieu.

CHAPTER 18

Letters, Packages and Red Cross Gifts

ON THE 15th of each month, I filled out an application for our monthly supply of writing paper and package stickers. Each man was entitled to two letters of twenty-five lines, two cards of five lines, and two blue labels. Every fourth month, we could ask for an extra red sticker. Blue meant food only; red, clothes only. They were now distributed free, and required no postage.

Members of the Sanitation Corps, and army chaplains, were allowed a double number of both letters and stickers; non-commissioned officers, fifty per cent more than corporals and privates. These special measures were unpopular. Weren't we equally hungry for news and food, and weren't we equally prisoners?

Not only should these be reckoned separately, but the application had also to stipulate how many men belonged to Occupied France and to Unoccupied France, and how many were Belgian. According to the case, their writing formulas would bear the stamp: Fr. *Besetztes Gebiet*, Fr. *Unbesetztes Gebiet*, or none in the case of the Belgians. The system was ridiculous. Until the 10th of the following month, when this material would arrive from the *Kontrollstelle*, our number would have varied three or four times. We would have more or fewer prisoners on board, and the respective proportion of Belgians and Frenchmen, from both zones, would be changed. The result was that we hadn't the proper paper for everyone, and sometimes not enough of it. It would have been much simpler to print the three words: *Besetztes Gebiet, Unbesetztes,* and Belgium, on each formula, and let the prisoner strike out the improper zones.

A further complication came from the fact that minor regulations varied from *Kommando* to *Kommando*. In some of them, the letters and cards were distributed on Sunday, one at a time; in others, all at once. One man having received his monthly supply here, then being sent to another *Kommando,* might have the luck to receive a couple of weekly formulas extra. But, on the contrary, if he came from a *Kommando* where the monthly distribution had been delayed two or three weeks, as was frequent, he would simply lose the privilege of writing those two or three back-letters. And, as the families could write only on the reply sheet attached to the prisoner's letter, he would lose an equal number of letters from home.

Sometimes the *Vertrauensmann,* or the sentry of his new *Kommando* if it were a small one, would write to me about it, and I would do my best to persuade my *Kommandoführer* to let me mail them a few formulas if we had any extra. The process was far from satisfactory. Many injustices and irregularities resulted from it, and nothing annoyed the men more than not being able to write every Sunday. Even if the average number of formulas distributed during a year was correct, it made a great difference if, not having written for several weeks, the prisoner had to send many letters all at once. A prisoner has little to say, but is greedy for news, which he can get only as often as he himself writes.

A *Stalag* regulation renders the *Vertrauensmann* responsible for the correction of the letters: the zone-mention must be exact, the address clear, and the prisoner's identification complete on the back, according to the instructions printed on every formula.

A letter had twenty-five lines for the prisoner, and twenty-

Forced Labor

five others for his family. Though each was clearly marked, one out of fifty prisoners wrote on the wrong sheet. I have done so twice in succession. The complete formula was lost. Censors would return it torn, it would not be replaced, and the *Kommandoführer* got a very unpleasant blame, which would finally fall on me. Another crime was to add a couple of lines to the twenty-five prescribed, or to write in very small or illegible characters. Any language other than German or French was forbidden.

We had a little forty-five-year-old mason who was a Spaniard. He had fought on the Loyalist side in Spain, and later migrated to France, but, because his wife lived there, he hadn't been interned. He had enlisted in the French Army in September 1939, and fought in Belgium, but hadn't learned any French. He spoke to no one, but a Southerner who spoke Spanish, took care of him, and wrote his letters in French. I had asked the *Stalag* in vain, to grant him permission to write in the only language he knew. I tried to interest the *Sonderführer* in his case, and have him demobilized as a member of a nation belonging to the Axis; but after inquiries, this officer warned me that, as a Spaniard, he would have to return to Spain, which was, in his case, more dangerous than captivity.

The greatest difficulties came from forbidden contents. I warned my comrades repeatedly that they were not allowed to complain of anything, or criticize Germany, or indulge in political comments other than those most favorable to our captors. This was a written regulation and, though 100,000 cards or letters passed through our *Stalag* censorship every week, it was rigidly enforced.

While I was in Hammerstein (*Stalag* II B) for two days, during the first winter, one of our comrades had written his wife that he didn't doubt the British would get the best of the Germans, and that the latter would be compelled to ask the

French for help, after this war, as they had had to ask the British and Americans after the last war. As soon as his letter was picked out by the censor, he was convoked by the *Sonder-führer*, and ordered to correct his statement. He only reiterated it, at the cost of thirty days in jail. Thirty days with bread and water for having written what he, as a prisoner, had a perfect right to think! When two guards came in the barrack to take him to jail, all his comrades lined up at attention, as a mark of respect and affection. Even the guards understood that it was not for them.

We were now old prisoners, and everyone knew that such open antagonism could not help us; but we used the censorship as a means to provoke attention from the "big shots" of the *Stalag*, to our worst problems: the fleas, for instance.

One Sunday, a score of comrades agreed to write the accurate truth:

"Each of us is devoured by twenty fleas at least. We can hardly sleep. We have to wake up every hour to fight them."

Two weeks later, the controlling officer arrived.

He must have been sixty years of age and his love of uniform was touching. His cap stood perfectly horizontal on his lean head. His long thin body fit in his impeccable uniform without a wrinkle. He even had a walk that hardly creased his perfect boots. The brief case in his grey gloved hand didn't sway.

He was a painter by profession, but appeared to spend all his imagination and all his art in achieving a deeper submission to Hitler. In the Army, he was only one point; but he wanted that point perfectly correct, exactly in its place. His manners were accordingly dry, but his voice was kind. When he politely inquired about the sort of art I practiced, I answered by naming some of the German artists I admired.

"Thank God," he said, "Hitler has expelled them all from Germany."

Forced Labor

Having taken the *Kommandoführer's* chair, he extracted the bunch of guilty letters from his brief case.

"This," he said, "is an outrageous scandal. All these men complain that they have fleas. Haven't they been told about the regulations?"

"I've told them so many times, *Herr* Leutnant. Besides they are posted foredeck, afterdeck, and in the distribution room."

"Then why do these men complain that they have fleas?"

"Because they *have* fleas, *Herr* Leutnant."

That he couldn't possibly admit. It had been stipulated that no complaint should be mentioned in letters home. Weren't the French intelligent enough to understand that? It never occurred to him that they might not accept it, as he was sure every German would. Our lack of obedience showed how uncivilized we were.

"And why in the world would they want to spend three lines of their weekly letter to their wife, talking about fleas, when it could only prove unpleasant to her? Do they want to bother their families? They should all write home that they are well and satisfied."

"If my wife were sick, I'd prefer knowing it, sir; and I'm sure she'd rather be informed about my condition than ignore it. The French may have the reputation of being romantic, but they are accustomed to stating facts as they are: they call a cat a cat. My comrades fail to realize why they should call a flea a butterfly."

The lieutenant was most kind not to get angry with me, though I spoke with all possible deference, and though he had admitted, to begin with, that he and I had something in common. But I couldn't dare tell him that the incident had been created on purpose. I got around it by saying:

"Wouldn't it be possible to give us better means to get rid of the fleas?"

"It's their fault" said the *Kommandoführer*. "If they were cleaner they wouldn't have any."

"There were no fleas in Germany before the war" said the *Kontrolloffizier*. "They have been brought here by the captives. The circus used to pay as much as eight marks a dozen for fleas, to renew their trained teams."

"We..."

"What?" inquired the lieutenant.

Damn my tongue! I had almost said:

"We pay only one mark for a dozen chosen lice to throw at some people."

Finally he agreed to speak to the doctor about it, and have our allowance of antiseptic increased as much as possible. But there was another letter that shocked him even more:

"Our horse sausage is awful" one man had written "we receive it in the evening, and it stinks the next day at lunch time. I have thrown mine away almost every day. We haven't enough to eat."

"Send for this man" ordered the officer.

The boy came, with the cold portion he had just received, and showed it.

"It's edible," the officer said.

"But it won't be tomorrow" I suggested.

"Then why doesn't he eat it now?"

It was hopeless. He thought it fine to eat only dry bread for lunch.

"Besides, with all the packages we let you receive from France, you are in no way short of food."

That was it. Our wives should deprive themselves in order to give us the strength to work for our captors! That is the price of defeat. Not only we, but our families, belonged to them.

Forced Labor

He came again a few weeks later. Having had no help from the doctor, we had agreed, this time, not to mention the fleas, but asked for insecticide to be included in our next package. The letters were all torn, and the lieutenant, after blowing up each of the guilty prisoners, warned them that if they wrote anything wrong again, not only would their letters be destroyed, but writing would also be suppressed for six months. Was that understood?

How mad he would have been if he had realized that we had many ways to disguise what we meant, under sentences innocent for the censor. Some of us had agreed with our wives on secret codes, before going to war. One can always explain many things by allusions to facts known only to the sender and his wife, especially if the information is divided in several weekly messages that the censor will not see together. Knowing of this practice will not help the Germans to find what is implied, in vague sentences, in 1,300,000 letters written, every Sunday, by French prisoners only.

Letters from home bore the censor stamp *"Geprüft"* and his number, but were less carefully controlled. We would find open statements in them that would not have been allowed otherwise. Nevertheless, they stayed in his office, one, two, or three weeks, for we received two or three together, and very rarely one at a time, as we should have preferred. Letters came from France in about four weeks, sometimes five, and from America in two, three, or four months. Mine bore the British control mark, the regular *Stalag Geprüft*, and often an extra stamp from the *"Oberkommando der Wehrmacht."* I had the honor of reading my letters only after many people were through with them. I have received eight or nine out of every ten sent me.

The letters arrived by packages, through the mail, in the

morning. I remitted them to Lamy, who hung a list of the lucky names in the distribution room. As soon as their firm was dismissed, after the evening re-entry control, our comrades raced there. If they found their name, they went foredeck to the infirmary. It was a corner of the first floor, ten feet by fifteen, with a table, a few benches, a cabinet, no bed, and enclosed by a heavy lattice. It served as general storeroom for shoes, sabots, uniforms, and as depot for packages and Red Cross gifts, as well as a post office.

Lamy arranged the letters in little piles, and handed them out to the callers, through the lattice. Two or three patients lay on the benches and, between other clients, he cleaned their wounds and abscesses. One third of our men suffered constantly from carbuncles, many of which degenerated into ulcers. They read their letters while Lamy pressed the pus out.

The packages were brought in special trucks, or in horse-wagons, 100 or 200 at a time. The drivers were dark-blue-uniformed women, who chatted in the office with the *Kommandoführer*, while the cleaning squad and the sick unloaded the precious freight. It was taken up the ramp, and down one flight of stairs, to the infirmary, under the disgusted eye of a sentry counting them with me. They were locked up there, under the responsibility of Lamy.

Their distribution began at 7 P.M. Six or eight sentries called the numbers written on the blue or red labels, and they opened the packages in the presence of their owners, and, theoretically, of me. As I was often busy, I delegated the Interpreter II, Maurice, to witness the control. Every wrapper was torn open, every item pawed, a few cigarettes occasionally cut in two, in search of hidden notes. Only one can of food could be allowed each prisoner at a time. The rest was packed up with his name and number, and locked up under my responsibility, while the prisoner signed a receipt for his package.

Forced Labor

Thus the Germans hoped to prevent us from accumulating food for an escape, or selling it to the black market. It must be stated that official rules protected our packages very well. Any German soldier convicted of stealing one of them, could be shot. Out of the individual packages coming from France, not more than five or ten per cent failed to reach their destination. Personally, I received three-fourths of what my wife sent me from America. The Germans knew that we were not fed enough by them and needed contributions from home badly. It was ultimately to their advantage.

The prisoners went away delighted with the wrappings smelling of home, and what they had been allowed to take. They formed small associations for the pooling of their packages. Contents were divided equally between the members, no matter what their contribution had been. It helped the least fortunate. Some fifty men never received more than one small package a month, and thirty received none. Later in the week, each associate called at the storeroom for another can or bar of chocolate, and finally obtained enough for a little banquet. They preferred spending all at once, on a real meal, to dividing it patiently between fourteen lunch sandwiches.

*   *   *

If individual packages were properly distributed, the same cannot be said about collective gifts. The French Red Cross contributions were principally: hard biscuits, sardines or cans of meat, and tobacco or cigarettes. American Red Cross contributions that reached us in 1941, were small, but substantial, and generally reserved for the Belgians: chocolate, fat, coffee, cigarettes, cocoa, condensed milk. As we had always shared with them what the French Red Cross sent us, monthly, in the name of Pétain, our Belgian comrades were only too glad to share with us their occasional American delicacies.

Both French and American Red Cross gifts arrived at the *Stalag* in sealed freight cars. They were controlled by the *Vertrauensmann* of the *Stalag*. This privileged prisoner had once been allowed to visit the large working camps and, I have no reason to doubt that this first distribution that the International Committees have sometimes controlled, was correct.

What no commission has seen, I believe, is what happens between the *Stalag* and the *Kommando;* that is to say, how the *Kontrollstelle*, to which the gifts are forwarded, divided them in its district. There is the principal leakage point. In our case, in Stettin, this second division — allegedly made according to the number of men present in each *Kommando*—was controlled by no one. The *Vertrauensmann* of the sanitary barrack, a man representing only the sick of the infirmary, was considered by the *Kontrollstelle* our guarantee that everything was done well. He went with a squad of Germans to the railway station, to open the freight car destined for the district, and sign the receipt. That was all. He was not given any real opportunity to do, or see, anything else. He was not always present when the different lots were prepared by a German sergeant and, anyway, had no possibility of knowing if the figures given for each *Kommando* were correct. When the *Vertrauensmann* from the working camps, called for their share, our comrade was not even there. A German sergeant handed the goods out to us, under the eyes of our own sentry, blew him up and blew us up, hurried us along, gave no explanation, and accepted no protest. We had to sign the receipt before counting the stuff. The receipt did not always stipulate for how many prisoners this was, and often we found that we had not even quite the number of items listed.

It was so easy for this German sergeant to dispose of a few cases of biscuits or meat; and a proof of this is that our own Slobberer, the half-witted *Wachmann* who took the sick to the

Forced Labor

sanitary visit, rarely came back from the *Kontrollstelle* without pocketfuls of French biscuits and cigarettes, that he was too simple to hide. Contrary to what the *Stalag Vertrauensmann* had said to me, we never received an even number of anything: there would be, for instance, thirty-five cigarettes, one and three-fourths packages of tobacco, two cans of sardines for three, and so on.

American cigarettes and chocolate were especially popular with the Germans. When one saw a sentry with some of these, one knew where they came from. Prisoners coming to us from other *Stalag*, reported that they had been distributed American shoes, there. One of them showed me a pair with rubber heels of a well-known brand that I recognized immediately. The only other similar pairs I saw in our *Kommando*, were not on the feet of prisoners, but in the hands of a sentry who sold them to Ehlert for ten marks per pair. I told Ehlert they were American shoes and he let me look at them. They were the very same shoes sent by the American Red Cross to the other *Stalag*.

"I bought them" said the sentry.

I didn't doubt his statement, but he had bought them from someone who had no right to sell them. Blushing as he was, he knew it, too.

I couldn't help that. In my year as *Vertrauensmann*, I had found that sometimes I could minimize the wrongs done to us, but not suppress them. Even if the German high officers gave orders that the distribution be absolutely fair, they couldn't prevent a succession of minor officers, noncommissioned, and privates, taking their cut any time the gifts were handled in their vicinity. It was sometimes done with the help of prisoners easily impressed by threats, or bribed.

In Hammerstein, thirty or forty comrades repaired old shoes for the various *Kommandos* of the *Stalag* II B — torn, miserable shoes, covered with pieces that would last a week. In a storeroom behind the shop, were several hundred beautiful, brand-new French-Army shoes, of chrome leather, supple and strong. I know, because I managed to steal one pair! They were not handed out to prisoners, but two of the best shoemakers in the shop were busy, constantly, dismounting and rebuilding them—custom made — for the officers of the *Stalag*. This also I have seen. I am willing to believe that the German colonel commanding the *Stalag* didn't know about it.

CHAPTER 19

Night Life on SS. Nordenham

AT 9 P.M. the *Kommandoführer*, or his assistant, or both, made a last round of the boat, to make sure that everything was in order, and everyone in bed. When they were in a good humor, they would grant my request to allow ten or twenty pupils of a late class to stay up a little longer, after ordering them to hit the hay immediately afterwards.

All lights went out except a thin line of bulbs along the stairs, and here and there, to maintain a dim visibility, on each floor. Outside, the silence and the night were broken only by the monotonous steps of sentries; by the occasional flashlight of the sailor on duty in the castle, and by a streak under the office door where we kept late hours.

Then a mysterious and concentrated life began.

While the great dual body of the *Kommando*, foredeck and afterdeck, lay inert in sleep, its nervous centers stirred and appeared. Long legs, inelegantly wrapped in the extra long underwear customary in the French Army, shot from under the blankets and, like a silly kind of ivy growing in reverse, crept down the corner post of a bunk. Others seemed to dismount from an unsaddled horse. Like capes, old overcoats were thrown over shoulders. Feet were pushed in slippers made of rags, burlap and cardboard, and sold by thrifty comrades for three marks a pair.

Noiselessly, two score men whose mental energy survived all compulsions and fatigue, went towards passionate rendezvous. The meeting points were located in corners well protected from views and drafts. Some of them were permanent. From behind the loosened board, concealed flying cords, sockets, and bulbs were extracted. The main line had been tapped by our electricians. Wire and other material had been picked up while cleaning ruins caused by the last British raid. The lamp was hooked on a bar between two bunks. A shade of newspaper finished the job, and crowned the conventicle with a large cone.

*   *   *

Here was a poker game. Every night, on each side of the boat, five or six players sat around a crate, or a stool with a cardboard suitcase on it. They rarely spoke, but showed on their fingers how many cards they wanted. To refuse, they tapped a knuckle on the table. They threw their bids briskly — a little bunch of crumpled notes that creaked: five, ten marks at a time. Two hundred marks were won or lost in a few hours: a fortune, a year's salary. One part of it came from their gains at smaller evening games with amateurs timidly bidding ten or twenty *pfennige* (ten or twenty pfennigs), and getting out when they had dilapidated five or ten marks. Another part came from various trades. They would sign I.O.U. notes, and ask me, later, to legalize them. I accepted if only *Stalag* coupons were involved. I have refused in the case of notes amounting to 20,000 francs, the yearly salary of a French mechanic. They bet their packages-to-come, for one, two and three months, as well as their personal clothes.

Winning or losing, winking or looking blank, wriggling on their stools with a pair of fives; or sighing with a royal flush; they spent ardent hours. The emotions of the game shook them all the deeper because no other conflicted with it. When they had no more coupons, they put on *Reichsmarks*. I have seen piles of these that would have turned the heads of all the women in the *Lagerführung*, and abashed the *Kontrolloffizier*. Several men have thrown in the pot, and lost, the money saved for their escape.

321

Forced Labor

A neighbor, returning from the night privy on deck, and shivering with the cold, gave a sleepy look at the hands and, discovering suddenly the fortune of forbidden *Reichsmarks,* shining between the rough fingers like stolen diamonds, shuddered.

Once in a while, one of the players would get up, say "Washed up," and go to bed, to dream of fabulous sequences, or subtle tricks to defeat the luck and science of the others. Or, perhaps, he would only fumble through his belongings, get hold of his last pair of woolen socks, and seek the dark corner where the black market went on.

*   *   *

Black market was an adequate name. One saw only a few shadows, and heard only a murmur. No one sat. Most of the transactions had begun during the day, at work or in the yard. The goods were now delivered and the money paid.

The prisoners' black market is only an extension of the German one. One day, while digging or shovelling with a German civilian, the latter would say to you:

"Coffee, chocolate?"

It was dangerous, especially for the civilian. Only specialists would risk it — men who were masons or carpenters only as a blind. They bought a pound of coffee for thirty-five, forty, fifty *Reichsmarks;* a pound of chocolate, thirty *Reichsmarks;* a cake of soap, five or ten *Reichsmarks;* a can of beef, six or eight; a pair of new socks, ten *Reichsmarks* and an all wool pullover, twenty-five marks or more. They would resell for double.

Certain prisoners specialized in these contacts. For the whole boat, four or five men handled most of the deals because they were gifted for it, or because their daily work allowed them opportunities to communicate with these Germans. They paid you twenty-five or fifty per cent less than they received; but they took many risks while smuggling the goods out of the camp, or bringing in the precious money. They could handle very little at a time. The process was slow. The most daring exchanged the food for civilian clothes, which they would later sell to comrades preparing an escape. Clothes are made of ersatz fabric, and the supply is very limited, in Germany, but considerably easier to obtain than delicacies. The black market agents knew what the trousers and coats they exchanged for coffee or tobacco, were meant for. Even remote complicity in a prisoner's escape would cost them their head, if caught. They would not always take such risks. A pair of old trousers was reckoned at fifteen or twenty marks; a coat, thirty or forty; and an overcoat, sixty or eighty. It was difficult to bring them to the *Kommando*, but it could be done.

One sentry is watching twenty prisoners; but twenty prisoners are watching him. They know more about him, his habits, his weaknesses, his mistakes, than he can ever learn about them. While he surveys one group, something passes behind his back. While an incoming firm went through the gate, between two guards, and marched towards the middle of the yard where the *Kommandoführer* stood, I have seen packages shot from the ranks, very low, at a prisoner tying his shoe five yards away. When he got up, the package, attached to his belt, had disappeared under his overcoat.

The Germans cannot stop such deeds. It would require five times more sentries than they can afford and better ones.

Eventually, half of the clothes smuggled in the camp will be found during various searches; but such odds are not discouraging. In order to escape, the shadows, pressing the black market dealer with new demands, were ready to risk the worst.

The exchanges were swift. As soon as he had taken in all the

Forced Labor

stuff he could hide at one time — that is, one or two pounds, or one or two pieces — the dealer returned to bed, or went to the poker table and poured into the pot the best of the money he so dangerously earned. Meanwhile, the fugitive-to-be, having advanced one step in his preparations, treasured his last acquisition.

How sumptuous a civilian garment looked in the dim light of the boat. I cannot forget the rayon tie, shredded with use, that I bought for five *Reichsmarks*, a bargain: grey, with heavy blue stripes. It was so soft under my fingers. I hid it successively in my socks, under the strip covering the electric wires in my corner, in a ventilation pipe, and finally in the latrines.

*   *   *

While poker games and black market sessions were open to anyone with the necessary nerve, money, or material, other gatherings were strictly private. One could recognize the latter easily. Two or three men would be precariously installed under the shelter of a blanket and engaged in mysterious activities. They were sure to keep a partner at the foot of the stairs, standing guard, and when a discreet whistle announced a coming sentry, the blanket fell upon things that should not be discovered, while the men pretended to be going up to the privy or, stretching and yawning, to be returning to bed. The same signal would warn all others, and poker games would collapse in sudden darkness. The danger passed, the bids continued, on a sequence of hearts, or on a box of tobacco, and the smaller parties would resume their work: forging papers, transforming clothes, trying them on, rehearsing in costume, the approaching venture. When they tore up photographs, so dangerous because they bear the *Stalag "Geprüft"* on the back, they were not far from breaking out — one or two days, at the most.

They were not seen any more at lessons, theatre exercises,

sport teams. One let them alone, tacitly, unless they asked for help. One looked at them in awe, but from a distance. They were almost gone already. One was impatient to learn how far they would go before being stopped.

*   *   *

Private clubs met too, on regular nights. They were small and based on a unique interest.

"The Lice Throwers" were seven of different ages, origins, and professions. They were interested in lice. They knew the unfortunate boys whose fat skin nursed the biggest specimen. They had dates with them, to find out how the stock was coming on. On Saturday night, they would come to choose. For twelve healthy-looking lice — presumably full of eggs — they paid as much as one mark. A matchbox — it should be exclusively a German one — constituted a sufficient stable, if closed at both ends with adhesive paper.

On Sunday morning, they came down to the general review, fully armed. Between each index and thumb, they held snugly one of their champions. When the *Kommandoführer* or the sentry passed in front of them, standing at attention like all other comrades, they would briskly snap up one index and catapult forwards the live dose of itch. It can be done very well, with a good chance of hitting the victim below the belt, and little chance that the quick motion of the finger be noticed at all. While practicing on a black Dutch army overcoat, they had found that at least one projectile out of three stuck on the target.

This could also be done while raising the hand for military salute. It would be especially indicated for officers, if one could approach near enough. Good guards, like Kellner and

Forced Labor

Grün, were never treated so; but swine like Schlegel, and madmen like The Gnome, were literally bombarded. The club declined all responsibility if, in the sentries' barrack, undiscriminating little guests tried one pyjama after another.

*

Five men called themselves "Scavengers." They collected portraits of the *Führer*. Photos printed in "Slave Papers," as we called those published in French, in occupied territories, under the title of good old French newspapers, but now devoted to the exclusive art of bootlicking, were especially valued by the Scavengers. They cut the pictures out neatly, folded them, and put them in their pockets. Before going to work, they met and showed them to each other, while asking such questions as:

"What is your's today?"

"A fine one; a bust, five by eight inches."

"I beat you. Mine shows the feet as well."

"You aren't in it, men; look at this. Not only a full picture of Adolf, but one of his club-footed pal, also."

If they failed to produce an adequate picture, they were bound to contribute one mark, in *Stalag* coupons, to a common fund reserved for buying color-reproductions.

Every day, at some time between 7 A.M. and noon, each of them would lay down his tool, and say to a neighbor:

"I have to think about Hitler," and would retire for a few minutes to the lone little barrack present on every work-yard.

In the evening, the club met again, and the members asked each other:

"Gotten rid of it yet?"

"No," said one, "I have to go to see Lamy," and to the puzzled prisoner-nurse would be said:

"Give me a little ersatz castor oil. I haven't been able to kiss Hitler for at least two days."

*

There was also the club of the Black Crosses, somewhat more intellectual. There were eight members who managed daily to buy a *Pommersche Zeitung* from an overseer, second hand, when he was through with it.

Their night meeting was not meant to decipher the news, but only to count the black crosses, on one of the inside pages; little black crosses with a large swastika underneath, and a mention, covering two square inches:

"For the *Führer* and for the Fatherland, our beloved son, [father, brother, nephew, uncle, cousin So-and-So] died on the . . . victim of the cowardly Russian snipers."

There was an average of eight or ten every day. The club convention was as follows: all individual packages were strictly pooled. When the newspaper carried fifteen crosses, a small tin of sardines would be opened, emptied on a few biscuits, and then eaten as a celebration. When twenty dead were admitted, that day something as important as a can of meat should be opened. For thirty, as happened once or twice a month — it would be an all-out banquet: every available delicacy on the table. Lacking drinks, they would toast the brave Russian snipers with a mouthful of meat. The newspaper served as tablecloth.

Then they indulged in statistics. I had furnished them with the following information obtained from civilians: only distinguished Nazi families inscribed their war-dead in the paper. A police authorization was required, and every obituary announcement cost thirteen marks. When two women in the kitchen had lost their brothers, and when the sympathetic

Forced Labor

civilian who came in the office had told me of the death of his fifth friend, I had asked to see the announcements. The three mourners told me there were none. After talking it over with several other Germans, I had concluded that no more than one half of the war losses were represented in the daily paper.

Two hundred and fifty crosses monthly should mean 500 deaths for only the city of Stettin, with a population of a little over 250,000 in normal times. During the five months of hard fighting, every year, the 80,000,000 Germans suffered a proportionate loss of two for every 1000, which is about 160,000 dead every month. A minimum of 800,000 dead during the violent period, plus a couple of hundred thousands more during the rest of the year, seemed to be an acceptable figure. When the Black Cross Club said around the camp, in February 1942, that 900,000 Germans had been killed in Russia alone, and 1,500,000 wounded, it was sound information that one could use to make fun of the ridiculously small losses announced in the communiqué.

One repeated the figures with enthusiasm. It meant that the walls of our prison were crumbling. Tears were shed in every house in Germany, but wasn't it so in France, too? It would be a few more years before we could realize again how miserable this all was.

Now we could only rejoice.

We rejoiced.

*

I was wondering what new club this was, when one of the men called me. It was a midsummer night, so hot, so damp, and so full of mosquitoes in the hold, that they had sneaked out on deck, with their blankets, in the vain hope of being more comfortable behind the tiller room. In spite of the little breeze coming from the Baltic sea along the Oder, they weren't, and had squatted against the planks, like terra cotta targets lined on a rifle stand, at a county fair.

They were four, and talked of the time when they had a gun in their hands instead of a pickaxe. The first one was Desprez, a Belgian chemist, very popular in the camp on account of a series of rows with the *Lagerführer*. He had converted his school-Dutch into fairly good German, and never missed an occasion to say something unpleasant with it. One evening, the *Lagerführer* who was in a good mood, had come in the distribution room and shown a large photograph of burnt and twisted bodies of Ukrainian old men, women and children, allegedly victims of the Bolshevic terror. Desprez had come near, and looked carefully at the picture.

"Isn't this frightful? Aren't the Russians ruthless murderers?" Opferer had asked.

"I've seen worse than this," said Desprez.

"Where?" asked the other, rather interested.

"In Belgium, in 1914, 15, 16, 17. and 18."

The *Lagerführer* left the room without even a single oath.

Now, Desprez was telling about the eight men he had killed during the war: two with a bayonet, six with an automatic — all fifth column agents dressed as civilians, and shooting at retreating Belgians, especially officers, from trees and attics.

"I crawled behind them," he said, "very near, so as to down them with one single shot or blow. Afterwards, I took their weapons and their papers. That's what I've done."

The second comrade, Riffain, was a handsome youngster; and this was his story:

"I was lost in the Vosges Mountains, with ten men and two light machine guns. It was the day of the armistice, but we didn't know it. We had escaped capture twice, and marched south, through the woods, in hopes of meeting a friendly regi-

Forced Labor

ment. We woke up at sunrise to find that, during the night, a company of Germans had camped 200 yards below us, by a narrow road turning around the hill. They were already drinking coffee; several hundreds of them, standing in groups around a kitchen wagon. I aimed one of the light machine guns, a corporal the other, while our comrades prepared the ammunition. In thirty seconds, we had fired our complete supply: 400 cartridges. They fell on top of each other down there. It was disgustingly easy. I was so mad that we had no more ammunition. The survivors got one mortar in position, and the first shell cost us two men, so we fled, abandoning all equipment on the spot. Three days later we were taken prisoner.

" 'The armistice is signed,' cried the Jerries, waving white flags. 'We'll send you home immediately.'

"Here we are, but you have heard that kind of stuff too. Anyway, I've downed at least a hundred of them. On the hill, they looked like little patches of grass."

Duclos, the third one, was a professional boxer. He had gotten out of a burning tank with his colonel. Having fallen in a deserted trench, they found a case of hand grenades.

"Let's not surrender," said the colonel.

They let the attacking tanks pass over them, and waited for the motorized unit that followed. These were compelled to stop and lay planks over the trench. That was the ideal moment: one after the other, they tossed the hand grenades at the squad of trucks until several of them burned and exploded. Then the Jerries overpowered them. They shot the colonel immediately, because he had fought like a soldier, and they beat Duclos unconscious. When he came to again, he was a prisoner, and quite surprised that his life had been spared. But his jaw ached as it never had before, in his years of prize fighting:

"I'd like to know the blow that knocked me out for the first time in my career," he commented.

The fourth comrade was named Moineau.

"I have killed only one man," he said. "I pushed him in the river, and he was drowned. I stayed long enough to make sure he'd never come up. He was no German. This was a little before the war. He had . . . but why should you care about what he had done to me? Much more than your victims had done to you. I'm a murderer, and you are heroes: two bloody sorts. Only mosquitoes torment my sleep, on this convict ship, and I don't believe that visions of squadrons of ghosts, with shrouds of pale green, like German uniforms, masquerade around your bunks. But here is our own *Vertrauensmann* who has confessed to nothing yet. What are you guilty of, Jean?"

Had I aimed as well as I did at moving targets on the training field?

"I don't know exactly. I have fired six shots, one June night; three on my left at one man, three on my right at a group running towards me. It was dark. It happened fast, and then I ran. When I try to remember, I see two of the shadows falling. Do you think I am entitled to the benefit of the doubt? May I believe that no grey-haired mother is crying because of me? But if I have been awkward, and only wounded those 'falling shadows,' I am, nevertheless, guilty of intention. Even now, there are others — many others — that I want to kill, calmly, with my own hands, making sure, like Moineau, that they wouldn't come up again."

So we murmured, a hot midsummer night, about our homicides; gently, like schoolgirls about furtive kisses and promised dances.

The fog had fallen. One after the other, we curled up in the blankets and fell asleep.

*　　　*　　　*

Forced Labor

I headed the Central Committee of the boat. It was composed of three members, and its existence was known only to thirty of our comrades. It had the same characteristics as all other groups of prisoners: it was naive and passionate, earnest and inconstant. It expressed our willingness to fight with the means still accessible to us.

We three were very different men. We had in common only one thing: in the past, a strong taste for solitude and individual interests. We met with the opposite attitude in view. Perhaps because we had had no political affiliations, and because we represented no particular class we could now express the strange collectivity of the captives.

We met in my corner, very late, when all others had retired. I had at my disposal, a few square feet enclosed with lattice of two shelves and a cabinet, where I kept the *Kommando* lending library, and various papers concerning my public functions as *Vertrauensmann*. There was constant danger that the *Kommandoführer*, as well as a sentry on duty, would call on me there, at any hour of the night.

As my two colleagues worked with firms, they were physically tired, and I woke them up at the proper moment. They came, one at a time, cautiously, and we three fought sleep, confusion and despair out of our heads. We tried again to conceive our *Kommando* as a unit, as well as a part of the millions of European prisoners. We considered it under its various aspects that we only could realize all at once: firms, classes, groups, teams, clubs, committees, not completely independent of each other, because the same men might belong to two or three of them.

We appraised what we had accomplished so far, and what we had failed to accomplish. We planned insidious actions and violent ones, many of which never lived beyond the enthusiasm of a night.

I was older, and perhaps more objective, than my two associates; and yet I can't say that I ever saw clearly where our efforts led. The only point that was clear was that, our present condition being unacceptable, and our future dark, we should fight off mental and physical anemia, and try to survive. Most of us would have been glad not to wake up any more: we were already that low. We should move, get back to intense life, at all cost; become proud and confident again. We should resist. We should fight. Anything was better than poisonous resignation. The desire for a more intense life — that had formerly led us out of the crowd, in fear of its everlasting agitation — now took us back to the crowd, though we were aware that it was only temporarily purified by despair. To-morrow it would be as healthy, but also as careless, as ever; concerned with fashion rather than beauty, with news, rather than truth; and ready for fresh catastrophes.

So we drove our ship in the dark, without instruments and without help, between two streams: one of love, the other of hate. The love for our comrades we felt strongly. The *Kommando* was a mass of oppressed beings, with old uniforms, uncouth, bitter, tender, dreaming and craving hope, exactly as we were. The hate for the enemy was in no way spontaneous. I hated and wanted to kill the sergeants who had made me run, one night in June 1940, through a woods, after marching 147 miles and fasting five days. I have sometimes wondered how I could drown the *Lagerführer* Opferer without having to pay for it. Our last *Kommandoführer* I wanted simply to strangle. There were others whom I liked as individuals, whom I wished to meet again when Europe would be cured of the leprosy of uniforms. Now I hated them collectively, because there was nothing else to do. It would have been too ridiculous to feel happy when the British bombs fell on the Germans, and yet pretend to love the victims; and most of all, too confusing.

Forced Labor

If I loved my comrades, I had to be against their oppressors, and whoever stood with them. Only hatred was positive, sound, and healthy.

The *Sonderführer*, so happy because I liked the *Uhrfaust* of his Goethe; the *Unterlagerführer*, so sad because I refused to take his preaching seriously; the old drunkard of a guard Kellner, who touched me for cigarettes; and the dreamy corporal Grün, whose grandmother was French — each held a gun or a pistol with a swastika on it. They, too, were trumps in Hitler's hands. They, too, embodied subjugation, destruction, misery; what I had always hated.

So, we opened our meetings by talking about our hatred of the Germans. It was a kind of warming up before the bout.

Ours was similar to any other underground organization. We had one man in every secondary unit of the *Kommando*. One of the best, kept his eye on the foredeck half; another, on the afterdeck half. One man acted in each "firm," hidden in the shadow of the official firm-leader. A boxer, a singer, an actor, a pupil of each class, devoted himself to helping our comrades in what we thought was the right direction.

It was imperfect, inasmuch as we knew these different trustees unequally well, and some had to act in several groups. Though I did everything possible, in the office, to postpone their mutation elsewhere, we lost one fourth of them every two months. We met with them separately and at different places: in the latrines, in a corner of the yard, by the canteen, under a stairway — and always with an obvious excuse, such as exchanging books.

The Germans had no way of finding these men, even if some sentries suspected their existence; and we did indulge in a little romantic foolishness. For instance: among the replacements allowed us monthly by the *Kontrollstelle*, were excellent English shirts, trousers, blouses, coats, seized in stocks at Dunkirk, in Crete, or taken from prisoners. I saw that each of the thirty men on our staff wore an item of British clothing. Sometimes it was only a brass button.

We were proud to wear a bit of the uniform of a nation still at war. I can write it without danger, now that the *Kommando* XIII/226 has been divided and transferred to other camps, its secret organizations transformed, and the old banana freighter packed with Russians who will invent other ways to fool their *Kommandoführer*.

With this understructure as means of action, our activities bore on three main points: raising the morale of our comrades; lowering the morale of the Germans; working for victory over them, as much as possible.

*   *   *

The distractions now available in the camp, had succeeded fairly well in restoring some mental alertness in our comrades. Only news: *real fighting news* could do more.

Our sources of news were papers and information obtained through Poles and anti-Hitlerian Germans. I subscribed to the *Pommersche Zeitung* and *Das Reich*. The official communiqué gave some valuable indications. I have later found that they didn't lie on enemy shipping losses and prisoners taken, but would often repeat them several times and give the superficial reader the impression that they were new. By reading carefully and comparing successive communiqués, I could extract some acceptable indications, and move the swastikas on their pins, across the map of Russia, thus discovering the approximate importance of the first German setback, in the winter 1941-1942. I collected Hitler's speeches. From a distance of a few months, the successive contradictions and omissions pointed to new events. Occasionally, I heard the official broadcast in the *Lagerführung*.

Forced Labor

I had been unable to obtain a radio set for the camp. There was none to be bought, in Stettin. It would have been operated from the *Kommandoführer's* office, but I might have been able to hear the British broadcast, once in a while. We had tried in vain to reconstruct radio sets, with parts picked up in ruins; but essential pieces had always been missing.

Newspapers other than Hitlerians, could be obtained occasionally from neutral ships coming into Stettin harbor — especially Swedish. Several of our "firms" unloaded those ships daily. Though constantly watched by sentries, overseers, harbor police, and plain-clothes men, the prisoners managed to communicate with sympathetic Swedish sailors.

I had provided our trustees with an assortment of miniature notes, written in both German and English, numbered and progressive (all sailors know a little English; and Swedes usually understand a little German). If, while carrying sacks or crates, our comrade noticed a sailor looking at him with interest, he would try note number one on him, by dropping it casually at his feet. It said:

"Have you any bread to sell?"

If the man didn't pick up the note, or shook his head to say no, it meant that he didn't care, or wasn't willing, to take any risk. Otherwise he would disappear inside, and soon bring a little sandwich, look carefully around, and then give it to the prisoner. He would immediately receive note number two:

"Thank you for helping me. Is there anything I can do for you in exchange?"

The sailor read the note and would shake his head. Sometimes he'd dare to write something on the back of the paper, such as:

"Do you need anything else?" or some comment showing his good will. If his manners proved reassuring, this was our man. The next note would say:

"The next time you come to Stettin, could you bring us some

British or American newspapers? If you don't recognize me, leave them crumpled up somewhere on the deck. One of us will pick them up."

Thanks to this tedious system, I have read the *London Times* during several months. It was quite a feat to lounge on my bunk with a copy of this newspaper, bought in Göteborg, and in which everything was the counterpart of the Nazi publications. The boys gathered around me with imprudent enthusiasm. It felt so good to give them proof of the seriousness of the British efforts, as well as results of Allied bombings of Germany. Alas! the news was two or three months old, and talked about Allied victories in Greece, when I knew already that Crete had fallen into Nazi hands.

As everyone in my *Kommando* knew I had some knowledge of languages, any foreign newspapers, found anywhere, were brought to me. Huge loads of old papers were unloaded from Finnish or Swedish boats, and transferred to freight cars by prisoners. They picked out the bales of American, British, and Spanish publications, often unopened. I can state that an important reporter of the largest Stockholm newspaper, didn't read his *London Times*. I have had at least two dozen issues of it, still wrapped in their long tube of paper, with his name and address on it.

Our night committee condensed the principal news thus obtained, into a few clear facts; and we set them in circulation. We had a special medium: the washroom meeting. Every evening, between 9:30 and ten, twenty or twenty-five boys sneaked out on deck, and hid in the damp, cold washroom, to smoke and discuss. So avid were they for information, that any item told them, was sure to be known to the whole boat, by the next evening: it travelled fast, from bunk to bunk; from firm to firm; from group to group, and even from *Kommando* to *Kommando*.

Forced Labor

We also compared the various newspapers published in Belgium and occupied France. There were points where they differed from the strictly German ones. We could learn something from these differences.

I was suspicious of information obtained from the Poles, because it contained so much wishful thinking. Many of our comrades worked together in cellars with Poles, who often knew a little French or German. It was posted in the *Kommando* that we should never speak to them, except on business. They wore a conspicuous "P," in yellow and violet, sewed on their coat, and were despised by the Germans as much as Jews, and far more than French and Belgian prisoners. Posters, in every street, warned the public that the Poles were a foul race; that it would be a crime to make friends with them, and other cruel stupidities.

There was considerable emotion on the boat, one evening, when several of our firms told of having met a German woman being promenaded through the Stettin streets, tied on a carriage; stripped to her waist; her hair shaved. Huge signs, hanging from the wheels, said:

"She has soiled herself with the love of a Pole."

According to the newspaper, she had received the very lenient sentence of thirty years in prison, while her accomplice had been shot. Such information appeared once or twice a month.

Living in camps, the Poles were allowed in the streets during their free hours, but could spend the money earned by forced labor — a little more than we received — in their canteens only. Or they could send it to the wife or mother they had been compelled to leave somewhere.

One Sunday, when I had been with forty men to a delousing center, in March 1941, we had met, on the way back, six Polish girls on Adolf Hitler Place. They looked at us. I gave the

French command reserved for generals, flags and monuments to war dead: *"Tête, droite!"* and, at the same time, the marching prisoners turned their heads briskly towards the girls, as a mark of supreme respect. They joined their heels, and answered us with military salutes. Their smile, their raised hands, their pluck, were splendid; they shone as a warm, friendly light in the enemy city. It had happened so fast that the German crowd had been more puzzled than indignant; and the Slobberer, busy hitting the tail of the column, hadn't understood what was going on, fortunately; for it would have cost me my post of interpreter, at least.

The older Poles were often seen giving the Nazi salute; but we presumed they were compelled to do so. The young behaved especially well. They hid their intense hatred behind smiles, and promulgated, extensively, anti-Nazi information. They must have belonged to strong underground organizations. They announced, as early as December 1941, that there would soon be a war between Germany and Russia. America was to come in at the same time; and Hitler to beg for peace within three months. For them, Berlin was already entirely demolished, the Ruhr didn't exist any more; the Allies were going to invade Stettin the next morning!

So we liked and admired them, but couldn't use much of what they said. It was through them, however, that we had had news of the Russian prisoners while they were terrorized, in special camps, for three months before being sent to work. When the first columns of these appeared in the streets, they looked worse than we ever had. I exchanged a few words, in English, with a wounded Russian prisoner, brought, as an exception, to our sanitary center. He was an Ukrainian flyer, and volunteered this surprising information: on the Sunday that the war began for them, hundreds of planes were ready at a large airdrome near Kiev. The order to start had come.

Forced Labor

They had jumped in their planes. Not one propeller turned. The tanks were half full of water. There had been a powerful fifth column in Ukraine, also.

The anti-Hitlerian Germans I have met, especially sentries, would tell me some news given by the British Broadcast, to which they listened at homes of their friends. They, too, had a tendency to be over-hopeful; but they provided us with priceless data about the scandals in Nazi organizations, and the violence of racial and political repression. A German plumber, working in the camp, has told me this, while sitting on a bench, on deck and eating his lunch snack:

"Suspected of knowing some Communists, I have been arrested, attached to a table, and beaten with a stick, from toes to knees, for half an hour. When they let me loose, I fell, and they had to send me to a hospital. My legs are still weak, even now. One month later, they arrested me again. They took me to a room where a man I knew had been stripped and attached to a post, with strings so thin and so tight, that they had penetrated the flesh. The cuts had become infected, the flesh swollen between the bonds, and blackened. They had let him die. It smelled horribly. When I remember it, I can't eat. They showed me a post, and said it would be for me if they found out that I had had any relations with the corpse. I lied; I swore; I promised anything they wanted. I hate them, but I don't work underground any more. I'm so afraid they'll get me, and torture me, also."

The man didn't even shiver; he would have been afraid to be seen if he did so. He dared speak to me, on account of my white armband, and because he was supposed to ask me where the other leaks in the waterpipes were.

Such were the stories we heard, and repeated to our men as accurately as possible.

*　　*　　*

To lower the morale of the Germans, we formulated short slogans that our most daring comrades would try on the civilians working with them. They were based on the headlines of the Nazi papers. When the British Government signed a war pact with Russia, all newspapers published in red the following statement:

"Churchill has sold Europe to Stalin."

Our answer was:

"Bad news; but hadn't Hitler already sold the world to the Japanese?"

We had noticed that such a slogan worked well only if beginning with a confirmation of the German point of view. While digging or shovelling beside civilians, our men would repeat the above remark in very simple words, learned by heart:

"*Die Zeitung sagt das Churchill am Staline Europa verkauft hat. Schlechte Nachricht! Aber hat Hitler nicht schon genau so die Welt den Japaner verkauft?*"

It worked especially well in conjunction with:

"There is a yellow peril for Germany, also."

Whether it was true or not, we didn't know; but, like soldiers in a trench casting hand grenades blindly to another trench, we used everything we believed could hurt.

I have had the satisfaction of hearing one overseer comment on both of these propositions with one of our *Kommandoführer*. From worker to worker, they had reached him. Bad news always travels fast. Only a few words had been improved upon on the way. The slogan that our men preferred to use on the civilians was:

"For every prisoner compelled to slave for Germany, there will be one German corpse in the plains of Russia."

They watched while the other wondered, and they could see the sadness in his eyes when he caught the implication:

Forced Labor

"We are put in your place so that you can be sent to your death."

*　　　*　　　*

The Central Committee argued endlessly about the third point of its activity. One night, we failed to find anything useful to do; the next, we engaged in schemes impossible to carry out. Member three wanted to start a revolution of prisoners immediately; kill the guards, and paralyze the principal centers of the city. We could have done part of this. Killing all the guards was possible: I could have suppressed those on duty, one after the other. Then putting on their uniforms, we could have stabbed the others in their sleep. Our thirty men could also have disguised themselves as sentries, and led the boys out, as if going to work, at night, at important buildings, which they could have set on fire. What next? We'd be massacred; but worse, a great toll of prisoners, innocent of our revolt, would be taken to account for it. Families in the occupied countries would be shot. Such action could be helpful only if timed with an Allied landing on the Baltic border. We hoped there would be one; we dreamed about it, but knew nothing. Getting in touch with Allied agents was essential before starting anything like that.

In vain did I try, for a whole year, to get in contact with one of them. I let any German I ever met know that I lived in America. I bothered the *Kontrollstelle* and the *Stalag* with repeated demands for authorization to buy English books. They were never granted; but my only reason was to raise the interest of someone, in the military offices, who might be in British pay. If we had at last contacted one, while preparations were made for a revolt of prisoners, we could have been of considerable help to an Allied spy. One hundred and fifty of our men worked exclusively on the piers. They knew every transport

342

going in and out of the harbor. They knew how many soldiers it carried, and what sort of equipment. They knew how long it would be before it came back — presumably from Norway, Finland, Eastern Prussia. They have seen, between March 1941 and September 1941, hundreds of thousands of troops leave the harbor. Before the declaration of war on Russia, the inhabitants of Stettin wondered where they could be going. A sailor has sworn to me he "knew," from a reliable source, that these troops were going through Russia to line up against British India. At that time, Stalin was thought to be Germany's friend. Several Soviet ships were constantly unloading wheat, rubber, cotton, raw material, and loading crates of machinery. On the day that Hitler invaded Russia, three large freighters were seized in Stettin, together with tankers of oil.

Two hundred yards below the *Nordenham*, an important railroad bridge crossed the Oder. Train after train of troops, material, ammunition — so easy to recognize by the care taken to camouflage them — passed on it. We had established concrete plans to blow them up. What was needed now, was only a small charge of melinite, and a few feet of cord.

We were incredibly angry because these transports, these trains, staying for two or three days on the piers, were never bombed. Only once, during 1941, did we hear that an arsenal had been blown up, thirty miles north of Stettin. Several prisoners had been mutilated by the explosion, and sent back to the *Stalag*. They had met one of our comrades there.

I have seen many warships on the Oder — including cruisers — and collected some information about them. I kept the information as long as I had hopes of passing it out to British agents; but later, destroyed the dangerous notes. About the enormous plant for artificial gasoline of Pölitz — one of the five principal ones in Germany if I were to believe the Stettiners — we could have known much. Fifty of our men had worked there several

Forced Labor

months. They had told me where the protective balloons were anchored; where the various anti-aircraft batteries were hidden; where the most vulnerable tanks were located. We never had the pleasure of seeing it burn, though we looked in its direction, during the air raids, with ardent hopes.

We had warned our boys that it was their duty to wreck as much as possible, being careful, though, that the blame couldn't be laid on prisoners. They slowed down the work as much as they could; they undermined tracks, so that a small wagon would fall in the river; they broke their tools; they dropped sand in delicate machinery; they cut electric wires, and ruined waterpipes, but on a small scale. Perhaps we failed to give them the enthusiasm necessary, or rather, after giving it to them, failed to keep it alive. Exactly as the conditions in the camp went up and down with the temper of the *Kommando-führer*, the secret activities rose and fell with the energy of the three members of the Central Committee, who fought sleep, anemia, and despondency in my corner, every night. We were so tired of waiting. Wasn't anyone interested in us?

We needed instructions and encouragement from outside. They could have come to us through many channels — from France and from England — through the growing flux of civilian workers imported to Germany. It can't have been a mystery to the Germans that this was a marvelous opportunity to introduce spies; but they couldn't help it, any more than they could help keeping a huge army of prisoners on their territory, at the most vulnerable points, i. e. where there was urgent work to do.

Isn't this a deadly contradiction of the Nazi system, to be compelled to constitute great bodies of men united by oppression and barbed wire? Still organized as an army; conscious of the discipline of an army; couldn't the prisoners be the basis and medium of a fantastic revolt? There were 5,000,000 of them, at the least, of all nationalities, working in contact with Germans, tools, machinery; national wealth and power. If a little organization, such as ours, had been developed in each *Kommando*, and given a day and a "zero hour," those 5,000,000 prisoners could, in half an hour, have killed 250,000 sentries; 1,000,000 to 2,000,000 civilians, and set the whole country on fire beyond any possible help. Wouldn't the anti-Nazi Germans have risen too; and could the German Police and Army handle such a revolt if it occurred everywhere simultaneously? We didn't believe they could.

Millions of men would have been slaughtered in one day; but weren't millions of men going to be killed, in the long run? Wouldn't it be less horrible than to keep the fate of the oppressed in suspense for years, while their bodies decayed and their minds weakened? Could Germany have survived the sudden death of a few million working civilians and prisoners? Certainly not.

How much easier to die, on one grandiose day, than remain here for two, three, four more years! Each of our thirty men felt the same — one out of twenty in the camp. Wasn't it enough to inspire the others? Hadn't each successful revolution started with the exaltation of a few men, in an attic, or in a beer cellar, looking crazy and useless at first, and taking on body, consciousness and direction from the very opposition it encountered, until it became the symbol of all the oppressed, and, from a useless speculation, became a full reality?

So we murmured passionately, while the hours passed, as passed the Oder under the boat, without our advancing one step, until fatigue seized us and, with it, the consciousness of being only three exasperated fools, condemned to throw lice, instead of bombs, and to push, occasionally, a lone wheelbarrow into a lone canal!

*   *   *

Forced Labor

It was after 3 A.M. and it was cold. The meeting had just ended and I had never felt more desperate. I went on deck and hid behind the night privy, to breathe and to look at the sky and the oily water. Then I found I wasn't alone.

With flaps down on the ears, collar turned up, and fire between the lips, all prisoners look alike in the dark.

"Who are you, comrade?"

"Marquet, of Kronibus. Is that you, Jean? I hadn't seen your white armband."

"Yes. Dreaming?"

"Too many fleas in the straw; too many bats in the belfry; so I came up to inspect my line. Feel it; there's something on it."

He put the string in my hand, and I pulled it up. There was an eel on it, wriggling like a mad belt; struggling uselessly. It was prisoner of a little hook that Marquet had cut and forged out of a piece of our own barbed wire.

"Don't you want it, *Dolmetscher?*"

"No thanks, Marquet; you keep it. I'll have it fried in the kitchen for you."

"Some other time. Tell me, isn't the guard on duty, at the ramp, Corporal Grün? Please take the eel down to him, and tell him it comes from the Frenchman with a coffer shaped like a boat. He'll remember. He was swell to me last Sunday, during the general search."

"*Was? für mich? Danke, danke sehr, Johann*" (what, for me? Thank you . . .), said Grün, and he stuck the fish in his coat pocket. In the silence, his steps seemed to resound younger, happier.

*   *   *

Two quarts of ninety-four per cent alcohol were brought to the boat one evening. A small group of prisoners had loaded

346

big jugs, all day, and managed this extortion. They added water and sugar to it, and offered me a sip. It was bad. It tore the tongue, the throat, the stomach; and as soon as this first effect had subsided, a sudden flame rose inside of you, up to the brain, as if you had become a torch inside, only.

Finot drank a full cup of it, and fell. We undressed him and put him to bed. He fell out of it, and we let him sleep on the floor, with his blankets and clothes over him. Around midnight, a comrade came to my corner. (I was, I remember, reading again *The Knapsack*, an anthology of poetry and prose published for English soldiers, that was my devoted companion until the last day.)

"Trouble with Finot," he said.

He had awakened, white as lard. His eyes were closed, but his limbs shook and waved like trees in a tornado. He spoke. The words, too, seemed to be brought by the wind, and taken away by it: they buzzed in an incomprehensible murmur, and suddenly roared back. They roared like the engine of a plane diving at you, and a little meaning became clear in them, grew, and grew, as grows the figure of the bandit in the machine-gun tower, when the plane passes over you, thundering and murdering, and then disappears slowly, through a little black hole, at the other end of the sky; and as it falls again on you, from the clouds, a mad bird with four, eight tongues of fire, thirsty for your life.

So roared and hummed our comrade, fighting a battle all alone in the corner. He had broken a stool and a bunk. He had thrown all his clothes and blankets away. His naked body was obscenely pitiful. He clenched his fists and next, raked his skin and whatever else he could reach, with his nails, like claws.

We built a wall with many blankets, to deaden the noise he made. Several comrades stood in the stairway, to divert the attention of the night sentry, if he came in.

Forced Labor

Standing around Finot, we listened hopelessly to the confession coming out of his mouth like a foam: like a slaver, all that he had hidden before, under a soft little smile: a mixture of German, of English, of French, a nightmare of rage, of hate, of threats, of sneers, of misery, with little bits of love in it, like pink ribbons caught in a maze of thorns.

Until morning we watched.

When he had said it all, he sank into a peaceful sleep, pale and thin, looking so young — and so old.

*   *   *

Foltin never knew what time it was. He got up in the night, and went down the exit ramp. The sentry yelled at him, and pushed him back inside the boat. Then he wandered around the floors until a late poker player, or anyone discreetly busy in a corner, stopped him and saw him back to bed. His neighbors pulled his blankets off him in the morning, and found that he had forgotten to undress. He would even forget to eat. One boy kept his food card, brought him his rations, and told him when it was time to take some nourishment. He never washed. When he became too black or too smelly, two or three others took him gently to the washroom, and scrubbed him from head to toe. They washed his laundry for him. He didn't write to his mother. His friends had to fill up his letters. They made him sign at the bottom of the page. When her letters came, they got them from Lamy, and read them aloud to him. He nodded.

We sent him periodically to the doctor, without obtaining any other result than a fresh order for delousing. Even the overseer of his firm could see he couldn't work. His hands couldn't retain anything heavy, and his knees were always bleeding from frequent falls. He was employed at sweeping floors or watching stoves.

Somewhere on the Albert Canal, Foltin had been shell-shocked.

*   *   *

David wanted to become a priest. He had made the decision while working on the roads. Life had seemed so excruciating to him then, that he had realized the role that spiritual consolation could play, but did not. He had obtained a *Gospel* from home, and because there was no light in his corner, he sat on a stool, under the stairway, for half an hour, reading, while the others slept.

He was seeking words of hope that could be words of action. He wanted to save the world again; but he also wanted to escape.

*   *   *

It was rare that we liked to be awakened but when, instead of the customary: "*Aufstehen, aufstehen!*", the sirens of an air-raid alarm sounded, everyone stirred, and sat up on the bunks. Laughs replaced the snores. When dozens of antiaircraft batteries knocked the skies to pieces, the real fun began. Small bits of shell fell on the decks, and on the roofs around. The guards ran to the heavy concrete shelter built for them in the center of the yard. We stayed on board with the guards at the ramps. It was forbidden to get out of the hold, but dozens of men dashed through the doors. "Latrines!" they cried to the protesting Jerry, and, while pretending to wait by the little hut, they enjoyed the fireworks.

It was a superb feast. Ten or twelve searchlights dug deep ruts in the night. The batteries fired four shells at a time: we saw the flames at the mouth of the guns, and in the sky,

Forced Labor

everywhere; fugitive stars, among which we sought, passionately, the raiders. They were so high we could rarely see them. We had to be content with the purr of their engines — British, American, Russian engines, they sang of home, of hope, of sweet horror for the others. They dropped powerful flares. The bombs whistled so well, just like the German bombs when they used to fall on us. No one feared that they might hit the boat; or at least, no one said so. We wished to see the coal depot, the city gas tanks, the electric works, the high silos, the rows of apartment houses, the barracks, the churches, the hospitals, all of it blow up, pop, jump in the sky as a rabbit, full of shot, makes his death somersault. And we wanted to hear the stones, the bricks, the pieces of wood, falling. And we craved the shrieks of the wounded, and the laments of the terrorized.

How splendid, how refreshing if, next morning, the whole city should be only a maze of smoking wreckage!

One went to work the next day with joy, to see, to hear, to know the results. Alas! as long as I stayed in Stettin, we never had much success. Of one hundred bombs, so many fell astray, in empty yards, in the water, or in the street; some fell on small buildings; and only four or five did substantial damage.

They also fell on barracks full of prisoners. Twenty-nine of them were killed in a single night, in October. The *Stalag* sent them a wreath with an inscription on it. The last word in publicity!

CHAPTER 20

Story and Midnight Trial
of a Barber

GENERALLY despised by his fellow prisoners, Tribaut, our little Belgian barber, would have been hated if he hadn't been so patient and considerate with everyone of his customers. You came back from work, dusty with cement, angry because of a fight with an overseer, or because your soup was all rutabaga — no potatoes in it — and your piece of meat was exactly suited to fill the smallest hole in your shoe. Perhaps, also, the last letter you had sent home had come back, torn by the censor, because you had written two extra lines. You sat on a stool. Tribaut would arrange your own towel around your neck, overlook a louse or two, and lowering his voice as if ten boys waiting around couldn't hear anyway, he would tell you the latest news: how many packages So-and-So received from home; what the interpreter had read in the Stettin paper about so many millions of Russians taken prisoner, and that the German top corporal had said they were coming to take our place. So we would go home soon. Tribaut would insist that this was no story.

You didn't much believe it, but it made you feel good, and you were soon ready to answer some polite questions about what happened that day at work: who got a kick from guard Schlegel; who hid a whole hour in the latrines while the others overworked; and who had taken on mysterious airs la⁺ely, as though getting ready for one of those disappearances that drove the *Kommandoführer* frantic, and would mean, for a month at least, curfew at 7:15 P.M., plus whatever punishment could be invented. When you went out and left five *pfennigs* — perhaps

Forced Labor

ten — he would say "Thank you" to anybody; but he knew how to make you feel that his consideration was proportionate to your importance in the camp life. He had picked up enough German to get along with the guards, and produced information coming, he said, from people placed to know what was cooking.

Every three months we received a new *Kommandoführer;* and Tribaut managed his beard and his temper. He would have kept on growing bigger and redder in the face — hardly happier than the others, though, for even more food and lighter work don't render acceptable a life deprived of freedom and joy — if fierce *Unteroffizier* Jurk, assisted by two guards, hadn't suddenly searched our comrade Dutheil's belongings, and found 180 marks hidden in a toothpaste tube.

At twelve o'clock, on a cold January night, Tribaut found himself awakened brutally by Finot, dragged out of his straw sack, told I wanted to speak to him, and, grumbling and yawning, pushed towards the infirmary. The padlocked door was open. Finot pushed Tribaut in, snapped the lock behind. Then he went to the top of the stairs so as to take care of the guard who was tapping his freezing feet on deck, and might take it into his head to patrol his beat inside. Eventually, if necessary, Finot would pretend to slip on the steps, and his falling shoe would be the alarm signal.

With a shirt stamped in thick black letters "*Stalag* II C," shorter in front of his hairy thighs, a large mantle thrown over his shoulders, the funny tuft hanging from his Belgian cap, and his small bewildered eyes, Tribaut was a sight for the thirty-two men awaiting him; but none laughed.

Fifteen men stood on each side, forming an alley. I motioned him to the end and made him sit on a stool. He was going to need it. The electric wires had been tapped, and a small bulb hung above him. If Finot's shoe ever bounced on the steps, the light could be turned out promptly, while we crouched against the walls. The room reeked of chemicals, ill-washed laundry hanging from the beds around, and of hundreds of bodies lying exhausted on decayed straw. Men snored, each in his own key. The ever-turning dynamo roared a gentle bass.

Dutheil arose from the darkest corner of the infirmary, pointed a finger at Tribaut, and said in a low voice:

"I told David yesterday, at six o'clock, that I had just taken 180 marks to the boat. Then I saw that Tribaut was there listening. Two hours later, I was searched, my money taken, my plan of escape ruined. I accuse Tribaut of letting guard Reipsch know that I had money."

David stepped out and said:

"I've been helping Dutheil with his scheme from the beginning. I would not and have not, said a word to anyone. I accuse Tribaut."

"I . . . What? . . . . No, no . . ." muttered Tribaut. He had gotten up, and he shook his small fists, madly. "I haven't spoken of it to anybody!"

"Sit down barber. I, *Vertrauensmann* of this camp, have found out that you cut guard Reipsch's hair at seven o'clock yesterday. At seven-thirty, when I came back to the office after handing in the names of sick prisoners, Reipsch was talking eagerly with *Kommandoführer* Jurk. They hushed immediately and went out. At eight, they searched Dutheil's corner, and found the toothpaste tube in which he had rolled up the bills, and which, imprudently, he had left in his coffer."

"I couldn't hide them better until night," said Dutheil.

"It's a lie," repeated Tribaut. "I have never done anybody any harm!"

It sounded like hollering, but his words were low. The most violent life of a camp expresses itself, at night, in murmurs and shadows.

Forced Labor

"Tribaut, you are accused of treason. This is the ship's council, and I preside over it. Do you know these thirty men?"

One after another, stating his grade, his nationality, the firm he worked for, and his activity in the camp, I named them.

"Do you object to any of them? No? Indeed no! No one could object to them. For months they have come back from work as tired as any of the others, and just as sore; but they have found time and energy to help me build up the morale of our *Kommando*. They have made efforts you have no idea of, Tribaut. They have given others courses without documents, so that the time of captivity would not be entirely lost; they have organized sport teams, card tournaments to amuse you; they have written sketches, composed songs, lectured — often for the first time in their lives — and on all subjects. They have brought me material and information, patiently extorted, from the city, with which I have composed the anti-Nazi propaganda that they have also diffused. In the firms, they have fought for the rights of the others — whatever small rights could be imposed on the Germans by slowing down work, day by day, imperceptibly; and provoking difficulties until the guards and overseers, out of patience or utterly puzzled, would grant tacitly what had been claimed.

"Here they stand, features drawn, tired, looking as ridiculous as you and I, with their bare legs or long torn underwear, coats of all colors, and headgear cocked in all directions, as conscious as I am, perhaps, of the possible grandiloquence of this scene, but ready to play at judges, as the Germans make us play at slaves, with a feeling that is no make-believe. They represent — they are indeed — the soul of the camp.

"This is no play, though it looks like one, and though there is something tragically toy-like in any part of a prisoner's life. Our meat portion seems cut to play with; our clothes are fit for clowns. Many of us have been made, and kept, prisoner with bed-time stories of prompt liberation. All day, we play for the guards a comedy in which we pretend to be working; and at night, the best of us play at escaping, secreting, like magpies, odd objects, buttons, pieces of cloth, anything with which one may compose a disguise and be mistaken, for a few minutes, for a civilian. And then for days, for weeks, they will play hide-and-seek with peasants in the fields, the policemen in the street, the sharp-shooters and their fierce dogs on the borders.

"But being caught is no play, Tribaut. At best it means weeks in jail, with bread and water, and a single blanket with which to sleep on the floor. And being convicted of destruction of any material, theft, or worse, means the disciplinary company for a long time, with minuscule rations of food, and exercises at all hours of the night. Then too, if they happen to win, in spite of our hopes, the Germans have not failed to warn us that captured fugitives will be freed only after all the others.

"Do you realize that escaping is the ultimate goal of all prisoners, and that it is to this end that we have been trying to build up their courage, and awaken them from the mental torpor of captives? Everyone carries a scheme of evasion; even you, perhaps. It begins like a fairy-tale that you tell yourself, one day, when the longing for those you love becomes unbearable, and the work too hard. You nurse it, day by day, night by night. For many, it will remain vague, and sink into mere fantasy; but a few will be able to transform it into reality. Suddenly they will go; shoot through Germany; reach home, perhaps. And that day, the guards will be enraged — and the remaining comrades will gladly pay for it!

"Tribaut, a man preparing an escape is taboo in the camp. He is a sort of saint, and symbolizes the hopes of the others. Doing anything to ruin his chance is a crime against the whole camp. Denouncing, to a German, a comrade ready to break out, is the worst of all treasons. We have to be sure that it can-

Forced Labor

not happen. The penalty for it must be the maximum. Do you agree, my friends?"

One by one, the thirty men said "Yes; I agree."

"Tribaut, you have not confessed, but appearances are against you. Many comrades have already reported you as dangerous. I have warned you several times to stop gossiping and investigating the affairs of others. You are envious, and ready to do much to maintain your credit with the *Kommando-führer*, and get more to eat. You may hate the Germans, as you have said, and yet help them, out of jealousy or stupidity. It is also possible that you are today the victim of an exceptional coincidence. It is my conviction, however, that it is through you that *Unteroffizier* Jurk has been able to effect this search at the right time. If you are guilty, it is, to my mind, in one of the following respects:

1) Wilful denunciation in order to get advantages for yourself.

2) Telling guard Reipsch something concerning Dutheil that may have confirmed suspicions existing about him. A pair of civilian trousers had already been taken from him, long ago. You might have tipped off the guard by, say, laughing in a certain way, or hinting that somebody who works in the kitchen, as Dutheil does, is a pretty smart fellow.

3) Answering, out of stupidity, questions put to you by guard Reipsch concerning Dutheil and leading to the same conclusion.

"If your thirty comrades decide that you are guilty of any of these crimes, I propose that the punishment be as follows: For wilful treason, death. You will be thrown in the Oder."

Here David stepped out and said:

"There is an exhaust pipe for hot water coming from the ship's machinery. It has melted a small hole in the ice, two feet thick on the river. If Tribaut were dropped from exactly above, he would sink, and never come back. I could testify that he had fallen accidentally."

"If your judges find you guilty on the second count, I propose that you box six rounds, in this infirmary, with Duclos, our best boxer."

Duclos stepped out. A former professional boxer, flat nosed and damaged ears, he lifted up his arms and shook his hands above his head, as fighters do when they enter the ring. Then, picking up the training gloves that hung from a nail, he threw them at Thibaut's feet, and said:

"He may defend himself if he wishes."

Tall, lean Lamy, the *Kommando's* nurse, added:

"I'll patch him up afterwards. Perhaps I can make him look as though he had fallen down the steps."

"And if you are found guilty in the third manner, I propose that you be ostracized completely, as utterly dangerous."

Here, Desprez, the chemist, stepped out and said:

"As one Belgian for another Belgian, I demand that this ostracism be extended to his civilian life. With your agreement, my comrades, I shall see that the shame he has brought on us be known in his village."

"Tribaut, do you still deny the charges?"

"I haven't betrayed him," he cried. "No! No!" and he buried his face in his hands.

"Look at us, and say so again."

He looked up. Despair and fear alone could not seem so ugly.

*   *   *

Five taps on the door. Finot came down, opened the door, closed it behind me, and we sneaked together to the water-room on deck, to smoke a pipe, in silence. Again five taps, and I went back to the infirmary.

Forced Labor

"Friends, have you found him guilty?"

"Yes; we have."

"Do you believe that our procedure has been fair, that we have acted for the best, to protect this camp from demoralization, and those preparing an escape, from denunciation?"

"I do," said each one.

"Then whatever you have decided — whether death by drowning in the icy Oder, a pounding of face and ribs by our expert comrade, or the most despicable ostracism — I take the responsibility for it. To the Germans, by way of denial, though I have no doubt that any decent German officer would approve of this in his heart; to the French, by complete admission, if they ever claim us from here, and ask me for the count of your pains; to God, if any, above!"

Marquet, the oldest of us, a mason and a clear headed man, stepped out and said:

"We believe that Tribaut has acted from stupidity; that he is dangerous and should be ostracized. We shall let it be known tomorrow to each of our comrades, in our firms."

"Then go, Tribaut; and go alone! Except for the indispensable matters of service, nobody will speak to you any more."

Between the lines he went, red, furious, and a little relieved also. One by one, clapping their wooden shoes and tightening their topcoats against the stairway drafts, the others went down to their beds of straw and lice, for a few hours of sleep, before another day in slavery.

CHAPTER 21

My Last Kommandofuhrer

As A corporal, almost a year ago, Jurk had perturbed the boat with his galloping furor. Now that he was back as *Unteroffizier* and *Kommandoführer*, with no one to curb him, he was far worse.

He had chosen as assistant a corporal whom we called Judas. Something worn out in Judas' face made one think of an old shoe. He never looked anyone in the eyes, so crooked were his own. He was constantly drawing his eyelids down, for fear that his venomous thoughts would show. He entered the office and closed the door with exaggerated care, as if an unknown danger had been threatening. He crept noiselessly towards his boss who, squatting nervously on a stool, had a lot of a bulldog, and a little of a dachshund. Judas spoke with his head so close to the other's that he seemed to be spitting eardrops, when he reported what he had seen through a keyhole, and overheard in the latrines.

The team was as indignant at the importance that their predecessors had given Paul and me in the office, as the others had been glad to be relieved of most of their work. Judas, who could hardly write, dreamed of being a secretary; while Jurk was convinced that he could handle the problems of a large camp, as he had handled stones, as a mason's helper: one at a time. He forgot that his mason had set them according to a plan, and that it wasn't a mere scribble on a sheet of blue paper. As no love affair called either of them out of the camp, they spent sixteen hours of the day undoing what had been done before they came.

Forced Labor

As soon as I left the office, they fumbled through my papers, and took half of them away. They believed that something mysterious was hidden in the file of identification cards. They pawed the cards constantly, mixed them up in no alphabetical order, and even locked up some of them concerning prisoners of whom they were especially suspicious. They thought, perhaps, that it was like hexing them, and that if their description and data were safely put away, the prisoners couldn't escape.

As a result, when the *Kontrollstelle* called up for information about any current problem, it couldn't be given any more, and Jurk engaged in virulent and endless tirades in his effort to place the blame of the miserable bureaucracy of his predecessor:

"Everything is wrong here," he said. "I've never seen so many papers in my life; and you must give me a little time to straighten them out."

In two weeks, most of the documents formerly laid on the shelves in tolerable order, had disappeared in his chest of drawers, or in the stove. Files were broken, references lost, and no one could help the marvelous mess any more. As a solution to every trouble — one occurred every ten minutes — he telephoned: to the overseers, the bookkeeper, the *Kontrollstelle*, the *Arbeitsamt*, the *Amtmann*, the captain's office. He vituperated, complained, and asserted what he didn't know, with a remarkably quick imagination; thus impressing his auditor with his exceptional vitality.

Soon the mistakes and contradictions had multiplied to such an extent that he received a succession of unpleasant telephone calls that made him very angry. Unusually afraid of his superiors, for a German soldier he gave way to unrestricted language. To criticism on the daily report, from the *Amtmann* — the same correct gentleman who had received me a few months before — Jurk made such insulting remarks that the other hung up his

360

phone, and notified the *Kontrollstelle* that he would not deal any more with such a beast. Jurk complained about this ostracism:

"I represent the Army," he cried over the phone. "and this paper-monger represents only the civilian administration! We are at war, and the Army should come first everywhere. Couldn't you ask the captain to reprimand this pretentious *Amtmann* and. . . ."

As much as I had been annoyed with Schumann's endless telephonic romances, they had at least the merit of being expressed in a low key. Schumann was chewing rose petals; but Jurk was chewing T.N.T.

He had regular scraps with the *Lagerführer* in the yard. He thought it a shame that there should be two masters in the camp.

"I should handle the kitchen business, too."

"I am the *Lagerführer*, and I represent Hitler here!" hollered the *Lagerführer* while waving his vermillion armband in the other's face.

"I am the *Kommandoführer*, and I represent Hitler more than you do!" screamed Jurk, while pointing at the little swastika embroidered on his chest.

They told what they thought of each other, in great detail; and so fast that I could translate only the most colorful insults, for my comrades, who were eating their rutabagas to the rhythm of this music.

This kind of self-sabotage of the *Kommandoführer*, would have been amusing if all the disorder he created didn't affect us directly. Everywhere that the ambitious little brute turned his suspicious and jealous mind, disaster was in store.

I had handled the clothes distribution for ten months, with the help of Interpreter II — the capable and devoted Maurice. We kept exact lists of our comrades whose outfits were really

Forced Labor

the worst, and we made sure that they were helped first, when a replacement lot arrived from the *Kontrollstelle*. One afternoon, the *Kommandoführer* and his pet demon transported, themselves, all the material kept in our storeroom, to a cabin in the ship. Thereafter, they assumed the distribution, according to their caprice, without order, fixed date, or effective control. It would have been interesting to investigate how many pairs of the best shoes were sold by Judas, outside of the camp, and how many packages of cigarettes and *Lagercoupons* he collected from prisoners, who bribed him in order to make sure of getting a pair of trousers.

Jurk and Judas raided the boat constantly. Having remarked that a certain number of shoes remained under the bunks during the day, they took them away. Didn't the *Stalag* rule stipulate that no prisoner could possess an item of uniform in double? When the boys came back from work with the old sabots they wore on dry days, so as to economize their one pair of shoes, they found they were gone. Others who had received the missing shoes from home, lined up by the office door, with their certificates of ownerships. I raised as much of a scandal as I could, and threatened to write to the *Kontrolloffizier*. The two imbeciles had to give way, but it proved impossible to restore the shoes to their exact owners, and men who had before a fairly comfortable pair, had to be content now with one that was too small or too big.

*   *   *

Provoked by the setback, Jurk and Judas excited the guards against their men, with more or less stupid stories, about which corporal Grün kindly warned me. Individual searches were multiplied. Every evening, one or two men were brought to the office by their sentry, who reported:

"I suspect this man of having received civilian money. I've seen him exchanging something with a civilian."

This was an opportunity for a rather nice bit of foolishness.

Swivelling on his stool, Jurk ordered me to make the man understand that it was much better for him to surrender his money before being searched. I got up, went near my comrade and told him:

"You are asked to surrender your money, if you have any, and you know what you should do."

He answered:

"I have no civilian money."

I turned on my heels, as if on a pivot, and translated this in German.

"Tell him," thundered Jurk "that we are going to search him; and if he has lied, he will be punished: jail, bread and water."

I turned again, and repeated the threat.

"I have none," reiterated the prisoner.

So they stripped him. They looked in his wallet, in his pockets, in his socks, in his underwear, in his sleeves, in his cap. They felt the seams. They made him open his legs wide and looked underneath. They didn't find any money there, either. They became angry. They knew that nothing could have possibly escaped their investigation. The sentry looked shocked. My comrade put on his clothes, saluted, and left. As soon as he was on the other side of the door, he laughed. So did I, inwardly.

You couldn't find it, master Jurk, for one of many reasons. First of all, I had warned my comrades against bringing money to the camp on the day they had obtained it. They should hide it in the work-yard — that's always possible — and pick it up only the next day, or whenever they were sure their transaction hadn't been noticed and reported.

Forced Labor

Another reason was located in my own back. Didn't you ever notice that I had a low hip pocket that no other French army trousers boasted? Someone had cut and sewed it for me; and all comrades who should know, knew about it. When a prisoner transports money, it's rarely in his pockets. It's more likely to be crumpled up in his hands, or under his sleeve, so that he can pass it quickly to someone else, in case of trouble. It's only rarely that the whole camp can be searched at once. There aren't enough guards for that; and as it must be done outside work hours, it's not likely to occur in the evening.

If the suspected prisoner hasn't rid himself of his precious load before being brought to the office, he still has a good chance to push it in my hip pocket while I turned my back repeatedly to him, especially the first time when I came quite close, or when I distracted the sentry by asking him, as was my right of *Vertrauensmann*, if he had actually seen my comrade taking money.

When the crumpled note was not in my hip pocket, it might be under the counter — a rich idea of Jurk to prevent casual visitors from coming near our tables. It had a door, and while he went through it, our comrade had his first chance to pin his bill underneath it, with one of the thumb tacks lining the walls of the corridor through which he had just passed. There was also a little box outside, allegedly to throw butts into, before entering the office. Indeed, we were tolerably well equipped, and, with a little alertness, our comrades could get through the difficulties of execution.

Only the black market dealers and the few dozen men engaged in active preparations for an eventual escape, handled large sums of civilian money. They were careful, fully instructed, by me, of the dangers they ran, and gave so much thought to such problems, that they could be considered as specialists. They did accomplish marvels. When "amateurs" were caught, it would be with only a very few marks; and it was good policy to let Jurk find something, once in a while, to feed his vanity.

"I know much more than you think," he would tell me. "I see what your comrades are up to. They aren't fooling me."

He was bragging; but primitive as he was, he was decidedly harder to manage than cultivated people. He didn't fall over some of the obstacles that I laid in his way to distract his attention, because he was too crude to see them. He didn't trust anyone, including Judas, whom he knew to be as treacherous as he was himself. He crawled under the prisoners' beds, felt the wall joints with his knife, and always made sure the coffers had no double bottom. He never went through a pack without finding some forbidden item, such as a bottle of ink, or a few French bills hidden in an old pipe.

The firms working on the piers worried him very much. Though it hadn't yet been proved, he suspected that some of our boys managed to open the crates of food they loaded for the German Armies fighting in Russia, and lay hands on a few cigars, a bar of chocolate, or a bag of sugar. The boys immediately put the cigars in a French package, ate the chocolate on the spot, and brought the sugar back to camp through a stratagem too good to tell while there are war prisoners. The incoming firms were usually searched in vain.

One man, though, committed the indiscretion of innovating on the matter. Wearing long underpants, like the rest of us, he tied them around his ankles with strings, drew his socks up over them carefully, and tied them too. Then he filled all the space that his legs didn't occupy, with the contents of a bag of sugar. He must have felt like an insulated pipe, and it must have been very trying to walk two miles with the sugar against the skin. He had hardly entered the gate when his group was lined up for a regular search. Where a sentry might have

Forced Labor

thought nothing of the queer feel of his legs, Jurk smelled a rat, and made our boy open his trousers. Between the front buttons of his underwear, little rivulets of sugar ran accusingly. Some sight! Jurk made as much noise as an antiaircraft battery. Then he compelled the guilty prisoner to run in the yard, around the concrete shelter reserved for the guards. Quite a torture, especially between the legs. The seams of the underwear burst and the running man left a little trail of sugar. Jurk kept him going from the center, with a sentry's rifle as a whip. I protested violently, asking for military punishment only, but was ordered, several times, to shut up. I called for my colleague, Paul, and we both set ourselves rigidly at attention. For the twenty minutes that his punishment lasted, we saluted our comrade uninterruptedly. The whole camp watched. When the sneering Jurk had returned to the office, we saw our man to the infirmary, where Lamy washed the sugar off the scratches on his thighs.

*   *   *

Jurk never ended a Sunday review without delivering a speech that he insisted on my translating in detail. He gave way to his imagination and his entire lack of scruples. Once, he made me announce that he had received a phone call from the *Stalag* informing him that we should all be liberated in the first months of 1942. A record was to be kept of the prisoners' behavior, especially at work, and those designated as unwilling to co-operate with the Germans, would not be freed. I was more careful than ever, during my translation, to emphasize repeatedly the fact that *he* had said so before. Jurk noticed a certain lack of enthusiasm in the crowd.

"Don't they believe it?" he asked me.

"They've heard such things quite often, for eighteen months, *Herr Kommandoführer.*"

"But why don't you tell them it's true? Don't you believe my words?"

"I'm not here to believe any words, *Herr Unteroffizier*, but to translate them. I have done so."

He was considerably vexed. The idea of not believing him! He couldn't bear that. I had been wrong to speak my mind, even so discreetly, for he took his revenge by fooling me quite well, the following Sunday.

He woke me up at 4:30 A.M. to tell the men that we were leaving the boat, and should pack up in a hurry. One hour later, all stood in the yard with their belongings. Not everyone had had time to unbury his hidden treasures and conceal them on himself or in his baggage.

Two sentries were placed at each ramp, and prevented anyone from going back on board. We waited two more hours, until two officers, twelve noncommissioned officers, and fifty soldiers arrived. This was a masterfully organized party, where the prisoners would provide the fun. For the first time, I hadn't been in a position to guess that there was going to be a general search.

I knew the captain. He was a good man, but didn't like difficulties. I had been taken to his office as interpreter, several times, when he wished to question a captured fugitive, himself, or a man condemned to a little stretch in jail. He called me, and ordered me to warn my comrades that if they surrendered, immediately, the civilian money in their possession, it would be refunded to them in *Stalag* coupons. This was certainly fair, and little man Jurk was not quite as pleased as he had expected to be. If they didn't surrender it, it would be confiscated as soon as found.

About one hundred comrades volunteered to hand out one or two marks each — ridiculous little sums indeed, but it pleased

Forced Labor

the captain very much. Only a few timid fools came out with ten, or even twenty, marks. The others held their treasure in their mouth, wrapped up in tinfoil, or under their feet in the sand — or in their hands, and passed it constantly to one another.

For one aware of it, it was marvelous to watch these sixty-two newcomers, reinforcing our own three dozen guards, in their search of wallets, pockets, and suitcases, where they discovered only some two hundred marks and five pairs of civilian trousers, while some 10,000 marks, mostly in high bills, kept flying from hand to foot, from cap to coat, from coat to pants, and from sack to coffer. It may be inconceivable for anyone having had the luck never to be in a position to learn the prisoners' tricks. Even the most indifferent among us knew enough, after eighteen months of captivity, to fool many a guard. To make this search successful, from a German point of view, it would have required at least four times as many guards, or have required three whole days, instead of one morning.

I have an idea that the captain was not unaware of it, for he came to me and said bluntly:

"You, *Dolmetscher;* how many *Reichsmarks* have you?"

"It is forbidden to have any, *Herr* Hauptmann. I have none."

"Fine, but I mean, how many do you have hidden, somewhere? 200, 300 *Reichsmarks?*"

His eyes were laughing, but I didn't trust him to the point of saying, as I wanted to:

"You know I shan't tell you."

"Just the same, we'll search you a little," he added; and calling the first sergeant in sight, he handed me over to him. How lucky that it was Schumann, our former *Kommandoführer!*

He looked at my wallet, fingered my photographs, stuck his hands in my pockets, looked absent-mindedly at my cap, and murmured in my ear:

"Don't you regret the time when I commanded this camp?"

(I did) while declaring loudly that I had no civilian money. How nice of you, *Unteroffizier* Schumann! You knew that I wouldn't have it on me, anyway. The captain had been very cunning, though, in guessing the amount of my fortune: I had then 230 *Reichsmarks* snugly enclosed in a little metal box lying on the bottom of the Oder. It was hooked on one of Marquet's fishing lines. When the show would be over, I would pull my fat little fish under the exhaust pipe of the ship, while pretending to be washing my soup bowl, as I would have done at the last minute, if we had really left the camp.

*   *   *

It was a mania with Jurk to draw out his pistol, make you see that it was loaded, undo the safety catch, and push the nozzle into your ribs.

We had a little tenor in the musical group, who was so timid that if one looked him in the eyes, while he sang, he blushed, lost his voice, and had to be excused from the stage.

Guard Reipsch brought him to the office, one evening, accused of having hit his overseer. The boy defended himself obstinately:

"He hit me first," he said. "I only protected myself."

Jurk had the pistol out already, and lifting up the boy's coat — a very unnecessary refinement — poked it against his shirt.

"Tell him if he says another word, I'll shoot."

I translated exactly.

The boy answered with his sweet and slightly nasal voice: "Tell him if he misses me, I'll strangle him."

He looked like a child, so simple; so dignified too; but his eyes were steady. This was no song. He wasn't impressed. What a coincidence that he, too, wanted to strangle Jurk! It was exactly what I felt. It must have been his short neck that

Forced Labor

one needed to elongate to a better proportion; or perhaps his words, so piercing, so brutal, that one wanted to smother in the nest, like a flock of young vultures. Here they roared out again:

"What did he say? What did he say?"

"The prisoner says, *Herr Kommandoführer*, that he has been in the war, and isn't afraid of firearms."

*　　*　　*

Jurk and Judas were very fond of poker games when they could find a couple of sentries disposed to lose a few marks; but they enjoyed, very much, enforcing the *Stalag* rule forbidding gambling in the camps. They went around the boat, every evening, with all the secretiveness they were capable of, and fell on the neck of innocent little groups playing a mere ten *pfennige* stud.

Jurk waved his pistol in the players' face, while Judas pocketed the *Stalag* coupons lying on the table, in true gangster fashion. They later sent them to the *Stalag*, according to the rules; but as they had failed to count them in front of the men and of me, and deliver a receipt, they could keep a substantial bit, with complete safety. Our comrades got around this danger by playing with pieces of paper instead of coupons, and settling the differences when they were sure none was watching.

What a pity for the two bandits that they didn't know about our night parties!

*　　*　　*

They both drank persistently. Judas became sick, rapidly, and disappeared, while Jurk became sentimental. He kept after me. I didn't understand him, he said; I didn't like him; he felt it. Why didn't I want to get along better with him? I'd have everything to gain.

There was some truth in this. While I had taken, from Schumann and Ehlert, many an unpleasant order, and witnessed many stupidities whose consequences would be suffered by my comrades, I had never been impatient with them. I felt that I was playing a game and that it was up to me to outwit them. They were on to the rules. They knew I wouldn't do anything, personally, to bother them, but, on the contrary, I'd warn them of their mistakes in the office. Similarly, they never did anything directly against me. When they left the *Kommando*, I had been sorry, as one is to lose an old adversary at chess; and I had even been glad — foolishly so — that it wouldn't be on them that my escape would be blamed.

I couldn't stand Jurk. The disgust that he caused me to feel, prevented me from finding what might have been the acceptable side of his temper. Anxious as he was to be a master — to redeem the compulsions and humiliations of his humble life as mason's helper — he would have reacted favorably to continuous flattery.

If I had never been guilty of open flattery with Schumann, I had, nevertheless, said many "*Schön*" and "*Ja wohl, Herr Unteroffizier,*" in the name of diplomacy; and with good results, too. Why should I lack the courage to go a little further, even with this repellent shrimp?

The reason was that I was weakening. I was overdriven, tired of dragging the mass of my comrades behind me, on a road I didn't see, or that I was incapable of building for them. I was tired of having two faces and two languages — one for the day, in the office, the other for the night, in the boat. It was time for me to break out. I was almost ready, and the last preparations absorbed some of the energy I had before devoted entirely to the camp. What a relief it was going to be, even if I didn't succeed, and were arrested.

I thought with delight of a few weeks, or a few months, of

Forced Labor

solitude, even in a cell. Then, perhaps, they would send me to a little *Kommando*, as far away as possible — perhaps in a village like Bornzin! I dreamed of a little girl like Irma, smiling at me from the steps of an old house; and of self-annihilation in physical fatigue. How much lighter it had been; how much lighter it would be, than my life at present. Yes, I was through. It was my fault if I lost ground, every day, to the diabolical pair now ruling the *Nordenham*. It was time that someone relieve me of the mission of which I was no longer worthy.

Around Christmas, I tried hard again. My comrades needed all possible distractions during the difficult period of traditional festivities. We were going to have only one day free, and not even an extra round of horse sausage to make a better meal; but we'd have the best show of the year!

I should improve Jurk's disposition: I should interest him in our theatre, and persuade him that the merits of its achievements would be attributed to him. I would let the *Sonderführer* know how much he had helped us. Would he be the one *Kommandoführer* in Stettin to obtain, from his superiors, permission for the prisoners of the *Kommando* located next door to us, to come to our show? I begged him to let us hold this unique show on Christmas Eve, and end it by a midnight mass. I promised him that there would be no trouble of any sort.

He gave in. His vanity was tickled. It was obvious that nothing else could ever soothe him. It was only when the "firms" came back from work, on Christmas Eve, a little earlier than usual, that I was able to announce the good news:

"Yes; we'll have our theatre tonight."

The property-men rushed to the stage to get it ready.

Our comedians, singers, and musicians were prepared to do their best. At 8 P.M. the curtain rose in a room incredibly packed with boys determined to forget their worries for a few hours.

At eight-thirty, the show was well under way when Jurk appeared at the door, drunk to the point of stumbling, and shouting for me. He wanted to sit with me, on the first row of stools. The boy on the stage interrupted his song, and as it was impossible to make a way for Jurk, he tiptoed on the benches, between loins and hips, somewhat hesitantly, until he fell between Paul and me. Then he praised our miserable Christmas tree, set on the left of the stage, and when our comrade resumed his song, endeavored to drown his voice with a German song. Finally, he passed his arms around my neck and vomited in my ears his foul confidence:

"I know I'm a beast," he said. "I know I do everything to poison your life, but it's your fault. You don't understand me. You don't want to be friends with me. You don't want to be my children. It's your fault, mark my word," and he pressed his tumefied nose with a soiled index.

Have I ever shrivelled with more disgust?

The smell of cheap liquor, cheapened even more by his own smell of sauerkraut and leather polish — his treacherous face, his sticky, tender eyes, were more than I could bear, even on that evening that I had begged from him with so many concessions already! The urge to kick him in the face, squeeze the ugly soul out of him, was rising fiercely in me, when, very tactfully, our master of ceremonies ordered the curtain down, and announced that the next act wouldn't begin for ten minutes. So everyone got up, and I led Jurk out of the room. Once in the dark yard, I ran away from him, but he chased me, slipped and fell in a large puddle of melted snow.

The reaction of the cold, made him sick; and he produced repellent noises while weeping and crying:

"*Franzose . . . Franzose . . . Kamarade . . .*"

*   *   *

Forced Labor

He was on our trail all right. With the scent of the dog he resembled, he searched for the secret organizations he felt hidden behind our shows and classes. He interrupted everyone of our weekly lectures on the pretext of recalling some forgotten point of the camp rule, but in fact to stand by the blackboard, like a lecturer, and to show everyone in the audience that I, their own *Vertrauensmann*, should bow to him at any time, and translate his words. When he had spoken uselessly for half an hour, he declared it was too late to resume the lecture, and ordered everybody to bed.

At eleven o'clock, every night, he made an extra round of the boat; and we had to postpone most of our meetings until the hour when I was reasonably sure that he had gone to sleep.

The men who were well-known as my personal friends — a little group I sometimes played cards with — were searched extensively. It was very good that none of them played any important part in the secret life of the camp.

On January 28, 1942, at nine-thirty, Jurk sent me to the *Lagerführung* with a piece of work requiring about an hour. When I came back a little later, to collect some complementary information, I found that he had ordered my colleagues, Paul and Maurice, to pack up in a hurry. They were leaving for another *Kommando* at ten o'clock. He had substituted their names on a mutation list at the last minute.

All I could do was to embrace my dear comrades, thank them in the name of us all, for their devoted help, and for the night classes they had given. I promised them that they would soon be avenged.

Jurk was going to be expelled from this camp.

I had a sensational piece of trouble in store for him.

*   *   *

PART IV

ESCAPE

CHAPTER 22

Exit One Kriegsgefangene

On the fourth of February, I arrived in the office at 8 A.M., saluted *Herr* Jurk with all the respect due a *Kommandoführer*, told him that all firms had regularly departed, and sat down beside him, as usual.

I lined the desk with papers, reports, individual cards, and began my clerical work. Jurk seemed to have drunk too much, the previous night. Between his elbows, the silent telephone rested like an empty bottle. He was watching a little black spot on the wall.

Around nine o'clock, I rubbed my cheek and sighed. At ten, Lamy, the postmaster-nurse, came in, clapped his heels, and inquired if a package of mail had arrived from the censor's office.

"No." I answered "but have you some aspirin in the camp pharmacy?"

He brought me two tablets. I took one immediately, and the other sometime in the afternoon.

On the fifth, I took two tablets again.

On the sixth, I took three.

On the seventh, Lamy said I had exhausted his supply: and I asked Jurk if he would allow a whole box to be bought for me by a sentry. I showed him my cheek, which was very red.

"*Ja!*" he barked.

He and I were not on speaking terms any more. Outside of questions and answers concerning the service, I had nothing to say to him. He didn't care whether I had a toothache or not. It was only an absent-minded curiosity that made him look at my cheek every morning, to see if the irritation increased or

Escape

subsided. As I rubbed it for half an hour before getting out of bed, it was bound to look quite sick! Pimples appeared under the skin, which was sensitive.

When, around the tenth, my cheek began to swell, I could see that Jurk expected me to break down, any minute, and beg him to let me go to the hospital with the sick, the following morning. But I did not. My table was littered with aspirin tablets. Any time that he looked in my direction, I picked up one, broke it carefully in small pieces, mixed it with a little water, and swallowed the tasteless medicine, while making a face. He knew that if I didn't groan, it was only to deprive him of the pleasure of hearing it!

But when, on the morning of Friday the 13th, I appeared with an enormously swollen cheek, and a mouth so distorted that I couldn't even speak, he rose and burst out loudly:

No, he wouldn't stand for this nonsense any longer! He had had enough of seeing me trying to commit suicide by massive absorption of aspirin. Only imbeciles or cowards were afraid to have their teeth pulled out! He himself had gotten rid of most of *his* teeth. (He opened his mouth wide, and stuck a finger, yellow-hued by tobacco, inside. His tongue looked like a shoe sole, and his last teeth like worm-ridden pegs.) Whether I wanted it or not, I should inscribe myself immediately for the medical visit the next morning! Now, I should clear out of the room, and go to bed!

It was as a favor that I asked permission to stay until lunch time, to finish the most urgent part of my work — the semimensual reports. At twelve-thirty, I asked him if I might go, and if the new interpreter could take my place, at night, for the inscription of the sick, and the control of the packages. Sure, sure! All he wanted was for me to take that obscene abscess of mine out of his sight!

So I arranged my papers, pens, pencils, and little bottles;

picked up my aspirin, and pushed my stool under the desk, noiselessly.

*   *   *

Marquet was waiting for me in my corner. His firm had worked until six this morning, but as I needed him he would sleep another day.

"Everything is all right," he said. "A comrade is lying on a bunk directly by the stairs. If anyone comes in, he'll cough, and I'll pretend to have brought you some water."

I undid my bed and messed it up carefully. On my stool, I sprinkled aspirin tablets and set two cups. In one I poured water from a pitcher. In the other, I spat out my abscess that consisted of a good hunk of cotton. It had been almost as uncomfortable as a real one.

"Fine, Marquet! Now listen to me. Go to the latrines and wait until no one is near you. Poke your hand through the seventh, ninth, and eleventh holes, to your left. You'll find that packages are hidden there, directly under the board. They are in a net of strings fastened with short nails. Get hold of the package first, then cut the strings and pull. You'll need your topcoat to hide them under."

He went, yawning and stretching his arms. Marquet was always thorough in any undertaking. None should wonder what he was doing around, instead of sleeping. His sabots clapped on the stairs.

"Hell! I have diarrhea again," I heard him tell someone on deck.

I inspected my suitcase: two pairs of woolen socks, two sets of underwear, half a pound of tobacco, and a package of all my wife's letters. I pushed it under the bunk, and set my shoes beside it not too orderly. Then I unearthed my briefcase and polished it. I had blacked out my name and address, written

Escape

inside a long time ago, when I was afraid the sentries would steal it from me, but they still showed. I blackened them once more, with ink and shoe polish. Inside I laid: a shirt, shorts, a little tobacco, two recent issues of *"Das Reich,"* a new toothbrush, a new razor that Marquet had bought for me in the canteen, a little cake of soap, a towel, two small sandwiches, and a heavy brown package.

Some one coughed. I slid under the blankets, hugging my brief case. It was only Marquet, looking pregnant.

"Here's one," he said "I'm afraid it smells a little. I have to return for the others."

Then I heard him groaning on the stairs: "Here I go again. I shan't sleep a wink today. Damn rutabagas!"

I had feared the odor all the time, so I had wrapped my packages in many newspapers which should have absorbed most of it. It would evaporate quickly, once in the open. Now, however, in this boat of a thousand stinks, I couldn't tell.

I had never realized before how splendid my overcoat was. Could anyone believe that it had once been a British officer's coat? Of course I had changed the metal buttons for large wooden ones and sewed them in a different place. I had retouched the collar and the half belt. Dyeing it had not been really difficult, but long. I had borrowed a large basin and obtained warm water in the kitchen, on the pretext of delousing my clothes. In the night, I had hidden in the tiller room and with a pail and some stolen charcoals, I had improvised a stove. It had taken the water two hours to boil. I thought it never would. I felt like an alchemist, while pouring the precious dyeing powder in it. I had paid twenty marks for each ounce of it, at the prisoners' black market, and it had taken me two months to obtain it. It was a priceless gold that I was after. I had to stir constantly in fear that the coat might burn at the bottom. With only the light of the stove, I hadn't been able to see if I had succeeded. I didn't dare turn on the electricity. I had wrapped up the coat in a sack and hidden it under a pile of chains, hoping that nobody would find it, before the next night, when I could come again to press it, if I could lay my hands on one of the kitchen flat irons. It was fortunate that the *Lagerführer* gave all sorts of jobs to his women! What an undertaking this had been: pressing in the dark, with the floor as a table. I felt with my hands to know if it was smooth enough.

Now I had my reward. I could see my masterpiece in the open. It had only two regrettable streaks, lighter in the middle of the back where, perhaps, the material had been greasy. Anyway, I adored it. I had it on when Marquet came back, holding my trousers under his coat, like a tummy-ache.

"Oh" he said, and touched it delicately, with withheld passion. He held up the straw sack, while I laid the garment on the boards, like a woman.

The trousers had cost me only fifteen marks one evening when, a search having been announced, one of my neighbors had become frantic and had offered them at any price. They weren't quite long enough for me; the seat was far too large, and the legs too narrow. They were black, or had once been black. Now they wavered between green in the top part, and brown for the rest. Fortunately, stripes of light grey, as large as a finger, ran vertically and provided unity to the trousers. They gave the impression of having been painted rather than woven. Even so, they looked much better to me than the most expensive ones that were ever made for me by a Parisian tailor. I put them on. Marquet adjusted the belt.

Two coughs. Danger. I jumped into my army knickers, and then into bed. Marquet was helping me to a fresh dose of aspirin when Judas entered. Gosh! I'd forgotten the cotton in the cup. Would he notice it? I held my cheek in my hand and twisted my mouth.

381

Escape

"You have to come to the office," he said. "The *Kontrollstelle* wants you on the phone."

"I'll follow you," I grunted, and he left. I replaced my abscess, and pulled down my trousers. The creator of the infantry knickers is someone who must own a controlling interest in a factory of khaki cloth. They are incredibly long. When not held up by puttees, they fall below the ankles. While listening to the questions of the *Kontrollstelle* secretary, I wondered more about the possibility of answering him without spitting out my cotton, than about the danger of my civilian trousers showing around my sabots. It was a painful moment. When I had finished, Jurk picked up the phone and explained that I had the biggest abscess he'd ever seen and that he would send me to the hospital the next day.

"Now, may I go back to bed?" I asked.

"*Ja,*" he sneered.

I found Marquet prudently lying on someone else's bunk in the vicinity of my place. It was only 3 P.M. and we had three more hours. I washed and shaved. Only at the last minute would I put vaseline on my hair so as to hold it completely flat. That would change my appearance and also enable me to stick my hat on. That hat was a gift of love: it had been stolen expressly for me by a grateful comrade on the pier, two months ago, at a time when I was trying an escape on a Swedish boat. The attempt had failed when the boat sailed ahead of schedule, but the hat remained. I had kept it rolled up, but the dampness of the hiding pit had penetrated the successive layers of paper and now it refused to stay straight. It waved around my head like a merry-go-round. It needed pressing with a hot iron that we couldn't possibly get now. This worried me very much and I fought with the brim for a good hour. Finally I set it flat on my suitcase and laid my books on top of it.

Another transformation was my mustache. By trimming my

hair, Marquet had obtained fine material, but I had stupidly figured that ordinary glue would hold it, and it did not. It dried in five minutes and peeled off. I should have gotten varnish. Disguising my face was now obligatory. Not only did every guard and civilian in the camp know me well, but dozens of others also had come too often to the office for my safety. The only solution left was to distort my face in a manner that could be kept long enough — until I was out of the zone of greatest danger, at least.

I was studying the effect of a lifted shoulder on my general appearance when Judas called me again, from the stairway. This time I was wanted by the *Kontrolloffizier* himself.

Goodness, did they suspect something?

I reported to the office with the most pitiful appearance I was capable of. I had hardly saluted him when he blew me up loudly.

Who did I think I was to have filed a petition, again, for the return of our noncommissioned officers to the *Stalag?* Hadn't I been told several times that it was out of the question? What kind of illusions had I kept about the Geneva Convention? Had France any German prisoners as bargain trumps? NO! Then we should take what was granted us and ask for nothing more.

I became as angry as my position and condition permitted, and defended my petition in a very embarrassed voice. I had never been so poor at words. The officer had easily gotten the best of me. I bowed under the shower. Jurk exulted. I held my cheek. When both ran short of saliva, I implored:

"May I go, *Herr Leutnant?*"

"Yes, you may go."

I clapped my heels for the last time.

*   *   *

Escape

At five-thirty I dressed completely. My apple green coat was much too small and certainly the worst part of my outfit, but it wouldn't show much under the brown topcoat. I put my spectacles in my pocket and my hat in my bosom. I covered my head with Marquet's large winter cap. Over my civilian clothes I slipped a large Belgian overcoat, borrowed for the occasion. With my fallen knickers, and my sabots, I felt no sentry would recognize me. I paused on deck, to see if the stage was set.

The snow had stopped falling. The firms succeeded each other every five minutes. I saw them coming from under the bridge, on Altdammerstrasse, then disappearing behind a barrack and finally reappearing opposite the camp. They turned and walked the fifty yards separating the street from our gate.

The gate was open permanently, now, and the sentry tapped his feet against its posts. He greeted his colleague when the latter passed with his prisoners. The incoming column advanced in the yard as far as the kitchen and stopped. Judas who had been warming himself inside, came out with his control sheet and the new interpreter. He counted the men and then dismissed them. The prisoners went to the boat to get their soup bowls; the sentries went to their own barrack to undress. All soon returned to the kitchen to get their evening meal. No, not quite all.

As on yesterday, a little group was gathering around the volley ball ground. Two boys had begun sweeping the snow away with a board. The sentry at the gate seemed to be watching them with interest, as far as I could see without my spectacles. Would this be tolerated again? Was it possible that none had noticed that the posts of the game had kept falling regularly during the last three months, and always being reset a little farther, until they had reached a spot just opposite the *Lagerführung*, and not more than forty feet from the gate? And didn't it seem strange to anyone that men who had worked out all day, would want to exercise with a ball, on slippery snow, in the bitter cold, instead of eating their rutabaga concoction that had at least the virtue of being warm? The teams were forming now, five on each side. A few other prisoners lined against the windows of the *Lagerführung*, ready to watch the game while eating.

Someone touched my fingers on the railing. It was David.

"Everyone's at his post," he said.

I went down the chicken ladder. I dragged my sabots by the guards' barrack, reached the latrines and entered by the only door. There was already a crowd inside, some on the seats, others watching the yard through the small side windows set high, just under the ceiling. Marquet waited for me in the very last cell and handed me my shoes. He had polished them too much, I thought. They shone like patent leather. An amateur shoemaker had bored many decorative little holes on the top piece, so as to disguise the many little patches of different kinds of leathers with which a completely useless pair of civilian shoes had been rebuilt. They were so big that I could wear two pairs of thick socks, which was good. They felt incredibly light on my feet. Could they really pass for shoes? To me, they looked like a Cubist collage and that was one more reason to be fond of them. I took off my army knickers and flung the big Belgian coat over my shoulders, like a cape, sleeves free. I held my hat underneath. Marquet said:

"Come on!"

I followed him out. I crossed the whole yard, waited to let a firm pass, and then joined the little group of spectators lined against the *Lagerführung*. I set my back between the last two windows. Finot, Marquet, David and Moineau stood in front of me. Opposite each window, one man was peacefully chewing his rutabagas and spitting out the cores.

Escape

Six o'clock: the sentry was being replaced. The hateful little Reipsch was taking his turn. He was already in a bad humor, and frozen. He began pacing the width of the gate, endlessly, from one post to the other.

"The man on deck is pulling out his handkerchief," Finot said.

Then I unbuttoned the Belgian coat. The volley ball game was becoming hot. I could recognize Desprez and Duclos, facing each other on both sides of the cord, and jumping high after the ball.

"The man on the latrine steps is blowing his nose," announced Moineau. "All clear. Here comes the Brandt firm. Get ready."

The thirty men passed by us. Their sentry followed, a little wearily. Judas came out of the kitchen. Four hands were stretched towards me behind my comrades: Marquet held my brief case; Finot held a wallet with my money and papers in it: Moineau and David held nothing but their fingers. I touched them. They felt rough, warm, and kind. At this moment, the ball hit the ground, two of the players slipped and fell, and Duclos ran towards Desprez with his fists raised:

"It's your fault, dirty cheater" he cried, and knocked him down brutally. All the prisoners around shouted. Judas ran towards the game. Reipsch advanced four steps in the same direction.

"Adieu," murmured David.

"Adieu everybody," and quickly placing the Belgian coat on David's shoulders, my hat cocked over my eyes, holding my brief case tight, I shot out, exactly three yards behind Reipsch.

I began to count, slowly. One . . . at two, I passed through the gate. At three I walked normally at right angle to the right. If Reipsch or Judas had seen me, this was the time when they would shoot. It would come in my back, a little on the right side. Do you hear the whistle of the bullet that bores a hole through you?

"Five!" shouted a voice inside of me, much more powerful than the commotion of the dispute, twenty yards away behind me. Five seconds! They had not seen me! I was now exactly opposite the private exit of the *Lagerführung*. From the yard, I looked as though I were coming out of it.

Joy, fantastic joy ran through me, a joy that I had never felt before in my life! Why had I waited so long, so long to feel it? Never had walking been so delicious. My feet balanced lightly under me. The twist of my face that I wore as a mask had no more weight than a smile.

The world around me was so bright, so loud, the steps of another firm coming towards me from the street sounded so clear: one, two, one, two . . .

I lowered my head so that they wouldn't recognize me and I looked at their shoes, their wooden shoes, their torn trousers, the patches of which I knew so well: these belonged to Jacques, these to Martin, these to Louis, dragging snow behind their weary steps; oxen driven back to the stable; slaves pushed back into their jails; my companions, my own companions whom I was abandoning to their fate.

Then I bumped into the *Wachmann*. He, startled, said: "*Verzeihen Sie!*"

"Pardon," I murmured — but not to him.

CHAPTER 23

Veillee D'Armes

ONCE on Altdammerstrasse, I followed the sidewalk, the one to the right, of course. One of my best comrades had been arrested because he had walked on the wrong side of the street. The policeman under the bridge had yelled something at him. He hadn't understood, had waved the Nazi salute and kept on until the other ran after him and, finding him a foreigner, took him to the police station.

I wondered if this were the same policeman on duty down there now and if he were already eyeing me suspiciously. Why should he? Why should anyone know by my face that I was an escaped prisoner of war? Only I knew that I should forget it. I should remove the barbed wires out of my mind as I had removed them out of my sight.

Another of our firms passed me. It was Mast, thirty-two men and one sick, today. I didn't need to count, so deep remained the office routine in me. The short firm behind was Müller.

I passed under the bridge over which so many troops and so many ammunition trains had succeeded each other. The steps of the sentry above resounded. That man could have seen me getting out of the camp, two hundred yards below, as well as anyone of the civilians living behind the windows of the high apartment houses on the left side of the street. If they had, they would call up the police. It would take five or ten minutes until the agitation began. I should near the Hansa bridge then, beyond which lay most of the city. A street car stopped by me but not knowing the ticket system, I didn't dare take it. Also, I dreaded sitting down and offering my costume and my face to two dozen people having nothing to do but look at my oddities. It was safer to walk, normally, not too fast, not too slow.

Bridges are dangerous spots. It is on bridges that, at given hours, the policemen begin asking for credentials from everyone. I dared look at the officer on duty on the Hansabrücke. He smiled at me and said:

"*Kalt.*"

"*Ja,*" I answered. It helped me. I was all right if policemen smiled at me. *Das Reich*, neatly folded, stuck out of my pocket. Who but an excellent citizen read Dr. Goebbels prose?

Beyond the bridge I should turn to the left, or was it after the next one? For an instant I feared I had confused the way. I had studied it on a map and verified it the last time I had been in the city, but it didn't look the same now that I walked on the sidewalk instead of in the gutter, and that no sentry held me on a leash.

I arrived at the railway station at six forty-five. The train I meant to board left at six fifty-five. There was a sign saying "Berlin" over one of the gates but an employee was writing something on a blackboard, while a long line of people, mostly men with rather odd luggage, handworkers obviously, pressed around. I went to the ticket window for main lines and waited behind a young man. He held his identity card. I could see the large violet stamp with a stiff broad eagle holding a swastika in its claws, but I couldn't read the name.

"One way to Metz," he said when his turn came.

"Sorry," answered the employee, "the train for Berlin is full, and I'm instructed not to deliver any ticket for the capital or any point beyond until we know there'll be room in another."

"When will that be?"

"Probably tomorrow morning at 5:50. Come early."

"*Merde,*" said the traveller, as if to himself, while withdrawing from the line. I followed him and asked:

Escape

"Warum, Merde?"

He looked at me, an open face with laughing eyes.

"Merde is what we say in Alsace, in such a case."

"That's what we say sometimes in Antwerp, though it would be more usual in Liége," I answered him in German, and we began to talk. I helped him out of the way with his numerous pieces of baggage, and he informed me that he was going home on his semi-annual leave, for ten days only. I told him that I was in the same case but going in the direction of Brussels.

"Then," he said, "we'll travel together as far as Berlin. Let's have a glass of beer."

*   *   *

It began to snow. I tramped alone along the river. What a pity! Anyway, I wasn't caught yet. I had foreseen this kind of possibility. Ever since December 15, the *Pommersche Zeitung* had given wide publicity to successive reductions in the railway traffic and its necessary irregularities, but it was a poor beginning for me.

Did the Alsatian really mean what he had said:

"Eight-thirty by the Catholic Church?"

Where the ice-breakers had passed, during the day, the river was freezing again. It made a scintillating trail that the snow was slowly softening. The freighters were retiring for the night into sharp silhouettes. The heavy sliding doors of the docks were already locked. Lone freight cars of ancient models, high on thin wheels, held to the thin tracks like benumbed fowls perched on a railing.

I had watched these piers from the top deck of the *Nordenham* and often dreamt of wandering among them, like this, except that I hadn't thought they could be so cold, or so silent. I had no idea where they led. There should be a busy corner, somewhere along the water-front, with at least one little bar. I would order whatever everybody else drank, hoping it would be *schnaps:* two or three glasses that one gulps quickly, one after another, because it doesn't taste good. It's the fire inside that's wanted.

A shadow by a door; it's a man, a civilian. He's looking at me, at me only. Danger! Fool, what have I done? I marched straight towards him, for the fight.

"Good evening. I'm glad to meet someone at last. Could you tell me what time it is?"

"It's eight o'clock," he answered, "but what are you doing in this forbidden area?"

"I? I work for the *Hafengesellschaft,* on the *Reiherwerder-hafen* pier, on the other side. We've been unloading Swedish ore today. I'm going home to Antwerp, on leave, in Belgium, you know. But I missed the evening train — it was full. Now I must try to catch another tomorrow at ... at ..." and I pulled out my wallet. The man turned on a flashlight. This yellow sheet ... no, this is only my *Urlaubschein.* I opened it enough for him to see the police stamp on it.

"It must be this; yes, 5:50 A.M. Isn't that painful? So I'm going to meet a friend at eight-thirty, by the Catholic Church, and we'll spend the evening together. As I've never worked on these piers I was looking around a bit. Fabulous cranes. They must lift at least one hundred tons, don't they? I hadn't realized this was forbidden area. I didn't see any sign. Anyway, I'm getting cold and would rather have a drink. Could you tell me where I can find a little *Bierhaus,* with good pre-war stuff?"

"Blame it on the British," he laughed. "The beer isn't what it used to be, but there's a fairly good place where I go myself. Come along, I'll show you how to get there."

"Thank you, but won't you have one too?"

Escape

"I wish I could but I'm on duty around here until midnight. You'd better clear off these grounds soon, anyway."

I didn't need to warm up any more. The beer was fair. I swallowed it slowly, in case he had changed his mind and followed me.

*   *   *

Pacing up and down the wide street, from the church to the bridge, and from the bridge to the church, was imprudent. Guards Reipsch and Grün had passed ten yards away from me, talking quietly, but another might come nearer and recognize me. Jurk would, I'm sure, with his devilish scent. I'd wait only five more minutes and then walk to the shed David had told me about, back of the work-yard of his firm, beyond the station. There was a hole in the fence and the watchman was old and deaf. The place would be sufficiently safe, but how cold.

Not until nine o'clock did the Alsatian arrive with another man.

"This is my Flemish comrade," he introduced me.

"How do you do?"

We shook hands, entered a door, climbed three flights of steps and sat in a warm little room under the roof.

"Men, you'll be better off waiting here for that early train than having to return to your barracks on the other side," said our host. We chatted pleasantly about our work: I, about the Swedish boats; they, about the factory where they were mechanics. Then the Alsatian engaged in a private discussion with his friend, and I didn't listen any more.

Sunk deep in a cheap armchair, I didn't feel the springs sticking out of the seat. I was exhilarated. My imitation of a Nazi police stamp was good if it had fooled a plain-clothes man. I had copied it from documents in the office, but nothing is more dangerous than a flashlight shining obliquely. The streaks left by the indelible pencil show like asperities even when they have been softened with a wet blotter.

My speech had gone well. I was listening to it as if another person had spoken for me. A policeman is like a fence: in order to pass, you have to walk up to him unhesitatingly. You mustn't allow him to form an opinion on you before you have told him everything he would ask you: why you speak with an accent, where you come from, and where you are going.

I knew also that no scandal had shaken the camp yet, otherwise Reipsch and Grün would not have been allowed to leave. The night was quiet and this little room was cozy. It reminded me of my youth in miserably furnished attics, the rent of which I never paid in time. I turned the chromolithograph's face to the wall, though, and never had such an ugly clock triumph over my mantelpiece. This one pointed to eleven o'clock.

This was the moment when Jurk made his last round of the boat. He would probably come to my corner, to bother me a little, and see if my cheek had grown more ridiculous. He would find my bunk empty, but normally so. It was messed up; half a dozen aspirin tablets dotted my stool. My shoes lay in the way. He should conclude that I had gone to the night privy. If he wanted to take advantage of this opportunity for a quick investigation of my belongings, he would find that my suitcase under the bed was full of underwear and letters, and that the door of my *Vertrauensmann* cabinet was covered with personal photographs. On the shelf, he could see my military identification booklet, another bunch of letters, a package of American tobacco, a razor, a toothbrush, and a small cake of soap. Nobody would go away leaving such precious items behind.

If I seemed a little long about coming, he wouldn't wake up the comrades snoring around, to ask them about me, unless he

Escape

suspected something was wrong. Why should he, though, when he himself had ordered me out of the office as late as five o'clock, in the presence of the *Kontrolloffizier?*

It would be only when he had retired to his cabin in the castle that Desprez and Duclos would arrive, take away my letters and photographs to burn, and my tobacco and underclothes to divide, as they had already shared the other pieces of my uniform, after their mock fight at the volley ball game. My *Dolmetscher* armband already lay at the bottom of the Oder, under the exhaust pipe, with my plate of control "87.461" attached to it as a weight, hardly half a mile away from this room.

Until a quarter to six in the morning, nothing would happen. Then, the Slobberer would look for me to line up the sick for him, as usual, and would be told that I was going along to the medical inspection. At six o'clock, at the latest, Jurk would be hollering around the camp, his pistol drawn, his eyes rolling furiously. The greatest danger would begin then. I would be sought everywhere in the city.

If there were no place on the five-fifty train, I'd try one of the trucks that Marquet had told me about as leaving for Berlin every day around 7 A.M. They were easy to recognize, but could I get inside of one without being seen? Germany is no country where you could thumb a ride. The civilian road traffic is very small, and severely controlled, as one of my predecessors had, unfortunately, found out.

If that didn't work, my last chance would consist in attempting to sneak on board a Swedish freighter. There was one in *Reiherwerderhafen* now. Coal would be loaded on it all day, and probably tomorrow. I knew exactly how to approach it, through a swamp, and I had conceived a plan for getting inside, based on information given by comrades working on this pier every day. It should be feasible, but the chances of avoiding discovery before the ship sailed, were hardly one out of ten, so intricate is the German inspection of neutral ships. I would risk that, or anything, rather than be caught here in the middle of Stettin, and be taken back to the poisonous sneers of Jurk. How he would hate to have missed a chance to spill the lead of his pistol in my back, but also how he would enjoy showing me to the whole camp and crying:

"You see your dear *Vertrauensmann?* You thought he was clever but he hasn't even gone one single mile. Now he's going to know what it costs to forge a Nazi police stamp. . . ."

No, that couldn't be. I'd be spared that shame. Wasn't this kind looking young Alsatian my protection, tonight? He, brother to the men whose Nazi salute had so deeply revolted me on the day of my capture, would now help me. He didn't suspect anything. He would even buy my ticket if I asked him, with some plausible pretext.

He stirred me up around 4:30 A.M. Without realizing it, I had dozed in the chair. He had shared his comrade's bed. We didn't disturb him. I carried some of the Alsatian's luggage and it gave me poise. The street was very slippery and our steps echoed against the walls. At five o'clock, we stood in line for our tickets, behind many others. The woman at the window hardly glanced at my yellow paper, stamped it, and gave me a ticket direct to Antwerp, for thirty-eight marks fifty pfennigs. I had suddenly realized that if there were an inquest, the bearer of the ticket for Metz would seem the probable fugitive.

The gate to the platform was closed again. The blackboard above said the train would be thirty minutes late, due to the snow, of course, but what a catastrophe for me! I hated waiting in this hall where so many men I knew could come: officers going to Berlin, overseers coming to work from the suburbs, sentries going to, or returning from, leave. In the night, I had

Escape

forgotten about disguising my face, and I couldn't do it now without the Alsatian noticing it. Only my lack of spectacles and my hat with a corrugated brim protected me. It was a slim chance. How endless an hour spent reading the time tables all over again, can be.

At six o'clock sharp we were admitted on the platform. At six-twenty, the train hadn't arrived. I knew what was going on in the office at this very minute. My neighbors on the boat had admitted that they hadn't seen me since last night. Jurk wouldn't search any more. He would go through the regular routine that I had witnessed before. My green identification card in one hand, and the telephone in the other, he would call up successively the *Kontrollstelle*, the Stettin Police Presidium, the Railway Police, the Highway Police, and the *Stalag* via long distance. He would give a succinct description of me until the *Stalag* sent copies of my photograph and of my fingerprints everywhere. The late edition of the *Pommersche Zeitung* would contain this mention:

> Warning. French prisoner of war at large. Jean Helion, 5 feet 6, 140 pounds, speaks German and English, presumably in uniform . . . [and the standard statement]: Escaped prisoners are always dangerous. They will steal food, clothes, bicycles, arms, and commit acts of sabotage. Report all suspects immediately to the nearest police station.

While waiting for the *Kontrolloffizier*, Jurk would fill out the "*Flucht Meldung*," in three copies, where along with the circumstances of my disappearance, the reason for the flight should be given. A reason . . . Was it naive or humorous?

At six-thirty, the station loud-speakers roared:

"*Achtung, achtung* . . ." but it wasn't yet about me. It was only to say that the train now entering the station was reserved exclusively for the *Wehrmacht*.

My companion swore loudly. I didn't say anything. It was already too late to have any chance with the trucks. It wasn't until six-fifty that another train arrived. I couldn't believe I'd ever board it, for crowds fought at every door. Greatly hindered by the Alsatian's baggage, I finally got in last of all. Someone on the platform said:

"*Glücklicke Reise.*" (Happy Trip).

To whom?

The corridor was jammed. Pressed against a window, I couldn't help looking outside. On a bench was a solitary man with a felt cap, a box of tools, and a bunch of lead pipes, a plumber. He was eating a sandwich. Where had I seen this same plumber eating a sandwich before? Lacking my spectacles, I couldn't quite make out his features, but I knew that man for sure.

Above him gaped a loud-speaker, black, like the mouth of a gun. The train started. I heard only "*Achtung! Achtung!*" The rest was lost, far away behind, in the noise of the steam and of the wheels.

CHAPTER 24

Berlin Express

PEOPLE surged from the car ahead of mine, and pushed me back irresistibly towards the middle of the corridor. Then, for a moment, no one could move a foot; but no train is ever so completely packed that a little room can't be made after patient adjustments. For a solid half hour, packages circulated between legs, suitcases above shoulders, in all directions, until they reached an adequate parking lot, either on the racks — provoking someone's protest about a squeezed hat or a mashed cardboard box — or under the seats, wherever willing legs volunteered for a little discomfort in favor of general interest. After a long time, an important piece of elbow was removed from the pit of my stomach by a stout old man who, realizing only then how unpleasant it must have been for me, apologized extensively.

Not at all, sir! Nothing could bother me for the time being — not even a flea diving down my underwear on a favorite spot just above my left knee. Damn it all the same! In such a crowd I should lose it promptly — and not even a certain neglect relative to dinner and breakfast.

The Alsatian was one man, two ladies, another man, and a pile of luggage away from me, and telling something about her suitcase to a rather pretty girl. I was glad he wasn't too near. We were in the center of the train. The control started probably at either end, or both. With the condition of the corridors, neither the controller of tickets, nor the controller of identification papers, could advance more than a car length per hour, I should think. This was a non-stop express, due at Berlin in two and a half hours, let's say three with the snow. If my speculation were correct, they would arrive at me only when nearing the capital.

Would I dare fight my way through fifteen feet of flesh and clothes? To say fifteen times:

"Pardon me, excuse me, I'm sorry! Thank you! I hope I didn't step on your foot. Please will you kindly let me pass?" In other words, tell this idle crowd:

"Guess where I picked up my foreign accent. Guess where I'm going, where I came from, who I am."

Who I was was my imperative reason for retiring for a while. I remembered my name, my day of birth, and that, without my spectacles and bushy hair I had lost fifteen years from my age, and was now only twenty-three. But did that make me born in 1919 or 1920. I couldn't remember, to save my life, and it's a favorite trick of policemen to ask you, when they are holding your papers:

"Born on?"

No one seems to be able to be sure of any birthday but one's own. I could read mentally the whole paper:

" 'Josef Vanuytrecht, crane driver, unmarried, living in Antwerp, now working for the *Hafengesellschaft* in Stettin, on leave until February 22, born on 2. 17. 19', or was it 20?"

I had to make sure at once, though people are so unwilling to move when their limbs are packed between someone else's. I stepped on a child's foot, and he bawled. His mother thought I had done it on purpose. Finally, the washroom door was unlocked and an indefinite number of people waited ahead of me for their turn. So did I, patiently, while the controller advanced towards me, towards me alone, irresistibly, like a dented wheel, with the click of his wet stamp on the papers, one man at a time.

Had I been right to choose facing the danger, instead of avoiding it by stealing rides only from freight cars, trucks or

Escape

barges, or resorting to walking? Since the fall of 1941, when thousands of war prisoners had attempted to recover their freedom, and been found everywhere, at large, the Nazis had tightened considerably their interior defenses, and created new ones. The rigid control of the trains dated only from last November. The roads were positively locked at all crossroads. Premiums were paid to civilians for causing the arrest of fugitives. I had figured that whichever method I used, I had to cross an equivalent number of police barrages, but that the dangers of unfortunate hazards should be reckoned in proportion to the time spent in flight, rather than in proportion to the distance to go. For instance, copies of my photographs and fingerprints would be made today only in the *Stalag*, and sent either this evening or tomorrow to the different special stations. If I could beat them to the frontier, my chance to succeed should be better.

When at last my turn came to enjoy a few cubic feet of solitude, I pulled out my wallet and reviewed my weapons: my yellow title of leave had already been under fire twice; it should be all right now that the Stettin station stamp was on it, even if I hadn't known about a serial number required in a corner, or some other detail. I had paid one hundred marks to have it stolen from a shelf, in the barrack of the Mast overseer, where I had seen a pile of them when I had been taken there about a question of Lohnlisten. A comrade had watched for an opportunity for two months, and then snatched it. It was well worth the money. It was easy to fill it out according to the printed indications. Where it said: police stamp, I had copied a Stettin police stamp of which we had several samples, on various documents in the office. After practicing for a few weeks, and with much patience, almost anyone can do the same.

I was more worried about the other credential: the passport; though I felt warmly about it. It was a gift from David. Every morning he took coal to each office in his firm. He had seen a stack of civilian workers' passports, (just handed in after their return from leave) on a table, and had taken one behind his employer's back. When he had returned with another load of coal, the passports were being transferred to a safe. He had presented it to me on February third.

"Why don't you keep it for yourself, David? Don't you know I've offered hundreds of marks on the black market for a passport of any nationality, for six months, without any success?"

"No, I'd feel like a thief if *I* kept it, instead of feeling proud. I want you to have it, if it can be of any use to you."

That was just like my David, ready to escape on certain conditions only, and not at any price.

The next morning, I had started on my toothache, which had lasted as long as it had taken me to duplicate the last of my exit visas cancelled on this passport. Desprez had helped me. In vain had I tried to persuade him to join me in several previous preparations. He didn't lack audacity, but faith in his own star, or perhaps he was as heavily intoxicated by the fatal force of habit, as most prisoners were: the habit of being a prisoner, of suffering, of hating, of hoping. Hope, taken in certain doses, is a poison for the best natures.

Desprez had spent hours every night copying exactly every little line. We had unglued the tax stamp from one of the oldest visas, and transported it to the new page. On the night of February 12, the job was completed, and it wasn't bad. What *was* bad, very bad, was that the description of this man couldn't be changed: he was twenty-three years old while I was thirty-eight; it was written in several places and an erasure would have been very obvious on the paper. Also I had no suitable photograph of myself to replace his, even if the stamp, in relief, on it could be successfully imitated. With my hair oiled flat, I

Escape

could perhaps be considered as having been flattered by the photographer, if only a quick glance were cast on the picture, but who would ever believe that I was six feet tall, when I lacked six inches? Only when sitting, could this pass.

Another impossibility was the date: how could a man, back fourteen days ago, according to the last immigration stamp, be going on leave already?

That passport was a good looking document, but should never be looked at closely. I didn't hope to pass the border with it, but it might prove sufficient to justify my presence on a west-bound train.

When I came out of the washroom, the controller was already there, sooner than I'd expected. He held out his hand. I put everything I had in it, ticket and papers. I smiled as bravely as I could and felt that the end had come. Instead, he only tore off part of the ticket and handed me back the papers, saying:

"Show them to the policemen over there."

There were two, coming from the rear, fighting their way slowly from compartment to compartment. They spent several minutes on each person. I had no chance to survive such an attentive examination. Then the train slowed down, the brakes ground, the Alsatian called to me:

"Give me a hand again, please! I'll pass you my bags through the window."

I was the first one off the train. It hadn't even stopped entirely. The policemen didn't yell after me.

CHAPTER 25

In the Shade of Swastika Blossoms

I REMEMBERED this railway station. I had taken breakfast in this beer hall ten years ago. Now, full of soldiers, it was as dark as ever, but more noisy. We sat right in the middle of the room.

"What will you have?" the Alsatian asked the girl.

"Coffee," she said, without laughing.

"And two beers," he told the waiter, without even asking me. I had carried all of his luggage, while he had carried the girl's. She was young and fresh, with a large black hat slightly raised in front, not without similarity to mine. He was courting her rather ardently. She sweetened her drink with little tablets of saccharin: they bubbled up to the surface, swam around and then sank to the bottom. Not until then would she drink. We had several beers. I couldn't possibly show my impatience, as I had already missed the train leaving from Schlessiger Bahnhof at eight-thirty, according to the Stettin time-table.

Anyway, it was good to sit there with these two gay youngsters, and to babble with them. She called him Peter, and he called her Truda. He had already told her about me for I was *Herr* Josef to *Fraulein* Truda. On the pretext of washing, I left them alone for ten minutes, and ate one of my two sandwiches so that my head would stop turning. This was ahead of schedule, and the next day would be one of complete famine.

Escape

When I went back, they were talking to three or four police-men, and laughing loudly.

"Here he comes," cried Peter, indicating me, "and I'm sure he'll give you more than I can afford to."

So the policemen turned towards me with large smiles. The first one pinned a beautiful swastika, in ersatz copper, on my chest — would I have believed such a day could come? — while the second shook his collection box under my nose. I dropped two marks in it, and the third persuaded me to buy the respective portraits of Hitler, Göring, Göbbels, Rosenberg, Von Schirach, for one mark each. For Himmler, I positively refused.

"I'm ruined," I insisted, but they were quite pleased with their business at only one table, and explained that this whole week end would be for the exclusive benefit of the police forces fighting in Russia.

As one peddler necessarily attracts others, a woman in uni-form came to me also. She was selling much prettier swastikas, according to her. There was a little wheel around it, with a ribbon attached, and it looked like a mean little flower. I couldn't refuse spending another two marks for the touch of a German woman's hand on my British officer's coat. Indeed, I had never felt so friendly towards any kind of police before. They assured me that they had much sympathy for the Flemish workers coming to the rescue of the German factories. That cost me an extra mark, which I gave very happily because, while all this bargaining went on, another party of policemen had asked for papers all around, and was now going away. They had been particularly insistent in the corners. That was something to remember, as well as this theorem:

"The best defense against a policeman, is another policeman."

With my chest littered with Nazi insignia, I looked like a Nazi version of a French recruit when, before the war, and after the medical examination, it was customary to celebrate your good health and fortune by parading with tricolor medals and ribbons, and becoming thoroughly drunk.

Peter telephoned for me to the two stations offering possible trains to Cologne, and I learned, to my disgust, that there would be none until possibly 11 P.M. He himself had decided not to leave until the next morning, perhaps because Truda was counting on spending the day shopping, and returning to Stettin late in the night.

A whole day alone in Berlin would be somewhat risky. I made myself as pleasant as I could. I tried to remember all the jokes I had ever heard, but had to watch my tongue, for many of them had something to do with prison camps and the others with artist models, two dangerous lines for a crane driver! In short, I would have made love to that girl if Peter hadn't been doing so himself with devastating success; but they weren't going to get away from me. In spite of the national drive against virtue for unmarried women, I firmly decided to chaperone these two as long as they would stand for it. I talked about going to the movies, theatre, no matter where:

"Germany has been good to me," I said unashamed, "I have made money here and would be pleased to spend some of it on two Germans if they'd give me a chance."

I was under the impression that Peter looked a little hard when I said so. Was he becoming jealous, or was I overdoing it? The girl was enjoying her whirl of popularity, and finally took the hint that I had a little niece and would like to buy a doll for her.

"I dare you to find one," she said "but why don't you two come shopping with me?"

So Peter checked his luggage. I wouldn't part with my brief case. We took the subway and I found that my railway ticket entitled me to free transportation.

On *Postdammerplatz*, what was once the biggest Jewish

Escape

store, had received a vague Aryan name, but there was nothing to be bought any more, or very little. Small posters, at every door, said:

"Entrance forbidden to all Jews. Between 5 and 6 P.M. Jews will serve Jews at gate number So-and-So exclusively."

Inside, the customers were few. Polite salesgirls said that no doll baby could be bought anywhere, and there wasn't even a wooden toy for my little son. There would be none until the Christmas period. Everything but books seemed to be rationed. All I could acquire in the store was another couple of Nazi medals: policemen were on the hunt everywhere. It was obvious that foreign workers would be the easiest victims. I saw real Flemish workers being assaulted. On the fourth floor I heard French spoken by a group of women, and it moved me, but I hated them for being there. Had they volunteered to work in Germany, or had they been compelled by misery, or by threats, to come? If I'd been alone, I might not have resisted the impulse to ask them if they knew what the prisoners thought of them.

Passing the photographic department, I inquired about the possibility of getting a quick picture. It wasn't done any more, but they could send me the proofs anywhere I wanted, within four days. No, that wouldn't do, for it wouldn't fit in with my foolish desire to send a picture of myself taken in front of a naively painted view of Berlin, to Herr Jurk, with a little dedication, such as:

"*Souvenir de voyage,*" with a discreet number of five figures as signature. It was probably my good luck that I didn't find an automatic picture booth anywhere.

*   *   *

At lunch time I left the cooing couple counting their ration tickets. I had none, and knew nothing about what could be gotten without them, if anything at all. They thought I was at last becoming understanding.

I fought hunger with more beer, and followed Leipziger Strasse, Unter den Linden, Franzöziche Strasse, any street whose name appealed to me. My poise was now good. Every half hour, by my watch, I walked up to the nearest policeman, told him I didn't know the city, was on my way home to Antwerp on leave, and could he indicate some interesting buildings in this vicinity to look at?

I trusted this would be sufficient to reassure any plain-clothes man who might not like my ways, my costume or my loitering. None fearing the police would be likely to speak to a policeman. Once in a while, in doing so, I opened my wallet where the yellow paper and passport were in full view, and pretended to be looking for an address, or for a mark to give to the endless procession of policemen collecting money with more or less threatening smiles.

I was directed to the Grand Opera where the roof, once badly torn by British bombs, was being completed again.

At four o'clock, I entered a barber shop and asked for a shave and a haircut. An old man took care of me and was very anxious to talk. He wanted to know everything about me, and I had to repeat a story that was becoming rather monotonous. He knew Antwerp a little and while filling my nose with lather — then very politely begging my pardon and removing it without consideration for the tenderness of my cartilage — he asked me if I knew any barber willing to earn reasonably good pay in Germany.

"If you ever run across a French one — you know, a Parisian — not only would I give him a fine salary, but also I wouldn't forget the man who sent him to me. Now, if you were a barber" — and then he cut my neck — "I'd hire you at once. I have more

Escape

work than I can do now, and my last assistant will have to go to the Army."

I was glad to hear the last part of his speech and thanked him heartily, but, unfortunately, I knew nothing about his profession. His spouse, at the counter, was perfectly suave. She charged me two marks for the various services, plus one mark eighty *pfennigs* for a very ugly little compact, the best she had, and wasn't it lovely? I hoped that my wife would find it lovelier than any other if we ever reached America, the compact and I, at the other end of the world.

At five o'clock, passably fresh, but angry with my stupid hunger, I met Peter and Truda in the same department store, and we had a funny-tasting herb tea. If a long time seemed to have elapsed for me since I had left the camp, a longer one had passed since these two had met each other in the train. They looked like honeymooners. I had a hunch that they were. How kind of them to tolerate my company. We wandered from café to café. Not one seemed to offer the kind of cosy corner they wanted. Once more I was being understanding and read *Das Reich* all over again.

Around 8 P.M. we sat in a *Bierhaus* near the station, in the fartherest corner of the second floor. It was crowded in a fashion that reminded me of some better evenings in Berlin, ten years ago, with the friends whose address I hadn't dared look up in the telephone book. They could have become Nazis, since the war, through patriotism, or if they hadn't they could be under police suspicion. It would be dangerous, for both them and for me to call on them in memory of a time when one chose friends without inquiring about their nationalities.

Even these two young lovers would run into endless trouble for being with me, if the police arrested me, though they should be able to prove, as I would swear, that I had seen neither one of them before this morning. Treason it would be called and meant facing a firing squad, far worse than I'd get myself, if I didn't resist arrest. I was sorry for I was beginning to like them both very much.

The café had almost the same atmosphere of noisy gaiety that formerly I had found in the cafés of big harbors, except that now uniforms prevailed, and the windows were blackened with a thoroughness of which no people on earth is more capable than the German.

That was one evening when I had no right to object to any sort of swastika when I was wearing four or five of them myself, and when my pockets were full of pictures that I could have sold to the members of the Scavenger Club for a handful of *Stalag* coupons, though . . . but I should never think about yesterday until I could be assured that no tomorrow would ever be like it.

After pilfering several small sandwiches and accepting my statement that I wasn't hungry in the least, Peter and Truda saw me to the station. It was a bit demolished on the side, but the black-out was so complete I couldn't enjoy much of it. At ten forty-five they couldn't wait any longer and decided to leave. Peter told the girl that as I was a good friend of his, she ought to give me a kiss; which she did without hesitancy.

"Look here," he said to me, "if you don't find things the way you want, wherever you go, how about paying me a visit in Metz. Every Alsatian would be glad to receive you, and to help you, you understand?"

As I looked up, thoroughly surprised, he added, very low, in French:

"Quite a joke, a German girl kissing a strange Frenchman good luck, isn't it?"

CHAPTER 26

With Thanks to
the German Police

THE train didn't leave until midnight. I wasn't impatient any
more. I'd been late everywhere, and it hadn't been for the
worst. I found a compartment with plenty of soldiers in it,
and asked them if they would mind a civilian.

"Not at all," they assured me. That was my chance to tell them
what they should know about me. I even offered them one
cigarette each, a "Juno round," from a package of twelve that
was soon as empty as it had been when I had picked it up in the
office wastebasket, three months ago. It had taken me all this
time to fill it up, one cigarette at a time, with what the most
polite overseers gave me when I made a list for them. Cigarettes were scarce inside of Germany, and considered very
valuable presents.

We joked a little. I wasn't afraid of soldiers. I knew their
uniforms. I had spoken to so many of them for twenty months
that I was accustomed to their habits. These looked like so
many Franzs, Grüns, Kellners, fine boys, fond of a laugh, and
relieved that no top sergeant was in sight.

Everyone in the train looked nice. I saw only smiles, heard
only polite words, comments on the latest movies, many things
sounding new to me and happy. These Germans said "we."
They were one people. They were not mean any more. There
was no enemy in sight. There were no barbed wires around
me to rouse their fear and anger.

Do the barbed wires render all men on earth fierce, whether
they are on one side of them or the other?

Germany, when I used to look at it from the yard, had been as unreal as a picture, and the fence had appeared to be a series of long scratches, nervously entangled across it by a discontented artist.

No, no, no! said each barbed line, tearing off the landscape.

Now it looked open and so different. This compartment scene around me was fine and peaceful. I was still very tense, ready for trouble, but a certain reflection of the outside tranquillity shone inside of me.

If only I could eat a little . . . . The night was going to be hard to spend. There would be no more beer to give my stomach a temporary plenitude. The water in the lavatory tasted bad. "Not drinkable" said a sign above the spigot.

I knew the inspection of papers was held about one hour after leaving Berlin. Two of my good friends had been stopped at that moment, two months ago. They had only one yellow *Urlaubsschein*. I had helped them to fill it out. Taken off at the first stop for inquiries in a police station, they had soon been compelled to confess. It had been a sad ride back to the *Stalag* in Greifswald, where an officer had complimented them on their pluck, but warned them that they would have to pay for it. The one who took upon himself the responsibility for the theft of the yellow title and the forgery, was sent to a punitive camp for several months. The other had done only four weeks in jail, and then been sent back to a *Kommando*, with the recommendation to be given hard work. He had ended in the hospital and a boy of ours met him there. When the latter was released and sent back to the boat, he had repeated to me the precious details of the unsuccessful venture. For one escape begins, so to speak, where another has failed. My experience was built of all the information I had gathered from men who had already tried once or twice. I knew more about what not to do than about what to do. Fortunately I had learned a lot in twenty-

Escape

four hours. I was as ready as I could ever be for the next obstacle.

"Boys," I told the soldiers, "I'm feeling mighty sleepy. Will you wake me up when the controller comes? My name's Josef. I guess you'll have to yell for I'm hard to rouse."

They laughed and I, rubbing my hair to make sure it was as flat as the picture of my passport, sank in my turned-up collar and curled up in my corner.

When they all started calling "Josef! Josef!" and at the same time pounding me on the back, I jumped, perfectly, authentically startled.

"Time to get up, Josef," they said, as if they had known me all the time. I yawned painfully, while looking at the inspector, pulled out my papers, all at once and presented them, at arm's length, very near his face. There was everything he could want, mixed up with much he didn't want, but he couldn't possibly afford to be disgusted at my disorder. On top was my ticket: that was good. Underneath was the photograph of Adolf Hitler. Let no one tell me that wasn't very good. Third came the first page of a real passport. The photograph on the following page was not mine, but how could he tell when I was yawning again at the time, stretching, trying in vain to open my eyes, and spitting in my handkerchief? And at the page of the visa were my *Urlaubsschein*, already identified, and Mr. Goering's paunch, even more decorated than mine, supplemented by the smile of Mr. Rosenberg. "Police Day," said the inscription across the glorious photographs.

"*Schön*," said the inspector, and he gave the whole pack back to me. I went to sleep immediately — that is apparently. Between my eyelids I watched him investigating the soldiers' documents. There was only one other civilian and I couldn't doubt that he was German, but he wasn't exactly like his own photograph on his identity card, for the inspector looked him over carefully, in the glare of an electric torch. The victim was thoroughly indignant but didn't let out a word until the police officer had gone to another compartment.

"*Schön*" sang my head. "*Schön*" sang my heart, and I celebrated with my second and last sandwich. But I went to the corridor for that. I was afraid one of these soldiers might once have been a *Wachmann* and would recognize the two sardines laid on my bread as identical with sardines in oil that prisoners received from the French Red Cross and that the guards coveted so much. I had been reminded early that night, that the least detail counts. Hadn't I given myself away as a Frenchman, with a single word said to Peter, in the station at Stettin?

Dear Peter! Peter the Alsatian, who had known all the time the risk he was taking in letting me spend the night with him, and hadn't even let on until the last minute!

*   *   *

The rest of the night cost me two marks fifty *pfennigs* more. One whole hour couldn't pass without a new policeman waking everyone up in the name of the glorious Russian Expedition corps. It was monotonous, and disquieting for many reasons. In vain did I show them the row of poisoned flowers on my coat — they thought I needed one more swastika, and kept on shaking their metal box until another coin had been dropped inside.

Since ten o'clock yesterday, morning, I had spent twenty-five marks on them, ten marks on beer, three marks eighty *pfennigs* at the barber shop, and my capital had been reduced to a mere sixty marks. How far would I go with it?

It was around August 1941 that I had begun selling the best part of the packages I received from home. I had discontinued the afternoon cup of real coffee, in the office, only after the

Escape

departure of *Kommandoführer* Ehlert, so that it wouldn't be noticed. In November, I had ceased eating any of the two loaves of bread allotted weekly to each prisoner. Thanks to my good relations with the kitchen crew, I replaced them by a few potatoes. My best woolen socks had joined these food stuffs on their complicated migration towards the German black market, through our mysterious channels, and brought me good civilian money in exchange. On the eve of my exit, I had sold all my books to various comrades, and this had brought my fortune to the peak of 350 Reichsmarks, carried successfully through many searches of all prisoners' affairs — even the cleverest organized by suspicious *Kommandoführer* Jurk. But the money had melted promptly: I had paid sixty marks for my English officer's top coat, fifteen for the trousers, ten for the shoes, five for the tie, one hundred for a few square inches of yellow paper and almost forty for my railroad ticket.

If my fortune were gone, so was I, or almost. Cologne wasn't very far away, and the border only fifty miles beyond. Even if I were taken now, my failure wouldn't be ridiculous. I had crossed the better part of Germany.

In Cologne I had to change trains and wait three hours. I wouldn't hang around the station as I did yesterday. I wasn't travelling in the shade of a German girl any more, and the fewer times I showed my papers, the safer it would be. I wandered in the city. It was dark at first, and foggy later. No shop seemed to be opening and that reminded me it was Sunday. Sunday should be a good day. Everyone should feel lazy, even the policemen; but I felt depressed. I wanted sleep and food without quite realizing it. My nerves were beginning to weaken after thirty-six hours of constant tension. Not until I found a few demolished houses did I cheer up!

One of them looked fresh, like a wound. The wallpaper showed clean as a new shirt, around what had once been a chimney, hanging three stories above a pile of ruins, but a little order was beginning; the bricks had been set in neat piles, the scrap metal was lying aside and it seemed as though the hole in the row of dwelling houses would soon be patched up.

I searched so passionately for demolitions, that I almost missed the 10 A.M. train to Aachen.

*   *   *

I was now running straight into the lion's mouth. Aachen was famous for its numerous police barrages. It was the last city before the border. Every hour or so, the whole station was carefully combed. It was a place to avoid.

Until October, the best trick had been to get off at the station before, and take a street-car to any one of the little cities lining the border. There, one would drink beer in one little café after another, until one met either a policeman — and then the end had come — or one of those racketeers who used to smuggle tobacco from Belgium to Germany, before the war, and now smuggle food from Germany to Belgium and, quite bravely, people who had no papers but a little money.

The Germans had caught on to this and not only did they inspect the street-cars but also they paid a higher price for the denunciation of fugitives than the latter used to pay to be smuggled into Belgium. Now, women and school children were constantly on the lookout for any stranger in the vicinity.

Our train was unbelievably full — mostly Belgian workers, talking loudly in either Dutch or French, and obviously going on leave. Very few of them wore Nazi insignias and I felt with pleasure, that mine were not too popular. I removed the most conspicuous, as discreetly as I could, but it was too early for a thorough cleaning.

415

Escape

I engaged in conversation with a couple from Brussels. Both worked in Cologne — he as carpenter, she as factory helper. I learned from them that this train went as far as Herbesthal and that all inspection of passports would be done there. It would be quite a job they said for they had never seen such a crowd in one single train.

My teeth were clenched, and I looked around slowly for anything that might prove a clue to a better solution than the one I had in view. It was time to get ready again. I opened my brief case and extracted the heavy package that was in it. I put it in my pocket and untied the string. Half of it stuck out but my sleeve covered it.

I let Aachen pass. Now the train ran very slowly, then stopped.

"Herbesthal," said huge letters on a low building.

"Everyone out" yelled German employees in German, while the Belgians yelled it in French.

A fence divided the platform in two, and the only opening in sight was the door of a low building saying: Passport examination. On the other side was Belgium. It was good to see it, if only for a little while.

As everyone fought his way out of the car, I discarded the brown paper and held the object in my sleeve. It was a hammer. My idea was to entrust my overcoat, my hat, and my brief case to someone else, on the pretext of going to the toilet. Then I'd lose myself in the crowd, return to this train and begin tapping the wheels with my hammer, as if it were my job to see that everyone of them was sound. As I would be bending my head very low there was a chance that no one would notice that I had no cap on. It was worth trying. I would follow the train from wheel to wheel, to the last wagon, and then mix with the men unloading crates over there, trusting that the Germans would take me for a Belgian and the Belgians take me for a

German. I would find a way across the fence, either at the extremity or by following the crates wherever they should be transported.

There were other trains, waiting on the Belgian tracks; and once on their side, I would promptly disappear.

Before the war, when leaving a country, I had often observed how easy it would be for anyone with pluck to escape the inspection, and though everything was tighter now, it should still be feasible, if not easy. It couldn't be any harder than getting out of the *Nordenham*, except that *there* I knew what I was up against while *here* I would have to find out quickly how the ground lay.

So I followed the Belgian couple to give me countenance, for a while. They concluded that I was trying to stay with them and asked me to carry some of their luggage. They knew their way around, for in two minutes I was incorporated with them in a line hanging from the passport office, and from their point of view, in good position — that is, very near. That, however, didn't suit me so well.

"Could you tell me where the lavatory is?" I asked the man.

"They won't let you go there now," answered his wife, and calling the nearest policeman, she inquired.

"No, you'll have to wait until you're on the other side" he informed her.

I hope I didn't show that little woman how exasperated I was with her for trying to be helpful out of turn. There was no use getting out of line now that she had attracted attention to me. The policeman would stop me, or follow. The scheme was ruined. Curses on her! I wanted to crack her on the head with the hammer! but instead, I pretended to tie my shoe and abandoned it under my feet. I had stolen it in vain from the carpenter's tool box on the ship. And now wouldn't the woman stumble over it? How could she be everywhere she shouldn't,

Escape

either with her tongue or with her feet? She picked it up and handed it to her husband:

"Look," she said "someone has lost a hammer."

"You don't have to let everybody know it. It's a good one and has found an owner" so he pocketed it.

Meanwhile the line advanced slowly, dangerously so, and a new collection plate was passed under my nose. I dropped only a small coin in it and the fellow wasn't pleased. He said so with little discretion but everyone around was growing much less interested in the fate of the German police corps in Russia, now that Germany was only a narrow strip away from Belgium. Though there would be Germans on the other side as well, it meant a substantial difference. These knew it was their last chance to collect alms, and insisted. A very tall one, six and a half feet, perhaps, with his cap abnormally cocked on the side, got out of the office, pushed aside the head of the line and shouted:

"Listen everybody. There's a big crowd today, and you'll have to wait a long time. Whoever will give five marks — five marks for our heroes in Russia — will pass right now. Who's first?"

He repeated in broken French:

"Five marks, *passer tout de suite.*"

Twenty feet behind me an impatient man shot out of the line, a five mark bill in hand; another; three others; and the big German pushed them inside, while calling to his colleagues:

"Look, pals! I've collected twenty-five marks in one second."

They thought it was a good joke and laughed, but the crowd was all the more angry because it couldn't even groan.

My turn came to get in. I threw my papers on the desk, exactly as I had shoved them in the inspector's face, last night, photos and all. At the page of the picture that should have been mine was a five mark note. When the officer saw it, I made the gesture of taking it back and said:

"Excuse me."

"What? No, that won't do" he said. "Give it to me in a hurry."

"But officer, look at my chest. Look at all these photos. I've spent a week's salary on you since yesterday."

"Come on," he retorted, "you can well afford one more fiver; you make a lot of good money in Germany, you all do."

But I wouldn't, and the tall man came to the rescue. They insisted and I fussed until the woman from Brussels, behind me, couldn't hold her tongue any longer, and complained that this tilt was causing hundreds of people to wait. So I turned towards her and apologized, and then said to the man at the desk:

"All right, you win! Keep the bill."

"That's a boy" he laughed. With one hand he stuck the bill in his box and with the other he stamped my visa. He hadn't even read the name on it.

I was out of Germany. This time the little woman had saved me.

*   *   *

Beyond this office was another one, opening on the Belgian platform, and a sign saying that here one could exchange a maximum of 300 marks for Belgian or French francs, according to the passport.

I was getting my money ready before presenting it when a man of my own age, a little smaller, with no overcoat, and a broad cap, put two ten mark bills in my hand and said:

"I, too. Please."

I changed seventy marks in all, and received 840 Belgian francs. The other followed me in the train. I gave him his money and he laughed softly.

Escape

"The worst is over," he said.

"I don't know. Better be careful."

His coat had once been part of a Norwegian uniform. I could recognize it by the shape of the pockets and the thin little stripe around the sleeves, though he had built up a civilian collar in front, and dyed the whole a very dark green. His shoes were French military shoes, but he had cut off the copper clips on the sides that make them so easy to spot anywhere. To give them a civilian appearance he had polished them remarkably well with an old bone, probably, while holding something smooth, such as a bottle, under the leather. His trousers were entirely homemade, from army knickers, also dyed green. His cap, I guessed, had been missed by a German worker, one evening.

He looked like a civilian exactly the way that a painting, made by someone inexperienced but enormously patient, looks like its model. His costume was naïve, fresh, romantic, and somewhat convincing. It didn't fit current patterns, but it fit current notions: Every detail was there, the holes in the buttons, the slit in the collar, and all. The expression on his face matched perfectly — a fixed smile, a professional look of honesty, a perfect picture postcard under which should have been written in gold letters: "Souvenir from Herbesthal."

I could understand why he had passed unseen, wherever he had been.

"I had a coat exactly like yours, but I've travelled on the axles from Aachen and ruined it. I had to leave it on the tracks, and I hope we'll leave before it's found. I was already standing on the Belgian platform when you came out of the inspection room, and I spotted you on account of your British coat. I wasn't sure, though, until I saw you turn towards the wall with medals on your chest, and turn again without any."

He had escaped inspection by walking openly along the tracks with a lantern he'd taken down from a post, until he found a way out of the station. Later he had entered it from the Belgium side. He knew about the money exchange, and had waited until he saw someone he thought he could trust.

Getting rid of the swastikas had been a mistake, and would have cost me my freedom if any German had noticed it, but instead, it had brought me a companion.

I was not through with the couple from Brussels. The man and his wife arrived, after looking for me in the various compartments, and she addressed me in Flemish dialect, instead of German, as before. I couldn't make out what she wanted. She laughed, and told me, in French, it was clear to her who I was; for she'd seen my Flemish passport lying on the desk. A little reluctantly I admitted it.

"I'm so glad," she said with a kind smile; and her husband shook hands with me. We made friends though I can't say I felt comfortable about her. Impulsive as she was, what would she do next?

The train tried to start, painfully, with much grinding of wheels and a succession of jerks; and then we had an accident. She had nothing to do with it, but almost became a victim. We were standing at the end of the corridor, when the coach behind us became disconnected, and three or four people who had been on the platform fell on the tracks. My new comrade caught her by the arm, just in time to save her bones. How much the others had been hurt, we couldn't tell — they had disappeared under the wheels. The tracks, between both sections of the train, stretched like rubber bands. With almost enough noise to cover the shrieks, we stopped. It took half an hour for the German and Belgian policemen to get the bodies out, and not before another half hour were the cars connected again and the train left at last.

Escape

"You're so pale," said the woman "are you sick? Are you afraid of blood?"

I was feeling sick, but it wasn't the blood of the others, but my own luck; this magnificent luck not to have been standing a little farther on the platform, wounded (if not killed) and taken to the hospital — in other words, back; a luck that seemed to me more incredible than anything I had gone through in the last thirty-six hours. It still seems so.

* * *

We spent the night in Brussels. There was no question of going to a hotel. You couldn't do that without first getting a permit from the German police, and I didn't feel strong enough to fool them once more. The couple insisted that we have a glass of beer together. We had several. Then they begged us to wait an hour for them.

"My name is Emile," said my colleague. "Let's play *belote*."

We played the most popular French card game, and drank a very poor substitute for the famous *"Gueuse"* of my souvenirs, as if we were living quietly in the city. The Belgian people around were as open as ever, but so thin, thinner than most war prisoners. They talked mostly about food, and the black market: a pound of butter cost 300 francs, thirty times more than normal. Bread was rationed to seven or eight ounces a day and was very bad, but not even a crumb was ever left on a table.

We hadn't really realized the damage done to our countries while we were away — Belgium was almost like home for us. We had counted on finding a happy feeling everywhere, instead of an atmosphere of cruel privation. We couldn't imagine the truth any more than one can realize the condition of a prisoners' camp without having been a prisoner. The health of the Ger-

422

man soldiers, passing in groups outside, was shocking: it was made up of all the pounds of flesh that the invaded people had lost.

When the couple came back we couldn't hide from them our feeling of depression. They reminded us of the joy we should be feeling, and took us to their little house in the suburbs. There, for the first time, we listened to a British broadcast, turned very low, for one never knew who might hear outside. The news was about two German battleships that had sneaked out of Brest and made their way through the channel, a few days before.

The woman wanted to cook something for us, but we wouldn't let her, and in spite of her insistence, we accepted only a very thin slice of bread, each, with a bowl of coffee substitute. We paid for our board with our full story, and they chuckled happily. Working in Germany had not rendered them Nazis. "What else could we do," they asked "Starve?"

I asked their advice about my passport, and they made me burn it. The real Josef Vanuytrecht could not be blamed for its loss; the firm would get him another one, for it would be the bookkeeper's fault. Keeping it would be dangerous for me. It was better, in case of trouble, to pretend that we had come from France, and always deny that we had ever been in Germany.

We stretched out on the floor, under one blanket. It was cold. Emile and I huddled against each other but we stirred endlessly. I didn't sleep but the tension of my nerves subsided a little. At times I heard the coins being dropped in metal boxes by every policeman I had met — threatening scarecrows along my flight. It sounded like bells rung beyond the horizon, whose song the wind brought by whiffs, and whirled away again.

At 5 A.M. our host shook us up. We washed, drank something

Escape

hot, and followed him out to the house of a friend of his — a friend he'd seen yesterday while we waited in the café. This man operated a truck for the Germans, and collected various products from other cities. He could take us along in the direction of the border, but wouldn't hear of any payment. We should walk to a given corner. He would drive by slowly, but not stop. It would be up to us to jump inside his truck unseen. If it proved impossible, he would come back a little later. We shook hands with both of them, cordially. The carpenter gave me a little package, long and heavy. My fingers recognized my hammer under new wrappings.

"Take it along. It's a good weapon," he said.

The plan worked all right. We hid inside, behind a generous stack of sacks. At the south gate of Brussels, the truck stopped for inspection. We heard the driver talking, about his orders and various papers, in German. A sentry poked his head in the back and didn't see anything wrong. I was so choked then on account of the fumes from the charcoal stove replacing gas as fuel, that I could hardly refrain from coughing.

Three hours later, after much bumping and rattling of gears, the driver tapped on the partition panel and said we were nearing Tournai. He would slow down again and as soon as the coast was clear we should jump out. Good luck to us!

We followed the road until we found a café. For five francs, a little glass of yellow alcohol with a pretension to the taste of apple jack, did us good. In the next café we drank beer and waited another half hour without meeting any customer. In the third we took alcohol, and with no more luck. We were fighting drowsiness when the owner of the fourth place, an old woman, sat down with us and quizzed us a little.

She could see we were French, and looking for something. She was Belgian. We had nothing to fear from her. Why not tell her what our trouble was? We did. She took us to her back room, kissed us both, and showed us the photograph of her son who was a prisoner somewhere in Austria. We told her the details, not too disheartening, about life in the camps, for instance, what we had to eat, and it sounded reassuring to her. She had feared much worse, but it was better than what most people got around here. She cried, all the same, and we couldn't console her. To take her thoughts away from her own sorrow, we told her we had money, and would pay any price for food. She put a scarf around her shoulders and left us alone in the house. She came back after a good while with two pounds of potatoes she had bought for forty francs. She fried them with a little grease she had left, and ate them with us. They tasted so good, and it was so refined to sprinkle salt over them, out of a salt shaker, that Emile and I began to cry, too. Perhaps it was because we needed sleep so badly, and were almost drunk.

At 4 P.M. a cousin of hers arrived, and she told him who we were, and urged him to help us cross into France that night. The quicker we went the better. "Fine" said the cousin, and we left the good mother. We boarded a streetcar going in the direction of the border only ten miles away. We left it a few stations before the end of the line, and began another wandering tour, from café to café. Fortunately they are very close to each other on this road. Almost every house has a counter: it's an extra occupation for the wives, between washing dishes and raising sons and vegetables. We drank French wine, at ten francs a glass because it was the most expensive drink and our only way to reward these kind people. We stayed longer in each than we wanted; their rhythm was not as fast as ours, but we had to bow to it. They wouldn't let us out on the road again, until someone smoking a pipe outside, had said that no German was looking this way. In the last place, the owner changed what was left of our Belgian francs for French francs, which were a little cheaper. We received 700 francs between us. When

Escape

dusk had fallen, we shook hands with everyone around, and the hostess kissed us good luck.

"*Vive la France*," she said.

"*Vive la Belgique*," we replied, in a very low voice, like a secret.

Then she threw over her shoulders the knitted scarf that no woman between the Somme and the Meuse can do without, opened the back door, and endeavored to lock her chicken house while we crawled at her feet. She disturbed her flock so conscientiously that its cackling covered the noise we made along the garden hedge. The ground was frozen, with little spots of snow, and hard on our hands.

Sixty yards to go, she had said, but it seemed so much more. When at last I reached the end, I passed my head very cautiously through the hedge, at ground level, and looked around. There was a dirt road. Ten yards to the right it turned between two houses and was stopped by a gate. Fifty yards to the left, the German patrol was tapping its boots around a little hut. Opposite us was another hedge and behind, the gable of a small house.

Emile got in position, and we both emerged at the same time, holding our shoes in our hands and tiptoed across. The Germans didn't see nor hear us, but a dog growled, and they swore loudly at him.

Their oaths echoed against the wall, where we were now crouching, on French soil.

CHAPTER 27

Reserved Quarters

ONE streetcar took us to Tourcoing and another to Lille. I knew this country well. It was fortunate that an early curfew had been lifted a few days before. At 8 P.M. we sat in a large café where I used to come, as a student twenty years before, with youngsters as noisy as these around us, pretending to be gay. Maybe they really were — the boys with their thin faces, and the girls with half an inch of cheap make-up.

We listened to their chatter: exams, dates, movies, and how someone had bought a pair of used trousers, or an ounce of candy without ration tickets, "can you believe it?"

I had hoped one of my classmates would still be in the habit of taking his evening *apéritif* at one of these tables, but I couldn't recognize a single face any more than I could recognize the furniture. Everything had changed — the men, the décor, and my eyes too. Pretty women and homely ones went in and out, followed by men of all ages, quiet, their breast pockets filled with adequate papers. No one seemed to be thinking about the other men who should have been sitting here too, but who, at this very hour, were being pushed back into barracks, holds, jails, and carefully locked up. No one, except an old woman, wearing a Red Cross armband, who came around shaking a metal box, the same shape, but smaller than the German police ones. The label on it said:

"*Pour nos prisonniers.*"

For our prisoners, the people gave fifty centimes, one franc, two francs, less than they would leave on the table as a tip, after drinking a glass of colored water. This woman probably

Escape

made daily rounds and, after so many months, had become quite a bore, with her little box.

"Here, Madame," called Emile, and she approached a little timidly, or wearily. We both stuck one hundred franc notes in the slit. The notes wouldn't go through. She had to take them out and fold them flat, then push them in, one at a time. Abashed at this unusual sight, the consumers at the next tables had stopped talking.

The "*Merci, Messieurs, merci,*" of the woman resounded in a little zone of silence. We looked around, Emile and I, with angry eyes, ready to fight. Then everybody began asking for "no trump," or writing paper, or another "demi," or the evening paper exactly as before, while we realized we had given ourselves away, one more time, uselessly. There might be — there should be — some plainclothes Germans around. We left immediately.

In another café we found too many green uniforms for our taste. In a small bar, Emile told me he had an idea, and that I should wait for him. He spoke to the waiter, went out, and soon came back with a woman. She was neither young nor old; neither pretty nor ugly; and she had on neither more nor less make-up than the others. She looked at each table with a possessive air, as if she had sat there often, and forgotten something on each bench. One, two men winked at her. She sank in a chair, ordered something special, and began to play with the rag out of which Emile had made a necktie.

"Say, you don't look very rich, my boy. Are you going to make me lose my time?"

"We have a little money if that's what bothers you, and you may get some of it, but what we want cannot be bought."

"How sentimental! You don't want me to tell you I love you, do you?" she sneered. "What are you two up to, anyway?"

He told her, very simply, in a few words. She didn't seem to hear. She was fixing her hair while looking in the mirror behind me.

"Let's go away from here," she finally said. "I don't like this joint."

She took Emile's arm, and led us to another place. In the back room, two young men were playing cards. She sat in the lap of one and said to us:

"This is my pimp, isn't he handsome?"

We laughed, as seemed expected of us, and she added, to him:

"These men need you, not me." Without another word she dragged her heavy hips out into the street again.

He arranged everything smoothly. He got us a meal for fifty francs each: dry fish, noodles, two olives, a little cheese, enough bread, and two glasses of wine, — quite a banquet for the time, and without ration tickets. We bought him a glass of poor kirsch, he offered us a better one, then took us out through the courtyard into a corridor leading to a sordid hotel.

"It's all arranged," he said, "This man will give you a room. You'll register under any name you want, and mention identification papers. If there is any trouble and you are arrested, you must swear you've thrown your papers in the toilet, because they were not good. If everything goes all right, your written declarations will be torn up. Get out early tomorrow. Good luck! "

Away went the pimp. We paid forty francs for the room, and went to bed, after inspecting the sheets attentively. They were grey and revoltingly spotted, but no bugs were in sight, perhaps because it was so cold.

Again we didn't sleep. Steps went up and down the stairs: dry little wooden heels, regular, accustomed to the way, and heavy fumbling boots, German ones, that we recognized by the particular clap of the iron horseshoe reinforcing the heels.

At six-thirty we bought tickets for Paris. We knew the

Escape

danger would increase around Amiens, half of the trip. There ended the "Forbidden zone," an extra division of the occupied territory thought to be what the Germans planned to annex, after the war. The train was not excessively full, and not heated at all, which is the contrary of German trains. The soldiers occupied cars reserved for them and, in spite of a few strange figures, we could feel at home among the civilians.

At Amiens, we watched through the window two uniformed men getting in the last car. "Here are the inspectors," everyone said. So we took our position at the end of the corridor where we could see them arrive. At the propitious moment we would open the door on the inner side of the tracks, get out on the steps, close the door, and hang there, as low as possible, until a reasonable time had passed. It would work, or it would not. That was simple.

An hour later they still hadn't come. We saw them getting off at Creil, with six or seven civilians, with no baggage but with anxious looks, obviously in trouble. The inspectors had enough work on their hands for the time being. So without having to indulge in acrobatics, we arrived in Paris at 1 P.M.

That was Tuesday, February 17. Only four days ago, I had thrown my identification plaque in the Oder.

CHAPTER 28

A Sick City

ONLY when Emile had left me and gone his own way, towards his family, somewhere in the suburbs, did I realize that we hadn't said anything to each other, except exchanging addresses through which we might eventually correspond. We had parted briskly, as we had met. I wanted to tell him something warm, and instead I had shaken his hand, absent-mindedly, and walked away.

Now I wished I had avoided Paris. The beloved city was there to meet me, outside the station door, but in what a state! It had become pale and thin, like the few civilians on the sidewalks. German uniforms spotted it, like fungus on an old watercolor fallen out of its frame. At every corner and in the middle of the squares, multiple signs painted in black, in German, pointed towards barracks, hospitals, airfields, *Kommandantur*, depots: a spider-web in the face.

Opposite some houses, the sidewalk and part of the street were isolated with white-washed wooden fences; white-washed like hog pens, and like rooms where someone has been sick with a contagious disease. Pedestrians turned clear around, passed in the very middle of the street, returned to the sidewalk well beyond, and hurried away.

Uneasy, I entered a café, and from the booth called several of my friends, without success. Either their telephone had been disconnected, or they were away. At last I reached one, and when I told him my name he said:

"It is impossible!" and I asked if I could come and explain to him why it wasn't.

"Immediately," he said, and I took the subway.

Escape

It was as before, except that some stations had been closed, and the Germans had added some new posters, threatening all sorts of penalties for any infraction of their rules. Others "cordially" invited the French workers to join their comrades, the German workers, in the war factories devoted to the defense of the New Europe, beyond the Rhine.

A group of young men boarded the subway at Chatelet, and sat by me. They were annoyed because they were late. They had been kept half an hour in the station when all the issues had been blocked, and German plain-clothes men had investigated the identities of every person. Only twelve had been arrested, they believed, and that was less than usual. I didn't dare ask what they meant by usual.

My friend positively fell into my arms and I into his. We were both so glad to see each other, and both of us had changed so much. Because the Germans visited his shop frequently, he took me to the kitchen, where a splendid meal had been prepared for me. I threw my sack, my coat, and my worries away, sat down and ate with enthusiasm. Between draughts of wine, I told him where I came from, and how happy I felt to be at home, in France.

"You aren't home yet," he said, "and far from safe. The streets, subways, stores, hotels are raided constantly and anyone whose identity is not attested by a recent card delivered under control of the Germans is locked up. If they get you, you'll soon go back where you came from. You must move as little as possible. I'll give you a room until we can get you some kind of papers."

He left me to see somebody about them, and came back, two hours later, frantic. Everything was more difficult than he had thought. No papers could ever be obtained for me, even with the greatest pull. The fact that I had no permanent domicile in Paris, rendered it even more impossible. I would have to resort to both false papers and false identity. But the worst was that the penalty for housing escaped prisoners of war had been raised to death, *immediate death* to anyone incriminated in the least.

I understood. The mad race was not yet over. A good meal and a few hours of rest in a comfortable chair, had taken the edge off my fatigue, but the carpet on the floor seemed to go up and down. It was the same drowsy feeling that had accompanied me during the last days of the retreat, two years ago. Again I would have to retreat, in the same direction, flee away from my own city, from the houses of my friends, even. That was clear. I'd set my teeth tight and go. But my head was lead. It was failing me. All I could think was that I still had a hammer and would sink it deep in the skull of anyone who tried to arrest me.

Meanwhile, a new hat was put on my head and the other burned in the stove because it was so bad looking, and as much money as I might want was offered to me. I was trying in vain to have an idea, to figure out how to contact someone in a position to help me, when another friend arrived.

She was an American and since her country had entered the war, only tolerated by the Germans in her own house. They paid her frequent visits, and she enjoyed causing them as many difficulties as she could, but she expected to be interned soon. She offered me asylum before I asked her, if I were willing to run the risk. I surely was!

Only when I reached her place and sat in front of a meagre fire that she had generously built with her weekly supply of wood, did I recover from my paralyzing exasperation. I had forgotten my English; German flew more readily out of my mouth especially when my thought returned to Stettin; so in a mixture of those two languages, on a background of French, I told her what she wanted to know. I explained to her that I

Escape

owed her part of my present freedom — as well as to our jittery friend — because I had sold some items from the packages they both had sent me. She was most annoyed because she had mailed me another package last week, and it contained all of her supply of cigarettes: four packs, bought at the bargain price of sixty francs each. Now she could only offer me butts, collected in a small tin box that stank, but a little smoke was decidedly needed to make the evening fully satisfactory.

Her delightful humor and brave coolness before the catastrophes that had befallen the country since I had last seen her, reduced my past four days to four times twenty-four hours instead of the thousand that they seemed and felt to me. I don't know if she realized how much I had to learn again. For instance, she showed me how *not* to hold my knife like a weapon, and how *not* to behave like someone just out of jail. I didn't tell her anything about the hammer. I didn't dare. She had news from my wife that was only six months old and tasted so deliciously fresh because it hadn't passed through the *Stalag* censorship!

She taught me also the various difficulties of the city: how to avoid centers as well as all deserted places and, most of all those white fences set around the buildings occupied by the Germans, to protect them from any contact with the French people they had expelled from them, because innocent looking passers-by threw bombs at them, quite often.

She helped me find those among my nearest friends, who had not yet been arrested, killed, or compelled to flee. They hastened to her house, as brave, as cordial, but as much in trouble as she. They all had done something very wrong, such as writing what they thought; painting what they felt; marrying Jewish girls; or belonging to political parties that were no longer popular. Everyone of them offered me shelter, money, and even their own food ration tickets.

434

With the richest of them I went out to fine meals, almost as wonderful as the meal we used to plan, so naively every Sunday, on the Bornzin prison farm, but at which, alas, none of my good companions could be present. They cost from 300 to 500 francs per person, about twenty times more than before the invasion.

With the poorest, I went to popular places where the greater part of the people entertained their paleness with one ounce of turnips, and a miserable stick of very doubtful sausage that, with a slice of bread worse than what we had in captivity, cost a minimum of twenty francs.

We arranged itineraries so that I could avoid the most dangerous zones and stay out as little as possible — especially after 8 P.M. the hour when Jews are not tolerated in the street any more. I couldn't show any paper to prove that I didn't belong to that persecuted race.

I had a strangely good time. In a week I was already well rested, but the comparative tranquillity had made me lose much of my previous alertness. During a police round-up, in the St. Lazare metro station, I fumbled my way out of it so awkwardly that it was only by hazard I wasn't caught. The danger was growing because I was weakening; and also because my description had certainly arrived at the Parisian Gestapo by now. It was urgent to undertake the last stage of my escape; but I was compelled to wait for a false identity card.

One old friend, among the first to turn up, was taking care of that. He had been very generous and helpful but, surprisingly was now quite prominent in the hated minority of men well thought of by the Germans and their stooges. He excused himself by saying it was only politics, etc. until help came from outside, but he went to a lot of trouble to help me out, and obtained all the information I needed.

I learned from him (and it proved to be true) that escaped

Escape

prisoners were well received in three military centers of the *unoccupied* territory: one in Châteauroux, one in Montauban, and one in Bourg-en-Bresse. They were demobilized, presented with a suit of clothes made of army cloth; a certain amount of money; a more or less suitable job; and became normal civilians. The Germans had agreed not to claim them unless they returned to occupied territory, in which case they would be arrested and shipped back to Germany.

He warned me about many dangers I hadn't yet realized, and I followed his advice to leave my American shelter. Staying longer would be exposing my hostess as well as myself to sure trouble. So I wandered from room to room, for some time. Once I slept in a bed where two British flyers had spent the night before, while on their way to Portugal, after having crashed in Northern France. I met three French underground agitators. How important they were I couldn't tell. I told them what could interest them about the part of Germany I had been through. They were brave — quite unafraid — but seemed surrounded by difficulties. I wondered if their enthusiasm was not a little of the kind that shook the nightly sessions of the now gone to ashes "Central Committee of the Boat" when we fought despair with illusion and exaltation and were readying ourselves, in a primitive and childish manner for sacrifices that were bound to be useless because no one outside appeared ready to take advantage of them.

I spent my last four days in a hotel. Some one had been there ahead of me and bluntly asked the woman proprietor if she would receive me without papers. She had agreed, on condition that I would not give my address to anyone, even if I were arrested in the city. She gave me a very good room, on the top floor, and said she would do her utmost to warn me in case the hotel were raided, so that I could flee over the roofs.

When, early on the last day of February, I came down with

a 500 franc note in my hand and asked how much I owed for my lodgings, she said the bill was paid.

"But Madame, I don't understand. Who did so?"

"We did," she said, simply. "We owe you more than that. Good luck, *Monsieur*, wherever you go."

CHAPTER 29

The Last Border

I WAS arrested twice, a few miles away from the line between the half of France where the Germans paraded in uniforms, and the half that they did not yet occupy openly. But my identity card looked so much better than a real one; I was so timid; I was so earnest; I had learned well the names of everyone living in the vicinity; and not knowing a word of German, it was so hard for me to understand their French, that they believed I was on my way to visit an uncle, in a little village where I had none. Was that forbidden? Did they want to read this letter in which he asked me to come?

They would check on that tomorrow. I'm sure they signaled all around my brown overcoat. That would be futile for it was in blue working clothes that I proceeded towards my goal. My briefcase and the rest of my equipment were inside a sack, and the sack was on my shoulders. My hands were soiled and my shoes caked with mud.

In a lone house I met a peasant. He took a pickaxe and handed me a shovel. Through the window, he showed me the road and, 200 yards above, a small group of German soldiers. He would go to the patrol and show his paper: the one with many stamps and swastikas on it, saying that he was allowed to cultivate his field in the zone forbidden to all strangers.

Then he would walk slowly, his tool on his shoulder, while I should leave by the back door and, taking advantage of every break in the ground, try to follow the direction he took. There were three miles to go. If I met any soldiers, it would be up to me. If I met only civilians, I should begin shoveling in the next field, until the coast was clear.

So, from hedge to hole, from tuffet to tree, I advanced as fast and as carefully as I could. The peasant kept in the open and stopped, at times, to blow his nose, or inspect a tree, thus giving me a chance to take my bearings.

The police dogs of the patrol growled loudly and pulled on their leash. The peasant turned his head in their direction, as if to say:

"What's the matter with you? Don't you see me?"

Then I reached a plain, dominated by a single house with a Nazi flag on the roof. There was no kind of protection except a large swamp, deepened by the melting snow. With my sack on the shoulder nearer the dangerous house, I entered the water. My feet slipped on the slime, or sank. My trousers were glued tight to my aching stomach. It took me one hour, at least, to get across.

A railroad line ran on a bank beyond. I didn't see the sentry, but I heard his steps, resounding on the tracks. The steel was so cold that it burnt my ear while I listened. On the other side of the bank, I paused a moment, holding my shovel tight, ready for anyone to come. But only the crows had seen me, and they turned above me — the brutes, the fools — as if to say:

"Look! Here's someone!"

At last I came upon a little thicket and for a while the way was easy. It was dusk when the peasant stopped, took off his cap and began to dig up a little tree. I watched attentively the direction in which he was throwing the dirt:

"Only one hundred yards beyond," he had said.

I planted the shovel upright, well in view. Then I walked so near the ground that he himself couldn't see anything but a lone sack wandering in the mud and snow. I stumbled and hit a fence, a last fence of barbed wires, along a road. It ground, and hissed, and sang. But the wind also sang, and hissed, and made the fence grind.

Escape

No car ever passed on that road any more. It was covered with beautiful snow. The boots of the patrol had dotted a line in the middle, as they had on the map. It was there that I crawled for the last time, on my hands, on my knees, dragging my sack, with my head very low, humbly, begging the soil of my country to receive me again.

The dogs began to bark, the crows began to caw, and I began to run. The sack battered my back, and the hammer battered my leg.

Let them bark, the dogs; let them caw, the crows; let them shoot, the guns!

They cannot have me now! They shall not have me!

THE END

The Nordenham, taken from the quay. © *Fonds Jean Hélion/IMEC*

A lineup of the graves of French POWs. © *Fonds Jean Hélion/IMEC*

Jean Hélion identity photo, with his prison number. © *Fonds Jean Hélion/IMEC*

an Hélion and his fellow prisoners in Stalag II C Stettin (Pomerania), 10 June 1941. *Left to right:* René aude, Jean Hélion, Paul Hostel, X, Paul Poitier, Paul Martin. © *Fonds Jean Hélion/IMEC.*

AFTERWORD
by Jacqueline Hélion

Escaping from a prison camp is not just a matter of walking out when nobody is looking, even though in Hélion's case it was that, too. An escape plan requires help and information, provided first by a few fellow-prisoners in the know and then by underground networks. In 1942, when Hélion finally reached the United States and began writing an account of his experience at the request of E. P. Dutton and the Office of War Information, the war was still on and VE-Day still twenty-five months off. Giving details of ways and means—by naming accomplices, pointing to those Germans who were deliberately or unwittingly cooperative, identifying friends and networks in occupied France—was out of the question. In Germany, the price to pay for helping escaped prisoners was either immediate execution, slow death in a concentration camp, or a much-dreaded transfer to the Russian front—the Battle of Stalingrad was just getting under way at the time. In occupied territories, to be caught helping escaped prisoners or shot-down Allied airmen could lead to a torture chamber, deportation, or execution.

Leaving the Camp

The plan devised by Hélion and his friends was an old classic, but it worked. Choosing a day when soccer was permitted within the enclosed area alongside the SS Nordenham, several men had agreed to pick a fight with the goalkeeper, the posts being placed conveniently close to the guarded camp entrance. The opposite team soon joined the fray, thus causing the guards to intervene just as a large contingent of prisoners returning from forced labor sites around Stettin were passing through the gates. The ploy had been carefully timed. In the general confusion Hélion quietly slipped out and made a dash for a shed, behind which another prisoner, at great risk to himself, had previously hidden a bundle of "civilian" clothes. Without these Hélion could not hope to cross the country.

Crossing Germany

Provided with forged papers, the few Reichsmarks he had saved up, plus information supplied by friends on work-shifts, Hélion was able to board a train bound for Berlin. Trains were dangerous. Controls on board could be frequent and haphazard. Luckily, no Brownshirts appeared on the Stettin-Berlin run, but they were all there at arrival, in a phalanx blocking the exits. Papers, passports, and wallets were scrutinized at great length while lines of passengers dutifully formed along the quay. Hélion's papers were rather crudely fashioned. In an effort to prevent the guard from looking too closely at them, he dropped his wallet. Its contents, including scraps of cut-out ads along with photographs of Hitler and Goering, lay strewn around the guard's feet. Hélion apologized and went about picking them up when the guard demanded to see them. Meanwhile the line behind him was getting longer. Finally, with an exasperated grunt, the guard shoved the whole batch back into Hélion's wallet, and all but kicked him towards the exit. Hélion, in a cold sweat, was about to thank his lucky stars when he saw, coming towards him in the crowd of outgoing passengers, one of the camp guards obviously returning from home-leave and about to board the train back to Stettin. Hélion and this man had spoken to each other on business for months in the office of the commandant. Hélion's heart sank; he felt sure the game was up. But as the two men passed each other, Hélion looked the other straight in the eye. The guard stared back for what seemed an eternity, and went on his way.

After that, Hélion relaxed somewhat. But soon he discovered that the train he was due to board to France had been cancelled. He could take a freight train later—but what to do in Berlin during the day and part of the night? Streets and public gardens were not safe. There were patrols everywhere. He decided that if he were going to be arrested, it might as well be in front of Rembrandt's *The Man With a Golden Helmet* in the Gemälde-galerie. When he found the museum, though, it was closed and sandbagged. The Nazis had moved all of the national collections to safe underground caves in Saxony. At a loss for another place to stop, Hélion walked into the nearest barbershop. The barber, who was Asian, spoke only broken German. Needing a shave and a shampoo, Hélion figured it was a cheap way of spending an hour or so. Behind a large towel and lots of lather, he felt emboldened to the point of exchanging small talk with a Wehrmacht non-com in the next chair. Accents were not a problem in those days as the country was flooded with "guest workers"—foreigners actually press-ganged into industrial jobs to replace Germans called up to fight.

Near the station, Hélion took refuge in a beer hall. Beer was cheap and he could make it last. A group of Luftwaffe pilots chose to sit down opposite him, and when one of them began staring at him with insistence, he left his unfinished beer on the table and made his way to the men's room. When he came out of the stall, who should be standing there waiting but the inquisitive pilot, now all smiles. The fellow was openly on the make and Hélion had some trouble shaking him off, all the while trembling with fear that he might betray himself by some slip.

The search for a freight train in the maze of a shunting yard was all but impossible for Hélion without drawing attention to himself by asking questions. Finally, he was able to board a passenger train "going west"—but "west" could mean anywhere from Karlsruhe to Antwerp. As on all German trains, there were coaches reserved for the armed forces. The rest of the train was packed full of families, school children, and foreign workers. By then, Hélion had acquired a technique and a certain ease in dealing with police controls. The train's destination turned out to be Belgium after all—the best of luck because, thanks to a Belgian fellow-prisoner on the SS Nordenham, he had a contact in that country. From Belgium and on into France, Hélion was in the hands of an underground organization. He spent that single night in Belgium with a few other runaways like himself, hiding in the cellar of a brothel near the border while a crowd of German soldiers caroused upstairs.

In Paris

Crossing France was equally dangerous. Escaped prisoners caught in the "occupied zone"—roughly two-thirds of the country—were shipped back to Germany and locked up in what amounted to POW concentration camps. The resistance network supplied escapees with a little cash, transport, bed and meals and, when necessary, passes, ration tickets, identity papers, etc. On reaching Paris, Hélion was directed to a small, very modest hotel in a corner of the Place de l'Odéon. The woman at the desk took him up to a tiny room on the top floor with a skylight opening onto the roof. She explained that it was the safest room because, in case the hotel was raided by the police (as hotels often were), he could climb out and walk across several adjoining rooftops to a building, where he would find another skylight left open for him. From there, a flight of stairs led to a door opening onto a street a block away. He understood that he must not spend more than two nights in any one shelter. On leaving the hotel, he asked how much he owed for those two nights and breakfasts. The woman replied: "You owe us nothing; we owe you."

Two other women played a part during the time he spent in Paris: one was Mary Reynolds, an expatriate American, a long-time friend of Marcel Duchamp, and a well-known bookbinder. She lived in a small detached house with a garden situated in a quiet part of the 14th arrondissement. She was one of the very few Americans who had decided to stay on in 1940 after the defeat of France. Needless to say, the German military authorities and the Gestapo kept an eye on her. As an enemy alien she had to report periodically at their headquarters in the Hotel Majestic. Reynolds was an important link in an underground network devoted to helping Allied airmen get back to England after being shot down. At the back of Mary's garden was a small tool shed where her protégés slept. A visit from the German authorities could occur at any time, day or night. Always on the alert, Mary was able to signal to whoever was hidden there, and while the police searched her house, she did her best to hold them up. Her "guest" could climb over the wall into one of the gardens or alleyways flanking her place.

The second woman was Gabrielle Picabia, widow of the painter Francis Picabia, who, like Mary Reynolds, was involved in a resistance group, possibly the same one. She lived in an apartment building in the rue Balzac, near the Étoile. With neighbors on all sides, she and her "guests" had to converse under a tent made of blankets stretched over chairs while Radio-Paris, the French collaborationist radio station, played loudly to mask their talk.

Crossing the Line (Vichy and Marseille)

The so-called "free zone" under the authority of Pétain's government stretched south of the Loire River from the Alps to the Pyrenees, excluding the Atlantic Coast. The border between the "free zone" and the "occupied zone" was in fact a wide strip of land fenced in and re-enforced with barbed wire. It cut across the country irrespective of roads, railways, bridges, fields or county limits. All around there were watchtowers and armed patrols with dogs. Within the occupied zone, one couldn't move without an "Ausweis," a permit issued by the Germans. The underground provided Hélion with all that was necessary; no names were ever mentioned, only codes. His first attempt at crossing the line failed, but on his second attempt, led by a wily farmer who knew his business, he succeeded. The Vichy authorities made a point of greeting escaped POWs with undisguised glee, providing them with new clothes, full fare to go home, and congratulations. When Hélion informed them that his home was in Virginia, in the United States, the functionary gasped but acquiesced. "After all, the rule says 'home' wherever it may be." With enough money to pay his way to America, Hélion realized it was going to be up to him to find a way of getting there. While in Vichy, he was questioned by Pétain's 2nd Bureau (or secret service, such as it was) and this led to his agreeing to meet "deux Messieurs anglais, two Englishmen," who were anxious to hear what he had to say about his imprisonment. These were British Secret Service or SOE agents. These fellows were most interested in information regarding rail traffic, troop movements, arms, and freight going east, or west, from Stettin or Berlin. The conversation was conducted in English even though the two Englishmen spoke fluent French. Hélion gave them all the scraps of information he had gleaned daily from prisoners working on the railways and for local industrial plants. He showed them photographs of the SS Nordenham and one or two of himself on deck taken by a naive German guard. What interested the British most was what could be seen of the port in the background with German warships at berth.

As he was about to leave Vichy, Hélion was approached by one of the bureaucrats he had been dealing with. This man gave him a letter addressed to a colleague in Marseille who could be of help if necessary. Hélion put it in his pocket and forgot about it. Marseille proved to be a set of hurdles not the least of which was a permit to leave the country legally—without it, no Spanish visa. Portugal, Bermuda, and Cuba only delivered transit visas subject to an immigration visa granted by the US consul. Visas were never valid for more than ten days, and the lines of people camping outside all the consulates were such that it could take more than a week to reach the right desk. After running around hopelessly for weeks, Hélion finally remembered the letter he still carried on him. It took him to an office with a cordial functionary behind a desk. When he had read the letter, the man expressed surprise that Hélion had waited so long before looking him up. And from then on, everything went very fast: permits and visas were granted, papers were signed and stamped. This was mysterious; but later in New York, a friend to whom he showed the letter drew his attention to three small dots arranged in a triangle under the signature. Without knowing it, Hélion had happened upon one of the two main Masonic lodges represented throughout France's administrative offices—universities, bar associations, magistrates, and last but not least, the police. Having unwittingly given the Masonic sign, Hélion was very soon on his way to Portugal via Spain, on the SS Serpa Pinto to Cuba and finally, to New York.

—Paris, 2011